D0759541

The Poetry of Kabbalah

The Poetry of Kabbalah

Mystical Verse from the Jewish Tradition

WITHDRAWN

TRANSLATED AND ANNOTATED BY

PETER COLE

CO-EDITED AND WITH AN AFTERWORD BY

AMINADAV DYKMAN

YALE UNIVERSITY PRESS ■ NEW HAVEN & LONDON

A MARGELLOS
WORLD REPUBLIC OF LETTERS BOOK

The Margellos World Republic of Letters is dedicated to making literary works from around the globe available in English through translation. It brings to the English-speaking world the work of leading poets, novelists, essayists, philosophers, and playwrights from Europe, Latin America, Africa, Asia, and the Middle East to stimulate international discourse and creative exchange.

Published with assistance from the Louis Stern Memorial Fund.

Copyright © 2012 by Yale University Press
Introduction, translation, and annotation copyright © 2012 by Peter Cole
Afterword copyright © 2012 by Aminadav Dykman

All rights reserved.
This book may not be reproduced, in whole or in part, including illustrations, in any form (beyond that copying permitted by Sections 107 and 108 of the U.S. Copyright Law and except by reviewers for the public press), without written permission from the publishers.

Yale University Press books may be purchased in quantity for educational, business, or promotional use. For information, please e-mail sales.press@yale.edu (U.S. office) or sales@yaleup.co.uk (U.K. office).

Set in Electra and Nobel types by Newgen North America.
Printed in the United States of America.

Library of Congress Cataloging-in-Publication Data
The poetry of Kabbalah : mystical verse from the Jewish tradition /
translated and annotated by Peter Cole ; co-edited and with an afterword
by Aminadav Dykman.—1st ed.
p. cm.—(The Margellos World Republic of Letters)
Includes bibliographical references.
ISBN 978-0-300-16916-4 (alk. paper)
1. Piyutim. 2. Piyutim—History and criticism. 3. Jewish religious
poetry, Hebrew. 4. Mysticism—Poetry. 5. Cabala. I. Cole, Peter.
II. Dykman, Aminadav.
BM670.P5P64 2012
296.4'52—dc23
2011041846

A catalogue record for this book is available from the British Library.

This paper meets the requirements of ANSI/NISO Z39.48-1992
(Permanence of Paper).

10 9 8 7 6 5 4 3 2 1

CONTENTS

THE STAKES COULDN'T BE HIGHER: extraction of light from the container of sound; ascent to the Throne of God and direct vision of His Glory; the eradication of coarseness and the forces of darkness; a path to redemption, sometimes through sin; the achievement of erotic union on high—which is to say, the sacred marriage of feminine and masculine aspects within the Deity.[1] "Great is the power of the poem recited for the sake of heaven," writes one late-seventeenth-century North African poet. "It unites all the [spiritual] qualities like a sacrificial offering, aligns the [heavenly] channels, and gives rise to effulgence in all worlds—above and below."[2]

In this Kabbalistic context, poems not only depict a mystical process, they produce it.[3] Seeking a return to the primordial harmony destroyed with the catastrophe of creation and Adam's transgression in Eden, those who compose and utter the lines of mystical hymns take part in the continual reconfiguration of the cosmos.[4] For the letters of the alphabet, or *aleph-bet*, are, a medieval Iberian Hebrew work tells us, nothing less than "the powers of God . . . engraved on the throne. . . . They are called the angels of the living God."[5] And according to late-phase Hasidic Kabbalah, the letters of the Torah are each "a palace or chamber inhabited by the divine presence": combined in the proper manner, they lead to the revelation of the Infinite's radiance.[6]

As with the gain, however, so with the potential for debilitating strain in the scheme of this at once conservative and truly experimental poetics, where the level of risk is raised to an almost impossible pitch. The Talmud warns of the threats that await a person who would hazard the halls of the upper palaces—apostasy, insanity, and death (spiritual or actual). Of the famous four sages who entered that place of esoteric interpretation seeking knowledge of this potent sort, only one returned in peace.[7]

Given the danger that attends to Kabbalistic inquiry, why submit oneself to an equivalent peril on the literary plane— the gauntlet of abstractions and the incessant mixing of mythic metaphors that dominate the textual landscape of Kabbalah? What, apart from a historical and armchair sense of the intense religious experience of spiritual adepts, does the poetry of Kabbalah have to tell us as readers today?

For one, long before Frenchified notions of trace and erasure took hold, a Kabbalistic poetics was drawing attention to aspects of language-in-action that slip readers into (as D. H. Lawrence put it in a wholly different context) a "dawn-kaleidoscopic" world of ramifying meaning where absence and presence evoke one another.[8] Contemporary literary culture tends to doubt the power of poetry and is suspicious of verse that takes as its subject its own medium. But hymns treating the (implicitly parallel) nature of divine and human creation, and the language that leads to that creation, lie at "the heart of the heart" of Kabbalah's country. No less an authority than Gershom Scholem—the great twentieth-century scholar of Jewish mysticism and a writer of almost clairvoyant powers—identified "the indissoluble link [in Kabbalah] between the idea of the revealed truth and the notion of language," calling this perhaps the most important legacy that Judaism bequeathed to the history of religions. He writes of the conviction held by many Kabbalists that "the language—the medium—in which the spiritual life of man is accomplished, or consummated, includes an inner property, an aspect which does not altogether merge or disappear in the relationship of communication between men. . . . In all such attempts there is something else vibrating."[9] So it is that Kabbalistic poems in Hebrew and Aramaic, Ladino, Yiddish, and Judeo-Arabic have moved generations of readers who may have understood only a small part of that literature's esoteric import. Working like verbal spirit traps, the poems of the Jewish mystical tradition precipitate a sense of transcendence, which becomes palpable long before it is fathomable.[10]

That core element Scholem discerned, out of which all other qualities of speech and the world are formed, points to the Name of God as "the metaphysical origin of all language."[11] Hence the Provençal Kabbalist Isaac the Blind's circa-1200 image of the inverted tree of divine might, whose roots (in heaven) consist of this Name, and the letters of which are branches and leaves that dangle down and appear as flickering flames of words and things. ("The letter," according to Isaac, "is the element of cosmic writing.")[12] And so, too, the idea put forth later in the thirteenth century by Avraham Abulafia—one of the major Kabbalists of the day and also the author of an astonishing long poem excerpted in this anthology—that letters are "the mystery that lies at the basis of the host [of all things]. . . . Every letter is a sign and indication of creation." As Abulafia saw it, the mind, hand, pen, ink, and parchment form a continuum analogous to that of the worlds on high and below.[13]

By the same token, as the principal Kabbalistic text of the period has it—depicting a literary situation of acute authorial susceptibility to the interaction of words—certain "inscribed letters" move the angels around the throne of the God whom they praise:

> One letter strikes from below, and that letter goes up and down and two letters fly above it. And that letter from below raises the order [of angels] below to above. . . . When the world was created, those letters from the supernal world generated all the actions below in their actual form. Therefore, the one who knows them, and is careful with respect to them, is beloved above and below. . . . These letters are male and female, to be contained as one, in the mystery of upper and lower waters. . . . Come and see: just as there are supernal letters of the supernal world [Binah, or the world of understanding], so there are other letters below [within Shekhinah, or Divine Presence].[14]

The passage as a whole points to the realm of the conceptually elusive *sefirot*—which is what Kabbalists call the ten primal channels continually emanating within the Godhead and the human soul, as they conduct energy and consciousness through a kind of spiritual circulatory system that reaches (down to the capillary level) every part of the universe and cycles back to the divine. "A world of deification by installments" is how Jorge Luis Borges describes the system of sefirot.[15] And Harold Bloom, noting that Scholem saw the God who manifests Himself as the God who *expresses* Himself, understands the sefirot as that expression, which is to say, language. "Popular Kabbalism," Bloom adds, "has understood, somehow, that the sefirot are neither *things* nor *acts*, but rather are *relational events*, and so are persuasive representations of what ordinary people encounter as the inner reality of their lives."[16] In another quietly marvelous image of literary incorporation, a major Kabbalist of Ottoman Palestine sees the five places of the mouth where speech is generated as the sources of the sefirot and "'the secret of the chain of emanation' of all reality": "Out of His love for man, God has fixed . . . letters in [his] mouth . . . in order to enable him to cleave to his Creator. . . . The meaning of the verb 'fixed' is similar to sticking the end of a chain in one place, and the other end in another place; the distance between the places notwithstanding, when a man shakes the end of the chain, which is in his hand, he shakes the whole chain." Sounds produced by a "twist of the lips," this Galilean visionary reports elsewhere in a related image, move like bodies and ascend through the network of the sefirot, bringing about changes within the configuration of heavenly forces.[17]

For most Kabbalists, Hebrew alone embodies the mystical properties of this primordial language in which God's Name is the text and texture of the universe. Abulafia and others, though, extend that understanding even into the secular sphere (as does Scholem's close friend Walter Benjamin); as they see it, all languages—through the prism of their transformations and permutations—offer glimpses of the mystery of existence, and this because they emerge from the Active Intellect, which in this Judaized Aristotelian cosmology is the bearer of the original divine utterance.[18] However fallen or limited—after Babel, or simply because they are human—the languages of women and men at the very least contain a reflection of that mystery of the divine mind and its act of creation-through-speech.[19]

No wonder that Scholem, who as a young man entertained thoughts of becoming a literary translator, once wrote to the theologian Franz Rosenzweig of the way in which translation "is one of the greatest miracles . . . leading into the heart of the sacred order from which it springs."[20]

"The mystic," Scholem noted elsewhere, "discovers in language a quality of dignity."[21] So does the translator and poet.

*

There is, to be sure, more to the poetry of Kabbalah than an embrace of language as a pertinent subject for verse, and the poems in this anthology are also highly charged carriers of initial vision and actual practice — crystallizations of both the simplest and most abstruse notions that have occupied Kabbalistic circles from the early Middle Ages into the twenty-first century. While the conceptual range of the poetry seems at first glance rarefied (and in need of being "translated" by readers into a form fit for their own use), the questions that the poems engage could not be more substantial.[22] They cover a broad spectrum of timeless concerns, asking, for instance, what it means or has meant to maintain a vital connection through speech to the spirit and why consciousness of majesty matters in the world of an ordinary week. From early on, this tradition considers how first things are bound to what comes last, and where the present stands in relation to both. Beginning in the eleventh century — though some would say much earlier — Eros enters the esoteric equation, and the poems take up the question of how that might inform a faithful existence. (In fact, the erotic dimension of Kabbalah becomes so central that coupling, the endlessly complex interplay between masculine and feminine aspects of creation, has been described as being, for Kabbalists, "the secret and foundation of all existence.")[23] Later the tradition looks at the ways in which a perception of cosmic exile alters our sense of being in place, and where and how darkness and evil figure in this mix. From the start, however, the hymns of the Jewish mystical tradition demonstrate how song — almost magically, and at times with actual magic — can conduct and preserve transformative knowledge, even for those who don't quite know what they know. Moreover, they show how a vision of the manifold linkage of all things and all degrees of thought and feeling might be registered in the cadence and weave of a line of verse, a series of wedded sounds in the air.[24]

Kabbalah, in this reading, is not restricted to the currents of religious thought that began taking shape among small, select groups of men in the late twelfth or early thirteenth century in southern France and Spain (currents that were disseminated to points farther south and east and north and eventually west for the next eight centuries, as the Kabbalistic vision gradually entered the bloodstream of Jewish life). Kabbalah *is*, of course, that historically evolving thing; but it is also what the leading scholar in the field today, Moshe Idel, has identified as a tradition whose spiritual roots reach back to the Talmud and, according to others, even to Scripture itself.[25] Noting that the Hebrew term means "that which has been received," Idel explains: "In a more extended form, as used by traditional Jews, Kabbalah is an esoteric tradition of hoary antiquity transmitted through the centuries. . . . It was regarded as both the most sublime and eventually also the most dangerous form of study found in Judaism."[26] It is in this more capacious manner that the term is used in this volume's title, for as with Torah, so with Kabbalah: in neither is there "early or late" (as the rabbis put it).[27] Hence, the presence in this book of numerous poems that predate the emergence of Kabbalah proper, but which Kabbalists themselves have looked to as in one way or another imbued with the spirit and insight of Kabbalah.[28]

Like Kabbalah, the term *mystical* resists clear-cut definition, and while articulate calls have recently been issued to avoid the word and its derivations in serious discussion of the Jewish esoteric tradition, the subtitle of this gathering includes it for fairly straightforward reasons. Certainly in the West it has been the adjective of choice when it comes to characterizing Kabbalistic literature in ordinary language.[29] So it is that the principal work in the field by its preeminent writer is called *Major Trends in Jewish Mysticism*, and so it is that—however imprecisely—we use a word like *mystical* to describe certain kinds of literature that, as the author of that book characterized it elsewhere, "seek an apprehension of God and creation whose intrinsic elements are beyond the grasp of the intellect, although this [intellect] is seldom explicitly belittled or rejected by the Kabbalist."[30]

Generally speaking the spiritual tradition of Kabbalah is understood in this volume along the lines set out by Scholem and his successors (even as they refine and in some cases sharply differ with him).[31] That line of Jewish tradition is characterized by, among other things, the return of a mythic dimension to religious consciousness; ardent involvement with inwardness and intimate knowledge of the divine; and engagement with esoteric teachings.[32] While one might argue over elements of the landscape and where a given border should go (is there "mysticism" in the Bible; do the Dead Sea Scrolls qualify?)—the basic map is clear, and that is the territory this book explores.[33]

Another way of putting this is that mysticism—and, curi-
ously, translation—tries to say what it seems can't quite be
said, what is hardest to say, or what some feel shouldn't be
said. By surrounding the unsayable with techniques of speech
or silence, the mystical work seeks to construct allegories of
inwardness and understanding, to catch at least a reflection
of that elusive essence of experience and so to tell us what it
might mean to be more profoundly awake to our lives and all
they ride on.[34] Granted, because in a certain sense an ordinary
conversation can seem or feel miraculous—much like a kiss or
a magic trick, or the flipping of a switch—all experience (and
achieved poetry) might be deemed mystical. (And one scholar
has written eloquently of the tradition of "normal mysticism"
in Jewish life, which practitioners discover through observance
of the commandments and the rituals of the day, the week,
and the year.)[35] In a more specific and obvious sense, however,
the various religious traditions of the world have distinct sub-
traditions that function like research institutes for specialized,
often classified investigation into high-energy and somehow
extraordinary spiritual encounter.[36] And as with almost all areas
of human life, this speculative activity sometimes produces
poetry. Not a great deal of poetry, and not always great poetry,
but the literary products that emerge from the place where
these specialists in trapping the unsayable meet are often pro-
foundly strange and, at their best, strangely profound.[37]

As to which of the tradition's literary products count as
poetry, by and large we have chosen to include in this anthol-

ogy what Harold Bloom calls (in a discussion of the work of William Blake) "poems that are always poems."[38] That is, our emphasis has been on the made verbal thing in which formal considerations—structure and frame, tension and release—are central to the development of the passage in question. Exceptions are made in several instances, and these are explained in the headnotes and the commentary at the end of the volume.

Throughout, we've taken our cue from Scholem's 1977 description of the great richness and "the tremendous poetic potential within Kabbalah." Scholem on that same occasion noted his own "secret longing" and unfulfilled desire to explore that potential and to further our "understanding [of] the lyric plane within the language of the Kabbalists."[39] While early in his writing life he savaged certain German expressionist translations of Kabbalistic poetry, and implied that philology was better equipped than poetry to carry out such exploration, toward the end of his career he reversed course and noted that in a time like our own, when God has withdrawn from language, the worth of that language might best be determined by the poets—"those who still believe that they can hear the echo of the vanished word of the creation in the immanence of the world."[40] In its way, *The Poetry of Kabbalah* tries to address Scholem's wish and bring together at least some of what is best about all three of these worlds—those of the Kabbalist, the philologist, and the poet. While the anthology is very much a poet's take on this body of work, it also owes a serious debt to scholars who have labored long and hard in what the Kabbalists themselves have called "the Field of the Holy Apples."

*

Though they conduct and transform a single spiritual current, the poems gathered in this volume respond to very different cultural terrains and take up multiple tacks. They emerge from three continents over a period of some fifteen hundred years, and so side by side we find cosmological masterpieces and occasional poems; erotic charms and epic phantasmagoria; ballad-like lyrics and didactic mottoes; simple hymns of the purest devotion and gnomic verse of numerological intrigue. Formally we encounter quantitative monorhyme, quantitative strophic rhyme, rhymed and unrhymed free verse, sonnets and hymns in syllabics, and more—all within a shifting spiritual framework.[41] The pleasures and problems that presented themselves to the translator were, then, various in the extreme, and a word about the translations themselves is in order.

English renderings of poetry deriving from Jewish and other (largely Near Eastern) mystical traditions have, for the past half century, tended to dispense with the apparent interference of the original verse's formal elements so as to better zero in on what translators took to be the more relevant spiritual essence of the poetry, which was then reprocessed and packaged along the lines of a new (or latterly New Age) aesthetic. Rarely, however, has this been done while accounting in responsible and responsive—let alone inspired—fashion for the key formal and musical implications of the original verse, which often reflect broader social, aesthetic, and even ethical or theological concerns. As a result, far more often than not we've been left with homogenizing poems of empty abstraction, porous vessels filled with translators' projections and readers' fantasies of spiritual liberation.

In the case of the poetry of Kabbalah—a widespread religious tradition whose very being has by and large been predicated on the passionate adherence to and visionary application of prescribed acts of religious observance, or mitzvot, and which at times developed in reaction to historical crises—it seemed important to highlight less the liberatory and sometimes antinomian impulse so commonly associated with contemporary mysticism than the dialectical tension between the planes of essence and enactment that characterize Kabbalistic tradition on the whole. Accordingly, I have chosen to work with the given formal elements of the verse rather than reconfigure them radically or melt them down in a search for an occluded poetry that might lie at their core: in other words, I've sought to release the religious experience at the heart of these poems not *from* form, but *through* form—that is, within diverse prosodies that echo those of the original poems emanating from Palestine, Babylon, Ashkenaz, Spain, Yemen, Turkey, North Africa, Italy, and eastern Europe. In order to reflect both that diversity and the predominantly conservative emphasis on observance in the Kabbalistic tradition, the structural integrity of the Hebrew poems has on the whole been maintained in these translations, and the musical elements of the poetry have been incorporated in more or less straightforward fashion. Poems that rhyme in the original are rhymed in the English, though far more freely. Likewise I have not attempted to "Xerox" the various meters of the original Hebrew, Aramaic, Yiddish, or Ladino, so much as to take my cue from them and seek out rhythmic equivalents in the English. Depth of content—ecstatic, vatic, or elegiac—tends to impress itself on the surface of a poem, as do concentration and intensity, along with specific densities of texture and timbre; by absorbing that surface, I have sought to register these qualities within the English weave. Throughout, I've done my best to keep in mind what Gershom Scholem called Kabbalah's "paradoxical emphasis on the congruence between intuition and tradition."[42]

It is also crucial here to remember that many of these compositions—these spiritual machines made of words, to adapt William Carlos Williams's characterization of the modernist poem—were, and still are, *used* as devices of meditation and prayer.[43] The act of devotion, the turning and recalibration of a reader's attention, is determined by the turns of the poetry, the shape and sound of the verse itself. It is an experience of this tension and shape, this turning and sound, that I've tried to offer in the translations that follow.

Peter Cole
Jerusalem and New Haven

Poems of the Palaces & Early Liturgical Hymns

Jewish mystical tradition once held that by reciting the visionary hymns known as the Poems of the Palaces (or Heikhalot) a man might, if he didn't fall prey to any number of potentially fatal obstacles along the way, ascend through the seven heavens to the innermost chamber in the palace on high and approach the throne of God. There he could behold the Divine Glory and participate in the celestial liturgy. Collected in a group of compact, strange, and spiritually turbocharged texts that recount the experience of that ascent, these hymns surface among magical incantations, prose accounts of the process of creation, and elaborate descriptions of the divine abode. Seen as a whole, the Heikhalot writings served as a kind of manual for mystical encounter.

This is, in other words, a poetry written for men who would become like angels, serving and praising God. It is *not* a poetry of "personal voice" or "a meter-making argument" with a "self." Rather, it is a verse rooted in the magical power of letters and words—their shapes, sounds, and the cadences they create in combination. Experience in this literature is acoustic rather than psychological in the conventional sense—though this does not mean that emotional struggle and insight aren't at the core of the work (where hearing leads to seeing, even if few are granted the ultimate vision). "No man shall see Me and live," says the biblical God to Moses in Exodus. But precisely that sight is what the spiritual adepts of this literature seek. And central to that quest is their verse's ability to animate what we today would think of as "abstraction"—to set up a palpable, percus-

sive current and timbre linking syllable to syllable and word to word
in a progression toward heightened perception and, in some cases,
ecstasy.

Just who the authors and editors of these hymns were and when
they lived we don't know. Scholars date the hymns to the early rab-
binic or post-Talmudic periods—anywhere from the second or third,
but generally the fourth to the eighth or ninth centuries C.E. Most
place them in Palestine, but others have argued that the material may
have been edited, and to an extent composed, in Babylonia. What-
ever the provenance of these poems, their authors came to be known
as Merkavah writers, and the practitioners they depict were called
Yordei HaMerkavah, "those who *descend* to the *merkavah* [chariot]."
(Gershom Scholem suggests that the somewhat puzzling expression
parallels a synagogue idiom meaning "to go before the ark"—*yored
lifne ha-teivah*. Elsewhere he proposes that it might indicate "those
who reach down into themselves in order to perceive the chariot.")

Alluding to the imagery of Ezekiel 1:15 and that prophet's fiery
visions of the wheels within wheels and the spirits of the four liv-
ing creatures that move with and within those wheels, the term
merkavah—which might also be understood as "vehicle"—first ap-
pears in the mystical sense in the early-second-century B.C.E. Book of
Ben Sira 49:8: "It was Ezekiel who saw the vision of glory, which God
showed him above the merkavah of the cherubim." Elements of the
Merkavah tradition appear in the scrolls of the Dead Sea sect, and
"the Work of the Chariot" is discussed explicitly in the Mishnah and
Talmud, where it is regarded as dangerously potent—a playing with
metaphorical fire that, if strict precautions aren't taken, could easily
become all too literal and lethal.

To ride or descend to the merkavah is, in short, to engage in vision-
ary activity. One gets the impression from the texts and the scholar-
ship surrounding them that the mystics who made use of this vehicle
of vision were elite practitioners and possessors of a carefully guarded

sort of esoteric knowledge. While some suggest that the Heikhalot literature emerged from the rabbinic mainstream of the day, which absorbed "practices that fell under the immediate spell of the pagan syncretism of the time," others see it as part of an oppositional movement, perhaps one that involves a development of ancient material by descendants of priestly families after the destruction of the Second Temple in 70 C.E.; in this latter scheme, the chariot-throne surrounded by angels represents a third, heavenly temple, or sanctuary (*heikhal*), which is lifted in the visionary imagination beyond the limits of time and space and whose priests become like "ministering angels." At least one scholar has proposed that Heikhalot literature comprises "a revolutionary manifesto" of another sort altogether and is essentially an esoteric expression of a social and intergenerational, psychosexual rebellion by less privileged members of the lower classes who, in Babylonia (or Palestine), were attempting to resist the ruling rabbinic establishment.

Whether the practice was esoteric or democratic, emerged within the mainstream or along its margins, it posed a threat not only to the individual but to the entire worldview of traditional Judaism, as the worshipper in this scheme acts as Israel's emissary who, according to the scholar Peter Schäfer, "constitutes anew the communion between God and Israel." No longer content to draw near to the deity through ordinary prayer, patient study, and the observance of the revealed law, the authors of these hymns and those who recited them sought, says Schäfer, "physically or psychically" and by means of "a grandiose literary effort . . . to storm heaven and force direct access to God." As usual, the wizard-like Scholem put it best when he noted that these poems, whose "immense solemnity of style is unsurpassed in Hebrew hymnology," act as an "Open Sesame of religion."

You who cancel decrees and unravel vows,
    remove wrath and bring fury to failure,
recalling love and friendship's array
    before the glory of the Palace of Awe:

Why are you now so wholly fearful
    and now given over to gladness and joy?
Now so strong in your exultation,
    and now overcome with terror?

They said: When the wheels of Majesty darken
    great dread and fear overwhelm us—
and when the glow of the Presence appears
    we soar in tremendous bliss.

A measure of holiness,
    a measure of power,
a measure of awe,
    a measure of terror;
a measure of trembling,
    a measure of dread,
a measure of anguish,
    a measure of horror—
a measure of the robe
    of Zoharariel,   10
the Lord, God of Israel,
    who is crowned and approaches
the throne of His Glory,
    engraved and covered entirely
without and within
    by His Name Divine:
and the eyes of every living thing
    are unable to gaze upon it;
neither the eyes of flesh and blood
    nor the eyes of those who serve Him;   20
for rounds of fire take hold of the eyes
    of one who beholds it directly,
or merely reflects and glimpses it;
    the balls of his eyes then flame

and send forth torches of fire,
and he's set ablaze and wholly consumed;
for the fire that issues from the man who gazes
burns and devours him utterly.
Why? Because of the robe of Zoharariel,
30   the Lord, God of Israel—
who comes
crowned to the throne of His glory.

Awe and Adornment	for Life Everlasting;	
Brilliance and Blessing	for Life Everlasting;	
Council and Crown	for Life Everlasting;	
Daring and Dread	for Life Everlasting;	
Endurance and Ease	for Life Everlasting;	
Firmness and Faith	for Life Everlasting;	
Glory and Greatness	for Life Everlasting;	
Honor and Hymn	for Life Everlasting;	
Intent and Instruction	for Life Everlasting;	
Justice and Joy	for Life Everlasting;	10
Knowledge and Kingdom	for Life Everlasting;	
Learning and Luster	for Life Everlasting;	
Mercy and Modesty	for Life Everlasting;	
Nobility and Name	for Life Everlasting;	
Oneness and Order	for Life Everlasting;	
Purity and Pride	for Life Everlasting;	
Quintessence and Quality	for Life Everlasting;	
Redemption and Rule	for Life Everlasting;	
Splendor and Sanctity	for Life Everlasting;	
Triumph and Tribute	for Life Everlasting;	20
Understanding and Utterance	for Life Everlasting;	
Valor and Vision	for Life Everlasting;	
Wisdom and Wonder	for Life Everlasting;	
eXtent and eXpression	for Life Everlasting;	
Yielding and Yearning	for Life Everlasting;	
Zenith and Zeal	for Life Everlasting.	

9

EACH DAY

1

Each day as dawn approaches,
the King sits in majesty
and blesses the holy creatures:
To you, my creatures, I speak,
before you I declare—
Creatures who bear the throne of my glory
with all your heart, and willingly with your soul—
Blessed is the hour of your creation,
and exalted is the constellation
beneath which I gave you form.
May the light of that morning continue to shine
when you came into my mind—
for you are a vessel of my desire
prepared and perfected on that day.
Be silent, creatures of my making,
so I might hear my children pray.

2

Day after day as the time
of the afternoon prayer arrives,
the King sits, adorned,
exalting the holy creatures.
Before He has finished speaking

the holy creatures come forth
from beneath the throne of glory.
Their mouths are full of exultation,
their wings are full of celebration,
they clap their hands, their feet dance,   10
and they encircle their King:
one on His right and one on His left,
one before Him and one behind,
and they embrace Him and kiss Him
as they uncover their faces.
As they uncover their faces
the King of glory covers His.
And then the firmament splits—
because of the King of glory,
of majesty, of luster,   20
of beauty, desire, and form,
and because of the longing
for the splendor of the crown
in which their faces appear.
 And so it is written,
 Holy, holy,
 holy is the Lord of hosts.

When one stands before the throne of glory, he begins reciting
the hymn that the throne of glory sings each day:

King of kings,
God of gods
and Lord of lords,
encircled by braided branches of crowns—
encompassed by branching commanders of radiance—
who covers the heavens with wings of His splendor
and in His majesty appears on high;
from whose beauty the depths are lit,
whose glory flashes across the sky—
proud envoys shoot forth from His form
powerful creatures explode from His crown,
and princes course from the folds of His robe.
All the trees rejoice at His word
as the grasses delight in His joy—
and His words pour forth as fragrance
in flames of issued fire,
proffering pleasure to those who search them
and peace to those who make them live.

10

TO RISE ON HIGH

To rise on high
and descend below,
to ride the chariot's wheels
and explore in the world,
to wander on earth
and contemplate splendor,
to bask in the blessing
of the Crown
and sound Glory,
to utter praises   10
and link letters,
to utter names
and behold what is
above and below,
to know the meaning
of the living
and see the vision
of the dead.
To ford rivers of fire
and know lightning.   20

Blessed is the eye that has seen
and blessed the man who was granted that vision.
Blessed is the mother in whom he was held
and blessed the breast at which he was suckled.
Blessed is the womb in which he grew
and blessed the teaching that gave him instruction.
Blessed is the wisdom that he passed down
and blessed the arms that embraced him.
Blessed is the peace he pursued
and blessed the eye that has glimpsed it.

Blessed are you, O Ishmael,
who has been granted this vision.

The rich tradition of Hebrew poetry written for the synagogue in late antiquity is distinct from the Merkavah literature, although the Byzantine-era liturgical verse does incorporate certain mystical elements found throughout the "Poems of the Palaces." The result of that meeting of margins and center is a verse of quietly spectacular power—one in which experience of the Divine Presence is registered with particular intensity, and often across the surface of the work.

Among the most famous of the Heikhalot-inspired early-medieval hymns that have come down to us in prayer books is "The Priest's Appearance" (below), which concerns God's Glory (*kavod*). The central image of this poem—the emergence of the high priest from the holy of holies on the Day of Atonement—derives from the apocryphal Book of Ben Sira (Ecclesiasticus), which contains an elaborate description of the priest Shimon ben Yohanan performing the Temple service. This passage appears just after Scripture's earliest mention of the merkavah, or vehicle of mystical vision (Ben Sira 43:7; see previous headnote). "The Priest's Appearance" is followed here by a gently ramifying hymn that accounts for some of the vicissitudes and psychological trials of the mystic's ascent and service. It is put into the mouth of the angel Metatron, the discloser of secrets, who guides Moses through the first heaven, which is made up entirely of windows in which angels stand before God's greatness.

These anonymous poems are complemented by others in the early liturgical tradition that were copyrighted, as it were, with the embedding of their author's name into signature acrostics along the poem's spine, and several of these are translated here as well. Yannai is the first great payyetan (liturgical poet) identified in this way, though his name is all we know about him for sure. He is believed to have lived in Palestine, around the late sixth or early seventh century. His work was completely lost until the early twentieth century, when it was discovered (as the upper layer of a palimpsestic text) in the chaos of the Cairo Geniza. The poems of Yannai printed here were part of much larger serial compositions known as *kerovot* (singular *kerovah*), which were based on the weekly readings from Scripture according to the triennial cycle observed in Palestinian communities in late antiquity. (That is, the hymn is part of a tradition in which poetry was expressly composed for a given congregation week after week, much as Bach's cantatas were composed weekly for worshippers in Leipzig.) Compositions of this sort were intended to intensify the experience of prayer for worshippers by "making new" the contents of the weekly reading. In fact, these hymns were valued so highly that they were likened to angels, which rabbinic tradition views as being created by God for specific missions and which vanish after completing them. A convincing argument has also been made that the hymns were originally intended not to ornament the standard liturgy but to replace it. The first poem by Yannai translated here treats the story of the burning bush. In Yannai's stunning vision, the heart of the unconsumed flame is understood as the embodiment of the Shekhinah, the Divine Presence, or immanence of God in the world. This sacred fire, as one commentator has noted, comes down from the heavens bearing with it the entire alphabet.

The second poem by Yannai is part of a serial composition attached to the weekly scriptural portion that relates the Tower of Babel episode; in other words, it deals with a theme that would become central to Kabbalah proper as that evolved from the late twelfth century on — the meeting between upper and lower worlds, especially through song. In a neat inversion of the theme of hubristic aspiration that drives the people at Babel, this section of the kerovah describes the majesty and power of the recitation of the Kedushah, or sanctification, during the Sabbath (and also daily) liturgy: "*Kadosh, kadosh, kadosh* . . . Holy, holy, holy is the Lord of hosts" is what the angels encircling the throne of God say (in Isaiah 6:3), and in imitation of them the worshippers in the synagogue recite these lines as the third part of the central prayer of the liturgy, the standing prayer, or *amidah*. The power of this utterance is such that it succeeds in reaching up through the entire universe to the throne of God in a way that the Tower on the plain of Shinar could not. This upper–lower world connection is reflected in the principal prose text of the Kabbalistic tradition, which notes that "there is a *kedushah* that we recite in praise, praising the supernal angels, and because of this praise they allow us to enter the upper gates" (*Zohar* 2:129b).

Yannai's most accomplished student, Eliezer Kallir, continued this liturgical tradition and went on to become the most prolific and celebrated of the early Hebrew synagogue poets. Again, little is known about him, though legend holds that in a fit of what the Talmud in another context calls *kinat soferim*, or writer's envy, Kallir's mentor Yannai murdered his gifted and probably already famous student by putting a scorpion in his sandal. Kallir too, it seems, was at the height of his powers in late-sixth- and early-seventh-century Palestine. The prayer books of many communities are still filled with his extraordinarily allusive and often virtuoso hymns, which attracted large crowds to synagogues in Late Antique Palestine.

Like many of the Heikhalot hymns, "King Girded with Might" is a poem almost exclusively concerned with images of majesty and manifestations of kingship. The piyyut, which most scholars attribute to Kallir, appears to be a poetic reworking of a rabbinic—and, as Moshe Idel describes it, a *theoerotic*—tradition according to which "God dons ten garments [*levushin*] corresponding to the ten places in Scripture where Israel is referred to as a bride . . . [and] Israel is said to crown God with ten garments corresponding to the ten times that God refers to Israel as a bride." The theme of the sacred wedding (*hieros gammos*) is also common in the later Kabbalistic literature.

Lines 10 and 11 of the Hebrew are a classic example of the highly worked-up, convoluted, and mannerist style that came to be known as "Kallirian." Even without knowing Hebrew one can try to pronounce these lines and attend to what is happening on the level of sound (the Hebrew letter *het* is transliterated "ch" here and pronounced roughly as in "Bach"): *Melekh talito kasheleg metzuhtzach/tzach u'vetzachtzachot yetzachtzach/metzachtzechim pa'alam lenatz'ach//melekh ya'at kinah/kano kinei ga'o ga'ah/ke'ish milchamot ya'ir kinah.* Virtually every image in this hymn alludes to a scriptural or rabbinic passage, and listeners' knowledge of these sources was presumed in Kallir's day. That said, the poem can be understood on its own terms, and the images also speak for themselves, in large part because of the poem's musical properties. It was once extremely popular throughout the East and is still recited in certain communities on the morning of Rosh HaShanah.

The second poem by Kallir is an *ofan*—a hymn about the angels (*ofanim*, which also means "wheels," again as in Ezekiel). The poem's pronounced cadence and monorhyme create a kind of tympanic return at the end of each line to "the Throne." While Kallir is drawing largely on scriptural and midrashic sources (including the Talmudic association of angels, song, and making it new), the influence of the Heikhalot material is again clear, and we know that the poet was eminently familiar with this literature. Like some of the Heikhalot writers, Kallir is said—according to one mystical midrash—to have "ascended to heaven and question[ed] the archangel Michael on the manner in which the angels sing and how their songs are composed." A mid-thirteenth-century writer reports that while Kallir was composing "Creatures Four-Square About the Throne," fire surrounded him.

Also apparently emerging during this period, though mostly likely from the later part of it, and farther East (tenth-century Babylonia or earlier), is the poem "Ana beko'ah" ("Release, please, by the power"). With this hymn it would seem that we are solidly back in the land of the ordinary individual speaking directly to his or her God. In fact, we are and we aren't. A plea for strength employing gentleness, or a gentle poem invoking might, the hymn is an important and well-known prayer by an unknown author, though it is anachronistically attributed to the second-century rabbi Nehuniah bar HaKana, to whom the mystical book of the *Bahir* is also ascribed.

The poem has been inserted into the daily and Sabbath eve liturgy, and can be read in both straightforward and mystical fashions. That double aspect is mirrored in the progress of the verse itself, which begins simply, develops through numerous epithets for God, and then returns to a direct and affecting conclusion. The plain meaning of the text involves a call for God to come to the aid of the People of Israel, who are suffering in the shackles of exile but nonetheless continue to sanctify God's Name in prayer and observe His commandments. The "mysteries" or hidden things of the final line hint at the mystical reading of the poem, though that reading turns out to have been encoded in the prayer and its structure from the start (in the Hebrew, though not in the translation). The seven Hebrew lines of the poem each contain six words. Combining the initial letter of each word yields a forty-two-letter Name of God, which is usually divided into seven groups of six letters (for the six wings of the seraphim of Isaiah 6:2 and, some say, the seven days of the week). The tactile and intentional presence of this Name of God runs throughout the prayer and links the worshipper with this Divine Name and its supernal power. The Name is never pronounced, but the conscious worshipper is aware of it during the reading. Even without this talismanic encoding, however, the poem—with its subtle insistence and simplicity of petition—achieves a consoling and focusing magic.

THE PRIEST'S APPEARANCE

How wondrous the high priest was as he emerged
from the holy of holies in peace, without being harmed

Like an Angel alighted by the edge of the road—
            was the priest in appearance;
Like the Bells of gold on the skirts of the robe—
            was the priest in appearance;
Like the Creatures clothed in the Rock's resplendence—
            was the priest in appearance;
Like the Descent of grace to the bridegroom's eyes—
            was the priest in appearance;
Like the Enclosure covered in purple and blue—
            was the priest in appearance;
Like the Form of the Temple and the curtain of witness—
            was the priest in appearance;
Like the Garment of strength that cloaks the pure—
            was the priest in appearance;
Like the Heart of the Rose in the garden of pleasure—
            was the priest in appearance;
Like the Instant of sunrise seen in the Land—
            was the priest in appearance;
Like Justice's robe which shields like armor—
            was the priest in appearance;
Like the King's brow adorned with its crown—
            was the priest in appearance;

Like the Length of the fringes upon the shawl—
was the priest in appearance;
Like the Miter made pure and with pureness worn—
was the priest in appearance;
Like the New moon sighted and the blessing begun—
was the priest in appearance;
Like the One who waits for a glimpse of the king—
was the priest in appearance;   30
Like the Pleiades arrayed aloft—
was the priest in appearance;
Like a Question posed to the sages of old—
was the priest in appearance;
Like the Rainbow's ascent through clouds in the sky—
was the priest in appearance;
Like the Shine flashing from the heavenly beings—
was the priest in appearance;
Like a Tent stretched taut in the heavens' heights—
was the priest in appearance;   40
Like the Urim and Thummim lit with direction—
was the priest in appearance;
Like Venus's glow on the eastern horizon—
was the priest in appearance;
Like the Windows between which the candles are kindled—
was the priest in appearance;
Like the eXultation of the hosts of heaven—
was the priest in appearance;

Like the Young lily among the thorns —

50   *was the priest in appearance;*

Like Zion aligned with the Lord in glory —

                  so was the priest in appearance.

WINDOWS OF WORSHIP

And Moses asked Metatron . . . What are these windows
[of the first heaven]? And he said to him, These windows are:

Windows of worship
Windows of beckoning
Windows of weeping
Windows of joy
Windows of satiety
Windows of hunger
Windows of penury
Windows of wealth
Windows of peace
Windows of war
Windows of bearing
Windows of birth

and he saw —
windows without number and end

ANGEL OF FIRE

And the angel of the Lord was revealed to him
(in the heart of the flame):

Angel of fire devouring fire
Fire Blazing through damp and drier
Fire Candescent in smoke and snow
Fire Drawn like a crouching lion
Fire Evolving through shade after shade
Fateful fire that will not expire
Gleaming fire that wanders far
Hissing fire that sends up sparks
Fire Infusing a swirling gale
10   Fire that Jolts to life without fuel
Fire that's Kindled and kindles daily
Lambent fire unfanned by fire
Miraculous fire flashing through fronds
Notions of fire like lightning on high
Omens of fire in the chariots' wind
[Pillars of fire in thunder and storm]
[Quarries of] fire wrapped in a fog
Raging fire that reaches Sheol
T[errible fire that Ushers in] cold
20   Fire's Vortex like a Wilderness crow
Fire eXtending and Yet like a rainbow's
Zone of color arching through sky.

FROM THE SKY TO THE HEAVENS' HEAVENS

From the sky to the heavens' heavens
From the heavens' heavens to the darkness on high
From the darkness on high to the upper dwelling
From the upper dwelling to the heavenly halls
From the heavenly halls to the doors of heaven
From the doors of heaven to the highest heaven
From the highest heaven up to the throne
And from the throne to the chariot

Who is like you
Who could reach you
Who has seen
Who has been
Who would hold his head high, or raise an eye
Who would insist
Who would persist
Who would dare
Who would consider
Who would be so coarse and proud
Who would plot and build

When you ride a cherub
And glide on the wind
And wander through thunder
And move within storms

10

20

25

Making your way through the waters
And sending yourself through flames
A thousand thousands and tens of thousands
becoming men
and becoming women
and becoming spirits
30   and becoming demons,
becoming every likeness
and carrying every mission out

With reverence and awe, trembling in fear,
shivering and shaking,
they open their mouths extolling
your holy name, and as it is written, calling:
Holy, holy, holy
is the Lord of hosts—
The world is filled with His glory.

THE KING

sits on His throne, high and sublime.
He dwells forever, and His Name is exalted and holy.
And it is written: Sing, righteous ones, to the Lord,
it is fit that the upright acclaim Him.

May you be lifted in the mouth of the upright
and be blessed by the words of the righteous.
May you be hallowed by the speech of the pious.
And among the holy may you be praised.

King girded with might
your Name is great with might
your arm is firm with might.

King on the day of vengeance
who dons garments of vengeance
and renders foes their due.

King clothed in majesty
King who dries up seas
and quiets rushing streams.

King of the ten garments   10
strengthened among the congregants
and feared among the holy council.

King who dwells in brightness
and covers Himself in light
and brings our Law to light.

King harnessed in strength
whose right hand alone is strength
against which no man can prevail.

King clothed in justice
20   and sanctified in righteousness—
yours, Lord, is righteousness.

King glorious in His apparel
Salvation's helmet is His crown—
God in holiness on His throne.

King in crimson garments come
to trample traitors down
and curb princes' spirits.

King in immaculate dress
who cleanses His clan with clearness
30   making their works forever fresh.

King who was clad with zeal like a cloak
and in that zeal is exalted forever—
as a man of war will waken fervor.

King to the ends of the earth
King to whom the earth will bow
when He comes to judge the world.

King whose day of reckoning
every creature awaits, trembling—
for He on high in eternity dwells.

King who rules the world by might   40
and with it makes the mountains swell
so they skip like rams.

King inspiring awe in kings
across the earth, who shakes the earth,
King enthroned upon the cherubim.

King whose power can't be stopped
as with power He bears all
bestowing power upon the faint.

King who renders judgment—
and on the Day of Judgment   50
will bring the proud to judgment.

King who plumbs the deep-ones' secrets—
those who seek the depths to hide
and in the depths will be revealed.

King who summons the winds
on every side will sweep the haughty
tyrants away in anger.

King who gathers kings on earth
into the storm of Dumah's burden—
60   He will punish the hosts on high.

King on high in judgment
who in strength desires judgment—
Justice is His throne's foundation.

King bringing vindication—
before whom Justice goes
protecting those pursuing Justice.

King whose rule endures
whose throne in heaven is hung
whose kingdom reigns supreme.

70   King who brings down with His glance
who stirs foundations with His glare
whose gaze reaches every thing.

King who searches all that's done
and seeks out all that will be done
above and so below.

O King, God of old,
enthroned by a people of old—
forever reigns the Lord.

And the creatures four-square about the Throne—
Begirding with two hundred and fifty-six wings the
    Throne—
Circle in swarms, face-to-face before the Throne
Dwelling on an image of heaven (their heads directed
    toward the Throne)
Etched like ice, containing a spark discharged from the
    Throne
Floating above the firmament, like the appearance of the
    Throne
Going in fear and trembling, forever on account of the
    Throne
Hurrying back, then forth in the face of the roaring
    Throne—
Instantly flying, like lightning, without disturbing the glow
    of the Throne,
10 Just as they know—no place could contain the place of the
    Throne
Kept alone, a five hundred and fifteen–year journey
    straight to the Throne
Leaping to laud Him—as they're released from beneath
    the Throne,
Made faint with fear of He who is high upon the Throne,
Not only bearing, but also being borne by the Throne
On arms of the world up to the Throne

Proud with the people's risen prayer, they lower their
    wings toward the Throne
Quelling the swell of sin, they beat their wings and touch
    the Throne
Repelling their foes, as the Lord sends clouds across the
    Throne
Sounds of the ram's-horn reach the Throne
Tender mercies beseeched, for those inscribed in the frame   20
    of the Throne
Under the aegis of the Judge — seated within the hall of the
    Throne
Verging upon: an image carved into the Throne.
Wondrous creatures, carrying and carried by the Throne,
eXerting all effort, not to dishonor the glorious Throne,
Yearn — and soon they will hear the voice of the Throne
Zealously urging: Remember those who served the King
    with you before the Throne.

Evince compassion for the world's pillars, on which the
    King's Throne was Laid,
As all in their Zeal will feel the terrible trembling and Roar
    of the Throne —
angel to angel uttering, with creature to creature facing
    the Throne:
      Blessed be the Glory of God from His Throne.   30

RELEASE, PLEASE

Release, please, this bound one
    by the power of your right hand.
Receive the song of your people,
    exalt us, Lord, and make us
pure. Almighty one, protect
    those who seek your oneness:
Bless them and cleanse them—bestow
    upon them your merciful justice.
Mighty one, holy one, in your
    goodness guide your assembly.
Turn, sole one on high,
    to those who remember your sanctity,
and accept our cry and plea—
    You who fathom all mysteries.

The Book of Creation

While not "a poem that is always a poem," and in fact not really a poem at all, *Sefer Yetzirah*, the Book of Creation (or Formation), is very much a cosmic or divine *ars poetica*, and the term "prose" hardly begins to account for what we find there. The analogy to artistic and, especially, poetic creation is all the more tempting as letters and the order one can make of them (through measure, registration, and arrangement) lie at the heart of the book's esoteric doctrine. Some writers have even described *Sefer Yetzirah* as a treatise on the power of sound and its magical capacity for "making" and "world building." In fact, the book takes on as its subject the grammar of creation rather than standard religious concepts such as the Sabbath, the People of Israel, ethics, sin, redemption, the Messiah, and the like. Thematic preoccupation apart, the intense concision and pronounced rhythms of the text, along with its particular focus on making, suggest "poetry" rather than prose, and Yehudah Liebes, among the leading authorities on the work, sees *Sefer Yetzirah* as a product of its own theory of poetics—that is, a poem, and a highly accomplished one at that. The graphic arrangement of the translation here is, then, not as arbitrary as it might at first glance seem, and there are Hebrew precedents for it.

This short and highly potent composition is, scholars have found, a peculiar literary phenomenon. Some of the oddness might owe to the book's having been assembled from discrete and very different strands that were forced together by an editor; but that only scratches the surface of its strangeness. Collaging a variety of learned opinion, we might sum up the book's oddness by noting that it has been described as an ancient non-Kabbalistic treatise that later became "a *vade mecum* for the Kabbalah." Since the tenth century the book has circulated widely and proven to be highly influential in diverse and by no means exclusively mystical circles. Scholars such as Liebes see a direct line between the book and later Kabbalah, as the proliferation of commentary around the short text evolved through, among other things, the Kabbalistic vision of the later Middle Ages.

When it comes to the book's provenance, however, we know even less than we do about the Heikhalot hymns. Tradition attributes the book's teachings to the patriarch Abraham, who is the only person (let alone biblical or postbiblical protagonist) mentioned in the text, and who as the "first philosopher" and the "ideal mystic" in one version of the book imitates the divine poesis in spiritual and intellectual fashion. Scholars have placed the writing or redaction of *Sefer Yetzirah* anywhere between the Second Temple period to the tenth century C.E. While many scholars favor a third- to fourth-century C.E. dating, probably in Palestine, a compelling case can also be made that would suggest a later, Islamic provenance. The earliest *historical* evidence of the book is from the ninth century, when the great polymath and Jewish communal leader Sa'adia Gaon translated it into Arabic and wrote an important commentary to it.

All agree, however, that this "earliest extant speculative text written in the Hebrew language" is at once enigmatic in the extreme and among the most important works in the history of Jewish mysticism—one whose elusive poetics of dynamic conduction and restraint would go on to have a profound influence on central writers in the tradition, from Eliezer Kallir to Shelomoh Ibn Gabirol and Yehudah HaLevi, up through the author or authors of the *Zohar*, and on to the first great modern Hebrew poet, Hayyim Nahman Bialik. The early-twentieth-century scholar Louis Ginzberg claimed that it had "a greater influence on the development of the Jewish mind than almost any other book after the completion of the Talmud" — a hyperbolic formulation that is all the more startling when one takes into account the book's style, which Scholem describes as "at once pompous and laconic, ambiguous and oracular."

Scholars have sought to explain the work's difficult surface as at least in part a result of its author's or authors' attempt to account in Hebrew and within the context of Jewish thought for a way of thinking and experiencing the world that Hebrew culture and the Hebrew language could not yet accommodate. "The author undoubtedly wished to bring his own views, clearly influenced by Greek sources, into harmony with the Talmudic disciplines relating to the doctrine of the Creation and of the *merkavah*," writes Scholem, who notes in particular strong connections to the speculative tradition concerning the paths of Sophia — divine wisdom — or *hokhmah*. Another recent reading, however, sees the book as a kind of Wisdom literature squarely in the Hebraic tradition. Still others suggest that the redaction reflects a circa ninth-century and Shi'i- and Gnostic-influenced Jewish "attempt to enter the mind of Abraham" (the "first philosopher"). That said, the book itself clearly integrates ancient material as well. Liebes even detects a possible Indian influence on the linguistic aspect of *Sefer Yetzirah*, and that notion has been tentatively and tantalizingly supported by recent scholarship.

Sefer Yetzirah introduces terminology and concepts that would become central to later Kabbalistic thought to such an extent that, noting the proliferation of medieval commentaries to the book, Liebes comments, "The Kabbalah didn't give birth to the commentaries to *Sefer Yetzirah*, rather, the commentaries to *Sefer Yetzirah* gave birth to the Kabbalah. In other words, the interpretation of *Sefer Yetzirah* is itself the teaching of the Kabbalah." As that teaching (in *Sefer Yetzirah*) has it, thirty-two paths of wisdom are the instruments of creation

through which God engraved (or hewed out) the world. These chan-
nels consist of the twenty-two consonants of the Hebrew alphabet
and the ten *sefirot*, or primordial numbers (1–10 — zero came later,
from the East, via the Arabs). The term resists translation. Despite the
Greco-Judaic source of the book's content, the word *sefirot* doesn't
derive from the Greek *sphaira* (which gives English its "sphere");
rather, it comes from a Hebrew root that yields, among other things,
the verbs "to count" (*lispor*) and "recount" (*lesapeir*), and the nouns
"number" (*mispar*), "border" (*sfar*), "tale" (*sippur*), and also possibly
"sapphire" (*sappir*). (Through the Arabic *siphr* it gives us "cipher.")
In this possibly neo-Pythagorean scheme, it is not, says Scholem, "a
question of ordinary numbers, but of metaphysical principles of the
universe or stages in the creation of the world."

So much for the math. The key to *Sefer Yetzirah's* worldview, if
one can call it that, is linguistic, and at the heart of that view is the
notion that heaven and earth were created by means of letters and
speech. The world itself is, in short, a literary creation and, not sur-
prisingly, *Sefer Yetzirah* devotes an astonishing sort and amount of
attention to the individual letters of the Hebrew alphabet and their
various properties in combination. Like the sefirot, the Hebrew let-
ters are in this manual of cosmic poetics vehicles of creation for the
continual construction (and deconstruction) of reality. By implica-
tion, human beings in the image of God act like God, or partake of
divine poesis when they create and above all when they create (or re-
create) with words. Jewish tradition contains at least several examples
of this: Scripture tells us that Betzalel, the builder of the Tabernacle
(which reflects the structure of the cosmos), was "filled with the spirit
of God, in wisdom, and in understanding, and in knowledge, and in
all manner of workmanship," and the Talmud explains what this wis-
dom consisted of: "[Betzalel] knew to combine the letters by which
the heaven and earth were created" (*Berakhot* 55a). And in one of the

longest and later Merkavah texts, the circa fifth- or sixth-century 3 Enoch, Rabbi Ishmael tells us:

> [The angel] Metatron said to me:
> Come and I will show you
> > the letters by which heaven and earth were created;
> > the letters by which seas and rivers were created;
> > the letters by which mountains and hills were created;
> > the letters by which trees and grasses were created;
> > the letters by which stars and constellations were created . . .
> > the letters by which the throne of glory and the wheels of the chariot were created . . .
> > the letters by which wisdom and understanding, knowledge and intelligence, humility and rectitude were created, by which the whole world is sustained.

In *Sefer Yetzirah* we encounter nothing in the way of this sort of midrashic reportage or transmission; instead, in this new and revolutionary line of writing, it's all principles, blueprints, and brass tacks—a radically theological take on what Ezra Pound said was the poet's central task: to build a world.

Through thirty-two hidden paths of wisdom,
YAH, the Lord of hosts, engraved
His name—the Lord of Israel,
Living God and King of the world,
merciful, gracious God almighty,
on high and dwelling in eternity,
    His name is holy
    and He is sublime
    and created His world
10   out of three words:
        sefer, sfar, sippur—
        letter, limit, and tale.

Ten spheres of restraint,
ten ciphers of Nothing—
and twenty-two letters at the foundation:
    three arc mothers
    seven doubles
    and twelve are elemental—

    Ten spheres of restraint
20   like the ten digits of a hand—
       five against five
    and the sole one's bond

aligned in the middle
with the pact of the circumscribed word
and the pact of the circumcised flesh.

Ten spheres of restraint
ten, not nine or eleven —
    fathom through wisdom,
    be wise through knowing;
judge through them and with them search,   30
set a word straight
and restore the Creator to His place.

Ten spheres of restraint
whose measure is ten without end:
        a depth before
        and a depth behind,
        a benevolent depth
        and a depth that harms,
        a depth on high
        and a depth below,   40
        an Eastern depth
        and a depth to the West,
        a northern depth
        and southern depth,
        the single Lord and faithful master
        reigning over all

from the dwelling
of His sanctity
into eternity;

50   Ten spheres of restraint—
the sight like lightning,
their reach without end,
and His word within them
     runs and returns;
His speech they pursue like a storm,
and before His throne they bow.

Ten spheres of restraint—
their end contained in their beginning,
their beginning in their end,
60   like coals and a lambent flame;
for the Lord is One
     and there is no other.
And before One—what would you number?

Ten spheres of restraint.
Bridle your mouth and keep it from speaking,
your heart from wondering,
     and if it wanders,
     return to the place—
which is why it is said:
70   *and the creatures race and return.*

Over this a pact was made.

. . .

Twenty-two letters to start with.
He engraved, quarried, and weighed,
    exchanged and combined—
and with them formed all of creation
and all that He was destined to fashion.

Twenty-two letters
carved through voice,
quarried in air,
and fixed in the mouth   80
    in five positions:
certain sounds in the throat,
certain sounds on the lips,
certain sounds against the palate
and certain sounds against the teeth,
and others along the tongue.

Twenty-two letters fixed
in a wheel like a wall
with two hundred and thirty-one doors—
    the wheel whirrs   90
    back and forth
    and the sign bearing its witness is:

No good is greater than *oneg* (pleasure);
no evil greater than *neg'a* (plague).

How did He
combine, weigh,
and exchange them?
Aleph with all
and all with Aleph;
100　Bet with all
and all with Bet.
Over and over and on again,
through two hundred and thirty-one gates—
with every creature
and also speech
issuing from a single Name.

He created substance from Nothing—
from *absence* making *what there is*—
He hewed tremendous columns
110　out of air that can't be grasped,
combining, exchanging,
and fashioning
all of creation
and every locution
within a single Name,
and the sign

bearing its witness is:
twenty-two longed-for things
in a single body bound.

. . .

From here on in consider   120
what a mouth can't utter
and what the ear can't hear . . .

Al-Andalus & Ashkenaz

Kabbalah proper would not emerge until the late twelfth century, in southern France, but important poets were, as we've seen, deeply engaged long before that with the metaphysical and psycho-spiritual hints and traces, the insights and experiences, that Kabbalists would later develop into a full-fledged symbolic system. One of these outstanding forerunners, and in fact one of the greatest poets in the history of Hebrew literature, was Shelomoh Ibn Gabirol, the second of the major Andalusian Hebrew poets. He was born in Malaga circa 1021 and died sometime after 1056, possibly in Valencia.

From the thirteenth century on, central personalities in the Kabbalistic tradition looked to Ibn Gabirol as a stellar figure in their lineage, much in the way that André Breton and the surrealists reached back into the past to claim Poe and Sade as surrealists before their time. The sense of affinity and influence was so strong that these later mystics not only read Ibn Gabirol's poems anachronistically according to their own system but, on occasion, put forth far-fetched arguments that Ibn Gabirol was a secret Kabbalist who, among other things, fashioned a female golem and engaged in various forms of magic.

Bracketing the problem of locating Ibn Gabirol with any precision in the history of Kabbalah, one can't but be struck by the recurrence in the great poet's Arabic-inspired liturgical work of elements drawn from esoteric Jewish doctrine, including Merkavah literature, *Sefer Yetzirah*, and the quasi-apocalyptic *Pirkei deRabbi Eliezer*, which in turn may have roots in the tradition of Greek Gnosticism. Also of interest in this regard is the intense Greco-Arabic Neoplatonism of Ibn

Gabirol's poetry and prose alike, where thought and feeling, keen reason and religious passion, are integrated to such an extent and under such a high degree of pressure that the boundary blurs between philosophy and mysticism. This is no doubt what led Scholem to speak of Ibn Gabirol's "mystical spirituality" and the way in which both he and Yehudah HaLevi were "motivated in the last resort by mystical leanings." And Moshe Idel has recently commented that "there can be no doubt that major Jewish thinkers active in the [Iberian] peninsula like . . . Ibn Gabirol were acquainted with mystical concepts and writings stemming from Arabic sources." Those leanings and that spirituality run through everything Ibn Gabirol ever wrote, and with his colossal literary gifts harnessed to a powerfully metaphysical scheme of his own, he seems to have anticipated the Kabbalistic inclination for complex networks of layered meaning. Within that scheme he unfurls a majestic vision of divine creation echoed by human re-creation, which is to say, his imaginative world developed around notions of order on micro and macro planes of the real, and with language as a cosmic power central to both. All this comes to unforgettable expression not only in his explicitly devotional work ("He Dwells Forever," "Angels Amassing," and *Kingdom's Crown*) but in secular poems such as "I Love You," and even—though this is more controversial—in what on the face of it appear to be straightforward court panegyrics (such as "The Palace Garden") and sui generis meditations such as "I Am the Man." In other words, whether one defines the term *Kabbalah* in a strict historical fashion, as the scholars must, or reads it ahistorically, as the Kabbalists proper (and poets) often do, it is clear that Ibn Gabirol and the later mystical thinkers form part of interlocking constellations in the night sky of mythic Judaism.

*

Yehudah HaLevi (ca. 1075–1141) is perhaps the best-known literary figure in Jewish history, though a large part of his fame derives from extraliterary factors, some of which bear directly on his relevance to the history of Jewish mysticism. Called in his own day "the quintessence and embodiment of our country . . . our glory and leader . . . a unique and perfect devotee," as an 1130 letter from the Cairo Geniza has it, he wrote a poetry that gave voice to national longings for a return to the Land of Israel, where he believed Jews could live in unmediated fashion in God's presence. Like Ibn Gabirol, he was precocious and supremely gifted, and in time his talent took on what many have identified as a distinctly mystical bent. Having inherited Ibn Gabirol's complete set of literary tools and modes, however, HaLevi ended up building a world of another sort altogether, and when push comes to poetic shove, the two poets could not be more different. Where Ibn Gabirol saw the sublime in complexity and endless and often agonized reflection, and possessed a universalizing cosmic sort of consciousness on the order of Walt Whitman's almost perfectly and inexplicably merged with that of Emily Dickinson, HaLevi found ultimate meaning in simplicity, surrender, and a kind of transcendental parochialism.

HaLevi's contribution to the development of Kabbalah is threefold: First, his prose treatise known as *The Book of the Kuzari* (the original Arabic subtitle of which might be loosely rendered as *The Book of the Defense of a Despised Faith*) is in places powerfully informed by *Sefer Yetzirah*. HaLevi reads that work in light of his intense belief in the unique and divine powers of the Hebrew language, which is "the language created by God . . . without a doubt the most perfect and most fitted to express the things specified." Second, the ideas worked out in his verse and prose about the nature of Israel and prophecy proved especially compelling to the Kabbalists of thirteenth-century Gerona and Guadalajara, or Castile generally: Israel is to the nations of the world what the heart is to the body, and Jews possess an "extra" or "second" soul that raises them over others and becomes a faculty for prophecy. And third, and perhaps most important on the literary level, the Sufi-like cast of HaLevi's lyric poems and the ardor of his poems of longing for redemption—in which complete surrender to

God was central, and where prophecy rather than reason or aesthetics was the source of ultimate value—marked him as a supplicant of the sort we will find again and again in this tradition, though no subsequent poet would approach the intensity of his awareness or the sonorous quality of his devotion.

HE DWELLS FOREVER

"Thy kingdom is a kingdom for eternity . . ."

He dwells forever, exalted, alone,
and no one comes near Him
    whose kingdom is One—
from the light of His garment He fashioned His world
  within three words that are sealed.

He yearned, longing for the teacher's counsel;
thought to reveal the ten spheres and their circles;
and against them inscribed
    ten without end—
  and five against five now depend.   10

Who fathoms the mystery is shaken with fear.
From this He discerns who's beyond all compare.
Prior to "One"—what does one number?
    He's prime to all primes—
  and to all that's exalted He's higher.

For the ten are as-
    if caught in a siege;
Who dwells upon them knows and sees:
He's the Creator and within them rules.
  His witnesses' claims are made clear.   20

And so by means of the twenty-two letters,
He stretched out fire at the uppermost border;
    at the lower extension He gathered water;
and He sent out between them the wind of measure
    and set the twelve constellations aloft.

It's He who brought forth Being from Nothing,
    and then from Chaos substance was formed;
He set up huge pillars beyond comprehension,
established an azure and inlaid circumference —
30   the abysmal waters flow forth from its stones.

He fixed six directions sealed with His Name:
From water hurled fire with heavenly strength;
He established within them
    His host and His throne
    for signs and seasons and days.

His Name which is raised and borne over all
    He placed in all with desire and labor;
the earth He hung like grapes in a cluster;
from His lofty place He's the place of all:
40   The Lord is a Rock everlasting.

On the upper spirit He established His throne,
where His kingdom's glory is eternally home;
there His dominion

over all is defined:
the spirit of God is Life beyond time.

High above all, and of all the strongest,
He sees the cosmos and over all watches;
above all holds sway,
      surrounds all there is;
      by means of His Name all creatures exist.   50

He fashioned all with a blemishless word;
He alone leads, He's instantly heard;
the Lord carries all
      without growing weary—
      within their own wisdom He captures the wise.

He gives revolution to the belt of the skies;
it's He who suspends earth's lands where they lie.
He says: Let there be . . .
      and it is by His might:
      All that's hidden He brings to light.   60

It's He who parts and He who gathers;
He who enriches then brings on disaster;
He who crushes
      and He who congeals—
      He who gives form to matter revealed.

Know that it's He who brings light and shadow;
He who exalts
    then He who brings low;
He who swells and He who collapses
70   the greatest of mountains and hills;

He who brings
    subsistence to men;
He who ripples their fields with grain;
He who gives them water to drink;
   it's He who brings down the rain;

and He who gives life to men of the world;
He who gives strength
    to the frame of a child;
He who over our sinew sends skin;
80   He who lengthens our bones within;

He who breathes through the body His breath;
He who keeps it upright in health;
He who deep
    into earth returns it;
   and He who will wake us from sleep.

ANGELS AMASSING

Holy, holy, holy is the Lord of hosts,
the whole earth is full of his glory.
—Isaiah 6:3

Angels amassing like sparks in flames,
their brightness like burnished brass in their casings,
before the exalted throne in a throng
    one to another in vision turn
    to laud their Lord the Creator in longing—
O sons of strength, give glory and strength to the Lord.

Sublime creatures beneath the throne,
charged carriers encased in light,
in four quarters acknowledge your glory
    and glow in entreaty and word and awe—   10
    on guard over day, keepers of night—
O sons of strength, give glory and strength to the Lord.

Leading the camps of your hordes they look on,
with Michael your eminent prince at the front—
a myriad of chariots set to your right—
    and they gather together to seek out your palace
    and bow before your partition in service—
O sons of strength, give glory and strength to the Lord.

The hosts of the second camp stand on the left,
20   and Gabriel over its army looks out:
thousands of seraphs, a tremendous force,
together surround your holy throne—
of-and-through fire on fire they roam—
O sons of strength, give glory and strength to the Lord.

From the third camp's ranks there rises song
with the Lord's prince Nuriel a turret before them,
at the sound of their rushing the heavens tremble,
in their seeking the place of I-am the Creator,
the reward of a vision of glory and splendor—
30   *O sons of strength, give glory and strength to the Lord.*

The fourth bears witness in majestic array,
with Raphael chanting your psalms and a prayer,
they wreathe the bud and crown of power
and the four lift in perfect accord
hymns you inspired to stave off despair—
O sons of strength, give glory and strength to the Lord.

In trembling and fear the assembled sparks
cry out as one with their will set strong,
they plead for your faithful, a people pursued,
40   and send a thunderous noise toward the void,
three times invoking your station apart—
O sons of strength, give glory and strength to the Lord.

I LOVE YOU

I love you with the love a man
    has for his only son—
with his heart and his soul and his might.
And I take great pleasure in your mind
      as you take the mystery on
    of the Lord's act in creation—
though the issue is distant and deep,
and who could approach its foundation?

But I'll tell you something I've heard
and let you dwell on its strangeness: 10
    sages have said that the secret
      of being owes all
to the all who has all in His hand:
He longs to give form to the formless
    as a lover longs for his friend.
And this is, maybe, what the prophets
meant when they said He worked
    all for His own exaltation.

I've offered you these words—
now show me how you'll raise them.   20

9

You are wise,
and wisdom is a fountain and source
   of life welling up from within you,

and men are too coarse to know you.

You are wise,
and prime to all that's primeval,
   as though you were wisdom's tutor.

You are wise,
but your wisdom wasn't acquired
   and didn't derive from another.

You are wise,
and your wisdom gave rise to an endless desire
   in the world as within an artist or worker—

to bring out the stream of existence from Nothing,
   like light flowing from sight's extension—

drawing from the source of that light without vessel,
giving it shape without tools,

    hewing and carving,
    refining and making it pure:

He called to Nothing—which split;   20
    to existence—pitched like a tent;
    to the world—as it spread beneath sky.

With desire's span He established the heavens,
as His hand coupled the tent of the planets
        with loops of skill,
        weaving creation's pavilion,

the links of His will
reaching the lowest
        rung of creation—

the curtain   30
at the outermost edge of the spheres . . .

24

Who could make sense of creation's secrets,
of your raising up over the ninth sphere
        the circle of mind,
the sphere of the innermost chamber?

The tenth to the Lord is always sacred:

This is the highest ring,
    transcending all elevation
        and beyond all ideation.

This is the place of the hidden
10   for your glory above in the palanquin . . .

You formed its frame from the silver of truth;
from the gold of mind you created its matter;
on pillars of justice you established its throne:
    its reality derives from your power;

    its longing is from you and for you,
    and toward you ascends its desire.

25

Who comprehends your thinking
in transforming the radiance of intellect's sphere
    into a glow
of souls and spirits on high?

These are your kingdom's soldiers,
angels serving your will with their forces,
holding the flaming sword that revolves
    every which way—

as they work in all manner,
wherever the spirit moves them: 10

all are glass-like forms,
all are transcendent creatures,
guarding without and within,
    watching over your presence.

From a sacred place they descend,
from the source of light they extend,
    splitting into their ranks,
    each with its standard's signs,
engraved with the pen of a ready writer—

among them princes and servants,   20
and armies that depart and return
    with neither fatigue nor pause
    —seeing yet not-to-be-seen.

Some are hewn from flame;

others are wind in air;

some are fire and water paired;

some are seraphs, some electrum;

some are lightning, others a flare;

each rank bows down before the One
30   who rides the heavens and stands

in the heights before His hosts;

By watches they issue out—
at first by day, and then by night,
    sending up song and praise

to the One who's wrapped in power.

All in awe and trembling,
bow and kneel before you, saying:

We offer up thanks to you,
our Lord, who is God,
40   that we are able to serve you;
that you are the sole Creator
and we alone bear witness;

that you it was
and is who gave us form—
    not we on our own—

that we are the work of your hand.

26

Who could approach the place of your dwelling,
in your raising up over the sphere of mind
    the Throne of Glory
in the fields of concealment and splendor,
at the source of the secret and matter,
where the mind reaches and yields?

On high you were raised and rose
        to the Throne of your Power —
    and beside you no man might ascend.

27

Who could accomplish what you've accomplished
in establishing under the Throne of Glory
    a level for all who were righteous in spirit?

This is the range of pure soul
gathered in the bond of all that's vital.
For those who've worked to exhaustion —
this is the place of their strength's renewal,
where the weary will find repose;
    these are the children of calm,

of pleasure that knows no bound in the mind: 10 this is the World to Come,

a place of position and vision for souls
    that gaze
into the mirrors of the palace's servants,
    before the Lord to see and be seen.

They dwell in the halls of the king,

    and stand alongside his table,
        taking delight
in the sweetness of intellect's fruit
    which offers them majesty's savor.

This is the rest and inheritance
that knows no bounds in its goodness and beauty,
    flowing with milk and honey;
      this is its fruit and deliverance.

29

Who could grasp your intensity

in forming the radiance of purity
    from the glow of your glory,

    from a rock the Rock has hewn,
from the hollow of a clearness withdrawn?

You sent the spirit of wisdom along it
and gave it the name of soul,
 and formed it out of the fire
  of intellect's ardor
whose spirit burned on inside it;   10

and you sent it out through the body
  to serve it and guard it—

and you watch as it acts like a flame within it,
 though the body isn't consumed

which was formed from the spark of soul
and was brought into being from nothing

when the Lord came across it in fire.

TRUE LIFE

I run to the source of the one true life,
turning my back to all that is empty and vain.
My only hope is to see the Lord, my king—
    apart from Him I fear and worship nothing.

If only I might see Him—at least in a dream—
I'd sleep forever, so the dream would never end.
If I could see His face in my heart's chamber,
    I'd never need to look outside again.

WHERE WILL I FIND YOU

Where, Lord, will I find you:
your place is high and obscured.
  And where
      won't I find you:
  your glory fills the world.

You dwell deep within—
    you've fixed the ends of creation.
You stand, a tower for the near,
    refuge to those far off.
You've lain above the Ark, here,   10
    yet live in the highest heavens.
    Exalted among your hosts,
    although beyond their hymns—
        no heavenly sphere
            could ever contain you,
    let alone a chamber within.

In being borne above them
    on an exalted throne,
you are closer to them
    than their breath and skin.   20
Their mouths bear witness for them
    that you alone gave them form.
    Your kingdom's burden is theirs;
    who wouldn't fear you?

And who could fail
    to search for you—
who sends down food when it is due?

I sought your nearness.
    With all my heart I called you.
30   And in my going out to meet you,
        I found you coming toward me,
as in the wonders of your might
    and holy works I saw you.
    Who would say he hasn't seen
    your glory as the heavens'
        hordes declare
            their awe of you
without a sound being heard?

But could the Lord, in truth,
40   dwell in men on earth?
How would men you made
    from the dust and clay
fathom your presence there,
    enthroned upon their praise?
    The creatures hovering over
    the world praise your wonders—
        your throne borne high
            above their heads,
as you bear all forever.

LORD,

all my desire is here before you,
    whether or not I speak of it:
I'd seek your favor, for an instant, then die —
    if only you would grant my wish.
I'd place my spirit in your hand,
    then sleep — and in that sleep find sweetness.

I wander from you — and die alive;
    the closer I cling — I live to die.
How to approach I still don't know,
    nor on what words I might rely.
Instruct me, Lord: advise and guide me.
    Free me from my prison of lies.

Teach me while I can bear the affliction —
    do not, Lord, despise my plea;
before I've become my own burden
    and the little I am weighs on me,
and against my will, I give in
    as worms eat bones that weary of me.

I'll come to the place my forefathers reached,
    and by their place of rest find rest.
Earth's back to me is foreign;
    my one true home is in its dust.

Till now my youth has done what it would:
    When will I provide for myself?

The world He placed in my heart has kept me
    from tending to my end and after.
How could I come to serve my Lord,
    when I am still desire's prisoner?
How could I ask for a place on high,
30   when I know the worm will be my sister?

How at that end could my heart be glad,
    when I don't know what death will bring?
Day after day and night after night
    reduce the flesh upon me to nothing.
Into the winds they'll scatter my spirit.
    To dust they'll return the little remaining.

What can I say—with desire my enemy,
    from boyhood till now pursuing me:
What is Time to me but your Will?
40   If you're not with me, what will I be?
I stand bereft of any virtue:
    only your justice and mercy shield me.

But why should I speak, or even aspire?
    Lord, before you is all my desire.

A dove in the distance fluttered,
  flitting through the forest—
    unable to recover,
she flew up, flustered, hovering,
  circling round her lover.
    She'd thought the thousand
years to the Time of the End
  about to come, but was
    confounded in her designs,
and tormented by her lover,   10
  over the years was parted
    from Him, her soul descending
bared to the world below.
  She vowed never again
    to mention His name, but deep
within her heart it held,
  as though a fire burning.
    Why be like her foes?
Her bill opens wide
  toward the latter rain   20
    of your salvation; her soul
within her faith is firm,
  and she does not despair,
    whether she is honored
through His name or whether

in disdain brought low.
Let God, our Lord, come
and not be still: Around Him
storms of fire flame.

In the wake of Crusader persecution and its attendant Jewish martyr-
dom, and under the influence of mystical Christian currents, a novel
Pietistic movement took shape among German Jewry toward the
middle of the twelfth century. The adherents of the movement and
its various strains became known as Hasidei Ashkenaz, "the devout
of Ashkenaz," or the Rhineland—a territory initially comprising the
banks of the Rhine and gradually extending outward east and west.
(This "Hasidism" is not to be confused with the later movement that
gained popularity in eighteenth-century Poland.) German-Jewish Pi-
etism made an immediate and lasting impact upon the character of
medieval German Jewry, and it became a critical link in the chain of
Jewish mystical tradition.

External historical and cultural influences apart, specifically Jew-
ish factors were also at work in the emergence of German-Jewish
Pietism. The ninth-century arrival in Ashkenaz of a leading Italian-
Jewish family, the Kalonymides, for instance, appears to have in-
troduced to German-Jewish communities the Merkavah tradition,
knowledge of the *Sefer Yetzirah*, and other devotional or esoteric
writings relating to "the mysteries of prayer." Though not all the ele-
ments of the new Pietistic morality and theosophy were necessarily
"mystical," several rang interesting changes on the esoteric literature
that preceded the movement; the Heikhalot poems and prose tracts
in particular they read as "news that stays news," in this case a valid
report from distant parts that would guide them on the path to the
divine realm.

The texts produced by the different Hasidic streams in Ashkenaz stressed both a preoccupation with the manner in which an essentially unknowable God is and might be revealed on earth, and a mystical understanding of prayer as the principal means to direct experience of that divine reality. The Pietists' call for humility, restraint, and intimacy of address in worship presented a striking contrast to what has come across to some as the prideful selflessness and exclusivity of the Merkavah-like ascent by adepts. This notion of an intensely focused and private turn to God by an individual in isolation (or by an isolated group) was far more compelling to mystically inclined worshippers than was the repetitive ritual of standard public prayer, and it would go on to have a powerful influence over Galilean Kabbalah and even twenty-first-century Judaism. In all three contexts, *kavannah*—the intention and concentration with which one focused on a given prayer's words—was a dominant value. Though German Pietists didn't yet use the word in this sense, the idea was already taking hold, and they believed that one had to understand the contents of one's prayer and pray in a language one understood. For this reason the Pietists of Ashkenaz "to the consternation of neighbors in the synagogue . . . prayed in slow motion," so as to better dwell on the esoteric and especially the numerological associations of the words in their prayers. Along similar lines, the German-Jewish Pietists emphasized distinct ethical elements that sometimes took on a Christian coloring, including ascetic renunciation; the cultivation of patience, serenity, and martyrdom in the face of trial; and adherence to principles of justice taken to extremes. Their moral ideal was, in other words, downright monkish. Their theology too was characterized by what looks like a Christian refraction, in its assumption that there were multiple aspects to the Godhead (an understanding that would be developed intensively by later Kabbalists).

The role of poetry in this cultural context is curious. On the one hand, the German Pietists emphasized the quality of the worshipper's concentration and purity of impulse. Suffering was seen as a prerequisite for attachment to the inner meaning of the prayers, the primary goal of which was to awaken the community, not to impress it with the beauty of a prayer leader's voice or the skill with which a poet rhymed or dealt with form. Accordingly, the movement also rejected a good deal of poetic material on principle as inappropriate and "un-Jewish." Nevertheless, several important poetic or poetry-related compositions did emerge from German Hasidic circles, most conspicuously a group of poems known as Poems of Unification (*Yihud*) and Glory (*Kavod*), which have been incorporated into the daily and Sabbath liturgies of many communities.

By far the most popular of these works is the "Hymn of Divine Glory" (*Shir haKavod*), which is frequently attributed to Yehudah He-Hasid of Regensburg (d. 1217). Yehudah was one of the most prominent members of the movement and occupied an almost mythic position within it—such that his standing has been compared to that of Saint Francis of Assisi. (The jury, though, is still out on the question of authorship, and some scholars propose that the poem may actually be by his father, Shmuel HeHasid ben Kalonymos; others suggest that one of Yehudah's disciples, possibly Eleazar of Worms, may have written it.) Yehudah is best known for a massive work called *Sefer Hasidim* (The Book of the Pious), a sprawling guide to Jewish piety grounded in daily life and illustrated through a mixture of tales, scriptural exegeses, and homilies. His embrace of modesty was extreme, and he forbade writers from including their own names on their books. His hymn—if it is his—takes as its subject man's desire to know the unknowable God and to understand the dynamic between three aspects of His being: His transcendence, in which, as Eleazar of Worms put it, "He maintains His silence and carries the universe"; the higher "inner glory," which is formless but has a voice and is identified with the Shekhinah and the holy spirit (sometimes as a kind of Logos); and a lower "visible glory," which takes on continually changing form that prophets and mystics alone can see. The Pietists understood the relation between these elements in erotic terms, according to which the upper glory was male and the lower glory female. In the poem's charged erotic scheme, the lower glory prepares a crown which is then lifted along the armature of the verse toward the upper glory, or the hidden head of God. Both the composition and recitation of the hymn, in other words, bring about unification within the divine realm and between God and those who seek Him in prayer.

HYMN OF DIVINE GLORY

I offer up songs
and weave these hymns —
　　for you, Lord,
my soul now yearns:

it yearns for the shadow
and shelter of your power,
　　to know the secret
of your mystery's plan.

Whenever I speak
of your glory and honor,　　　　10
　　my heart moans
and sighs for your love.

Therefore I praise
your glorious splendor
　　and honor your name
with songs of love.

I'll tell of your glory
though I have not seen you —
　　name and compare you,
whom I've not known.　　　　20

*

By means of your prophets'
and servants' secrets
   you've given your glory's
resplendence form,

they limned your greatness
and strength in creation
   in accord with the force
of your wondrous cause.

You were drawn in words
30   but not as you are,
     depicted in light
of what you have done,

in limitless visions
your likeness was cast,
   but through all comparison
you are One.

They saw in you youth
and then old age—
   your hair was black,
40   and then it was gray,

in judgment age —
and in battle youth,
    as a man of war
whose hand held sway.

On His head He set
salvation's helmet,
    His arm of right
and holiness prevailed,

His locks were filled
with the dew of light—   50
    with splintered drops
of night, His curls.

I adorn Him as He
delights in me:
    He'll be a crown
of splendor for me:

like choice gold
is the glow of His head:
    engraved on His brow
is His name and glory.   60

In majesty's splendor,
for glory and honor,

for Him His people
fashioned a crown,

the plaits of His hair
like those of youth—
    His black and twisting
locks flow down.

Righteousness is
70   His majesty's splendor:
    set it forever
as His highest joy—

His treasured nation
in His hand is resplendence,
    a royal miter
of beauty and awe.

He bore them and then
adorned them with grace:
    in His sight they were precious
80   and He brought them glory.

His glory is on me
and mine upon Him:
    He is near
whenever I call Him.

He comes out of Edom,
ruddy and bright—
    from treading the winepress
His robes are red,

to the meek one He showed
the phylacteries' tie: 90
    an image of God
at the back of His head.

He delights in His people
and adorns the humble,
    dwelling in praises
and among them raised.

Your word's inception
is truth through the ages,
    so seek out a people
who seek you in faith   100

and let the mass
of my hymns ascend—
    and my song's sound
approach your presence.

And may these praises
crown your station

as my prayers
like incense rise —

may the song of the poor
110   have the worth in your eyes
of the praises sung
by the offering priests

and this blessing come near
the one who provides,
who in righteousness brings
on action and birth.

Receive my words
as the finest fragrance
and before them nod
120   your head in turn,

and may my musing
be sweet to your ear,
as my soul for you,
Lord, now yearns . . .

The Kabbalah in Spain

The development of Kabbalistic circles in the late twelfth and early thirteenth centuries is a particularly complex and elusive phenomenon, and this isn't the place to unravel it or even to explain how others have tried to. For our purposes, it should be enough to say that, while some recent writers have found "Kabbalistic" phenomena appearing several centuries earlier in the East (and along the Rhine), scholarly consensus now holds that Kabbalah as we've come to know it crystallized around this time in southern France and then, nearby, in northeastern Spain. The Provençal school of Jewish mysticism appears not to have produced any significant mystical or Kabbalistic poetry, at least none that survives, though most scholars believe that it played a pivotal role in the bequeathal of a compact volume of literary prose that is generally considered to be the first properly Kabbalistic work.

The *Sefer Bahir* (the Book of Clearness, or Radiance), which was probably assembled around 1185, most likely from older fragments, introduces mythic elements that would become central to the worldview and vocabulary of Kabbalah: first, a divine world consisting of ten specific powers—which would soon become known as *sefirot* with particular names; second, the feminine nature of the lowest of these powers—the Shekhinah; and third, the depiction of the divine realm as an upside-down tree—its unreachable roots in heaven and its branches extending toward earth. The *Bahir* also introduces the notion of the transmigration of souls, along with a far more dramatic sense of evil than had hitherto been seen in Jewish thought and which would be taken up in great detail in later Kabbalistic writing.

The following passages from the *Bahir* show how the sefirot and an increasingly eroticized Shekhinah (which, say some scholars, betrays the influence of Christian veneration of the Virgin Mary and her role as intercessor, restorer, and savior—or daughter, mother, and bride) gradually become part of the mythopoetic world of Kabbalistic thinking:

They asked him, What is the meaning of the verse (relating to the prophet Balaam): "And he took him to the Field of Tzofim" (Numbers 23:14)? Meaning, not "the field that is *known as* Tzofim," but the field *of* the *tzofim*, which is to say, of the seers and vision [those who see, in Hebrew: *tzofim*]. It is written, "Come, my beloved, let us go into the field" (Song of Songs 7:12). What does that mean, "Come . . . let us go into the field"? Do not read "the field" (*sadeh*), but rather "the fold" (*shidah*), as in the carriage or vessel [through which higher powers flow]. He said to him: "Come my beloved, let us go into the field (meaning, let our hearts be borne toward God), lest we remain in a single place. And what is this "heart" (*lev*) . . . whose numerological value is thirty-two (*lamed-vav*, which spells *lev*)? The thirty-two [concealed] paths through which the world was made [created].

A parable: There was a king in his innermost chambers. Now there were thirty-two chambers in all in his palace, and each had a path (or hall) that led to it. Was it fitting for this king to allow all to enter his rooms by these paths? No. Was it fitting for him not to reveal his pearls and tapestries, his treasures and secrets and hidden things at all? No. What did he do? Touching [taking] his daughter, He concentrated the various paths within her and her garments, and anyone who wished to enter the innermost chamber had to gaze upon her. . . . In his great love for her, he sometimes calls her "my sister [my bride]" for they come from a single place; and sometimes he calls her "my daughter," for she is his daughter; and sometimes he calls her "my mother."

A short time later these and other similar ideas took hold in Jewish circles not far to the south, in Gerona, where another if related sort of Jewish renaissance was under way. The central figure of the early-thirteenth-century Jewish Catalan circle was Moshe ben Nahman, known as the Ramban or Nahmanides (b. 1194). An important writer in diverse fields that included Kabbalah, biblical commentary, religious law, philosophy, poetry, and communal affairs, he was one of medieval Spanish Jewry's outstanding intellectuals. He spent most of his life in Gerona and Barcelona, though after defending Judaism before the king of Aragon at the Disputation at Barcelona in 1265, he left Spain under somewhat mysterious circumstances. Two years later he set sail for Palestine, where he died in 1270.

Ben Nahman was part of what scholar Ezra Fleischer has called the Gerona school of poetry. With their "counter poetics," Fleischer notes, the writers of that school "sought to uproot secular poetry from its historical ground and transplant it to another, more fertile soil. In Gerona, for the first time in the history of Spanish Hebrew literature, poetry was composed far from the main centers of Jewish political life, and by poets lacking any but oppositional contacts with the Jewish oligarchic upper class." The poetics of this new "oppositional aristocracy" eliminated much of the ornamental, metaphorical richness and conventional practice of the by-then epigonic Andalusian school and shunned the humor and frivolity of the rhymed-prose and often picaresque form that had come to dominate the Hebrew literature of the day (the *makamah*). As a result, says Fleischer, "poetry became poetry again"—that is, it returned to verse and regained its serious, contemplative aspect, as in "Before the World Ever Was."

Perhaps Nahmanides' most famous poem, this magisterial hymn on the fate of the soul makes plain his considerable literary gifts and contains full-bodied expression of his thought, including—some have argued—his immersion in the mystical doctrine of the Kabbalah. Others believe the poem is purely Neoplatonic. Nahmanides was, however, known for his tendency to conceal the new esoteric doctrine within the cloak of standard religious practice, and here too he seems to be riding the cusp between mystical Neoplatonism and a new Kabbalistic vision. As one scholar has put it: "[In] the magnificent opening stanzas . . . the soul makes its descent through the world of the sefirot, . . . [At the conclusion of the poem the] 'return of all things to their original state' . . . establishes the spiritual and literary symmetry required by Andalusian sensibility—but it establishes it on Kabbalistic terms, as all things are in the end reabsorbed into the realm of the sefirot." According to Scholem, the poem is "a mystical hymn" that depicts "the birth of the soul in the depth of the divine spheres from where its life streams forth."

The three short poems that follow the hymn represent an intermediary stage of Kabbalistic speculation. They have been attributed to Ya'akov HaKohen, the elder of the medieval "Kohen brothers" (as they're now known), who were active in mid-thirteenth-century Castile (Segovia) and Provence. The brothers were at the center of an important new circle of mystics who were dedicated exclusively to Kabbalah and exerted a powerful influence on Moshe de León, the writer who, most scholars now agree, played a central role in the composition of the *Zohar.* Ya'akov appears to have maintained ties with the German Pietists. The varied and often pseudepigraphic prose writings of the brothers are characterized by, among other things, a dualistic Gnostic aspect (involving "mythic descriptions of evil"), a focus on the mystical properties of the Hebrew letters and their shapes, and "the first Kabbalistic myth of the apocalyptic and messianic end-time," which would entail a struggle between the forces of good and evil on the cosmic and not merely the individual level. The poems translated here are taken from a longer prayer that Scholem describes as "a mysterious hymn"; they employ symbolism characteristic of thirteenth- and fourteenth-century Kabbalah, including magical or numerological permutations of the Divine Name and mention of the *kelippot*—"shards," "shells," or "husks" that embody the forces of evil in the world. Scholem adds that if this poem is in fact by Ya'akov HaKohen (he is skeptical), it would constitute one of the earliest uses of that term, which would become central to the later Kabbalistic worldview. Scholem also notes what seems to be an allusion to the dire historical circumstances of the prayer's composition, as one of its sections mentions sixty-five Jewish families of a certain community that clearly faced an existential threat at the time. In fact, it's likely that the entire prayer—which takes up the theme of "divine aid" from the start—was a plea for the deliverance of that community and, as Scholem puts it, "for the opening of the heart." "With the Kohen brothers," Dan observes, "the first hundred years of the development of Kabbalah [proper] came to an end."

From the beginning, before the world ever was,
I was held on high with His hidden treasures;
He brought me forth from nothing and in
    the end I will be withdrawn by the King.

My life's course flowed from the heaven's foundation,
which endowed it with form in evident fashion.
The hands of the craftsman that weighed out creation
    shaped me then for the vaults of the King.

He appeared to reveal what once He'd concealed,
on the left and then the right as well;
and He sent me down the stairway leading
    from Siloam's pool to the garden of the King.

I was formed from dust, though your breath in me burns.
You've known this stranger's thoughts in these lands.
How long will you journey until you return
    and delight with your deeds, my soul, the King?

You set a lamp at my feet for the path
and searched to see if my spirit was willing;
I set out before you, and you warned me, repeating
    "Fear, my child, the Lord and King."

My heart was given judgment and choice:
if it brings me to mercy—in that I'll rejoice.
But if it brings wickedness, derision will reign,
  for this is not the will of the King.

I hasten, trembling, to confess my transgression
before I'm brought to the house where all end.
My name will bear witness before me then
  and who could deny the decree of the King?

I was drawn to a land of drought and starvation,
and nearly buried in wanting's tomb;   30
but I turned back, feeling contrition,
  for I had not kept to the counsel of the King.

He set great love in my heart for the world.
I pursued days and their vanity's whirl;
and so I'll be judged for all I've concealed
  and go in fear of my Lord and King.

Knowing iniquity, and anxious with guilt—
aware that fortune will fade—heart waits
in terror for mercy, for how can man's spirit
  corrupted come before the King?   40

In weighing out wrong that your servant admits,
place your mercies in the scales with his merit,

as against his will, he'll face an accounting
    before the Master, the Lord and King.

Yours is the grace of benevolence, Lord:
with it alone is refuge secured.
Yours is forgiveness with which one is rescued,
    its measure determined by the King.

I've trusted *you*, and not my power,
50   and know your mercy endures forever.
Before I call, somehow you answer.
      I'm ashamed to bring my requests to the King.

Your ways are a comfort, you crush all baseness,
so soul in its refuge will know no disgrace.
For the body interred will surely be vanquished,
    while soul will ascend to the halls of the King.

She knows you will plunge me into the mire,
knows you will take as pledge her attire —
but that you'll restore it, once she has suffered
60   the judgment soon to be judged by the King.

Steady and strengthen the weak one's hand,
and when to their former state things return
bring her forth from the palace's garden
    through the paradise groves that belong to the King.

1

May the Name send its hidden radiance
    to open the gates of deliverance
to His servants—and shine in their hearts,
which now are shut in silent darkness.

May the great King be moved
    to act in perfection and righteousness—
to open the gates of wisdom for us
and waken the love of old, the love of ancient days.

2

By the power of the hidden Name *I-Am-That-I-Am*,
and by the dew of Desire and Blessing, the dead will
    live again. . . .

3

I-am is the power of your Name in concealment,
and one who knows its mystery dwells in eternity's instant.

Over the world, it pours forth abundance and favor,
and on it all worlds hang, like grapes in a cluster.

Send the dew of blessing, the dew of grace;
renew my dispensation, and grant me length of days.

Bring light to my eyes with your teaching, and let not
    the husks that surround your hosts obstruct me.
May Heaven and Adam's children judge me with mercy.

Sustain me with their strength and fortune—
but do not leave me in need of the gifts of men.

Within the framework of the "normal mysticism" of rabbinic Judaism and its readily accessible literary canon, the poetry of prescribed prayer tends to serve as a relatively quiet, often personal expression of man's love of, and subservience to, God. Sincerity of expression, rather than what is actually said, is paramount. In the *extra*-ordinary and largely esoteric mysticism of the Kabbalistic tradition and its precursors, hymns constitute the suprapersonal building blocks from which the cosmos is continually constructed. In the Heikhalot literature, for instance, we find God described as a "King bedecked with robes of song," whose "Name *is* Song and Song is His Name." In this innovative Merkavah scheme, the song itself is what matters, and failure to sing or compose hymns involves less a transgression (for which one will suffer) than a deprivation on the level of spirit. The mystic must, therefore, risk a deadly ascent in order to learn and continually "bring down" the songs containing the secrets of existence.

Poetry as it's conceived in *Sefer HaZohar* (The Book of Radiance, or Splendor) — which would become the Book of Books in the Jewish mystical context, achieving a nearly canonical status alongside the Bible and the Talmud — falls somewhere between the two Jewish traditions of hymnology that precede it. In the *Zohar*, poetry's efficacy depends above all on the aspirant's ability to interpret strongly and find the secrets of existence in extant texts (rather than to rise in perilous ascent into uncharted regions). That is, the reader or supplicant bears responsibility for understanding how a given hymn he recites might affect life in the divine realm; then, through comprehension and recitation he has to bring his prayer into alignment with the world on high. In short, as the *Zohar* sees it, "man doesn't need new poetry," only a new way of understanding poems that have already been written.

While this conservative perspective might account for the paucity of verse within what is otherwise an intensely and even wildly imaginative literary compendium, song itself, as Moshe Idel notes, was valued highly by the Spanish Kabbalists for its ability to "sweeten" the "unbridled and hence baleful impact" of the sefirah of Gevurah, or stern judgment. Along these lines, Idel cites one of the major Kabbalists of the late thirteenth century: "Now we must understand that the secret of the quality of the Levite song was its ability to improve and gladden, to soften their own attribute in order to bind the 'left' to the 'right' through the pleasantness of song's sublime harmonization, and thereby to perform their service. Thus, with respect to all manner of song, it relieves despondency, cools anger, and brings joy as a result of the bonding of the attribute of the 'right side' to all else. For in the joy of this unification, the sorrowful influence of stern judgment is removed from the world."

The author of these observations, Moshe de León (b. ca. 1240), was for much of the twentieth century credited with having written a visionary multivolume pseudepigraphic Aramaic work attributed to the Mishnaic sage Shimon Bar Yohai. Today most scholars accept Yehudah Liebes's argument that "Bar Yohai's *Zohar*" was actually compiled by a limited if not elite circle of Spanish mystics that included de León. Some believe that the book also includes earlier strands that may have been brought from the East (and some of which were initially composed in Hebrew and then translated into Aramaic), and still others argue that it isn't a book at all but an assortment of discrete fragments that were later assembled as a collection. However it came to be, it aroused passionate interest among a select group of Jewish mystics, initially in Castile and, after it was printed in the mid-sixteenth century in Italy, throughout the Jewish world. "For centuries," wrote Scholem, "it stood out as the expression of all that was profoundest and most deeply hidden in the innermost recesses of the Jewish soul."

Alternately open and exclusive, naive and highly abstruse, surprisingly sensual and numbingly abstract, the *Zohar* is a daunting text, noteworthy for its free flow of associations which combine narrative, lyric, exegetical, and speculative modes. Its primary themes—the relation of the lower world to the upper, the phenomenon of spiritual awakening, the nature of the Godhead and the dynamic interaction of the sefirot (though the *Zohar* proper doesn't use the term per se), the power of evil and darkness, and the sexual dimension of the divine realm and cosmic processes—are expounded as Bar Yohai and his companions wander a fictional Palestinian landscape. There they hold forth on the Torah, which is seen in the *Zohar* as "the divine force cloaked in words, letters, and stories." In a metaphor that becomes a highly unusual lens through which to see the world, the revelation of the grammatically feminine Torah's secrets is, in this context, likened to the removal of garments that cover a female body. And with this image we come to what has been called the great myth of the *Zohar* (and which also characterizes the gist of its approach to song)—the fundamentally erotic nature of its interpretive enterprise and its contemplation of the Torah's secrets. As the characters in the book itself see it, however, they "do not 'interpret' verses [of the Torah at all]. Rather, they *are aroused toward them*—and in turn they arouse those verses." As the *Zohar* itself tell us, "[The Torah] reveals herself to no one but her lover." Just as what takes place on earth and in man affects what happens in heaven, so too what is in the reader's consciousness changes and is changed by *what happens in the text.* For the text in the world of the *Zohar* is hardly a static entity. "Under the gaze of the *Zohar*'s protagonists . . . the Torah shimmers, grows, and expands. [And] just as in an intensified erotic state, there is no part of the body of their beloved (the Torah) that does not evoke their interest, curiosity, wonder."

And so on and on for sometimes remarkable, sometimes intolerable page after page and volume after volume, almost all of which is cast along the sprawling lines of the standard early-medieval Hebrew model of textual interpretation, or midrash. The *Zohar's* artificial and on the whole not particularly elegant prose is, however, far more variable and also uneven than are the standard collections of midrashim. And though its associative reach and sometimes extravagant imaginative descriptions often lead readers to speak of its poetry (Scholem, by contrast, describes it as "almost . . . in the form of a mystical novel"), one has in fact to scour the text for anything remotely resembling signs of a *poem* as a made thing held together under tension and propelled by structural and linguistic principles. That is, only rarely do the formal elements of the text that one normally associates with "poems" make themselves felt in the *Zohar*.

One of the places they do is in a group of short introductory or concluding passages to the standard exegeses known as *toseftot* (additions) and *matnitin* ("mishnas," or teachings), which are cast in the voice of a heavenly herald calling to a sleeper to rise from his torpor. This awakening and arousal is at once spiritual, intellectual, and — again — erotic, and it too is intended to bring about the alignment of divine and human realms, which is one of the principal goals of Zoharic consciousness. In that alignment the sefirot are also roused — first the feminine aspect of the Divine, which in turn awakens the masculine dimension, drawing him to her. That union within the upper world results in the riverlike flow of the Divine Presence and blessing downward to the world below. The dynamic involved — "the actualization of divinity in the world" — is central to the mystical transformation at the heart of the book, and its vision of life experienced in fullness ripples out not only to the mystics themselves but to an ever-widening circle of readers. The language of these heraldic units (which have been translated below as prose poems) tends to be charged, tactile, taut, elevated, and enigmatic.

The *Zohar* also contains poetry in the more conventional sense in a few passages that include magical charms. With the incantation against Lilith we find an ancient Babylonian or Sumerian myth alive and most definitely kicking in a popular form of high-medieval verse. Lilith first appears in a Jewish context in Isaiah 34:14, where she is counted among the signs of vengeance and a land laid waste: "The wild-cats shall meet with the jackals, and the satyr shall cry to his fellow; yea, Lilith shall repose there, and shall find her a place of rest." In the Talmud she has long hair and wings, and poses a serious threat to men sleeping alone in a house. By the eighth century the well-known legend takes shape that Lilith was Adam's first wife. Created from the earth with her husband, she refused to give up her equality, fought with him about how they should have intercourse, then pronounced the four-letter Name of God and flew off. Henceforth her goal, she declared, would be to harm the newborn. In Kabbalistic lore Lilith is both a strangler of children and a seducer of men. From the nocturnal emissions and spilled onanistic seed of the latter she gives birth to a vast, black host of demonic sons. ("The Muse of masturbation," Harold Bloom calls her, "bearing endless imps to those guilty of self-gratification.") The consort of Sama'el, the satanic angel of death, she reigns as the queen of the Sitra Ahra, the Other Side, or realm of evil forces. Lilith is, then, the dark mirror of the Shekhinah—which had by that time emerged in the literature as a full-fledged feminine aspect of the Divine Presence. As the Shekhinah rules over the realm of purity (as mother of the House of Israel), Lilith reigns over the kingdom of impurity.

The incantation that follows emerges from this larger legend and its background, and it is one of many that surface in Kabbalistic writings that recognize Lilith's tendency to "infringe on the domain of

Eve" and threaten the consecrated union between husband and wife. For Lilith grows jealous of pious couples, whose sexual congress on the Sabbath evening brings about the union on high of the sefirot Tiferet (beauty) and Malkhut (kingdom and the Shekhinah). That pure double union—below and in the divine realm—draws down a holy soul, which enters a newborn's body. Envious of all this, Lilith prowls the earth, looking for husbands and wives who violate the sanctity of their intimacy by having intercourse by lamplight, and in doing so leave themselves vulnerable to "the Other Side." When she finds such a couple, Lilith pounces and takes possession of the soul of their offspring—striking the child with epilepsy or slaying it altogether. So it is that the incantation below is meant to be recited, as the text itself makes clear, "in the hour when the husband enters into union with his wife." At that point "he should turn his mind to the holiness of his Lord . . ." and address the she-demon directly.

ON AWAKENING AND DRAWING NEAR

1

Aspiration to action and the bonds of faith. A voice, the voice of voices, awakened on high and below. Our eyes were open: a wheel turned on high all around, and a fine voice was aroused. Awaken, those who drowse— with sleep in their hollows—and neither look nor see nor know, their ears sealed, their hearts thick, they drowse and do not know. The Torah and teaching stand before them. They cannot comprehend, and do not know what they behold. Scripture sends forth voices. Look closely, fools, open your eyes and understand. But none notice and none hear. How long will you dwell in the dark of your desire? Look and discover—the light that shines.

2

Fabulous constellations. Indomitable fortifications. Those whose eyes and ears are open. A voice—of voices—descends from on high, shattering mountains and stone. Who are they who see without seeing, whose ears are sealed, whose eyes are closed? They neither see nor hear nor know through contemplation the one held by two within, and by them cast away. To these two they cling. While one—the master maker—lies not within them. In memory's books they are not written, and from the Book of Life they're erased.

3

We were drawing near, and heard a rolling sound on high coming down and reaching through the world. A sound shattering mountains and stone. Great whirlwinds arose. Our ears were open and it was said along the way, The end of the end has come. Mute sleepers, in the sleep of their holes, hold fast to what they know. . . . They cannot sense, and do not understand, a book is open—and a name will be written.

4

The voice returned as before and said: O high hidden ones who roam throughout the world, occluded and with open eyes, Behold and see! And you below, eyes closed and drowsing—arise. Who among you—before it arrives—can turn darkness into light and a bitter taste to sweetness? Who among you awaits each day the light that streams when the King, coming in glory into the Doe, is declared King of all kings in the world? He who does not await this, day by day in the world, has no portion here.

INCANTATION AGAINST LILITH

Veiled in velvet, is she here?
   Leave off, leave off:
      You shall not enter,
         you shall not emerge.
   It is neither yours nor your share.

Return . . . Return:
   The sea is swelling;
      its waves are calling.
         I hold to the holy portion—
   I am held in the holiness of the King.

Avraham Abulafia's work represents a wholly distinct and often astonishing school of Kabbalistic thought. His language-centered mysticism makes little use of the sort of symbolism that came to the fore in the Castilian *Zohar* circle and earlier Kabbalah—both of which focused on the role of the sefirot and the structure of the Godhead. In fact, wrote Abulafia, "the sefirot are worse than the Trinity" (because there are ten of them to the Christian triad). Abulafia is, in other words, a Spanish Kabbalist whose Kabbalah isn't particularly Spanish. Less interested in the question of first things than in the mysteries of the present and the endtime, Abulafia focused on what Moshe Idel calls "the inner road that emphasizes . . . the transformation of the human psyche or intellect." As Idel puts it, "The main message of his Kabbalah is that there is a way to attain the life-of-the-world-to-come within this life," or, in Abulafia's own words: "Life is the life of the world to come, which a man earns by means of the letters."

Born in 1240 in Saragossa and raised in Tudela, Abulafia distinguished himself as a maverick early on. Two years after the death of his father he left Spain for the Land of Israel, from where he hoped to set out in search of the ten lost tribes and the mythical river Sambatyon, beyond which, legend had it, large parts of these tribes had been exiled by the Assyrian king Shalmanaser. Abulafia believed that finding them would help usher in the messianic age. He made it no farther than the port town of Acre, however, and headed home, passing through Greece and Italy, where he spent some ten years. In 1270, in Barcelona, a mystical experience led him to believe that he had attained prophetic inspiration, and he began preaching his doctrine to a small group of disciples, some of whom converted to Catholicism. Three years later—apparently misunderstood in his homeland—he returned to Greece and Italy.

During the final decade of his life, under the influence of a variety of non-Spanish mystical trends, Abulafia did almost all his major and utterly sui generis work. In 1280, he experienced a still more shocking vision and set out for Rome, where he sought to meet with Pope Nicholas III on the eve of the Jewish New Year and, it seems, explain to him the mystical essence of authentic Judaism. (Some scholars believe that his goal was to take the pope to task for Christianity's treatment of the Jews in their exile or to persuade the pontiff to convert to Judaism.) This foolish adventure nearly cost Abulafia his life. He was condemned to be burned at the stake and was spared at the last minute only because of the pope's sudden death. He returned to Sicily, where his troubles continued, and he was attacked within the Jewish community for a unique sort of messianic speculation, proposing among other things that "the Messiah is the human intellect" (the Aristotelian *nous poetikos*, or Agent Intellect) and that redemption entails not "the arrival of the time of the end" so much as "the arousal of the soul . . . to a spiritual life."

As Idel has written, Abulafia believed that "the Messiah is dormant in every person and this capacity should be realized." The implicit suggestion was of course that—with his own extraordinary intellect, and as a supreme sort of prophet, superior (he believed) even to Moses— Abulafia was that realized Messiah. Since Abulafia's concept of Messianism also included a more traditional historical-national aspect, it is hardly surprising that his self-appointment, or anointment, gave rise to fierce opposition. When in the midst of that controversy the most influential rabbinic authority of the time—and himself a Kabbalist—called Abulafia a charlatan, he was forced to flee to the desolate island of Comino, near Malta. There, in 1288, he completed the apocalyptic — even hallucinatory — fourteen-hundred-line *Sefer HaOt* (the Book of the Sign, or Letter), the only surviving example of several prophetic works he composed late in his life and, according to Idel, "one of the most interesting apocalypses ever written in Hebrew." Abulafia also wrote many language-centered mystical texts and handbooks of ecstatic meditation, whose aim was, as he put it, "to unseal the soul, to untie the knots which bind it." Untying the knot in this context means, says Scholem, breaking through "the natural and normal borders of human existence . . . [which] guarantee [the soul's] normal functioning" in order to "perceive the existence of spiritual forms and things divine." Abulafia died around 1292.

Though he composed only a handful of poems, Abulafia was obsessed with the mysterious mechanism of language, and his writings about its inner workings are fascinating for students of poetry. Just as Rimbaud called for the systematic derangement of the senses in order to tap the visionary powers required to be a true poet, Abulafia insisted on the need for the systematic disturbance and rearrangement of the plain senses of the text through numerological and other permutations in order to break through to the esoteric, visionary plane of understanding. His radical, contrapuntal readings dissolve the text as we know it, shifting the focus from surface narrative not just to its associative field of imagery but to the architecture of the individual words and the dynamic play between their letters. As Idel writes: "The principle of language [for Abulafia] is not its meanings, intentions, or grammatical rules but the . . . various transformations [the linguistic] medium has undergone." Considering the relevance and resonance of Abulafia's formulations, Idel likens them to Walter Benjamin's notion of translation as a process that, rather than distancing one from the gist of a linguistic moment, brings one into its heart: "Translation is removal from one language to another through a continuum of transformations. Translation passes through continua of transformation, not abstract areas of similarity and identity."

A similar strategy informs the poem at hand. While numerous elements of the *Book of the Sign* defy translation, or come across as merely bizarre, the prophetic and even literary thrust of the work is self-evident and, in places, breathtaking. Blood and ink in Abulafia's thought stand, respectively, for imagination (soul) and intellect (spirit), and the ongoing battle between them involves an effort to raise the individual imagination to the power of the Active Intellect, which is the conduit to eternal life and the divine. This transformation is brought about through — among other things — manipulation of the letters of the Divine Name. The poet likens their recombination to the harmonization of sounds in music. Also of interest to the literary minded is what Abulafia considered the highest grade of meditation, which he called "leaping" or "skipping" — whereby one jumps in writing from one association to another by adhering to a set of formal if flexible considerations that are intended to bring about the "widening of the [initiate's] consciousness." This leaping "brings to light hidden processes of the mind, [and] 'liberates us from the prison of the natural sphere and leads us to the boundaries of the divine sphere.'"

Abulafia's prophetic vision involves a synthesis of these and other often-conflicting forces through a kind of psychomachia wherein the inner processes are externalized through imaginative figuration. (The commandments, too, are understood by Abulafia as allegories for the spiritual process.) And this can be palpably sensed, if not quite fathomed, in the excerpts from the *Book of the Sign* that follow, where the struggle is, in part, between the imaginative faculty (represented by blood) and the visionary faculty (represented by ink). While the incantatory lines of *Sefer HaOt* are neither metrical nor rhymed, the cadence throughout is so pronounced, and the poem's various sections combine such a heightened sense of language and so vivid a visual panoply, that the whole suggests a Miltonic or Blakean poetics. Both in style and form, this mystical epic in miniature, like its author, is unique in Hebrew literature.

For all his uniqueness, Abulafia wasn't alone. He was a teacher, and his finest student was Yosef Gikatilla. Born in Medinaceli, Castile, Gikatilla lived for many years in Abulafia's town, Segovia, and he was greatly influenced by the prophetic Kabbalah of his mentor before going on to become a major Kabbalist in his own right. His best-known book, *Sha'arei Ora* (Gates of Light, written before 1293), demonstrates a marked departure from Abulafia's thought and shows Gikatilla to be immersed in theosophical Kabbalistic teachings treating the sefirot and other elements of Kabbalistic symbolism that Abulafia eschewed. Though no direct link has been established, he also seems to have been close to Moshe de León (and some scholars believe he was among the writers of the *Zohar*). Gikatilla's other work—much of which remains in manuscript—includes a Kabbalistic commentary on the Passover Haggadah, two commentaries on the Song of Songs, a book about the observance of the commandments, some twenty liturgical poems, and proverbs. While Gikatilla is not considered a poet per se, his handful of extant hymns and didactic poems are of interest for their Kabbalistic content and the author's desire to cast that material in Andalusian verse forms. The poem below comes from the opening section of Gikatilla's earliest surviving composition, *Ginat Egoz* (The Nut Garden), which he wrote in 1274, at the end of his two-year period of study under Abulafia. The book constitutes a clear and detailed study of the mystical elements of Hebrew. The initial word of the Hebrew title (*GiNaT*, "Garden of") is an acronym standing for *Gematria* (numerology), *Notarikon* (acronyms or acrostics), and *Temurah* (permutation of the letters, as in anagrams). The implication of this acronym is that the esoteric manipulation of letters is like a garden wherein ultimate nourishment can be found.

And the sign sings
and sky is key
to knowing the Will
that moves him and lends
grace to spirit
and mercy to power
to rectify action,
Kingdom now foremost
and the teaching behind,
the teaching foremost   10
and Kingdom behind:
and the letter, vowels,
and song reveal
the mystery of Blood. . . .

*

And YHVH spoke to me when I saw His Name
spelled out and merged with the Blood in my heart,
separating Blood from Ink and Ink from Blood.
And YHVH said to me: "Behold, Blood
is the name of your Soul, and Ink the name of your Spirit:
Your father and mother are vessels for my Name and a sign."   20
I fathomed, then, the tremendous difference between
my Spirit and Soul, and enormous delight came through me.
For I knew that my Soul was dwelling in the redness as Blood,

and my Spirit was dwelling in the blackness as Ink. And
    there raged
a war in my heart between the Blood and the Ink—
the Blood from the wind and the Ink from the dust,
and the black Ink over the Blood was victorious,
and so—the Sabbath subdues the days of the week.

With this my heart rested within me. Now I offer
praise to the Lord, to His Name in my heart forever. . . .

30

*

The Lord revealed a new vision with a Name
renewed and a spirit revived, on the fourth day
of the seventh month, with the first moon at the start
of the eighteenth year from my visions' onset. I
was watching, and behold a man came up from the West
with a great force, and the number of men in his camp
was twenty-two thousand. That man's glory and strength
of heart and splendor shook the earth's foundations,
and the hearts of his soldiers trembled. Strong-armed riders
were with him, and men on foot—and the line of those men

40

came to no end, and his forehead was marked with Blood
and Ink at its edges, and a sign like a staff determined
between them, and this is the letter deeply occulted.
Black was the color of Blood and went red, and the color
of the Ink was red, and behold it darkened, and the color
of the letter determining between the two was white.

He unveils wonders—the sign, the key, within
the forehead of he who comes, and from his mouth
it rolls forth and the whole of his army set out.
And I, when I saw his face, was alarmed at the sight,   50
and my heart within me withdrew and leapt up
from its place, and I sought to speak—to call on the Name
of the Lord for His help, and the matter fled from my spirit.

And it came to pass, when the man saw the strength
of my fright and my terror mounting, he opened his mouth
and spoke, and my mouth too opened to speak,
and I answered him. And as I spoke my strength
returned, as though I'd turned into another
man, and I opened my eyes and looked, and behold
a stream of seventy tongues emerged from within   60
the sign that was on his forehead. The sign was a potion
of death, he called it, and I called it the potion
of life, for I changed it from something dead to alive.
When the man saw the reversal enacted to honor
the God of Israel, he was pleased, and blessed me
with the world's blessing. He opened his mouth before me,
with a voice that was clear, and said:
                              "Happy is he
who grows in righteousness, and happy are his teachers,
and his people who are with him, and happy are the people   70
who turn to his teaching's discipline, and blessed be YHVH
the Lord, God of Israel, his God who blessed them

with eternity's blessing, from which all living things
come to be—mercy and grace all around,
justice and right within. The arrows of compassion
are shot by its bow; over the blood of hearts
it passes its sword. Your heart, that warrior, is a blossom
in Eden, a bud sprouted from the highest heavens
that you vanquished in battle, and the blood of my
  forehead
80 you marked and its color you changed—and my trials of
  thinking
you understood. Ink you raised, and over
ink you will rise, a sign you sanctified, and by
virtue of a letter you will be made holy
in the great Name known as YHVA YHVH YAHV
  renewing. . . .

                                This illustrious
Name will come to your aid, and the sign of the forehead
will lend you knowledge—and nourish your spirit from
the source of the heart, and hand you the golden scepter,
which through the Glory will bring you life forever.
90 And this will be a sign for you when I come
to contest all the inhabitants of the land
which I will reveal to your ears. You'll see with your eyes
and know with your heart the letter occulted and set
in my forehead. This is the Law of the Sign, and its law
shifts from age to age—from generation
to generation it turns, and it wages the war

of the heavenly hosts. . . .

And from

the bow of knowing they shot arrows of learning,
sending insight toward the target of wisdom,   100
for the power of the blood in the heart is signed and sealed,
and the heart of he who is wise at heart is whole,
knowing his blood is alive and the slime is dead
within him, and so—slime and blood are enclosed
inside his heart. More bitter than death is slime.
His power is sunken within it, and sweeter than honey
is blood, and his spirit dwells in the heart's shrine.
And the soul of every creature of mind must journey
from slime's tent toward the tent of blood.
And from blood's tent toward the shrine of the heart   110
of heaven it travels, and there it dwells for all
the days of its life. . . .

*

And I lifted my eyes, and behold,

I saw three warriors pursuing each other and racing
one after the other, at a bow-shot's distance,
and each turned to the other and said, "Run
and fight against me." And then I saw, behold,
the first ran after the second and drove him away,
and as he was driven he shot a sharpened arrow,
and the arrow fell at his feet by a stone that drew it   120
and turned it there from side to side as it struck

his foot and clung to it, and the man let out
a tremendous bitter powerful shout and cry,
"Lord, God of my fathers, will this arrow
which struck me now bring on my death with its poison?"
And while he was speaking his foot swelled up like a
     swollen
goatskin full of wind, the pain mounting
and spreading throughout his body, till all of his limbs
and joints were swollen like yeast risen.

130   When I heard
his cry my heart was stirred, and I ran toward him,
drawing near, and whispering into his ear,
and his pain fled before my whisper. . . . And it came
to pass, when the first warrior saw how the second
by my whisper was cured, he ran holding
his spear, and struck him again through the navel,
and drove the blade into his belly, and his innards
fell forth to the ground . . . and there he died.

                          *

And when the third saw the second had fallen
140   at the hand of the first, he ran out, pursuing
the first, with his sword drawn. Once and again
and again, ten blows and he died . . .
on the tenth, and I went up toward the dy[. . .]
and said "tell me, my lord, if you will,
the meaning of this battle that I have seen
in a v.i.s.i.o.n." And he showed me an old man

seated upon a Throne of Judgment; his robes
were purple and blue, his hair was white, and he said,
"Go, ask that man on the Hill of Judgment
and he will tell you what these battles mean, 150
and what they will bring, for he is one of your people."
And I went up toward the hill and approached the man,
and bowed down and put my face to the ground
before his feet, and he set his hands upon me
and lifted me up to my feet before him and said:

"Peace be upon you my son in your coming, peace
to you and to all who love you for. . . .
You were saved from the war, and all my battles
you've waged. You have won. And now, know that these
   many
days and years I've awaited you here, until 160
you arrived, and now I will tell you what these battles
mean that you have seen. The three warriors
pursuing each other are three kings who will rise. . . .
"The name of the first is Kadri'el, and the name
of the second is Magdi'el, and the name of the third
is Alfi'el, and the name of the warrior you saw
at the start of the vision is Turi'el,
and I, I am Yaho'el—I have agreed
to speak to you for these several years,
therefore your name in Israel forever shall be 170
Ro'i'el, the Seer of God, the son
of the source of the Living God, Makor-el,

for you came from the place of life, and have chosen life,
and in life will live on—that life being
the children of Abraham and Isaac and Israel, our fathers.
All who hold to them hold to the Lord of Truth
and with us will live. Now, see: the fifth
king is my Anointed, who will reign
as the four kingdoms come to an end. This
180   is the meaning revealed to all, though only he
who knows will fathom the hidden meaning. My son,
Ro'i'el, this is what the Lord
of Israel has told you: You shall write what you've seen
in a book, and call that book the *Book of the Sign*,
for it shall be a sign to all who see it,
so that they will know of the Lord God's benevolence
over the People of Israel—He saw fit
to bring them salvation, and send the book to Spain.
Go in fear of no one, and be not ashamed
190   before any man, for you see that the Lord is your God,
in Him alone have you trusted, who holds up your arm,
that it may tell of His Name to the ends of the earth."

And I did what the old man told me to do in the Name
of the Lord, and I wrote this book, and here I have sent it
to you this day to [. . .] a savior to say
the Lord is with you in your returning
to him in the year of mind,
1288, with a heart that is whole.

THE NUT GARDEN

The Nut Garden holds things felt and thought
and feeling for thought is always a palace—

Sinai with flames of fire about it,
burning though never by fire devoured.

On all four sides surrounded so—
entrance is barred to pretenders forever.

For one who learns to be wise, however,
its doors are open toward the East:

he reaches out and takes a nut,
then cracks its shell, and eats . . .

The Safed Circle
(Galilean Kabbalah)

The most intensely erotic and, at the same time, ascetic phase of Kabbalistic development took place in the mid-sixteenth century in Safed, a dramatically pitched mountain town some ten miles northwest of the Sea of Galilee. During the principal sixty-year period of mystical activity there, Kabbalah evolved from a secret teaching promulgated among initiates to a more popular movement whose "peculiar doctrines" would, over the course of the coming centuries, reach almost every Jewish community on earth as they took up what Scholem called "their victorious march through the world."

Safed's emergence as *the* mystical center of Jewish Palestine is curious. The town isn't mentioned in the Bible at all, and the Talmud refers to it only in passing as a hilltop on which fires were lit to mark the new moon. It becomes important as a strategically located Crusader fortress in 1140, and a little over a century later the Egyptian Mamluk dynasty designated it as the provincial capital. By the beginning of the sixteenth century, as the Ottoman Empire embraced Spain's expelled Jews, the town easily outstripped Jerusalem in economic and spiritual significance. Commercial trade had been flourishing for nearly a century there, and the town was, above all, home to a thriving textile industry, a business in which Jews in Iberia and later in the Ottoman Empire had long been engaged at every level, and for which conditions were ripe in Safed, with its many streams and springs, and its location between major cities on the trade routes and not far from the coast. The political situation was also favorable, as the surrounding non-Jewish population and the governing authorities in the Galilee were less hostile to Jews than were the rulers in Jerusalem; taxes were lower, newcomers were welcome, and, because of its industrial importance, the town was well protected. One Italian-Jewish visitor to Safed in 1535 described the town as an economic miracle. Other miracles would soon follow.

Safed's Galilean setting and mythic history no doubt figured in its allure as well. Centuries earlier, the Mishnah had been redacted in nearby Sepphoris, and parts of the Palestinian Talmud in Tiberias. Legendary Talmudic rabbis including Shimon Bar Yohai (to whom the *Zohar* is traditionally attributed), Hillel, Shammai, and Tarfon, were buried in the hills around the town, and pilgrimages to Bar Yohai's grave in particular drew the region's Kabbalists. By 1536, when the Portuguese (and possibly Spanish) refugee Yosef Karo (1488–1575) arrived in Safed, having spent some forty years in a variety of Ottoman-Jewish communities (Salonika, Edirne, and Nicopolis — now parts of Greece, Turkey, and Bulgaria, respectively), the town was already known as an educational center. The arrival of Karo, one of the great figures of the day, gave Safed an exponential lift, and he was soon looked to as the leader of the town's Jewish community. While still in Salonika, Karo had begun a massive compilation of Jewish law that was intended to help people through the thicket of competing, confusing, and often contradictory customs and legal interpretations that held sway across the Jewish world. The famous abridgment of his work, known as the *Shulhan Arukh* (Set Table), is to this day considered *the* authoritative code of Jewish law and practice. Karo, however, was hardly a dry legal scholar. He was also a mystic, and, over a period of some fifty years, he received regular visitations from a *maggid*, or "celestial mentor," who communicated with him through a kind of automatic speech (warning against, among many other things, the neglect of the suffering Shekhinah and the demonic pleasures of food, drink, and marital relations). The messages received in these trances Karo recorded in a mystical diary.

While the nature and degree of the influence of the Expulsion from Spain on the Jewish mysticism that developed in Safed is a subject of debate—with Moshe Idel questioning Gershom Scholem's sweeping and not always substantiated claim that the crisis caused by the events of 1492 was the principal determinant of that mysticism's emergence and character—it is generally agreed that the Safed community and its Kabbalists saw classical Spanish-Jewish culture, with its rationalism and laxness, as being responsible for the weakening of attachment to "authentic" Judaism and especially to the observance of the commandments. In that post-Expulsion climate, Safedian Judaism picked up where the *Zohar* left off and defined itself against the Arabo-Iberian past: mystical thinking was cultivated, along with an intensified adherence to ritual practice and the observance of the mitzvot. This combination produced an asceticism the likes of which Judaism had rarely seen—certainly not since the Pietistic movement of twelfth-century Ashkenaz (which inspired the Galilean Kabbalists). Severe punishment was prescribed for an assortment of sins ranging from masturbation, adultery, and homosexual relations to the practice of magic or practical Kabbalah, the drinking of nonkosher wine, and transgressions such as vanity, haughtiness, and displays of anger. The neglect of positive commandments (such as the recitation of prayers) was also dealt with harshly. The punitive repertoire included rolling in the snow completely naked (for homosexual intercourse); rolling in nettles or thorns (for publicly humiliating another person); flagellation and sleeping on the ground for a period of fifty-nine days (for sleeping with a menstruating woman); wearing sackcloth and observing daytime fasts, sometimes extending up to almost a year and broken only by bread dipped in dust and the like (for adultery). In classic esoteric fashion, many of these sentences were determined by numerological correlations that linked the punishment to a sin.

Other rites that developed in Safed were at least slightly more uplifting. Prominent among them was the practice of *gerushin*—

literally, "banishments," though the term might be better rendered as "mystical peregrinations," on which the Safedian saints and their disciples would saunter (barefoot in summer) through the Galilean countryside and to the graves of the Talmudic masters who were buried there. Far from being romantic outings that involved "communing with nature," these redemptive excursions were fueled by fierce concentration on key passages of Scripture, and their goal was contact with something far beyond nature. The deep identification with the Shekhinah's exile, and perhaps the defamiliarization the change of scenery entailed, triggered a freer associative process than did regular study in a room. Moshe Cordovero (1522–70), the greatest Kabbalistic theoretician of the day, writes of the way in which, while wandering in the fields with his brother-in-law Shelomoh Alkabetz (author of one of the most beautiful hymns of this period—on which, see below), they would be discussing verses from the Bible when, suddenly, "new ideas would come to us in a manner that cannot be believed unless one has seen or experienced it many times." The verbal and distinctly detached aspect of the gerushin recalls the modern Jewish poet Paul Celan's description, in a famous essay, of two Jews walking in the mountains, silent among the silent stones: "So it was quiet, quiet up there in the mountains. But it was not quiet for long, because when a Jew comes along and meets another, silence cannot last, even in the mountains. Because the Jew and nature are strangers to each other." In a later ritual innovation, the Kabbalists would sometimes stretch themselves out near or actually atop the graves of masters in an effort to unite their souls with that of the sage in question, so that the secrets and mysteries of the tradition (*kabbalah*) would be communicated. On the whole, it's likely that this seemingly "un-Jewish" veneration of saints may (like several other elements that distinguish Galilean Kabbalah) in fact have developed under the influence of the Islamic mysticism of the day, Sufism, which would go on to play a major role in subsequent phases of Kabbalah.

Perhaps the most important and certainly the most far-reaching and moving aspect of Safed's legacy was its development of the ritual surrounding the welcoming of the Sabbath. The arrival of *the* Kabbalistic day (as it has been called, and which, like all Jewish festivals, begins at dusk) was seen in entirely mystical and mythical terms—and celebrated as a sacred marriage in which masculine and feminine aspects of God were joined through the religious practices and erotic enactments of the Kabbalists and their wives. Within this new rite of *Kabbalat Shabbat* (the reception or welcoming of the Sabbath), and through the hymns composed for it, the rhythms and sensual dimensions of nature and language were fused in sublime fashion.

*

Safed's most famous Sabbath hymn was written by Shelomoh Alkabetz, who was born in 1505 (probably in Salonika) and settled in Safed in 1535 or 1536, after arriving with his friend Yosef Karo. A prolific writer of sermons, works on the devotional rules of meals and the mystical significance of sexual union, and esoteric commentaries on the liturgy and Scripture, Alkabetz is known above all as the author of the Sabbath hymn "Lekhah Dodi" (the first two words of which give the poem its title and can be translated either as "Come, my beloved" or "Go, my friend"). A unique work in Alkabetz's canon, "Lekhah Dodi" spoke to the heart of both ordinary worshippers and esoterically minded initiates, and it was soon absorbed into the prayer book as part of the Friday evening ritual. The poem's fame spread—it was translated into German by both Johann Gottfried von Herder and Heinrich Heine—and for the past several centuries it has been sung in Jewish communities around the world.

It is at once among the simplest and most complex of the Kabbalistic poems. At first glance a fairly straightforward, four-square, and almost Protestant-sounding hymn sung at the end of the ritual welcoming of the Sabbath—a kind of bridge between profane and sacred times in the week—it is written in a clear, biblical Hebrew and contains no overtly Kabbalistic references. That plain surface, however, masks a highly coded composition that is rife with ambiguity and rich with mystical layering. Within the esoteric context of the poem, one means two, two means four, down is up, and vice versa. Action is always taking place on multiple planes, and all this is apparent at every turn: structurally, metrically, and thematically, as the poem plays out the drama of a sacred wedding in which the exiled and suffering Shekhinah is welcomed as a bride by God and the congregation of worshippers. Week after week, harmony is restored to the world through that erotic union—and humankind plays a vital role in bringing it about. Initially, it seems, the poem was sung by worshippers in Safed who would walk out into the fields to welcome the Sabbath bride. Later it was moved into the synagogue, where it is sung today (with worshippers turning at the final stanza of the poem to face the synagogue door and bow).

Like the transparent biblical register, the essential symmetries of the poem provide a sense of balance and reassurance (as with, say, an English hymn) that contributes in a major way to the poem's accessibility; at the same time, within that stability deeper esoteric figures are drawn without disturbing the surface of the verse and the more straightforward devotional experience of the average worshipper. Extensive notes at the end of this volume unpack the Kabbalistic depths of the poem, but the fact is that most readers—including the writer of these lines—have come to love "Lekhah Dodi" without knowing very much or even anything at all about that mystical background.

Another extremely well-known and much-loved component of the *Kabbalat Shabbat* ritual developed in Safed is the rhythmically enchanting and simple but potent hymn that begins "Shalom Aleikhem"—"Peace Be upon You"—which was sung in the home after the men of the house returned from the field. The hymn is addressed to the angels of the Sabbath. Today it is sung after the family members return from the synagogue and before they begin their evening meal.

"Yedid Nefesh" (Soul's Beloved) is also part of the Friday night lineup, which starts to look like a greatest hits of Hebrew poetry playlist. "It is the custom of passionate lovers to sing," its author Eliezer Azikri writes, "and since the love of our Creator is wonderful, passing the love of women (2 Samuel 1:26), therefore he who loves Him with all his heart should sing before Him." Azikri (1533–1600) also made it clear that "while God has given man a wife of flesh and blood whom he is to love, his real love must be for the daughter of the King, that is, the Shekhinah." (In a 1579 entry in his generally obscure mystical diary of meditations, revelations, and dreams—which is extant in his own hand—Azikri says that "the soul is a seat [or throne] for the Shekhinah.") Moreover, one must be prepared to suffer for the love of God "all the consequences of violent love," including sleeplessness and other trials. On the whole, notes a leading scholar of the period, Azikri represents one extreme in the range of ascetic Kabbalistic types found in sixteenth-century Safed—"a Sufi-like abandon to the love of God." In the Hebrew mystical tradition, that cleaving to the divine presence was known as *devekut*, and "the royal road to [it] was solitary contemplation and the reduction of all talk, business, and social intercourse to the barest minimum: 'The light of the face of the Living King rests on thine head . . . keep silent in His fear. And if thou speakest, speak to Him alone, and the listener [i.e., your partner in worldly intercourse] may hear. In this way thou wilt practice constant *devekut.*" On the evidence of his diary, Azikri himself appears to have spent the greater part of each day standing in motionless silence, wrapped in phylacteries, "his eyes focused on God" and trying to achieve that longed-for state.

While hardly a technique recommended for young writers, it did produce one great devotional poem, and the hauntingly lyrical "Yedid

Nefesh" soon became extremely popular in all Jewish communities, Sephardic and Ashkenazi alike, where it was sung (and continues to be sung) at a variety of times on the Sabbath. Sephardic communities have also recited it on a number of liminal occasions in the religious calendar—that is, the cusp between the Sabbath and the profane week, the passage from night to dawn, the middle of the night, and so on. Azikri himself introduces the poem in the first published edition of his major work, *Sefer Haredim* (the Book of the Reverent) with the description "A petition for union and the desire of love."

HYMN TO THE SABBATH

Come, my beloved, to meet the bride,
  we'll greet the Sabbath's arrival.

Observe and *remember* in a single utterance
    the singular Lord instructed us;
    the Lord is One, and One is His Name,
      for glory, for praise and renown.
        Come, my beloved, to meet the bride,
          we'll greet the Sabbath's arrival.

Come, we'll go toward the Sabbath now,
    for she is the source of all blessing;   10
    pouring forth from the fountain of time,
      creation's end, though first in conception.
        Come, my beloved, to meet the bride,
          we'll greet the Sabbath's arrival.

Royal city, shrine of our King,
    arise and depart from your ruin;
    you've dwelled in the valley of weeping too long:
      but He will show you compassion.
        Come, my beloved, to meet the bride,
          we'll greet the Sabbath's arrival.   20

Shake yourself from the dust and arise,
    put on, my people, the robes of your splendor,

through Jesse's son, of Bethlehem:
  "Draw near to my soul and redeem her."
    Come, my beloved, to meet the bride,
      we'll greet the Sabbath's arrival.

Awake, arise, your light has come,
  Rise up now, awake and shine:
  awake, arise, and utter a song,
30   through you has His glory been seen.
      Come, my beloved, to meet the bride,
        we'll greet the Sabbath's arrival.

You will not be abashed or shamed,
  why, then, be abject and mourn?
  Through you our afflicted will find protection,
    and the city be built on its ruins.
      Come, my beloved, to meet the bride,
        we'll greet the Sabbath's arrival.

Those who sought your ruin will be ruined
40   and they who'd destroy you be driven away,
    in you the Lord will find delight,
      as a bridegroom delights in his bride.
        Come, my beloved, to meet the bride,
          we'll greet the Sabbath's arrival.

Right and left, you'll spread abroad —
  in awe and worship, revering the Lord;

through Judah's son, the line of Peretz,
  we will exult in joy.
    Come, my beloved, to meet the bride,
      we'll greet the Sabbath's arrival.   50

Come in peace—O crown to her husband—
  in joyfulness come, in gladness, and song;
  among the faithful of this treasured people,
  come, my bride, my bride, come:
    My bride, my Sabbath Queen.
      Come, my beloved, to meet the bride,
      we'll greet the Sabbath's arrival.

Peace be upon you—
    ministering angels,
        angels of heaven—
from the King who is king of all kings,
    the Holy One, blessed be He;
    in peace be your coming—
        angels of peace,
           angels of heaven—
from the King who is king of all kings,
10   the Holy One, blessed be He.

Bless me with peace—
    angels of peace,
        angels of heaven—
from the King who is king of all kings,
    the Holy One, blessed be He,
    in peace be your leaving—
        angels of peace,
           angels of heaven,
from the King who is king of all kings,
20   the Holy One, blessed be He.

Soul's beloved, merciful father,
    draw your servant to your Will;
he'll run to you like a gazelle
    and bow before your splendor—
        for your love to him is sweeter
      than a taste of the honeycomb's nectar.

Majestic, magnificent world's luster,
    my soul is faint with love for you;
Heal her, O Lord, I beseech you,
    show her your brilliance's pleasure—   10
        then she will be strengthened and healed
      and serve your will forever.

Ancient of Days, may your mercies stir:
    take pity on him who loves you;
for long now has he yearned
    to see the glory of your power—
        Hasten, Lord, my heart's delight,
      do not ignore my desire.

Make yourself known, my spirit's treasure,
    spread the shelter of your peace about me;   20
let the world shine with your glory,

in you then we'll rejoice—
>   Hurry, my beloved, the hour has come,
be gracious as once you were.

Though he left behind him almost nothing in the way of theoretical, ethical, or confessional prose, and "seems to have lacked," as Scholem put it, "the literary faculty altogether," Yitzhak Luria comes down to us as one of the most vital figures in Jewish history—a mythmaker of major proportions and a charismatic personality whose recalibration of Jewish thought continues to alter the consciousness of Jews and non-Jews: doctors, writers, scientists, artists, mathematicians, people in business, Talmudists, and, increasingly, even Hollywood actresses and their acolytes.

In the popular Jewish imagination (and in tourist itineraries and guide books), Luria is virtually synonymous with Safed, though he lived there for less than three years. Born in Jerusalem in 1534, Luria moved to Egypt with his Sephardic mother when his Ashkenazic father died, and he studied Kabbalah there with a leading halakhic and mystical authority. He became a successful businessman and scholar of religious law, and then in his late twenties and early thirties began isolating himself on a Nile island and devoting himself to mystical pursuits. He moved to Safed in 1570, when he was thirty-six, studied briefly under Moshe Cordovero, and after Cordovero's death that same year replaced his teacher as leader of Safed's Kabbalistic community. Luria himself died of the plague in 1572, having transmitted the gist of his powerful vision directly to his students (rather than in books) and through a handful of haunting poems. Apparently he found it "impossible" to reduce his teaching to writing "because," as one of his students recalled him saying, "all things are interrelated. I can hardly open my mouth to speak without feeling as though the sea burst its dams and overflowed. How then shall I express what my soul has received, and how can I write it down in a book?"

The full articulation of Luria's mythic thinking is dizzying and, it seems, deliberately daunting, perhaps because it was intended to serve as a steep challenge to the mystics in his circle. It presents an almost bizarrely ramified vision of the erotic, psychological, and intellectual forces at work in the maintenance of the universe. Within that vision Luria depicts what Scholem calls a "process of cosmic restoration and reintegration (*tikkun*)" that follows the catastrophe of creation.

Creation, in the Lurianic scheme, took place when God desired to make Himself known, to ex-press himself—which is to say, literally, to step out of Himself and exteriorize His qualities. Prior to the creation of the world, however, there was no empty space whatsoever—no room for such expression; a limitless light—the presence of God— "suffused all of existence. . . . There was neither beginning nor end, but everything consisted of this one simple undifferentiated light, called Ein-Sof [endlessness, or infinity]." For a variety of reasons (ranging from beneficence to a desire for self-purification), that presence or endlessness sought "to issue forth the world of emanated entities . . . the fullness of His energies, names, and qualities." But in order to bring anything into a space that was already filled, God had to withdraw, as it were, into His own being. The infinite had to move toward definition, and the undifferentiated toward distinction. As Luria's student Hayyim Vital put it: "Ein-Sof then withdrew itself from its centermost point, at the center of its light, and this light retreated from the center to the side, and thus there remained a free space, an empty vacuum." This infusion of absence for the sake of presence is called, in Hebrew, *tzimtzum* (literally, "contraction" or "limitation"). Lurianic creation was, then, predicated on the Creator's descent into His own depths, and we might think of this divine concentration as the initial stage of a cosmic rhetoric. The entire vision is, says Scholem, "one of the most amazing and far-reaching conceptions ever put forward in the whole history of Kabbalism." As Harold Bloom reads him, "Luria had the originality of certain great poets—Dante, Milton, and Blake."

But the amazement was only beginning. Left behind in the empty space created in the wake of God's withdrawal into Himself were, as the Kabbalists saw it, "flecks" of the Divine Light, and these contained both Compassion and Judgment. The remnants of Judgment were transformed into "inchoate matter." In order to illuminate and animate that matter, which now lay in darkness, Ein-Sof sent a ray of its light back across the void at its heart.

Some aspects of the process described above had been part of the Kabbalistic vocabulary prior to Luria, though the Spanish Kabbalists' cosmology, for instance, was far simpler and involved merely the "straightforward" projection of God's power outward into space in a series of ongoing, one-way, and descending emanations. But in addition to refining the basal notion of tzimtzum, Luria introduced a new and startling element into the mix. So as to better control and conduct the return of the divine light, which held within itself ten gradations of illumination (the ten *sefirot*), God formed ten vessels (themselves made of a thicker sort of light). When the light from the ten sefirot began to flow into the vessels intended to shape, define, and transform their power in accordance with God's design, certain of the vessels shattered under the pressure of the unstable light, and in that catastrophe—that breaking of the line of Divine Light—sparks of holiness were scattered. (That cosmic rupture is paralleled on the worldly plane by Adam's sin, and by the transgressions of all who continue to sin in his wake.) As in earlier Kabbalah, the remnants of the shattered vessels—to which sparks of "exiled" holiness sometimes clung—became known as *kelippot* (shards, or shells), and they evolved into the world of material reality.

At this point, in an effort to bring the post-catastrophic situation under control, a new stream of light burst forth from Ein-Sof, which

Luria anthropomorphized as Adam Kadmon—Primal Man on the spiritual plane. (This new stream of light issues from his mouth, his navel, and his phallus.) Beneath Adam Kadmon, the primal light now assumed new and far more personalized configurations, known as the countenances of God, or *partzufim*. Together they constitute (or give birth to) the Living God. Luria's notion of the partzufim is too eccentric and convoluted to delineate here, but the outlines of the mythic picture are already clear, and the critical point is that this process of contraction and expression, or divine inhalation and exhalation, describes not only God's primordial creation, but every ongoing act of creation. And the rhythms of that creation—the ebb and flow of Divine Light, the dynamic of continual penetration and withdrawal—become in this scheme both increasingly complex and sexual. Mutuality, or at least reciprocity, is part of the cosmic process from the start.

While the divine realm seeks to work out its own restoration, or tikkun, of the primordial harmony that existed before the breaking of the vessels, it must be aided by the activity of devout men (and, to an extent, women) in the world, whose task it is to gather up the scattered sparks—that residue or exiled remnant of divinity in every being and bit of the created universe. This they do through spiritually focused acts, including prayer. And so, moment by moment, and for better and worse with every gesture and thought, each and every Jew becomes "a protagonist in the great process of restitution" and cosmic reconfiguration. As Scholem summarizes it, the main purpose of Lurianic Kabbalah was "the preparation of men's hearts for that renaissance the scene of which is the human soul."

In addition to his visionary theoretical teachings, Luria was known for his personal charisma and standing within the community of mystical aspirants. He considered himself the reincarnation of Moses, and legends abounded as to his occult powers and saintliness:

he went to inordinate lengths to respect the rights of others; demonstrated tremendous generosity and humility; could—it was said—decipher people's transmigrational auras, diagnose illnesses of the soul, and cure them; and was able to understand the language of birds and plants, see angels, and make past and future souls appear to him. He also predicted his own untimely death at the age of thirty-eight.

This is only a very rough sketch of the Lurianic saga and myth. But lest we think that the theory has to be mastered before the poems can be read or absorbed, it's worth remembering that, as Gershom Scholem notes, Luria first won fame as a poet, not as a theoretician—and that, as T. S. Eliot suggests, we're often taken with and drawn into poems before we understand them. Luria's three Aramaic hymns for the Sabbath meals—addressed to the baroque countenances of God as he envisioned them—have what Scholem called "the magnificent sweep of mind which visualizes a mystical process, half-describing it, half-conjuring it and producing it through [its] very words." Depicting the rituals that accompany the meals, and illuminating these rituals in mythic terms, with "the solemn drapery of their Zoharic Aramaic," says Scholem, "[the three poems] suggest the grandiloquent gesture of a magician, conjuring up a marvelous pageant for all to see." "They read," he says, "like the hymns of a mystery religion." For all these reasons, they were instantly embraced by Safed's Kabbalists and then—after they were printed in a Venetian prayer book—within a short time by other Jewish communities. Luria's principal disciple, Hayyim Vital, writes that his "master, of blessed memory" would sing the hymns "in a sweet voice" immediately after eating. In most communities today they are sung *before* the meals.

While the language, style, and content of "Why, My Desire" are strikingly different from Luria's Aramaic hymns for the Sabbath, A. M. Habermann, who published this poem and others attributed to Luria, writes that there is compelling evidence that the poem might in fact

be by the Ari—the "Lion," as Luria came to be known. And very re-
cent scholarship supports that attribution (noting that the poem was
attributed to Luria in the Venetian collection containing the Aramaic
hymns published just a few years after the writer's death). Still, as
scholars have also determined conclusively that one of the most pop-
ular of the poems traditionally attributed to Luria ("Yom zeh leYisrael
orah vesimhah") is *not* by the charismatic master—although it too
contains a full signature acrostic—caution has to be exercised when it
comes to determining the provenance of the other twelve poems asso-
ciated with him. Habermann himself leans toward attributing "Why,
My Desire" to one of Luria's disciples, and he characterizes the poem
as "a somewhat strange address to the *yetzer ha-ra*, the poet's evil in-
clination or desire," which he is apparently unable to control. Given
the ascetic practices of Luria and his disciples and the extensive rami-
fications of transgression (see the previous headnote), it isn't hard to
imagine a poem of this sort emerging from this milieu. Whether it is
by Luria himself or by one of his disciples, "Why, My Desire" is an
intense and potent poem that takes us into the heart of a universal
sensation.

*

Utterly distinct from Luria in both personal character and aesthetic
temperament was Yisrael Najara (1550–1625), who is widely consid-
ered the leading hymnist of the day. Unsubstantiated legend attrib-
utes to Luria a saying to the effect that a spark of David and the Holy
Spirit were with Najara (although, in fact, Najara was most likely too
young for Luria to have known much of anything about him or his
work). And while Najara came to be known in some circles as "the
great Kabbalist," and at least one important scholar has gone so far as
to state that "an examination of Najara's poetry in light of Kabbalis-
tic inquiry might well explain a good deal of his poetry's symbolism
and also its essence," Gershom Scholem and other modern scholars

have been more skeptical, questioning the extent of his involvement with Kabbalah proper. The issue of overtly Kabbalistic symbolism in Najara's work apart, his hymns were clearly composed and sung in an atmosphere imbued with mysticism generally and Kabbalah specifically, and the rapidly expanding Najara canon became part of the new religious rites that took shape in Safed and spread from there to other parts of the Jewish world.

Particularly compelling in that cultural climate were subtly mind-altering sessions in which worshippers, taking their cue from Job 38:7 — "when the morning stars sang together and all the sons of God shouted for joy" — would rise in the middle of the night or very early in the morning to sing devotional and sometimes erotically charged hymns. The tradition of these sessions, which were known as *bakkashot*, or "petitions," and some of which opened with Avraham ben Maimon's hymn about the sefirot, "Hidden God" (below), seem to have been influenced by the Sufi *sama'a* or *dhikr* ceremonies, ecstasy-inducing "spiritual concerts" in which poetry was recited to musical accompaniment. The singing of bakkashot continues to this day. "In the middle of the night on every Sabbath," one sixteenth-century account tells us, "[Rabbi Avraham Levi] would wander the streets (of Safed) and cry and call out with a great shout in a bitter voice and wail . . . calling to every *talmid hakham* by name and refusing to leave him alone until he saw him rise up from his bed. At that hour the entire community would come together and give voice to versions of the Mishnahs and Gemaras (the *Zohar*) and the midrashim, to the psalms and the prophets and to songs and supplication and petitions."

Najara's work soon became extremely popular with this audience, for whom he began to write; three different editions of his poetry were published during the poet's own lifetime (sometimes in multiple printings), beginning in 1587, when he was thirty-seven years old. Unlike earlier Hebrew liturgical poetry — such as had been written in Spain, for instance — Najara's work wasn't anchored to a particular part of the liturgy; nor does it seem to have emerged from the "classical" poetic tradition of Safed, where Najara was born—though clearly that poetry informed his work. Instead, the principal influence on Najara's poetry seems to have been Damascus's Turkish coffeehouses, which held Najara and other Ottoman Jews in their thrall. (Najara moved from Safed to Damascus when he was fifteen or so.) And so it is that the crucible in which his work was formed turns out to have combined—under considerable pressure—the mystical poetry of the Sufi tradition, the love songs of the contemporary Turkish popular repertoire, and the classical musical legacy of the Ottoman Empire (that is, Turkish, Persian, and Arabic musical traditions). Grafting the new Hebrew lyrics he composed onto the melodies of popular songs of the day—and often beginning his poems with Hebrew words that sounded remarkably like the Turkish or Spanish he was mimicking, so that *señora*, for instance, would become Shem Nora (the awe-filled Name, in Hebrew)—Najara operated provocatively and to great acclaim in the space "between sanctity and sacrilege." Even the great and anything but pious modern Hebrew poet Hayyim Nahman Bialik seemed taken aback by the practice, observing at one point that "what the Italian Don Juan with his bouquet of flowers in hand sings to this *signora* in Italian behind the inn on a spring night—R. Yisrael Najara with ashes on his head sings with the very same melody and in the Holy Tongue before the Holy One blessed be He and His Shekhinah, before the Holy Ark at the hour of the midnight worship and *tikkun.*"

The two hymns translated here reflect that seamlike quality of Najara's work. The first is an early erotic poem addressed by the masculine speaker to—it would seem—a radiant Shekhinah-like figure. If not for the poem's presence in a book of devotional hymns, each of which is followed by the line of Scripture that prompted it (in this case Isaiah 60, which conjures the luminous Divine Presence), most readers would have a hard time distinguishing the hymn from a secular love poem. And in that difficulty they would, one imagines, be precisely where the poet wanted them to be—as Najara deliberately sought "to raise the sparks of holiness from the Other Side to the Side of the Sacred" and to respond in his way to the call of Cordovero's disciple Elijah de Vidas, who wrote: "He who has never desired a woman is like unto an ass or less, for Divine Worship must be discerned from the sensual." This is what provoked the ire of Najara's rival, the Jerusalem poet and scholar (and Kabbalist), Menahem de Lonzano, who vehemently disapproved of Najara's loose ways with foreign verse and singled this poem out for scorn, characterizing it as "hocus pocus" (*ma'aseh ta'atu'im*) and "utterly defiled." In Najara's verse, de Lonzano notes, "God and the congregation of Israel speak to one another like adulterers."

Luria's disciple Hayyim Vital also developed a pronounced antipathy toward Najara. He wrote of the latter's way of reciting his psalms loudly and "in a frenzy of food and drink," waving his naked arms in the air. "The truth is," Vital continued, "that his hymns themselves are good, but it's forbidden to speak with him or recite any of [what] he has written, because he uses foul language and is always drunk. . . And even now . . . he gets so intoxicated that he engages in homosexual acts . . . and [recently] he fought with his wife and kicked her out of the house, then slept with a gentile woman he'd brought in to light his fire." Vital adds that he confronted Najara with these stories, and Najara admitted that they were true. That said, scholars doubt the veracity of the ever-envious Vital's claims. While Najara never responded to de Lonzano or Vital directly, his collections of poems contain both verse and prose that make it plain he isn't worried about offending certain learned men he considers pretenders. He knows exactly what he's doing—offering up, in his way, and in a way that spoke to masses of Jews in his day, prayers and poems of praise to God: "My mouth will condemn me if I do not praise and glorify its Creator." One scholarly observer's apologetic comment that "all he took from the foreign poetry was its surface and mood; the content itself he discarded" may be only partly true.

The second Najara poem below demonstrates just how slippery the territory the poet worked in was. Ostensibly a familiar kind of verse about the downtrodden and exiled People of Israel longing for revelation and redemption, the poem became one of Najara's most widely known hymns. Its subsequent history, however, takes it well beyond the mere "aura of Kabbalism" and devotional poetry and into a zone of transgression and sacrilege of a more blatant sort. Some two-thirds of a century after its composition, it was adopted by the Shabba-tian movement as a kind of anthem, one heralding the mystical mes-siah Shabbatai Tzvi's kingship (see below, "Jewish Muslims/Muslim Jews"). It was sung in secret gatherings in communities as far apart as Palestine, Poland, Turkey, the Ukraine, and Moravia. Moreover, it made its way into the Cathedral of Lublin in the mid-eighteenth century, where it was chanted by a chorus before the notorious Jacob Frank, a flagrantly antinomian, wife-swapping (or filching) Shabba-tian Jew who — covering all his bases — converted both to Islam *and* to Catholicism. At other times, it seems that Frank would sit, smoking and drinking coffee in the middle of his choir, as the singers stood around him and bowed in reverence. The "king" of the poem was, in that context, understood to refer to Frank himself, as an embodiment of the deity. That said, the poem remains extremely popular in the mainstream Jewish repertoire today.

HYMNS FOR THE THREE SABBATH MEALS

HYMN FOR THE FIRST MEAL

Prepare the feast
    of perfect faith,
the delight of the Holy King.
    Prepare the feast of the King.

This is the feast
    of the Field of Holy Apples;
the Lesser Presence and Ancient Eminence
    assemble with Her for the feast.

*

I sing in hymns
    of praise to enter
the gates to the Field
    of Holy Apples:

we call for Her now
    with a newly set table,
and a fine candelabrum
    that casts its light.

The Bride approaches
    through left and right: 10

She passes wearing
  Her jewels and gown.

She's embraced by Her husband
  in the sphere of foundation;
He gives Her great pleasure
  as His strength is pressed.

Cries and vexation
  are laid to rest,
as faces grow joyous—
20   and spirits with souls.

Great joy comes
  once and then twice,
and lights for Her shine
  as blessings increase.

Draw near, my companions
  and make preparations
for sundry pleasures,
  for fish and meat—

to take on souls
30   and new understanding,
along the three branches
  and thirty-two paths.

Seventy crowns
    are Hers, and the King
above crowns all
    in the Holy Shrine.

All worlds are formed
    and within Her impressed,
but all shine forth
    as the Ancient One strikes.   40

May it be His Will
    that Her grace be about us,
who delight in His Name
    with honey and cakes.

*

To the south I set
    the mysterious lamp,
and the table with bread
    I arrange to the north,

with wine in the cup,
    and bundles of myrtle,   50
to strengthen the weakened
    bride and groom.

We'll make them wreaths
    of well-chosen words—

seventy crowning
    Wisdom's gates.

By six loaves
    the Shekhinah is graced,
linked all around
60   to the sacred shrine,

as the impure powers
    are distanced and stilled,
and the menacing demons
    bound and annulled.

*

To break the bread
    like an olive or egg,
two *yod*s are taken,
    clear and obscure,

and the purest oil
70   is pressed from stones;
rivers are drawn
    in a whisper through Her—

for secret things
    have here been uttered,
although unseen
    and in mystery dressed

to adorn the Bride
    with supernal secrets,
within this holy
    messengers' feast.   80

HYMN FOR THE SECOND MEAL

Prepare the feast
  of perfect faith,
the delight of the Holy King.
  Prepare the feast of the King.

This is the feast
  of the Ancient Eminence;
the Lesser Presence and Field of Apples
  assemble with Him for the feast.

*

I've arranged this meal
  of the Sabbath morning
and call from it now
  to the Ancient Eminence,

that His light be cast
  through the Sanctification,
with fine wine
  which gladdens the soul.

May He send us goodness
  so we see His worthiness;

may He show us His secret
in a whisper expressed,

disclosing the meaning
of the twelve loaves —
His Name's letter
doubled and thin —

and the heavenly bond
all lives within.
May the power increase
so She reaches His head.   20

Rejoice, you reapers,
aloud and give voice —
and utter a word
sweet as nectar:

before the Lord
of all worlds,
in veiled words
you'll speak new things

to adorn the table
with the mystery's treasure,   30
deep and hidden
and not to be uttered.

These words will then
   be woven as heaven
and new horizons—
   and so that sun's

oil of anointing
   will flow from on high
as He turns to His Bride,
40   who has waited alone.

I wash my hands
   with a single vessel
for the other side
   which is insubstantial.

With three I call
   through the cup of the blessing
to the cause of causes,
   the Holy of Old.

HYMN FOR THE THIRD MEAL

Prepare the feast
  of perfect faith,
the delight of the Holy King.
  Prepare the feast of the King.

This is the feast
  of the Lesser Presence;
the Ancient Eminence and Field of Apples
  assemble with Him for the feast.

*

Sons of the Palace—
  you who yearn
to behold the radiance
  of the Lesser Presence—

be seated here
  at this Sabbath table,
adorned and crowned
  with the Name of the King.

Exult in your being
  part of this gathering   10

among the guardian
    angels' wings,

and rejoice now
    within this hour
of favor which knows
    not what anger brings.

Draw near me here—
    see my power,
without the judgments
20   of judgment's terror.

Those without
    may not enter,
for they are dogs
    of rancor and gall.

I hereby call
    to the Ancient of Days
to summon His will
    to drive them away—

for when His favor
30   in this room is shown,
the husks are rendered
    null and void.

He drives them into
   holes in the ground,
conceals them deep
   in caverns of stone.

And so it is
   now and till twilight—
within the Impatient
   One's delight.   40

*

Completed is the feast
   of perfect faith
of the seeds of the children of Israel.

Why, my desire, why do you always pursue me,
 and turn me, daily, into your enemy?
Why, my desire, why do you always pursue me?

Day after day you set out your snares,
 until in guile's pit you entrap me—
Why, my desire, why do you always pursue me?

You've been my enemy since I was young,
 gnashing your teeth and working against me;
Why, my desire, why do you always pursue me?

10 My soul sought to follow your path,
 for your hand's shadow, it seemed, would protect me;
Why, my desire, why do you always pursue me?

My eyes greeted the night with tears,
 and as you persisted, in anger you wrapped me:
Why, my desire, why do you always pursue me?

And if I imagine you'll come to save me,
 when I call on the day of distress you'll say to me:
(Why, my desire, why do you always pursue me?)

"Your words to me are sweeter than honey"
    —and so on your hook to doom you draw me.   20
Why, my desire, why do you always pursue me?

Hidden God in concealment's pavilion,
mind withdrawn from all conceiving,
cause of all causes, and crowned with the *Crown*
    of heaven, they'll offer you a crown, O Lord.

Within the beginning of your ancient teaching
your sublime and secret *Wisdom* was written.
It was formed from Nothing, in mystery's learning.
    The beginning of wisdom is fear of the Lord.

Faith's streams are paths to the river;
10   a man of insight will draw out deep water;
Discernment's fifty gates it delivers,
    and the faithful in turn are preserved by the Lord.

All eyes, God, are turned to your potency;
above the heavens great is your *Mercy*.
God of Abraham, remember who daily
    recalls your mercies, praising the Lord.

Sublime in glory, in strength and *Power*,
from changelessness you issue your luster—
with the fear of Isaac, may our judgment be rendered,
20   for you are mighty, forever, O Lord.

Who like you, O Lord, works wonders,
Jacob's proud one, in terrible splendor;
Glory of Israel, who hears the prayers
　　of the poor who cry out to their Lord?

Máy the Father's merit defend us—
Endurance of Israel, from darkness deliver us.
From exile's pit, save and raise us,
　　to see to the work of the House of the Lord.

The prophets left and right extend:
Triumph and *Majesty* within them sustained.　　30
Yakhin and Boaz they're called by name—
　　all your children will be taught by the Lord.

The font of the righteous is hidden in seven—
the covenant's everlasting token;
the source of the pools, the world's *Foundation*,
　　you are right and will triumph, O Lord.

Establish David and Solomon's *Kingdom*
with the crown with which their mother crowned them.
Israel is a bride to His wisdom—
　　a crown of beauty in the hand of the Lord.　　40

The strong unite the spheres as one.
Who cuts off their leader loses instruction.
As the gemstone's cuts aligned illumine—
may my song reach you, O Lord.

TO THE SHEKHINAH

Why do your eyes, my beautiful one,
out in the open draw their bow?
    All who see them tremble,
    like fish in a net with fear.
    They seek your nearness, afraid,
    though, to approach your radiance—
Star of Venus, in whose presence
the heavens' lights go dim with shame.

The night of lovers' pleasure you turn
to fear before your face's glow—
    and the light of your eyes that's held
    in hearts flares up in flames.
    Save those who've fallen
    into the net of your passion.
Spare them hell's torture, who burn
at the hearth of love like hissing coals. . . .

Let your Kingdom's glory be revealed
    over a poor and wandering people,
and reign, Lord who has ruled forever,
    before the reign of any King.

Ransom the nation that longs for your presence,
    Lord who dwells in the heights of heaven.
Over all gods you have dominion—
    Who won't fear you, O my King?

A living Lord, you surround me with favor;
10   my songs of praise have given you pleasure.
Into your city gather the scattered,
    for the people's greatness is the glory of the King.

I hope for the time of your redemption
    and wait with patience for your salvation.
If it tarries, Lord, in your absence
    I will look for no other King.

Without believing the good would appear,
    in no time at all, I would wither.
May my bud of deliverance be watered—
20   O my Living Lord and King.

Strengthen the bars of my gates and doors
  as you raise up the flock that remains.
Set my footsteps toward Sion's mountain;
  let me walk by the light of the King.

Bring my people back to you There,
  and I will rejoice around your altar.
With a new song, I will offer
  thanks to you, my Lord and King.

Extensions East and West

Yemenite and North African Kabbalah do not figure in Gershom Scholem's or anyone else's list of major trends in Jewish mysticism, and the poetry these esoteric traditions produced is minor (with regard to quality, if not quantity). Often boilerplate in both its didacticism and its devotion, it seems to be fueled by an Andalusian sort of urge without the original urgency, and it lacks the counterpoint one finds in the earlier hybrid Hebrew poetry. The best of its mystical verse is, however, distinctive for the particular timbre and density of its rhetoric and for its sensual qualities, as though its poets somehow maintained a low-grade but remarkably enduring contact high with the mystical tradition.

Despite its isolation, Yemen throughout the high Middle Ages stayed abreast of the latest developments in Hebrew literature. Manuscripts and correspondence discovered in the Cairo Geniza testify to the great esteem in which Andalusian Hebrew verse was held in Yemen from the eleventh century on. Books and manuscripts were regularly supplied by seagoing traders, and sometimes Yemenite Jews themselves ventured abroad to bring back the cultural and spiritual news. Zechariah al-Dhahari (c. 1513–c. 1578), perhaps the leading Hebrew writer in sixteenth-century Yemen, traveled throughout the Jewish world—from India and Persia and Iraq to Turkey, Syria, Egypt, and Palestine. In a rhymed-prose chronicle, he writes about his visit to Safed, where he seems to have met with several of the town's leading Kabbalists, including Karo, Cordovero, Alkabetz, and Najara. He was impressed and even humbled by the local methods of studying sacred texts, which involved a much more penetrating and philosophical approach than did the rote method practiced in Yemen (though he took some comfort in what he considered to be the Yemenites' superior knowledge of poetry). For al-Dhahari—as for Shalem Shabazi after him—the importance of Kabbalistic knowledge couldn't be overestimated. "If I hadn't held onto this [hidden] wisdom," he notes, anticipating by several centuries Maurice Blanchot's writing about literature and immortality, "I'd have fallen in grief toward the underworld. It raises a man from death to eternal life."

Though he was largely unknown beyond Yemen until his work was brought west to Palestine in the nineteenth century, Shalem ben Yosef Shabazi (b. 1619) eventually came to be thought of as Yemenite Jewry's national poet. No documentary evidence concerning him survives; we do know, however, that he came from South Yemen and was descended from an extended family of writers and scribes—the Mashtas. The contents of his nearly five hundred extant poems (half of which were recently discovered) suggest that he was poor, wandered for much of his life, and was—in the face of the difficult circumstances of Yemen's Jewry—preoccupied with questions of redemption and messianic expectation. Word of Shabbatai Tzvi's strange activities and self-coronation had stirred a disruptive fervor among the Jews of Yemen in the late 1660s. The kingdom's authorities reacted harshly, imposing increased taxation, restrictions of clothing, forced conversion, imprisonment, expulsion, and in some cases execution. Out of this highly charged cultural context Shabazi's poetry erupted, and—speaking in a sense for all of Yemenite Jewry—it expressed a deep-seated thirst for mystical knowledge and the spiritual revival that such knowledge might bring. Not surprisingly, Shabazi wrote on a wide range of pre-Lurianic Kabbalistic matters and frequently alluded to the *Zohar*, the *sefirot*, the Shekhinah, the permutations of letters, and the like.

"Who Kissed Me" is one of several quasi-Kabbalistic poems that begin with the image of a mysterious kiss. In a strikingly sensual and tactile manner (which echoes the erotic night visitation of the Arabic and Arabized Hebrew ode), it depicts the return of the soul to the body at dawn. According to Jewish tradition, the soul, whose origin is in the divine realm beneath the throne of God, leaves the body each night while we sleep; it returns each dawn with God's kiss, which wakes us and seals the bond of body and soul for another day. The poem blends the celebration of that bond and a plea for deliverance from the shackles of exile—not so much exile in the body as under foreign and oppressive rule. The second Shabazi poem is likewise immediate, this time appealing to the olfactory sense and treating the experience of exile in explicitly Kabbalistic terms. In these and other poems abstract notions are made palpable and vivid through sound, cadence, and concrete visual imagery—especially at the start of the poem: "The lovely doe in dispersion/brings me comfort—/at night in her lap I lie;/a cup of her wine/is poured for me always,/and hers is mixed with mine."

Confirming that sensual emphasis in this literature is the unexpected boost the work has received from popular culture in recent years: one of Shabazi's best-known (and also Kabbalistically inspired) poems, "Im nin'alu daltei nedivim, daltei marom lo nin'alu" (If the patrons' doors are barred, the doors of heaven are not), became a hit single when it was powerfully sung to a booming bass and synthesizer by the Yemenite Ofra Haza, one of Israel's leading pop singers of the seventies and the eighties. More recently, Madonna's *Paradise/Confessions Tour* featured a version of the song impressively rendered by an Israeli singer in a turban and galabiyya and preceded by soulful blasts from a long and serpentlike ram's horn. And in a particularly striking genre- and gender-bending twist, the transsexual singer Dana International, also of Yemenite descent (and winner of the Eurovision contest with a song whose refrain is "Viva la Diva"), sang a number of sacred Yemenite poems in a flagrantly profane setting. In a sense, these singers were simply continuing a long tradition, since most of the poems were—in the original contexts—performed musically, something that no doubt contributed to both their power and their appeal. Moreover, the poems were for the most part written with a certain melody in mind; and as is the case with the songbook cultures of nineteenth-century Germany and the first half of twentieth-century America, and also of American rock music, lyrics and melody can be separated, but usually with much greater loss to the verbal side of the equation.

*

Kabbalistic poetry in North Africa is in many ways similar to its Yemenite cousin: it came into its own during the seventeenth and eighteenth centuries, while the broader tradition it was part of flourished. Like Hebrew Yemenite verse, it developed under the influence of Iberian and Palestinian mystical currents, and as with the mystical poetry of the Levant, and also of Yemen, the North African poetry that was fueled by Kabbalistic passion was para-liturgical and popular. It provided a channel for a kind of trickle-down Kabbalah—so that while the broader swatches of the Jewish population didn't study the steeper and more abstruse texts (an activity that was restricted to more elite circles), they were regularly exposed to the increasingly accessible and even democratizing hymns that took up Kabbalistic themes and gave them broad dissemination. Late at night or early in the morning, on the Sabbath, holidays, or any number of festive occasions, worshippers in Morocco, Algeria, and Tunis (as in Safed and Syria) would gather to sing what might be thought of as a Jewish version of gospel music that encoded the most esoteric sort of associations and symbols behind a seemingly populist surface. "Bar Yohai," by the Spanish-born Shimon Lavi, is one of the poems they would regularly sing. Saturated with allusions to the *Zohar* and related texts, the poem uses the ten sefirot as a device through which to tell of the marvelous doings of the hero of the *Zohar*, the legendary second-century Talmudic sage Shimon Bar Yohai. At once esoteric in its allusiveness and appealing to the ordinary worshipper or devotee, Lavi's mid-sixteenth-century poem caught on quickly; it reached the visiting Yemenite al-Dhahari and other Kabbalists in Safed, and was disseminated widely throughout the East and eventually into Ashkenaz. Its popularity was such that it became the prototype for a new North African genre — "Bar Yohai poems" — all of which imitated the model in form, structure, and content. Scores of related North African poems take up standard Kabbalistic themes such as the sefirot and the permutations of letters. But North African poetry's most noteworthy contribution to the mystical canon is this no doubt Sufi-influenced verse treating the veneration of Jewish saints.

Lavi's poem about Bar Yohai is followed by a taut, esoterically didactic but lyrical riddle by Ya'akov Ifargan, an overlooked early-seventeenth-century Kabbalist. The poem takes us physically and psychically into the mystery of trying to name the divine, as it seems to ride the letters of the Tetragrammaton and the spaces between them.

Who kissed me with kisses of His love,
    in the king's chamber transporting me?
At dawn my soul's beloved came—
    she sighed the instant she felt Him near.
Had His compassion not come through me,
    she'd have left and abandoned my body.
How, my soul, have you bound my being,
    so I, as flesh, exist through your mercy?
You who have fathomed fate's trials, see
10   how body and soul are exalted in unity:
She is guided by the teachings' mystery—
    finding perfection and mind's intensity;
and the day she desires to return she'll turn
    back toward Metatron's banners and army.
Accept, my Maker, your servant's confession;
    so he might be inscribed for eternity:
Grant my offspring abundance and goodness.
    Attend to my predicament and plea.
You who save and redeem the poor—
20   have pity on one who has come to your door.

The myrtle's scent ascended—
    terror shook my soul:
at midnight I arose
    with my beloved guiding me.

I dwell in a desolate land,
    so why would my beloved—
while I am put to shame—
    choose to come and join me?

He wears desire's robe
    as His partner wanders,   10
and grateful for His treasure,
    I praise the One who made me.

Now between the branches
    Heaven's angels gather—
they're seen but do not see
    the Rock, my Lord who formed me.

Invisible on high,
    through them a soul has life;
it's known as Wisdom here
    in the mind's fathomless mystery—   20

resting within and involving
    thirty sacred degrees,
darkened and wholly contained
    within thinking's body.

The sinister aspect will turn,
    and fire toward me burn,
poised like hell itself,
    seeking to destroy me—

but I will flee to the right
30   in which I've put my faith,
and in that merit's grace
    my soul will rebuke me.

Turn, then, my spirit,
    and destroy evil's power;
to my palace's tower
    I know that you will raise me.

Through the gates of repentance,
    bound in the bonds of love,
my spirit will be summoned.
40   With wisdom you will lift me.

A flow of great abundance
    from rivers will surround us,

absolving those who turn
    back to the House of Prophecy.

Fathom this, my brethren,
    and you will be granted the vision
bright with illumination
    extending from eternity.

Remember, my friend, your beloved,
    hold to her, exalt her;   50
a garden with running water,
    she's light to all I see.

The people then will rise,
    all the scattered tribes,
and with a song of praise
    give thanks as they remind me:

Peace like a river will flow
    over the hills and plain—
and with it I will be cleansed
    and water my flock which is thirsty.   60

Blessed are you, Bar Yohai,
  you were anointed
    by your brethren with the oil of joy:

Bar Yohai,
        with the oil of a sacred share
you were anointed through holy measure,
    sanctity's bud you wore like a miter:
        its glory was set upon you.
          Bar Yohai, blessed are you, Bar Yohai,
10   *you were anointed*
                by your brethren with the oil of joy:

Bar Yohai,
        you found the perfect sanctuary
in your retreat when you had to flee;
    you attained your greatness and glory—
        in a cave of stones you endured.
          Bar Yohai, blessed are you, Bar Yohai . . .

Bar Yohai,
        the acacias about you stood firm,
20 deep in their study, disciples of the Name,
      they burned with the wondrous light of the flame—
        these were the teachers who taught you.
          Bar Yohai, blessed are you, Bar Yohai . . .

Bar Yohai,
>> to the Field of Apples you ascended
> in order to gather the blossoms' scent—
>> the learning's mysteries, like flowers' essence:
>>> for you He said, "Let us create him . . ."
>>>> *Bar Yohai, blessed are you, Bar Yohai . . .*

Bar Yohai,   30
>> you were girded with strength
> and fought at the gate with the fire of faith;
>> your sharp sword you drew from its sheath
>>> and you raised it against your enemies.
>>>> *Bar Yohai, blessed are you, Bar Yohai . . .*

Bar Yohai,
>> you reached the Palace of Marble
> and stood before the Lion in power—
>> you saw the stars and creation's pillars,
>>> but who there could see you?   40
>>>> *Bar Yohai, blessed are you, Bar Yohai . . .*

Bar Yohai,
>> in the holy of holies—
> that green region which is time's quarry—
>> with the seven Sabbaths and the fifty's mystery,
>>> you bound the Name before you.
>>>> *Bar Yohai, blessed are you, Bar Yohai . . .*

Bar Yohai,
> into the depths of His resplendence
50 you gazed at the point of wisdom's emergence,
> the thirty-two channels of creation's appearance:
> you were a cherub with outstretched wings.
>> *Bar Yohai, blessed are you, Bar Yohai . . .*

Bar Yohai,
> the wondrous light of heaven
you've feared—for its fullness is overwhelming;
> this is the mystery whose name is Nothing:
> "No eye," you said, "will see you."
>> *Bar Yohai, blessed are you, Bar Yohai . . .*

60 Bar Yohai,
> blessed is she who gave birth to you,
and blessed are the people on the path you pursued,
> and those who fathom the secret you knew—
> with the breast-picce of light's divination.
>> *Bar Yohai, blessed are you, Bar Yohai—*
>> *you were anointed*
>>> *by your brethren with the oil of joy.*

I will sing of God, and praise God—
    His name in His dwelling is holy—
through the letter *yod*, and the crown of the *yod*,
    hidden in the *yod*'s great mystery.

What's in the *yod* and at its end
    combine in the mystery of Knowing,
while the secret of *hey* is within the *hey*,
    buried there and hidden.

And so the initial, and then the middle,
    the one on high and below,   10
and the secret of *vuv*, and the limits of *vuv*
    toward its end that follows—

in the secret of four, linked to four,
    in four's secret is eight,
adhering through ten's mystery with ardor—
    the spell of dwelling, devout.

Being in the Name comes to be
    with the falling of *nun* at the start,
and the letter *ayin* at the end of the *ayin*
    is within the *ayin* at heart.   20

He who is frail will not fail
    to see the light of the Presence;
his voice will draw near, his speech offer pleasure,
    like fledgling pigeons and doves—

all of which is spelled out for all
    in the secret heart of the Law.

Jewish Muslims

*

Muslim Jews

On Saturday morning, December 12, 1665, an owl-faced, manic-depressive, forty-year-old Smyrna-born rabbi named Shabbatai Tzvi — who for the past decade had been at the center of serious religious turmoil within a number of Ottoman Jewish communities — marched with a mob of some five hundred followers toward his hometown's Portuguese synagogue. The rabbi was furious, as his orders to expel one of the synagogue's more esteemed members had been defied by the community's elders. Fearing the throng, the congregation barred the doors to the synagogue, at which point Shabbatai Tzvi sent for an ax and forced his way in.

Intellectually undistinguished but already notorious, Tzvi proceeded to read from a printed version of Scripture — a serious transgression, as Jewish law permitted reading only from a scroll during the prayer service — and then, in a gesture designed "to confound Satan" and disperse the evil powers all around, he "cupped his hands, put them to his mouth, and trumpeted in the directions of the four winds." It was, he announced, "time to work for the Lord." The smashing of the door, he explained, constituted — in "a profound mystery" — the crushing of the *kelippot*, and he began reviling various rabbis who opposed him, comparing them and their predecessors to particular animals: this one was a camel and another a pig; a third was a rabbit, et cetera; and all should eat the flesh of the animals they were. His batty sermon having come to a close, he approached the Ark of the Law, took the Torah scroll in his arms, and began singing — in what all who knew him say was a lovely voice — an old Ladino ballad about a young woman named Meliselda. Adopted from a secular Spanish/Ottoman context, the song was extremely popular among the Iberian-Jewish exiles of Turkey; and, just as Yisrael Najara had transplanted Turkish secular love songs into the soil of devotional verse, so for Shabbatai Tzvi the ballad took on mystical implications. The abbreviated version of the poem that Shabbatai seems to have sung tells how the speaker met the emperor's beautiful daughter by a river. In longer versions of the poem it is clear that the lover lies with the daughter by the river where they meet. For Tzvi, says Gershom Scholem, the poem was "a mystical allegory of himself." Meliselda was the Torah— the teaching, "the most lovely lady," as he once put it explicitly—and he was the bridegroom emerging from his chamber to participate in the sacred wedding and consummate this marriage to the Shekhinah and the book of sacred instruction.

This wasn't the first eccentric embrace for Shabbatai Tzvi. Some ten years earlier, after he'd been banned by the Jewish communities of both Jerusalem and Smyrna for a variety of blasphemous offenses, including having uttered the Ineffable Name of God and abolishing fast days, he moved on to Salonika and other Ottoman cities. There he aroused both ire and interest with his "strange actions." At one point he invited the leading Jewish dignitaries of one town to a banquet at which he performed a full-fledged wedding ceremony between himself and a Torah scroll. On another occasion he appeared in public with a large fish that he'd swaddled like an infant and placed in a cradle (indicating that the Redemption of Israel would in due course come under the sign of Pisces). And more than once he had arbitrarily reconfigured the Jewish calendar, moving the fall, spring, and summer pilgrim festivals (Sukkot, Passover, and Shavu'ot) to a single week and shifting the Sabbath to a Monday. For the more blatant of these transgressions he had been flogged, repeatedly.

Meanwhile, back in Smyrna, the song about Meliselda sung and explicated by the singer himself in Kabbalistic fashion (with reference to the Song of Songs), Tzvi then "revealed himself in clear and unequivocal terms as the Anointed of the God of Jacob, and the Redeemer of Israel." He was, in other words, and at least as he saw it, the Messiah—and he subsequently divided up the kingdoms of the world among his followers, appointed viceroys to Rome and Constantinople, and gave them all peculiar royal and often biblically based titles.

The notion of his being the anointed one was also not new. He'd had a vivid messianic sense of his calling ever since 1648, when he announced himself as just that—the redeemer. (As it happens, this was the year in which the *Zohar* promised the resurrection of the dead.) Little attention was paid to the twenty-two-year-old Tzvi, however, and the pronouncement was considered (like the incident of the fish) just another manifestation of obvious derangement. He seems to have repeated the messianic claim in 1658.

By 1662 Tzvi had settled in Jerusalem, and it's around this time that he came to the attention of a gifted and highly creative young Talmud student by the name of Avraham Nathan Ashkenazi (who would soon be known simply as Nathan of Gaza). A few years later, while Tzvi was off on a mission in Egypt, Nathan—now back in Gaza and immersed in the solitary study of Lurianic Kabbalah—was in the midst of a prolonged fast and had isolated himself "in a separate room in holiness and purity" when, as he tells it, the spirit came over him, his hair stood on end and his knees trembled, and he "beheld the Merkavah [the divine chariot] . . . and was vouchsafed true prophecy," the gist of which was that Shabbatai Tzvi was the Redeemer of Israel and would one day proclaim himself the Messiah. The vision lasted a full twenty-four hours, and it was said to have left Nathan with sacred and healing powers—including clairvoyant diagnostic skills—of the sort that Luria had possessed. Word of Nathan's illumination (though not the content of his vision) apparently got back to Tzvi, who went to Gaza "in order to find peace for his soul," which is to say, release from the vicious circle of psychosis. Nathan, whom Scholem in his magisterial biography of Shabbatai Tzvi likens to John the Baptist and Paul (the parallels between Tzvi and Jesus are also prominent in this story), tried over the course of several months to convince a skeptical or at least reluctant Shabbatai of the truth of his messianic calling. Finally, during the midnight vigil of Shavu'ot 1665, Nathan—in a trance and then again after he'd recovered—went public with his belief that Shabbatai Tzvi was "worthy to be king over Israel."

At this point, it seems, the idea took root in Tzvi himself, and he began finding mystical confirmation of his anointment in numerological readings of Scripture, seeing for instance, "the spirit of God moved on the water," in Genesis, as "the spirit of Shabbatai Tzvi" moved on the water, since the words in question were numerologically equivalent. He also called attention to the fact—by having it engraved on a ring that he wore—that the full spelling of "Shadday" (as in El Shadday, or God Almighty) and "Shabbatai Tzvi" were, in the *gematria*, interchangeable. In other words, Shabbatai Tzvi substituted his own name for God's. Likewise, he added to his signature the sign of a crooked (that is, subversive) serpent, the numerological value of the holy "serpent" and "Messiah" being the same. It was a fitting insignia for the man who would come to be seen as a "holy sinner." In one of many cruel rejoinders—which included an entire body of poetry composed to mock the Shabbatians—Tzvi's opponents pointed out that "Shabbatai Tzvi" and *ru'ah sheker* (the spirit of deceit) are also numerologically identical.

Shabbatai Tzvi then traveled to Jerusalem and the Kabbalists' capital of Safed, and from there on to Aleppo and back to his hometown of Izmir. Frenzied Jewish crowds rushed to greet the new and decidedly moody Messiah.

Boosting Shabbatai's spirit and tirelessly producing tracts that interpreted his quirks along mystical lines, Nathan himself soon emerged as the prophet and esoteric impresario of this new heretical movement. (Shabbatai, on the other hand, wrote almost nothing and left behind, says Scholem, not so much as a single memorable utterance—apart perhaps from the unforgettable performance of "Meliselda" and the occasional letter or two; he also either dictated or recounted certain visionary experiences that were then recast in writing.)

So much for background: In the weeks and months following Shabbatai's December proclamation in the synagogue, he widened the circle of his antinomian (and distinctly Reformlike) doings— abolishing additional fasts, calling women to the Torah, allowing men and women to dance together, and performing a sacrifice and then eating—as he had in the past—the forbidden and now highly (and sexually) symbolic fat of the slaughtered lamb. The latter act was accompanied, as were many of the others, by the benediction "Blessed art thou, O God, who permittest that which is forbidden [*matir issurim*]"—a play on the traditional morning prayer *matir asurim* (who frees the captive). As the Messiah, he had come to remove Adam's sin, and to that end he would have to descend into the kelippot, the realm of evil and transgression.

Kooky as it all sounds, this latest permutation of Kabbalistic possibility was utterly real to those involved, for and against the new Messiah, and Shabbatai's anointment addressed a deep-seated need in politically and spiritually besieged communities throughout the Jewish world. The movement spoke first, and with particular poignancy, to what Scholem characterized as "the unhappy dualism of the Marranic mind," which is to say, to the many Ottoman Jewish subjects who were descended from Conversos and had long lived with a profound and mournful sense of doubleness. (Idel calls Shabbatai "the *melancholy* messiah.") The story of the rapid growth and eventual dissolution of what would become the greatest messianic movement in Judaism since the time of Jesus and the "first serious revolt in Judaism since the Middle Ages" is of course long and complex. Suffice it to say that the movement's power was such that a full third of world

Jewry was caught up in the frenzy of belief in the mystical magne-tism of Shabbatai Tzvi—this man for whom the new Law was that of his own personality. As legends and miracles began to accrue around Shabbatai (pillars of fire, the appearance of Elijah, passing through walls, and so on) the rebellious gospel went viral, exploding through the communal networks of exilic Judaism, reaching the communi-ties of Asia Minor and Greece, including the Peloponnese and the Aegean islands, and then, astonishingly, spreading to Holland, En-gland, and even the West Indies, and eventually ranging across Italy, Germany, Austria, Poland, the Ukraine, Morocco, Egypt, Yemen, and Persia. Within two years it culminated in Shabbatai's conversion (under the threat of execution) to Islam, which in turn gave rise to what Scholem called "the fundamental doctrine of Shabbatianism, namely, that the apostasy of Shabbatai Tzvi was a sacred mystery."

At that mystery's heart was the supremacy of pure faith as the ultimate religious value, rather than observance of the Law. More-over, deliberate and increasingly flagrant transgression of that Law— "crooked ways" which, on occasion, included incest and other forms of highly questionable behavior—became a mark of that faith and a means of bringing about the unification of the upper worlds. All this, Shabbatians and Nathan believed, was of course carried out on sound theological grounds and in the manner of noble biblical predecessors in transgression, those who established the Davidic (that is, messi-anic) line: Judah and Tamar, Boaz and Ruth, David and Bathsheba. Apart from that legacy, deception in descent for the sake of ascent was familiar from the stories of Moses in Egypt and Esther in the alien Persian court.

Among the Shabbatians, Marranic doubleness evolved into even more complicated conscious duplicity, and it bequeathed to us the image of Shabbatai Mehemed Tzvi, as he came to be called after the apostasy, performing his Muslim prayers while wearing phylacteries, or sitting with a Torah in one hand and a Qur'an in the other. As one contemporary witness put it, "Sometimes he prayed and behaved like a Jew, and sometimes like a Muslim, and he did queer things." Or as one scholar sums up the situation, "The last ten years of his life can be understood as a prolonged effort . . . to prove to himself and the world that the two identities of Jew and Muslim can be fused in a single human being." Be that as it may, the circle of apostates around him grew. Amirah—as his followers called him, using an acronym for the Hebrew words meaning "Our Lord and King, may his majesty be exalted" and a name that recalls the Arabic word *amir*, "emir"— enjoyed the protection and even what seems to have been the affection of the Turkish sultan. After his conversion before the sultan's court in Adrianople, he received visitors from far and wide, preached in synagogues (often encouraging conversion and, on at least one occasion, reading from the Qur'an), and on the whole enjoyed freedom of movement. "We can easily imagine him," Scholem writes of Tzvi's erotic mysticism during his final years, "clad in phylacteries, singing psalms, and surrounded by women and wine."

In 1672, however, the situation changed. Bribed (it seems) by the rabbinic establishment, Turkish officers arrested Shabbatai for blasphemy, and he was imprisoned and eventually sent into exile in Albania, where he continued to communicate with his believers and to experience periods of illumination. Shabbatai Tzvi died (or as his believers had it, was occulted) on the Day of Atonement 1676, ten years after his apostasy and a few months after his fiftieth birthday. Nathan lived on in Sofia for another four years and then, apparently on his way to Turkey, and faithful to the end, he died in Macedonia.

*

Although many of the movement's "believers"—as Shabbatai's followers were known among themselves, as opposed to the "infidels"— returned to normative Judaism after the apostasy, and some remained steadfast as Jews who placed their faith in Tzvi the Messiah, a small percentage converted to the ambiguous sort of Islam that Shabbatai maintained after his conversion. This embrace of Islam was referred to among the believers as a Kabbalistic *tikkun* (in the light of Isaiah 28:21: "To do as he did, strange are his deeds, and to worship as he worshiped, for his worship is alien"). In time, and not long after the mass conversion of between two and three hundred families in Salonika in 1683—smaller groups followed suit in Adrianople, Constantinople, and other cities—these new converts, or Dönmeh (apostates), as the Turks called them, began to take on the characteristics of a sect. Various strains of Dönmeh emerged, and the members of the sect developed a complex double life as "voluntary Marranos" living "at the intersection of Kabbalah and Sufism." They worshipped in mosques as practicing Muslims, sometimes made the pilgrimage to Mecca, seem to have had close ties to particular Sufi movements, and spoke Turkish while taking Turkish names for all their dealings in the outside world. At the same time, with their fellow Dönmeh they spoke Judeo-Spanish (Ladino), used secret Hebrew names, forbade intermarriage with Muslims, maintained synagogues in ordinary-looking houses in the sect's quarters, and observed their own Shabbatian holidays—though only on the eve of a festival, so as not to disrupt a "normal" work schedule and call attention to themselves.

Also anxiously concealed in all this dissembling was the literature of the Dönmeh. Cognizant of their precursors' bitter experience with both normative Judaism and the Turkish authorities, and driven by a Sufi-influenced sense of the theological importance of their doubleness, the at-once fanatical and tolerant, insular and open sect managed to keep its literature from reaching anyone outside its circle for nearly 250 years. During the first half of the twentieth century, however, members of the sect began to assimilate into secular Turkish society in increasing numbers, and especially after the 1923 population transfer between Greece and Turkey (which relocated Salonika's crypto-Jews to Izmir the following year) certain Dönmeh began to pass on religious items that were in the possession of their families to Jewish friends in those two cities. Some of these, in turn, ended up in the hands of scholars. So it is that in the 1940s two manuscripts of Dönmeh hymns in Judeo-Spanish emerged (the larger of them was published in 1948, with annotation by Gershom Scholem and excellent Hebrew translations by Moshe Attias). In the 1980s a manuscript containing even more hymns was identified in a Harvard University collection, and since then two other manuscripts have surfaced. As a result of all these discoveries, we now have in hand more than 1,200 Dönmeh hymns—full-fledged literary embodiments of "an unprecedented theology of Judaism."

The hymnals themselves are compact (so they could be easily hidden) and look startlingly like Ottoman Turkish manuscripts, with flowing Hebrew characters that resemble calligraphed Arabic letters. While the hymns are on the whole written in Ladino, their Hebrew element is so conspicuous that scholars speak of their having been written in a combination of Hebrew and Judeo-Spanish. The odd phonetic spellings of the Hebrew words and phrases tell us that by the time the manuscripts were copied (the second half of the eighteenth century—some fifty years after the composition of the earliest of the group), the community had already grown distant from Hebrew and no longer really knew the language. By and large two forms are employed in the collections, which were probably family hymnbooks: rhymed quatrains with a refrain, or long-lined couplets that employ repetition—both strategies that facilitate memorization and recitation. The content of the hymns is often highly obscure (in part because of the coded language and also owing to the difficulty of deciphering the strange spelling and terminology). In fact, one scholar of the material characterizes them as perhaps the most esoteric poems in the history of Jewish literature. Be that as it may, they were clearly intended to transmit the Shabbatian legacy—its content, beliefs, and passion—and they were, says Attias, not "folk poetry," but the literary expression of the movement's "spiritual shepherds."

Particularly compelling and even haunting are the poems that weave Jewish and Muslim traditions together in the very fabric of the verse. Sufi influence on the Shabbatian movement appears to have been direct. There is evidence that while he was visiting Constantinople, Shabbatai Tzvi himself stayed at the monastery of one of the leading Sufi poets of his day, Mehmed an-Niyazi; and the Dönmeh of Salonika, in particular, seem to have had regular contact with their Sufi peers (especially the Bektashi order, which produced Turkey's greatest medieval poet, Yunus Emre, and which readily absorbed pre-Islamic, heretical, and Christian elements). As we know, the Sufi practice of dissimulation (*takiye*—maintaining a "normative" exterior to mask radical practice and private life) was central to the Dönmeh community. Most likely as a result of these various and numerous contacts, specific elements of the Sufi rite made their way into the Dönmeh hymns. For one, musical and conceptual elements of the Friday evening Sufi spiritual concerts (*sama'a*), as well as the *dhikr* ceremony, which is at the heart of Sufi ritual practice, are echoed conspicuously in a number of the hymns (see, for instance, the refrain to "The Ghazal of Goodness," below: "There is no God but Him"). We also find mystical ghazals, in the manner of Hafez, and poems that intentionally seem to confuse religious tacks (à la Ibn al-Arabi), as well as profane and sacred desire (as in "Meliselda"). The whole question of Dönmeh eroticism has drawn considerable interest, as rumors spread about the sect's libertine ways and wife-swapping rituals. Scholem comments that the accusations are most likely grounded in truth, and several of the poems below seem to allude in somewhat coded fashion to this practice, which was known as "the extinguishing of the lights" and took place on the Feast of the Lambs—a festival marking the start of spring.

For all of its subversion and syncretism, Shabbatianism, writes Scholem, remained "a specifically Jewish phenomenon to the end. . . . [And] beneath the surface of lawlessness, antinomianism, and catastrophic negation," he continues, "powerful constructive impulses were at work." Impulses of just this sort course through these quietly potent poems, which constitute one of the more surprising products of this utterly bizarre movement that, in its heretical way, contained the seeds of modern Jewish life.

MELISELDA

I went to the mountain
and down to the river
and there I met Meliselda—
the King's gentle daughter.

I saw that glorious girl
emerging from the water:
her brows were bows of night,
her face was a sword of light—

her lips were red as coral,
her milk-like flesh was white.

I HAVE FOUND BLISS

The hour is right
when the light dwells,
   in darkness
      I have found bliss.

And this is the place
where life's letter fell,
   and with that fortune
      I have found bliss.

Surely in love
and awe I've taken,   10
   as our teacher told us:
      I have found bliss.

For the soul in its longing
a hint is sufficient—
   peace is with him—
      I have found bliss.

Mercy is built
our faith tells us,
   and the *King* renews it.
      I have found bliss.   20

I've eaten fruit
from his garden —
   my soul is sated,
     I have found bliss.

Love has come
to terms with *Goodness,*
   in the *King's* praises
     I have found bliss.

Through you will the blessing be brought to Israel,
    through the secret of the valley of Ishmael,
        for the redeemer has come to restore
    through the secret of the valley of Ishmael.

He said, The Lord has heard
    his servant who has served—
        He, who within him has dwelled
    through the secret of the valley of Ishmael.

The letters hold redemption;
    for the jubilee year is his foundation;   10
        through sin he brought to sanctification
    through the secret of the valley of Ishmael.

Tzvi, our teacher, is the redeemer.
    It's he who established the upper splendor
        in primordial space in the shells' chamber,
    through the secret of the valley of Ishmael.

The letter of Life fell in a place
    where no one dies, the Truth is this—
        and all that is good within it exists
    through the secret of the valley of Ishmael.   20

These things are seen as though through a veil,
  and they are most abstruse as well,
    but in them I have found the real
  through the secret of the valley of Ishmael.

1

Here the table is set
and opens like a rose.
    Eat from all that's pure,
    and he'll in faith rejoice,
       arousing joy with song.

His bread is from on high
and fine food is holy.
    All with him are one,
    as he in faith rejoices,
       arousing joy with song.   10

In making she comes forth —
be generous with each hour.
    The King, our lord, allows it,
    and he'll in faith rejoice —
       arousing joy with song.

Our souls have been fulfilled:
He alters the lights on high.
    Goodness has eaten and served
    as he in faith rejoiced —
       arousing joy with song.   20

2

Our teacher's master announces
the mystery of the sanctity.
And like a rose it opens.
The mystery of the sanctity.

And then he ventures forth,
paying no heed to the petty.
This is the root of our lord:
The mystery of the sanctity.

He enters where he will
10   and neither rests nor wearies.
The time has been appointed:
The mystery of the sanctity.

He nullified the law—
destroyed the husks completely,
restoring all the worlds.
The mystery of the sanctity.

He's light that clings to Nothing.
He holds Esther's key:
Goodness—look and see:
20   *The mystery of the sanctity.*

SECRET PLEASURE

God created man on earth
    so he might live forever.
And from the Tree of Knowledge he ate.
    The angel Sama'el He gave power.

Through *Let there be* he fashioned all.
    Abraham's secret is our teacher.
An altered place, an altered name:
    Altered action is secret pleasure. . . .

The soul of our lord and exalted king,
    was prior to all that came to be;   10
and as the thread of light emerged,
    he was its equal in Eternity.

The Infinite having withdrawn its radiance
    left a void, a tremendous vastness,
from which the heavenly mantle was made
    there at the heart of a great abyss.

And as Infinity was gathered in,
    the twenty-two letters (in You) congealed
within the primal space of the void;
    it, in time, would be blessed by his soul.   20

The redeemer, our King and splendor, has come
    into the vale of Ishmael.
They broke away, defying Your Law.
    It was time to work for the Lord.

ON THE DESTRUCTION OF THE LAW

The light that lacks conception
    constitutes the occultation,
and with it He created
    all that in the world exists.
As it lacks conception,
    it's always in ascension,
for in it no rule holds,
    neither beginning nor end.

In strength he came to speak to us—
    he is Shabbatai Tzvi.
His nature is destruction,
    from one who knows I've heard.
Into the fourth husk and shell,
    from his place he descended:
for he destroyed the Law—
    in order to raise the Lord.

Fathom and hold to your faith, for there is nothing else
 but Him.
Circle and serve and you will find—not a thing but Him.

He and His name, which are the same (there is no other
 Creator)—
enter, observe, and understand: there is none but Him.

He vanquishes every evil thing: Sama'el and Belial.
Be filled with Him, see Him and say: there is no other
 but Him.

He is hidden, He is found—but not, to be sure, created;
Do not inquire, do not aspire, speak of nothing but Him.

He readies all, reduces all, decrees all—alone.
Do not weary, do not worry. There is no Lord but Him.

He is first, and He is last. Over all He reigns.
Read and read again what's written: There is no good
 but Him.

A thousand times, say it—poet—this is the heart of
 the Law:
There is no other to be discovered. There is no God
 but Him.

Italian Kabbalah

Italy played a central role in the dissemination of Jewish mystical thought and writing from early on, serving as a way station for esoteric literature that came from the East and was headed west, and also absorbing Kabbalah proper as it emerged from Spain. Merkavah traditions had taken hold in Apulia by the mid-ninth century; German Pietism can be traced back to the Kalonymos family's late-ninth- or early-tenth-century move from Lucca to the Rhineland; and in the thirteenth century Avraham Abulafia spent critical time in southern Italy teaching his brand of ecstatic Kabbalah. There is also clear-cut evidence that, from the late thirteenth through sixteenth centuries, Italy was already experiencing "massive direct importations of esoteric knowledge from Spain and Provence," all of which in time powerfully informed the work of Christian humanists, such as Pico della Mirandola, who developed a distinct stream of Kabbalah. Equally significant, the printing of the *Zohar* in Mantua and later in Cremona in 1558–60 (nearly a century after Hebrew was first set in movable type) made what had been a closely guarded work available to a much larger readership, and numerous other Kabbalistic books were issued by the flourishing Hebrew printing industries of Venice and other Italian-Jewish cities.

As early as the thirteenth century, then, Italian Kabbalists were in one way or another producing important works, and by the mid-seventeenth century Moshe Zacut was at the heart of that production. An editor, commentator, rabbinic leader, and proofreader for the busy Venetian Hebrew printers, Zacut was also seventeenth-century Italy's leading Kabbalist and its finest Hebrew poet. Born to a Portuguese Marrano family circa 1610 in Amsterdam, he was raised there, and after stays in Hamburg and Poland he eventually set out for Palestine, though his trip stalled in Italy. He settled in Venice in 1645 and remained in that city for nearly thirty years before taking up a rabbinic position in Mantua, where he died in 1697. It was in Poland that his interest in Kabbalah developed, and his poetry eventually came to combine elements of the Italian baroque with traditional Hebrew subjects and concerns, including the theories and worldview of Yitzhak Luria and his disciples. Dense, involving, and revolving—whether they are treating weddings or deaths, the anniversaries of important events or prayer vigils in the middle of the night—Zacut's mannerist poems act as brooding vortices that wind between opposing aspects: darkness and light, concealment and revelation, absence and presence, upper world and the world of decay. Riding the tension between these extremes, the poems—through their very composition and then by means of their recitation—participate in the process of cosmic restoration.

Among Zacut's most famous poems is "The Light Concealed," which was composed for the prayer and study vigil that runs through the night of the Shavu'ot festival. The poem was reprinted in numerous collections of religious hymns, in Prague, Venice, Livorno, Hamburg, and elsewhere (where it was often noted that it should be sung to the tune of Avraham ben Maimon's "Hidden God"; see above). It also appears in Dönmeh hymnbooks, where only the first three stanzas are included. The Dönmeh, it seems, understood the poem as alluding to Shabbatai Tzvi. While the connection is tenuous, the Dönmeh weren't inventing it out of thin air; Zacut himself, while in Venice, was very much bound up with messianic speculation and had initially been among the "believers" in Shabbatai Tzvi—although he was cautious and moderate in that belief. And once word of the apostasy reached him, he came out in unequivocal terms against Tzvi and Nathan of Gaza alike, calling their followers fools who kept up "a strange fire." By then, it seems, the Dönmeh had already included part of Zacut's poem in their hymnal. The full version, translated here, traces the tree of the ten *sefirot*, beginning with the hidden light of the Infinite and descending through each sefirah.

Also translated here, and focusing on the primordial light, is a poem for a pageant that took place on the first night of the Hebrew month of Shevat in 1675. On that night, members of the Jewish community came together to mark the sixty-fifth anniversary of the founding of Mantua's synagogue. They gathered in the sanctuary courtyard, which was lit with huge candles (in keeping with Isaiah's injunction to "honor the Lord with lights" [24:15]). Zacut, then the rabbi of the community, had composed a hymn for the occasion, and it was sung, with the members of the congregation echoing the refrain after each new stanza. What emerged in the lyrics of Zacut's occasional poem was anything but ephemeral, however. In his hands the events of the night were seen from a cosmic perspective — one that linked the goings-on in the courtyard with nothing less than God's creation of the universe. Once again, choreography in the world below was linked to the world on high. The primordial light, which left traces in the space created after God's contraction into Himself, and which then came to dwell in the Holy of Holies at Jerusalem's Temple, was in the wake of the Temple's destruction made to wander with Israel in its Exile. Ever since then it would attend to the Ark of the Law in synagogues throughout the Jewish Diaspora. As Zacut and his circle saw it, song itself, the right sort of song, fed by the primordial light that dwells in the Torah and in the sanctuary of their synagogue, participates in the formation or ongoing burning of that light. Hence the midnight regimen that had been maintained by members of the synagogue since its founding.

*

Moshe Hayyim Luzzatto was born in 1707 in Padua to one of the more well-respected Jewish families in Italy and educated in his town's Jewish ghetto. A prodigy who read widely in all the traditional Jewish subjects as well as in classical languages and Western literature, science, and philosophy, he was said to have committed to memory by age fourteen all of the writings pertaining to Yitzhak Luria, and by age seventeen he had composed at least one accomplished poetic drama and an important treatise on Hebrew poetics. Over the course of the next five or six years he wrote numerous works on rabbinic and mystical topics, in addition to his more occasional literary compositions. By then he was participating in an intense *Zohar* circle, which maintained round-the-clock relay-style readings of that book in an effort to bring about recalibrations in the divine world that might alter the status of Israel below. One day in the spring of 1727, as Luzzatto himself tells it, "while keeping in mind a Kabbalistic formula, I fell asleep; and when awaking I heard a voice saying in Aramaic: 'I came down to reveal hidden secrets of the Holy King.' I stood trembling somewhat, then I felt encouraged, and the voice did not stop revealing things mysterious. The next day at the same time I took the precaution to be left to myself in the room when the voice came again revealing another (Heavenly) secret."

And so began the young Luzzatto's frequent visitations from the same sort of *maggid* or divine prompter that had appeared to Yosef Karo and Nathan of Gaza—an angel or power who reveals the heavenly mysteries to select mortals steeped in Kabbalah. (Scholem describes the maggid as "psychologically . . . elements of the mystic's unconscious, crystallizing and coming to life, and behaving in an autonomous fashion.") The many visitations intensified the nature and scope of Luzzatto's Kabbalistic writings, which swelled to thousands of pages and soon aroused considerable opposition among the Venetian rabbis, who accused the unbearded and unmarried genius of harboring Shabbatian sympathies. His home was searched for evidence of engagement with magic, and in 1730 Luzzatto was forced to hand over his Kabbalistic writings and to stop holding forth on the subject.

The following year he married a woman named Zipporah—a marriage that was understood by the bridegroom in mystical terms: the match paralleled that of the couple's biblical namesakes and it was explicitly identified with sexual and ultimate union within the Godhead. In this and other ways, Luzzatto saw himself as an *ibbur* (the re-impregnation of the soul, or the mystical embodiment) of the Moses of old—which is to say, someone who would redeem the Jewish people from exile. Marriage, however, wasn't enough to quell his detractors, and—with his family in financial difficulty and perhaps also seeking to escape the persecution of the Venetian rabbinate—in 1735 he moved to Amsterdam. (The Venetian rabbis also had allies in Germany, where Luzzatto's Kabbalistic writings were banned and in part destroyed that year, as they would be two years later in Venice.) In Holland, among the more tolerant Portuguese-Jewish community, Luzzatto lived for the next eight years, writing extensively and powerfully on ethical topics and continuing to produce scholarly and dramatic work. He died of the plague in 1743, a short time after emigrating to Palestine (where he hoped to resume writing about Kabbalah). He was buried near Acre. After his death (as in certain circles during his life), he was looked upon as something of a saint.

Luzzatto's earlier Kabbalistic writings reorient the esoteric enterprise toward the world, as they emphasize the ethical implications of Lurianic theology for what scholars have seen as "a whole new philosophy of history"—one that views all things as moving dialectically (on both revealed and secret ethical levels) toward the messianic end of the perfect good and divine unity. "This movement . . . achieved within the very core of the divine will," involves at root "the wish to do good to another than the self." "The truth is," Luzzatto writes in one of his early Kabbalistic works, "for ever and ever the world-wheel turns always to one point, that is the final perfection. . . . While turning, it comes sometimes nearer to perfection and sometimes further away from it. And even after it has made a definite turn toward the better, it must return to a worse state of things. . . . But final perfection will be achieved with the coming of the redemption."

Though he would come to fight against the Shabbatian movement, Luzzatto—like Zacut in his day—appears to have been drawn to certain elements of its thought. That is, he viewed Shabbatianism and its messianic currents as vital spiritual phenomena, but he refused to accept the movement's antinomianism. In particular, he was interested in the dynamics of the messianic process and the characters that figure in it: the Messiah ben David (the anointed one of the Davidic line, who will redeem Israel, rule at the climax of history, and bring about the establishment of the Kingdom of David) and the Messiah ben Joseph (who will precede him and die fighting the enemies of God and Israel). The third figure in this triad is the biblical Moses, whose task is to strengthen, unite, and guide the two Messiahs as they carry out their mystical missions. As we have seen, Luzzatto viewed himself in no uncertain terms as Moses redivivus; it's also clear that two of his disciples saw themselves (and were seen by Luzzatto) as embodiments of the two Messiahs.

In the centuries since his death Luzzatto has been held in extremely high esteem as a poet and playwright. Hayyim Nahman Bialik considered him the first modern Hebrew writer, but as many have noted, he straddled several worlds, old and new, even as Padua links northern and southern Europe—and so he anticipates on the one hand both the secular reform of Moses Mendelssohn and the Haskalah, and on the other hand the extension of Jewish mysticism into a more popular, ethical context in the form of Hasidism and the

Musar movement. While Luzzatto combined in his person a hunger and talent for poetry and a passion for mysticism, his collected poems and plays contain little overtly Kabbalistic material (though some feel that he occasionally encoded esoteric elements within his dramatic poetry, as he may have at times into his ethical writings). In the 1960s and 1970s, however, ten new poems, along with other prose works by Luzzatto, were discovered, and — much to the surprise of scholars and certain streams of the religious Jewish community — these poems, which would seem to predate his departure for Amsterdam, and may well have been written around the time of his wedding, were unique in the Luzzatto canon; moreover, they were, in places, clearly Kabbalistic. The sonnet translated below, for instance, which was among that group, is driven by the same messianic fervor that characterizes the poet and Zipporah's recently discovered marriage contract. Both announce that the vanquishing of the demonic Sitra Ahra is imminent. And the poem, says the work's editor, comprises nothing less than "a message of encouragement" for the vengeful Messiah ben Joseph, who will wage war against the husks of evil and the enemies of Israel. The end of days, the poet implies, and with it the messianic victory, is near.

The light concealed in the clearing's whiteness
is longed for by its sacred effusions;
each in his place absorbs its profusion —
along a lustrous line of endlessness.

He set Delight beside Him in learning:
the store of treasure with brightness was filled.
And in it He formed hosts and worlds —
for the light anticipates angels and men.

There on high He set His pillars;
10   three above, then seven were fixed.
On them the throne of Eternity sits,
where the Ancient of Days longed to dwell.

Crowned with the *Crown* in a place unknown,
restorer of life, and mercy's guardian;
long suffering, show your compassion —
to all of Israel say, "I am."

Convey soundness to the living soul,
you who make all things happen.
Brighten the paths to learning and *Wisdom,*
20   where I might come in thanks to the Lord.

The Rock who rules over creation —
gives fools wisdom and prophets reason —
open the wondrous gates of *Knowing*.
Through them I'll reach the power of God.

Remember your *Mercy* to the House of Israel:
bestow magnanimity upon the poor.
Defender of Abraham, send a redeemer
who'll be with us — Emmanuel.

Strengthen, Mighty One, your flock as it yearns;
before your *Power* it goes in fear.   30
God of Isaac, let those who'd draw near
know, as you save them, that you are theirs.

Recall, Ancient One, that day of grace:
your *Glory* revealed in Sinai's flame.
Mighty One of Jacob, hear my plea.
Before you now I offer my prayer.

Set your feet on wonder's throne
and in your *Eternal Majesty* — respond:
Send, as in the desert, a sign.
You are the Lord of hosts, our God.   40

Tell my troubles and grief "No more,"
Shepherd of Joseph, increase my treasure.

Establish in Zion my *Foundation*
and the lot the faithful receive from the Lord.

Grant me the sight of *Kingdom*'s scion —
and with it Elijah, its zealous herald.
Hear my song, defender of David,
as befits your Name, O Lord.

Send the seraphs the glow of your bounty,
50　and over the heavenly hosts decree
joy's fullness for the hart's country.
And may my own meditation be worthy.

YOU READIED A LIGHT

You readied a light,
    Lord, for your people;
in the shrine of your Temple,
    you readied a light:
You readied a light
    as our companion—
    for us now
        you've readied a light.

The world's foundation
and eternity's perfection   10
    in dark contraction
and concealment is hidden—
the mystery's tracings
    and remnants of form
    illumine and shine
in the Unknown's depths.
Long ago, Lord,
    your utterance glowed
    with "Let there be light,"
and there was light.   20
You readied a light,
    Lord, for your people;
in the shrine of your Temple,
    you readied a light:

You readied a light
as our companion —
for us now
you've readied a light.

Your nation's merit

30   recalled as glory
through your greatness
alone ascends;
by you it was raised
as delight's testament,
and for your people's
future it stands.
It earned your nation
a name over nations,
from the darkness

40   dividing the light.
You readied a light,
Lord, for your people;
in the shrine of your Temple,
you readied a light. . . .

You set it alone
in the land of the living;
you drove out the nations
and readied good things,

planning a sanctum—
   for your glory a dwelling—   50
   between the walls
your light drawn in.
The House of Aaron
   was charged to bring
   the light's splendor
through lamps for the light:
You readied a light
   Lord, for your people;
in the shrine of your Temple,
   you readied a light. . . .   60

The Splendor went dim
as Israel transgressed,
   but your light and compassion
beside them remain—
and despite their being
   in enemy lands,
   the Presence holds,
a tower of strength.
Within that shrine
   you shine in the flame,   70
   a great abundance
where dwelleth the light.
You readied a light

Lord, for your people;
in the shrine of your Temple,
you readied a light. . . .

And so, as well,
Rock of the World,
    you've favored the faithful
80 in building your dwelling;
    its pleasure extends
        into this month,
        as the people gather
between its walls.
May their work find favor
        and their substance your blessing.
        Sweeten their fate
and their life with light.
You readied a light
90   *Lord, for your people;*
    in the shrine of your Temple,
        you readied a light. . . .

The Law was then given
to rise before dawn,
    maintaining the watches
within the pavilion.
Their council is firm
    through midnight's instruction,

with penance accepted
in hymns and songs —   100
which serve as a beacon
    unto the nation,
    delighting in you
    by the oil and light.
You readied a light
    Lord, for your people;
in the shrine of your Temple,
    you readied a light. . . .

But later came
those months of gall   110
    with the Rock's rage
at His nation abject.
Then with His grace
    the wound was healed —
    and salvation's phase
brought in the new year.
The host of the people
    assembled in Greatness,
    as in the darkness
He kindled the light.   120
    You readied a light
        Lord, for your people;
in the shrine of your Temple,
    you readied a light. . . .

God of Abraham,
pity the poor—
   as hearts holding fast
before you groan.
Stricken with sorrow,
130   they observe the commandments
      maintaining your covenant,
redemption's hope.
The enemy waits
   but our strength will reign;
   like the olive's green
which is pressed for the light.
You readied a light
   Lord, for your people;
in the shrine of your Temple,
140   *you readied a light. . . .*

The Land's glory
in your dwelling will shine,
   as when Solomon
built in Judah.
The service restored
   as it was then,
   through priestly offerings
love will awaken
with goodness through *man*

to *a* people appointed— 150
as by your light
we'll see the light.
You readied a light,
Lord, for your people;
in the shrine of your Temple,
you readied a light:
You readied a light
as our companion—
for us now
you've readied a light. 160

MESSIAH

Son of fruitful Joseph, precious Ephraim,
child of joy, lush grove of magnificence,
you will exult and rejoice — for, with a vengeance,
the Just will arise over the House of the Barren

when the time comes to crown the One who is righteous
with the blessing of mountains that bore you. The blessing
   of breasts.
The blessing of hills everlasting. Of the column's greatness.
Of sweetness hidden for you. Heaven's blessing.

His bullock's majesty will rise as one with the lion.
Hordes of foes laid waste, he will grow calm.
Laughing at fear, he'll sentence the serpent to oblivion.

You'll crush the power of tyrants. The wind will scatter them.
Those at ease in their wealth you'll bring to destruction —
and you will dwell assured of the peace to come.

Hasidic Devotion

"The earlier Kabbalah tried to bring man into heaven," wrote one recent observer of Hasidism. "The main idea of Hasidism was to bring heaven into man." Which is not to say that Lurianic Kabbalah and Hasidism were opposed to each other. On the contrary, modern Hasidism emerges out of the basic cosmic principles set forth by Yitzhak Luria—fullness, contraction, creation through catastrophe, and restoration (*tikkun*)—but it rings powerful changes on them. Instead of the sprawling Kabbalistic abstraction and stacked-up symbolic systems that seek to account for the dynamics of creation, in place of the mixed metaphorical registers of the *Zohar* and the nano-distinctions of theosophy that recall particle or post-atomic physics, one finds in the revivalist literature of Hasidism the aphorism, the parable, the person, and the world. After the mania of Shabbatian antinomianism, and in the wake of social upheavals brought about by political uncertainty in eastern Europe, charismatic Hasidism came into Judaism as a gust of very fresh air from the North.

Not surprisingly, it spread rapidly—beginning in the 1730s with the teachings of the Baal Shem Tov (the Master of the Good Name, or the Good Master of the [Divine] Name), and then with the work of his successor, Dov Baer, the Maggid of Mezeritch. By the late eighteenth century and the third generation of Hasidic masters, it had permeated Poland, Lithuania, Belorussia, and the Ukraine, and also reached Palestine. Hasidism would eventually become the way of life of most of eastern Europe's Jews and make its way to western Europe and the United States. With growth, however, came diversity, and various schools of Hasidic thought began taking shape under the leadership of independent and to some extent rival charismatic leaders, or *tzaddikim*.

Among that third generation of Hasidic tzaddikim was Levi Yitzhak of Berditchev, who was born in Galicia to a long line of rabbis that, according to tradition, spanned sixteen generations. His father was both a Talmudist and a Kabbalist. Soon after he married into a wealthy family and began settling into a life of conventional Jewish scholarship, Levi Yitzhak was drawn to the teachings of a Hasidic rabbi in a nearby town, and by his early twenties he was on his way to becoming a prominent member of the new movement. He joined the circle of the Maggid of Mezeritch, then took up a series of rabbinic posts in Polish and Belorussian towns, always in the face of serious opposition and even harassment by the rationalist Mitnaggedim. In 1785, at the age of forty-five, he became rabbi of the largely Jewish Ukrainian town of Berditchev, which was already an important Hasidic and commercial center. He served there till his death in 1810. Today Levi Yitzhak is considered the founder of Hasidism in Central Poland and a key figure in its development in Lithuania and the Ukraine.

As the rabbi of Berditchev, Levi Yitzhak became renowned as a much-loved, disarming, gentle, and charismatic Hasidic leader. In his writing and his practice he stressed joy, *devekut*, and the importance of passionate prayer that would elevate man's soul. He was also known for praying and speaking to God in Yiddish—as in the poem below, which is among the most popular of several that are attributed to him. In a marvelous translation from high to low, or angel-level to eye-level, Levi Yitzhak's Yiddish also mixes in elements from the Hebrew liturgy and a twelfth-century Hebrew poem by Yehudah Ha-Levi ("Where Will I Find You," above). Levi Yitzhak's poem—which became known as "Dudele" (i.e., "the little song of You")—embodies the cardinal Hasidic sense that, as Scholem put it, "God surrounds everything and pervades everything. . . . A ray of God's essence is present and perceptible everywhere and at every moment." Moreover, Scholem writes, "it is the communion with God through *devekut* that makes God an intimate friend of man, instead of a forbidding and remote stranger." Hence, Levi Yitzhak's intimate song to an anything but remote Deity, who not only created everything but continues to create all things and to be embodied in them.

For the Hasidim, this fundamental truth of God's nearness can be grasped not by learning but only by faith and in relation to other people in the world. Accordingly, notes Solomon Schechter in a now-classic essay on Hasidism, the three principal virtues of the movement are humility, cheerfulness, and enthusiasm. Though a strain of asceticism lingered on in certain schools of the new Hasidism, we are, with the Baal Shem Tov and Levi Yitzhak, light-years away from the flagellation and snow-rolling of the medieval Pietists (who were also known as Hasids), and of their successors in the hills of seventeenth-century Safed.

That said, Hasidism did develop a more scholarly stream, and this too emerged from that third generation of masters who were disciples of the Maggid of Mezeritch. The Belorussian Shneur Zalman, who in time became identified with the town of Liadi (some one hundred miles northeast of Minsk), was one of the Maggid's youngest and most gifted students. As someone with formidable training in Torah and Talmud, who had then been won over to the Hasidic ethos (because, as he put it, he knew "a little about learning, but nothing about prayer"), Zalman was chosen in 1774 by a committee of Hasidic leaders to defend Hasidism before the Gaon of Vilna, the preeminent Jewish figure of his day. Opposition to the Hasidim had grown intense, and the divisions it opened up in Jewish society cut deep. "Herems," or internal Jewish bans, against the Hasidim were passed in 1772 (and would be followed with others in 1781 and 1796); Hasidic books were burned; and oppositional tracts were composed and distributed deriding the "Hashudim" (or "suspects," as the play on *Hasidim* — "the pious" — had it), who were accused of magic, madness, treason, delusion, idolatry, irresponsibility, charlatanism, a residual Shabbatianism, and even Frankism. The Gaon refused to meet with Shneur Zalman.

Over the course of some twenty years, Shneur Zalman developed a distinct brand of Hasidism known as Habad — an acronym that stands for the Kabbalistic terms *Hokhmah, Binah, Da'at* (wisdom, understanding, and knowledge) — the three highest *sefirot.* (From the time of Luria and on, Da'at was sometimes added to the traditional sefirotic tree as a reflection of Keter, and so it is that eleven sefirot appear on the cover of this book.) Habad Hasidism sought to systematize Hasidic instruction, organizing it along more intellectual lines. Regular, ardent study, with the proper sort of desire for communion, or devekut, could lead the ordinary or average person to a kind of spiritual alignment with the divine on the practical plane of action, emotion, and even intellect. Meditation on the greatness of God the Creator would lift an individual onto a plane of more intense love and a reverence that is rational. As one scholar has put it: "Here the descent into the mystical realm is one of reaching out for ever more refined levels of mind, seeking that inner place where the mind of God will be joined to the most rarefied human intellect."

Shneur Zalman's writing was, then, known for its intellectual engagement, passion, common sense, and recombination of Kabbalistic elements. His collected sayings (*Likkutei Amarim*), which were published in 1796 and became extremely popular, were known as the *Tanya* (Aramaic for "It was taught"), as the first word of the book had it. The excerpt below embodies a central tenet in Shneur Zalman's worldview, namely, that true communion with the divine (or concealed) can be brought about only through attachment to what

has been created and revealed—God's Torah and the physical obser-
vance of its commandments by each individual. In this devotional
Kabbalistic scheme, in other words, expansion is achieved through
contraction, and the infinite encountered in the actual.

Lord of the World.
Lord of the World.
Lord of the World,
I'll sing You a little Song of You.

You-You-You

Where will I find You?
And where won't I find You?

So – here I go – You,
and – there I go – You,
always You, however You,
only You, and ever You.

You-You-You, You-You

East – You – West – You,
North – You – South – You.

You – You – You

The heavens – You. Earth – You.
On high – You, and below . . .

In every direction, and every inflection.
Still You. However You. Only You. Ever You.

You — You — You   20

All before Him is as nothing:
The soul stirs and burns
for the precious glory of His greatness,
to behold the light of the King
like coals of the fierce flame rising.
To be freed from the wick
or the wood to which it clings.

The Seeds of Secular Mysticism

Toward the end of his *Major Trends in Jewish Mysticism*, Gershom Scholem relates a Hasidic tale that applies in uncanny fashion to the final link in this book's literary chain of mystical transmission. Whenever the Baal Shem Tov was faced with a grave task, the story has it, he would make his way to a certain place in the forest, light a fire in a special manner, say a particular set of prayers, and—miraculously—the task would be accomplished. When his disciple the Maggid of Mezeritch faced a similar challenge, he would go to the same place in the forest and say: "We no longer know how to light the fire, but we can still say the prayers." He would say them, and the deed would be done. In the next generation, Rabbi Moshe Leib of Sassov was compelled to take up the challenge and perform the task in question. He went to forest and said: "We can no longer light the fire, nor do we know the secret prayers, but we know the place in the forest—and that is enough." And it was. But a generation later, when Rabbi Yisrael of Ryshin responded to a similar situation, he sat down on his chair and said: "The prayers have been forgotten. We cannot light the fire. And we do not know the place in the woods. But we can tell the story of how, once, it was done." He told the story and, remarkably, this too was sufficient.

"The Pool," by modern Hebrew's first great poet, Hayyim Nahman Bialik, is in a sense about that place in the woods and its story. In another sense, it *is* that place—though the miracle that attends to it in many ways constitutes a secular extension of the Hasidic story, as it shows the poet at the traditional site of power but removed from that power's tradition. In the poem, the consciousness of the artist, like the pool, absorbs, reflects, and transforms (in dreamlike fashion) all it is exposed to. And like the clearing in which the pool is found, artistic consciousness, in complex fashion, is a realm unto itself, and yet one that might lead to an understanding of the mysteries of existence.

While "The Pool" is a Romantic and even Wordsworthian poem about a solitary journey into the woods and toward a place of discovery in and through nature (where all is mystery and hints, splendor and wonder), it also integrates key terms from the vocabulary of Jewish mysticism: "cut off from the world," "the hidden light," "the great mystery of the kingdom," "in the secret chamber of its [his] powers," "secret scrolls," "this other world" (from the first part of the poem, not translated here); and "the Presence [*shekhinah*]," "[being] one with . . . heart and . . . god," "holy of holies," "the language of vision, revealed," "the hidden God," and more. As such, "The Pool" represents a transitional mode in which the traditional Kabbalistic lexicon and mythopoetic worldview begin making their way into a secular framework. Its revelation occurs, in other words, in a shadow-space of the sacred.

Bialik, who was born in the Ukrainian village of Radi in 1873 to a tavern-keeping father who died when he was seven, was raised by a strict and pious grandfather in nearby Zhitomir. He received a traditional Jewish education in a yeshiva and also read deeply in Hebrew and Yiddish literature, including translations of foreign works. After he left the world of the yeshiva and became a disciple of Ahad Ha'Am, the prophet of Jewish cultural and national revival, he steeped himself in all branches of humanistic and Jewish knowledge, everything from philosophy to history, religious law to Kabbalah. All of which is to say that he had full command of the entire Hebrew register of learning. Though he rarely wrote about Kabbalah in explicit fashion, his poems at times contain conspicuous allusions to mystical motifs, just as his best-known piece of prose echoes key Kabbalistic structures and concerns. "Revealment and Concealment in Language" is, therefore, sometimes looked to as a kind of Kabbalistic essay, since it attempts to peel back the outer husk of ordinary language and reach its kernel. But while, in the traditional esoteric context, that Hebrew kernel contains a holiness that replenishes itself (see Gikatilla's "The Nut Garden," above), the kernel of profane language, as the essay has it, is empty. Language itself conceals that terrifying fact. Poetry's task, then, is dual: it should expose the truth (the void and danger lurking beneath the words we use daily), and it should seek to reunite language with its place of origin and its primal power (the generative aspect of the Infinite or Nothingness).

This dialectical tension between emptiness and fullness, or absence and presence, is at the heart of Kabbalistic theories of creation (from *Sefer Yetzirah* to Luria), and it is central to Bialik's poetics as well. Hence one scholar's observing the somewhat remarkable frequency with which Bialik's poems begin in an acknowledgment of negation, absence, emptiness, or deprivation. And hence the poet's notion that writing or reading prose is like crossing a river that has frozen over with solid ice, whereas writing (or reading) poetry is like crossing a river in which the ice has already broken up into blocks that are moving rapidly along with the current. In order to cross safely from one bank to another, one has to skip from floe to floe above the depths of the river. In this way poetry—by revealing the nothingness out of which fullness flows—brings redemption of a kind, whereas ordinary language blocks the path to it.

"Bring Me in Under Your Wing," perhaps Bialik's most famous poem, was composed around the same time as "The Pool"—which is to say, just after he returned home to Odessa after a long and turbulent period of wandering. The two poems were published together in 1905 in Odessa's *HaShiloah*, the major Hebrew journal of the day.

Ostensibly a poem about love (though just what sort of love remains ambiguous), "Bring Me in Under Your Wing" deals at a deeper level with another sort of duality and tension—between exile and return, separation and a desire for restoration—as it explores the painful space of betweenness from which, it can be argued, poetry (like religion) emerges. As language is exiled from its own primal power in Bialik's essay, and as the Jewish people and the Shekhinah have been in exile from the spiritual and actual place where the presence of God would be felt most fully, so in this poem the speaker is separated from the place of youthful innocence, realized dreams, and the sense of connection that love bestows. At the same time he is also denied any consolation for that cataclysmic loss. At the liminal hour of dusk, the fact of exile from origin is most painfully felt, and the speaker longs for shelter beneath the wing of what seems to be the Shekhinah. "My soul dwells in exile," Bialik said of himself in another context altogether—attempting to explain why he wrote so little poetry once he moved to Palestine—"and who knows, maybe the Shekhinah descends upon me only out of sadness."

What did descend upon Bialik in Tel Aviv was a powerful desire for restoration of another sort. By the time he settled in the Middle East, he was fifty-one, and his best work was largely behind him. But he was still very much the national poet, and he was looked to as something of a literary messiah, or at least as "a modern Isaiah," as one contemporary put it. His sense of public mission loomed large— and he devoted the better part of his remaining years—he died in 1934—to the *kinnus*, or ingathering and extension of the great works of the (traditional) Jewish past into the (secular) Jewish present.

The two poems translated here reflect the private aspect of that ingathering, as a religious and sometimes mystical impulse is extended in precarious if exhilarating fashion into the realm of a nascent Hebrew modernism. This sacred-secular dynamic emerges in much of Bialik's work, but nowhere is it given gentler and, at the same time, more subtly ironic expression than in his most beloved piece of children's verse, which mirrors the suspension of the spirit exposed—perhaps like readers of this book—between distinct though not necessarily distant worlds:

> See, saw, see, saw,
> down and up, up and down!
> What's on high?
> What's below?
> Only I,
> you and I—
> both of us balanced
> on the scales
> there between
> the earth and sky.

When I was young and my days were sweet
and the wings of the Presence first rustled over me,
my heart knew longing and mute amazement,
and I sought a secret place for its prayer.
And so in the heat of the day I'd sail
toward the kingdom of majestic calm
into the heart of the summer forest.
There among the trees of God
no echo of a falling ax was heard;
10 for long hours I'd wander a path
that only the wolf and hunter knew—
one with my heart and my god until,
stepping over the golden snares,
I'd enter the sacred shrine of the woods.
Beyond the veil of the leaves lay
a green island with a carpet of grass,
serene—a world unto itself,
a holy of holies among the shadows
of the forest's trunks and tangled canopies.
20 Its ceiling formed a small blue dome
set and fastened over the trees—
its floor was glass: a pool of water,
a silver mirror within the frame
of the damp grass, inside which lay
another and second, smaller world.
And in the middle of that dome

and at the center of that pool
facing stones of jacinth shone,
large and carnelian: two suns.

And as I sat at the edge of the pool   30
and gazed at the riddle of the twin worlds,
not knowing which was prior—
my head bowed beneath the blessing
of the ancient grove, the play of shadow
and light as one, of resin and song—
I'd feel, palpably, the silent flow
of a certain freshness entering my soul,
and my heart, thirsty for sacred mystery,
would slowly fill with quiet longing,
as though it wanted more, and more,   40
and awaited the epiphany of His Presence.
Or that of Elijah. And as I listened,
and my heart shuddered and nearly gave way,
the echoed voice of a hidden God
exploded suddenly from the silence:
Where art thou?
And huge wonder filled the forest,
and the oaks of God, firmly rooted,
looked on at me from within their majesty
in amazement: Who is this among us?   50

A silent language of gods exists,
a soundless speech of secrets, but rich

with color, the magic of shifting forms,
a fabulous spectacle. And within that language
God makes Himself known to the chosen—
His spirit's elect. And the lord of the world
reflects as He will, and the artist gives shape
to the thoughts of his heart and dreams unspoken.
This is the language of vision, revealed

60   along an azure strip of the heaven's
expanse, and within its silvery clouds
and nimbus massed; in the corn's trembling
gold, and the great cedar soaring;
the white wing of the fluttering dove,
and the broad strokes of the eagle's wings;
in the simple beauty of a man's back
and the splendor of the look in his eye;
in the sea's anger, and its breakers' crash
and play; in the night's bounty and the silence

70   of falling stars; in the noise of fire
and the ocean-roar of daybreak's blaze
and dusk. Within this language, the language
of languages, the pool spelled out—for me
as well—its eternal riddle,
tranquil, and hidden there in the shade,
seeing all and also holding
and with it all always altering.
And so it seemed like an open eye
of the forest's lord—the greatest of mysteries

80   and the longest reverie.

BRING ME IN UNDER YOUR WING

Bring me in under your wing,
    be sister for me, and mother,
the place of you, rest for my head,
    a nest for my unwanted prayers.

At the hour of mercy, at dusk,
    we'll talk of my secret pain:
They say, there's youth in the world—
    What happened to mine?

And another thing, a clue:
    my being was scared by a flame.   10
They say there's love all around—
    What do they mean?

The stars betrayed me—there
    was a dream, which also has passed.
Now in the world I have nothing,
    not a thing.

Bring me in under your wing,
    be sister for me, and mother,
the place of you, rest for my head,
    a nest for my unwanted prayers.   20

NOTES

Citations from the Bible in this volume vary in their use of the standard translations: often the King James Version is cited, but at times I also quote the Revised Standard Version, the 1917 Jewish Publication Society version, and the 1988 JPS version (NJPS). All Talmudic translations are from the Soncino edition: The Babylonian Talmud *(London, 1952, 1990). Zoharic references are keyed to the standard pagination of the 1923 Vilna edition, as published in* Sefer HaZohar [Heb], *ed. Reuven Margaliot (Jerusalem, 1953), and* Zohar Hadash [Heb], *ed. R. Margaliot (Jerusalem, 1956). Where relevant, references are also given to* The Zohar, *trans. Daniel C. Matt, 5 vols. (Stanford, Calif., 2004–9), and* The Wisdom of the Zohar, *arranged and rendered into Hebrew by Fischel Lachower and Isaiah Tishby; introductions and annotations by Isaiah Tishby, trans. David Goldstein, 3 vols. (Oxford, 1997).*

Introduction

1. This litany of the poetry's desired effects is drawn from the following sources: Moshe Idel, *Absorbing Perfections: Kabbalah and Interpretation* (New Haven, 2002), pp. 183–84 (also pp. 131–32), Idel, *Hasidism* (Albany, N.Y., 1995), pp. 161–62, 215–18, and Idel, "Hermeneutics in Hasidism," *Journal for the Study of Religions and Ideologies* 9:25 (2010), pp. 3–16; Gershom Scholem, *On the Kabbalah and Its Symbolism,* trans. Ralph Manheim (New York, 1969), p. 144, and Scholem, *Kabbalah* (New York, 1974), pp. 139–40. On the question of Kabbalistic language, see Idel, "Reification of Language in Jewish Mysticism," in *Mysticism and Language,* ed. Steven Katz (Oxford, 1992), pp. 42–79, where he traces the notion of language as a link between the material world, human beings, and the

divine. Also see Scholem, "The Kabbalah of R. Ya'akov and R. Yitzhak HaKohen" [Heb], *Madda'ei HaYahadut* 2 (1927), pp. 165–290; Ibn Tzur in Hayyim Zafrani, *Hebrew Poetry in Morocco* [Heb] (Jerusalem, 1984), p. 19; and Idel, "Music," in *Contemporary Jewish Religious Thought: Original Essays on Critical Concepts, Movements, and Beliefs*, ed. Arthur A. Cohen and Paul Mendes-Flohr (New York, 1987), pp. 635–42. For more on the phenomena described here, see Scholem, "Redemption Through Sin," in *The Messianic Idea in Judaism* (New York, 1971); Amnon Shiloah, "The Influence of the World of Kabbalah on the Development of the Singing of Piyyut" [Heb], *Mekedem umiyam* 2 (1986), pp. 201–11; Lawrence Fine, *Safed Spirituality: Rules of Mystical Piety, the Beginning of Wisdom* (Ramsey, N.J., 1984), p. 162; Paul Fenton, "Les Bakkashot d'orient et d'occident," *Revue des études juives* 134:1–2 (1975), p. 106; and the notes to "The Kabbalah in Spain," below.

2. Moshe Ibn Tzur, *Tziltzelei Shama* [Ps. 150:5], in Zafrani, *Hebrew Poetry in Morocco* [Heb], p. 24, but see generally pp. 19–27. Ibn Tzur, who lived in the late seventeenth and early eighteenth centuries, is talking about the recitation of biblical poetry, especially David's Psalms. His own poetry, which has not been included in this volume, is saturated with Kabbalistic elements.

3. Gershom Scholem, *Major Trends in Jewish Mysticism* (New York, 1941), p. 271.

4. Shiloah, "Influence of the World of Kabbalah" [Heb], pp. 210–11.

5. From *Sefer Razi'el*, cited in Elliot R. Wolfson, "Letter Symbolism and Merkavah Imagery in the Zohar," in *Alei Shefer: Studies in the Literature of Jewish Thought, Presented to Rabbi Dr. Alexandre Safran*, ed. Moshe Hallamish (Ramat Gan, 1990), p. 199. Wolfson also cites another text from a similar provenance, which calls the Hebrew vowels the soul and the letters the body, indicating that the vowel that "receives the influence from the supernal grade" mounts, as it were, a cherub and soars. This alignment of sound and supernal energy, says the text, glossing Psalms 99:1 ("enthroned upon the cherubim") and 2 Samuel 22:11 ("He mounted a cherub and flew"), is "the secret of the cherubim." Wolfson cites numerous other related passages, including this one by Yosef Gika-

tilla: "Know that the vowels and the consonants instruct us about the form of the entire world . . . and the order of the chariots" (p. 208). "Chariots" here refers to the vehicle of vision in the Merkavah literature, about which see "Poems of the Palaces and Early Liturgical Hymns." As Wolfson notes, elsewhere Gikatilla uses the phrase "the chariot of the letters."

6. Moshe Idel, citing the late-eighteenth-century Hasid Mordekhai of Chernobyl, in "Hermeneutics in Hasidism," p. 12. See also Idel, "White Letters: From R. Levi Isaac of Berdichev to Postmodern Hermeneutics," in his *Old Worlds, New Mirrors: On Jewish Mysticism and Twentieth-Century Thought* (Philadelphia, 2010), pp. 234–47, and especially his "Reification of Language in Jewish Mysticism," p. 58, and "Perceptions of Kabbalah in the Second Half of the Eighteenth Century," *Journal of Jewish Thought and Philosophy* 1 (1992), pp. 55–115, esp. pp. 85–95. In a similar vein, from the seventeenth century on, Hasidim have understood the mystical import of Genesis 6:16 — "A window shalt thou make to the ark [*tevah*]" — as "A window shalt thou make to the *word* [*tevah*]," which should open onto essence (the really real) so souls can be joined. See Rachel Elior, "'A Window Shalt Thou Make to the Ark': Language, Memory and Culture as a Bridge Between the Secular Reader and the Jewish Library," in *Jewish Identity in Modern Israel: Proceedings on Secular Judaism and Democracy*, ed. Naftali Rosenberg and Eliezer Schweid (Jerusalem, 2002), pp. 61–62, and Elior, *Jewish Mysticism: The Infinite Expression of Freedom*, trans. Yudith Nave and Arthur B. Millman (Oxford, 2007), pp. 40–41; and Ithamar Gruenwald, "Reflections on the Nature and Origins of Jewish Mysticism," in *Gershom Scholem's "Major Trends in Jewish Mysticism" Fifty Years After*, ed. Peter Schäfer and Joseph Dan (Tübingen, 1993), p. 48.

7. *Hagigah* 14b: "Our Rabbis taught: Four men entered the 'Garden,' namely, Ben Azzai and Ben Zoma, Aher, and R. Akiva. R. Akiva said to them: When ye arrive at the stones of pure marble, say not, water, water! For it is said: He that speaketh falsehood shall not be established before mine eyes. Ben Azzai cast a look and died. Of him Scripture says: Precious in the sight of the Lord is the death of His saints. Ben Zoma looked and became demented. Of him Scripture says: Hast thou found honey? Eat

so much as is sufficient for thee, lest thou be filled therewith, and vomit it. Aher mutilated the shoots. R. Akiva departed unhurt." "The Garden" in this passage is, in the Hebrew, *Pardes*, a word that means "orchard," but which in the Kabbalistic scheme (and for that matter, generally in the Jewish context) becomes a figurative expression for a fourfold process of religious interpretation. Rashi explains that the four scholars ascended to heaven, and Tosefta adds that it only appeared to them that they did so. Others say it was "a vision." Aher (literally, "Another," which is how this person—Elisha b. Abuyah—came to be known) "mutilated the shoots," i.e., committed apostasy. The nature of his defection is controversial; he is talked of in the relevant literature as a Persian, a Gnostic, or Philonian dualist; a Christian; a Sadducee; and a "victim of the inquisitor Akiva" (see *Soncino Talmud*, commentary to 14b). In *Hagigah* 2:1 students are warned to steer clear of mystical inquiry. See note to "A Measure of Holiness," below.

8. Joseph Dan describes the world of Kabbalah as a place where "everything is the reflection of everything else" (Dan, *Kabbalah: A Very Short Introduction* [Oxford, 2007], pp. 33–34). See also Bialik's "The Pool," below, and the notes there. Lawrence uses "dawn-kaleidoscopic" in his poem "Pomegranate." As it happens, the pomegranate is, in the Kabbalistic context, a symbol of that intense and fecund proliferation of meaning.

9. Gershom Scholem, "The Name of God and the Linguistic Theory of the Kabbalah," *Diogenes* 79 (1972), p. 60. Moshe Idel also contrasts the attitude of Jewish and Christian mysticisms to language: for Augustine, he says, "it is language, or languages, that are to be surpassed in order to reach the acme of mysticism. . . . The mentalist and introvert mood that characterizes nonlinguistic mystical experiences seems to be exceptional to Judaism. Conceiving Hebrew as the perfect and divine language, there was no reason [for Jewish Kabbalists] to attempt to transcend, attenuate, or obliterate its use. . . . Words become the throne on which the deity dwells, ensuring the closest contact between the two entities" (Idel, "Reification of Language in Jewish Mysticism," p. 55). See also Idel, "Defining Kabbalah: The Kabbalah of the Divine Names," in *The Mystics of the Book: Themes, Topics, and Typologies*, ed. R. A. Herrera

(New York, 1993), p. 107, where he contrasts linguistic and nonlinguistic mystical trends *within* Judaism: "The emphasis on mystical metaphysics, that can be called theosophy, . . . as well as the centrality of the mystical intention during the performance of the commandments, [were] drastically marginalized by the ecstatic Kabbalist in favor of the manipulation of language that manipulates the soul." In a related manner, Joseph Dan contrasts Judaism and Islam with Christianity. Judaism and Islam are, he notes, traditions in which the language of revelation is an essential part of the revelation itself; in Christianity, on the other hand, the gospel, the message, the content of the transmission is its core. This "good news" not only survives translation, it is in many ways *born in translation*, or at any rate at a remove that all believers, or would-be believers, necessarily experience from the original Word (*The Heart and the Fountain: An Anthology of Jewish Mystical Experiences*, ed. Joseph Dan [Oxford, 2002], pp. 10–11). See also Steven Katz, "Mystical Speech and Mystical Meaning," in *Mysticism and Language*, pp. 3–41, esp. pp. 13–16 for Judaism's emphasis on the link between mysticism and language, as opposed, say, to Christianity's. Katz, however, notes the vital role of language in all mystical traditions, even those that seek to deny it. He also points out that Sufi and Hindu mystics make claims for Arabic and Sanskrit, respectively, that resemble those made by Kabbalists for Hebrew. Elliot Wolfson disagrees with Scholem about the distinctiveness of the Jewish relation to language (Elliot R. Wolfson, *Language, Eros, Being* [New York, 2005], pp. 26 and 421).

10. On the question of transcendence versus embodiment in this tradition and its scholarship, and also on the critical role of the reader in the dynamic of interpretation, see Daniel Abrams, *Kabbalistic Manuscripts and Textual Theory: Methodologies of Textual Scholarship and Editorial Practice in the Study of Jewish Mysticism* (Jerusalem and Los Angeles, 2010), pp. 129–33. See also note 22, below, for Arthur Green's comment along these lines.

11. Scholem, "Name of God," pp. 62–63; on the messianic aspect of the letters returning to their origin, see Scholem, "The Name of God and the Linguistic Theory of the Kabbalah," part 2, *Diogenes* 80 (1972),

p. 166, and Scholem's reading of Isaac the Blind's extraordinary commentary there.

12. Scholem, "Name of God," part 2, pp. 166–68. The image of the inverted tree is introduced in the *Bahir*, which is the earliest Kabbalistic text in the historical sense. For more on the *Bahir*, see "The Kabbalah in Spain," below, and the notes there.

13. Scholem, "Name of God," part 2, pp. 185–86, 188. As the ink links the world of the mind-hand-and-pen with that of the parchment, soul links the upper and lower worlds of creation. Idel cites Abulafia as saying that "beyond its practical use, . . . language contains a structure that conveys the true form of reality" (Idel, *Language, Torah, and Hermeneutics in Abraham Abulafia* [Albany, N.Y., 1989], p. 1). For more detailed discussion of Abulafia's language mysticism, see the section on Avraham Abulafia, below, and sources cited there, as well as his poem the *Book of the Sign*.

14. *The Zohar* 1:159a–b, trans. Daniel C. Matt, 5 vols. (Stanford, Calif., 2004–9), vol. 2, pp. 385–88. As Wolfson notes ("Letter Symbolism," p. 221), Abulafia and others understand the word *merkavah* as both a substantive and a verbal noun, indicating not merely "chariot" but the act of combining (letters). Continuing this implied move out from the explicitly Kabbalistic situation to the literary analogue, one might posit composition as the vehicle of a vision (or experience) of the sublime.

15. Jorge Luis Borges, "A History of Angels," trans. Esther Allen, in *Selected Non-Fictions*, ed. Eliot Weinberger (New York, 1999), p. 18. For more on this central concept, see Scholem, *Kabbalah*, pp. 98–116, and below, "The Book of Creation" and the sections on Moshe ben Nahman, and Avraham ben Maimon, and the notes there. The notion of the *sefirot* as being present "in each and every letter" is found in Isaac the Blind's writings. See Idel, "Reification of Language in Jewish Mysticism," p. 59.

16. Harold Bloom, *Kabbalah and Criticism* (New York, 1975), pp. 25 and 28.

17. The sixteenth-century Galilean is Moshe Cordovero, cited here by his student R. Elijah de Vidas (in Idel, *Hasidism*, pp. 215–16, and Idel, "Perceptions of Kabbalah in the Second Half of the Eighteenth Cen-

tury," pp. 92–93). The connection between "the five places in the mouth" and the metaphysical dimension of reality is first put forth in *Sefer Yetzirah* and the *Zohar*. See "The Book of Creation" and "The Kabbalah in Spain," below.

18. Scholem, "Name of God," part 2, pp. 186–88. Idel differs somewhat here, noting that that Abulafia attributed to the visual forms of the Hebrew letters a unique capacity for conducting prophetic knowledge and did in fact distinguish between Hebrew and all other languages, though the latter can "serve" the former. He quotes Abulafia: "The other languages are likened to Hebrew as an ape, who upon observing the actions of a human being wants to do likewise, and like a person who visually appears to another, through a mirror, and he mimics his actions and does not attempt to add to or diminish from them." Idel adds, "Apparently [Abulafia] implies . . . that it is also possible to use profane language to attain the results that are more easily achieved by means of Hebrew" (*Language, Torah, and Hermeneutics*, p. 21; see also pp. 11–28).

19. Scholem, "Name of God," part 2, pp. 190–91. At the same time, irresponsible manipulation of those languages can produce demonic and spiritually deadly effects as well. See also Idel, "Abraham Abulafia, Gershom Scholem, and Walter Benjamin on Language," in *Old Worlds, New Mirrors*, pp. 168–75. Referring to Benjamin's well-known 1916 essay "On Language as Such and on the Language of Man" (in Benjamin, *Selected Writings*, vol. 1: *1913–1926*, ed. Marcus Bullock and Michael W. Jennings [Cambridge, Mass., 1996]), Idel notes that "Benjamin anchors his view of language in the assumption that intelligible language is rooted in the divine 'primordial' language that imbues nature. Nature emanated 'a nameless, unspoken language,' which mankind, embodied in Adam, understood and transformed into the language of names. Thus for Benjamin language represents a move from multiplicity and variety, rooted in the intellectual and the nameless, toward a more unified existence in the transcendent linguistic realm that ultimately produces the divine word. Human language is an intermediary between the mental beings of nature and the divine word." Idel adds that Benjamin combines this notion that "the divine word is reflected in human language" with a

vision of "language as represented in a quintessential manner by a name
or names," and that this combination finds echoes in Abulafia's work.
He quotes the latter: "It is incumbent to dissolve all the languages into
the holy language in such a way that every speech that the speaker will
pronounce by his mouth and lips will be conceived as if it is composed
out of holy letters, which are the twenty-two letters" (*Old Worlds, New
Mirrors,* pp. 173–74). Scholem writes that "what we learn from creation
and revelation, the word of God, is infinitely liable to interpretation,
and it is reflected in our own language. Its radiation or sounds, which
we catch, are not so much communications as appeals. That which has
meaning—sense and form—is not this word itself, but the tradition be-
hind this word, this communication and reflection in time" ("Name of
God," part 2, p. 194). And this in turn—especially when combined with
the Kabbalistic notion that letters (at least the twenty-two letters of He-
brew) are "configurations of the divine energies" (p. 165)—recalls Ezra
Pound's comment that "three or four words in exact juxtaposition are ca-
pable of radiating . . . energy at a very high potentiality: . . . [these words]
must augment and not neutralize each other. This peculiar energy which
fills [them] is the power of tradition" (Pound, *Selected Prose, 1909–1965*
[New York, 1973], p.34). Daniel Abrams remarks that elsewhere, taking
up a similar approach, Scholem "comes close to adopting the Kabbalistic
view of the Hebrew language which identifies God's essence with His
name" (see "Presenting and Representing Gershom Scholem: A Review
Essay," *Modern Judaism* 20:2 [2000], p. 230). Idel, it should be noted, takes
issue with Scholem's analysis of the Kabbalistic view of language, stating
that Scholem's position derives not from the Kabbalistic texts referred to
in "The Name of God" but from Benjamin or an earlier German source.
On the other hand, he himself remarks on the close similarity between
Benjamin's views and those of Abulafia and, in some cases, Nahman-
ides. See headnotes and endnotes to the section on Avraham Abulafia,
below. With regard to translation's role in relation to this theory of lan-
guage, note Benjamin's comment: "It is necessary to found the concept
of translation at the deepest level of linguistic theory, for it is much too
far-reaching and powerful to be treated in any way as an afterthought, as

has happened occasionally. Translation attains its full meaning in the realization that every evolved language (with the exception of the Word of God) can be considered a translation of all the others" ("On Language as Such and the Language of Man," pp. 69–70).

20. Scholem, letter to Franz Rosenzweig, March 7, 1921, in Jeremy Adler, "There Stood My Mr. Benjamin," *TLS* (June 7, 1996).

21. Scholem, "Name of God," part 1, pp. 61–62.

22. See Arthur Green, "Religion and Mysticism: The Case of Judaism," in *Take Judaism, for Example: Studies Toward the Comparison of Religions*, ed. Jacob Neusner (Chicago, 1983), p. 90. Green writes of the way in which the reader of the Kabbalistic text "necessarily must also become a translator," in order to penetrate the impersonal (or apersonal) nature of most of the texts: "Kabbalistic literature in general should be viewed in large part as a projecting of states of soul and stages of consciousness upon the universe, a description of inner states in terms of 'upper' worlds. It is the reader's job cautiously to reverse the mirrors, as it were, so that the description of those numerous worlds above, often seemingly so utterly beyond meaning, will allow him to gain some insight into the mystic's own soul as well."

23. Daniel Abrams, *Ten Psychoanalytic Aphorisms on the Kabbalah* (Los Angeles, 2011), p. 23. Basing his remarks on work by the sixteenth-century Prague-born Kabbalist Isaiah Horowitz, who served as the rabbi of Kraków, Frankfurt, Prague, and — late in life — Tiberias, Abrams elaborates: "Every act of the Kabbalist is interpreted in light of coupling: the embodied performance of the commandments, his mental and emotional activities, the formulation of words of prayer before the Holy One, blessed be He, and conversations with his friend." See also R. Isaiah Horowitz, *Shnei Luhot ha-Berit, Sha'ar haOtiyyot, Ot Aleph, Emet veEmunah* [Heb] (Amsterdam, 1649), fol. 60b; and *Moses Cordovero's Introduction to Kabbalah: An Annotated Translation of His "Or Ne'erav,"* trans. Ira Robinson (New York, 1994), 2:1, where coupling (or unification) is discussed as what Abrams calls "a way of life."

24. See Moshe de León, *Book of the Pomegranate* [Heb]: "Everything is linked with everything else down to the lowest rung of the chain, and the

true essence of God is above as well as below, in the heavens and on the earth, and nothing exists outside of Him." See Katz, "Mystical Speech," p. 31, and Scholem, *Major Trends*, p. 223. As the *Zohar* has it: "He binds and joins the species with one another, above and below, and there is no juncture of the four elements except by the Holy One, blessed be He, existing among them" (*Wisdom of the Zohar*, arranged and rendered into Hebrew by Fischel Lachower and Isaiah Tishby; introductions and annotations by Isaiah Tishby, trans. David Goldstein, 3 vols. [Oxford, 1997], vol. 1, p. 250). See also Elliot R. Wolfson, *The Book of the Pomegranate* (Atlanta, 1988), e.g., pp. 95ff. in the Hebrew. For the series of wedded sounds in the air, see Basil Bunting's charge to poets in *Briggflatts*— "to sing, not paint, . . . /laying the tune on the air/nimble and easy as a lizard,/still and sudden as a gecko" (*Collected Poems* [Oxford, 1978], pp. 44–45).

25. That is, Kabbalah proper as it emerged in the Middle Ages extends certain trends that are, in a sense, already found in Judaism. The *Zohar* provides the classic confirmation of this extension, as the chief protagonist of this thirteenth-century pseudepigraphic text is a second-century C.E. Palestinian sage (*The Wisdom of the Jewish Mystics*, trans. Alan Unterman [New York, 1976], pp. 12–13). See Gruenwald, "Reflections on the Nature and Origins of Jewish Mysticism," pp. 29–30; Joseph Dan in his preface to Scholem, *On the Mystical Shape of the Godhead* (New York, 1991), p. 11; Idel, *Kabbalah: New Perspectives* (New Haven, 1988), pp. 112–99, and Idel, "Defining Kabbalah"; "Kabbalah," *Encyclopedia Judaica*, 2nd ed. (Detroit, 2007), vol. 11, p. 585; and Yehudah Liebes, "De Natura Dei," in *Studies in Jewish Myth and Messianism*, trans. Batya Stein (Albany, N.Y., 1993), pp. 55ff. Idel and others also discuss the tradition's extension into the Christian nexus. See especially his *Kabbalah in Italy, 1280–1510: A Survey* (New Haven, 2011). Lawrence Fine calls for a more historically bound use of the term in *Essential Papers on Kabbalah* (New York, 1995), pp. 5ff.

26. Idel, *Kabbalah in Italy*, pp. 21ff. Idel notes, however, that the use of the term in this "spiritual" sense begins only in the twelfth or thirteenth century. See also Scholem, *Kabbalah*, pp. 3ff.: "In its wider sense [Kabbalah] signifies all the successive esoteric movements in Judaism that

evolved from the end of the Second Temple and became active factors in Jewish history." See also Dan: "In this context, Kabbalah means a particular kind of esoteric, secret tradition concerning the divine world, which the Kabbalists themselves believed was given to Moses on Mount Sinai and was transmitted secretly from generation to generation. Kabbalah is an abbreviation of 'secret tradition concerning the divine world'" (*Heart and the Fountain*, p. 8). Earlier and parallel Hebrew terms include *sitrei torah* and *razei torah*, "the secrets of the Torah"; *ma'aseh bereshit*, "the work of creation"; and *ma'aseh merkavah*, "the work of the chariot" (all in the Talmud). In subsequent related literature one encounters *hokhmah penimit*, "inner wisdom," and the adepts themselves are called *ba'alei ha-sod*, "masters of the mystery," and *anshei emunah*, "men of faith," among other things. See Scholem, *Kabbalah*, pp. 6–7, for a full survey of the terms involved.

27. "There is no earlier and later in the Torah" (*Pesahim* 6b). See also Yosef Hayim Yerushalmi, *Zakhor: Jewish History and Jewish Memory* (Seattle, 1982), pp. 17 and 31–52.

28. All the poems in this volume preceding those of Moshe ben Nahman, in thirteenth-century Spain, are, in this respect, proto-Kabbalistic.

29. And that—its Western provenance—is precisely the problem. Noting the lack of a direct Hebrew equivalent for the word (which is originally Greek, and etymologically implies the closing of the mouth or the eyes), and the definitive employment of the term among modern Christian scholars, some writers have questioned its use at all in a Jewish context. Ithamar Gruenwald, for instance, prefers *spirituality* (in "Reflections on the Nature and Origins of Jewish Mysticism," pp. 28–35). See also Dan, *Heart and the Fountain*, pp. 7–8. Boaz Huss argues more radically for the elimination of the term from scholarly discourse altogether. See Huss, "Jewish Mysticism in the University: Academic Study or Theological Practice?" *Zeek* (December 2007), and, especially, Huss, "The Mystification of the Kabbalah and the Modern Construction of Jewish Mysticism" [Heb], *Pe'amim* 110 (2007), pp. 9–30, and the exchange about this article between Huss and Shaul Maggid, "Is Kabbalah Mysticism? Continuing the Debate," *Zeek* (March 2008). See also Idel, *Enchanted*

Chains: Techniques and Rituals in Jewish Mysticism (Los Angeles, 2005), pp. 3–30 and 205–27, for a general discussion of Jewish mysticism in the context of a universal definition by others; Idel, *Old Worlds, New Mirrors* (esp. p. 62), for discussion of Rudolph Otto and key concepts; and Idel, "Mysticism," in *Contemporary Jewish Religious Thought*. Almost all these scholars agree that *mystical* and *mysticism*, as they are used by Christian scholars to apply to Christianity and the religions of the East, are highly misleading when it comes to the very different and diverse practices of Judaism, where "union with God" is by no means a dominant consideration. On the whole, part of the objection is that the terms do not allow for Jewish particularity and instead see Jewish mystical experience as a subset of a universal religious experience. See Louis Bouyer, "Mysticism: An Essay on the History of the Word," in *Understanding Mysticism*, ed. Richard Woods (Garden City, N.Y., 1980), pp. 42–55.

30. Scholem, *Kabbalah*, p. 3. Scholem adds that "for some Kabbalists the intellect itself became a mystical phenomenon." And Borges called the Kabbalists "fanatics of reason" ("History of Angels," p. 18). As Arthur Green writes: "Even for latter-day Hasidim, where a certain anti-intellectual strain is to be noted, *da'at*, or knowing awareness, remains crucial to the religious mind. Only the one who comes to know that all contains His presence can truly participate in the ecstatic worship that is the Hasidic community's hallmark. The transformation of mind, called for by many of the Kabbalistic and Hasidic masters, required, first, mind's highest cultivation" (Green, "Religion and Mysticism," p. 75). Peter Schäfer has a very helpful and thorough discussion of the uses and abuses of the term in *On the Origins of Jewish Mysticism* (Tübingen, 2009), pp. 1–26 and 353–56.

31. There are numerous surveys of the field; see especially Moshe Idel, "Kabbalah," *Encyclopedia Judaica*, 2nd ed., vol. 11, pp. 681–92 and, most recently, Abrams, *Kabbalistic Manuscripts*.

32. See Scholem, *Major Trends*, p. 34; Green, "Religion and Mysticism," p. 68.

33. On scholarly disagreements regarding the map of Jewish mysticism, see — in addition to Scholem's *Major Trends* and *Kabbalah* — Gruenwald's "Reflections on the Nature and Origins of Jewish Mysticism"; Schäfer,

Origins of Jewish Mysticism; Idel, *Kabbalah: New Perspectives*, pp. xi–xix and 27–34; and the sources listed in note 24, above. See also the exchange between Bilhah Nitzan and Elliot R. Wolfson about the poetry of the Dead Sea Scrolls: *Jewish Quarterly Review* 85:1–2 (1994), pp. 163–83 and 185–202. Wolfson also contributes there toward the clarification of the use of the term *mysticism*.

34. See Katz, "Mystical Speech," p. 33. For more on the Jewish emphasis on using language and speech to say the unsayable, see notes 9 and 19, above. The proscription against articulation of the mysteries in so many mystical traditions testifies to this suspicion, which extends into the literary realm with the likes of Samuel Johnson's reported quip implying that if the German mystic Jacob Boehme in fact had, like Saint Paul, seen the unutterable, he should not have uttered it (James Boswell, *Life of Johnson*, 2nd ed., ed. George B. Hill [Oxford, 1934], vol. 2, pp. 122ff.). See in this regard Paul Mendes-Flohr's comments in his introduction to Martin Buber, *Ecstatic Confessions: The Heart of Mysticism* (Syracuse, N.Y., 1996), pp. xxiii and xxx.

35. Max Kadushin, *Worship and Ethics* (Evanston, Ill., 1964), pp. 13ff.

36. Which is not to say that these traditions always, or even generally speaking, resemble one another. On the contrary, the distinctions between them are often what is critical and of greatest interest.

37. Dan, *Kabbalah: A Very Short Introduction*, p. 40, talks about the price the Kabbalists paid for their blending into traditional Jewish culture: they had to forgo any individual expression, as this was not an acceptable part of the past. The obvious exception here is Avraham Abulafia and, prior to that, the Andalusian poets (who are not properly "Kabbalistic"). Pseudepigraphic works such as the Merkavah texts (see "Poems of the Palaces and Early Liturgical Hymns," below) made use of the first person, especially in their prose, but these were clearly masks. See Green, "Religion and Mysticism," p. 90. Green comments that most Kabbalists would have considered it (culturally) improper to tell of their own spiritual experiences in works for wider dissemination. Select works, and above all certain diaries, are, however, explicit about that personal dimension of experience (see comments below on Eliezer Azikri and Moshe Hayyim Luzzatto, in "The Safed Circle" and "Italian Kabbalah"). Regarding the

quantity and overall quality of Kabbalistic verse, several skeptical positions need to be registered: Both positions pertain to the composition of Kabbalah-related poetry in Spain (which admittedly produced much less work than did regions identified with subsequent phases of Kabbalistic thought, such as Safed, North Africa, Yemen, and elsewhere). Hayyim Schirmann, the preeminent literary historian of the Hebrew poetry of Spain, noted that Kabbalistic elements generally had a negative influence on the quality of medieval Hebrew verse, and that "a *superficial* [italics mine] examination of the material in question reveals that the combination of poetry and Kabbalah did not generally favor poetry" (Schirmann, *The History of Hebrew Poetry in Christian Spain and Provence* [Heb], ed. Ezra Fleischer [Jerusalem, 1997], pp. 325–26). Schirmann's distinguished student Ezra Fleischer noted that by and large the Kabbalists of Spain at this time had neither a need nor a desire for poetry, preoccupied as they were with the observance of the commandments; hence, Schirmann observes, the paucity of mystical verse relating to the subject of this elite group's speculations (pp. 321–22; see also Aminadav Dkyman's Afterword to this volume).

38. Harold Bloom, *The Best Poems of the English Language: From Chaucer Through Robert Frost* (New York, 2007), p. 302. In the scholarship surrounding this material, one often encounters calls—rather than convincing arguments—to treat certain prose texts, such as the *Zohar*, as poems. These calls are almost inevitably misleading, as they ignore the considerable difference between prose that is "poetic" or "lyrical" and a poem. Generally speaking, the poetic prose mentioned in this context seems to have been cut almost arbitrarily, like random swatches of fabric lopped off by the yard from a larger bolt. For more on this question, see the commentary and notes to the *Zohar*, below.

39. Scholem, "Understanding the Internal Processes" (1977), in *On the Possibility of Jewish Mysticism in Our Time* (Philadelphia, 1997), pp. 47–48. See also Scholem, *Kabbalah*, p. 77, on other Kabbalistic poetry.

40. The quoted phrase is Scholem's. His critique of Meir Wiener's *Die Lyrik der Kabbalah* is discussed in David Biale's *Gershom Scholem: Kabbalah and Counter-History* (Cambridge, Mass., 1982), pp. 30–31. Scho-

lem's "reversal" is really more a qualification of his remarks of some fifty years earlier—which seem to be driven in large part by his contempt for Wiener's fuzzy "poetic" work and its homogenizing Buberian inspiration. "Only in our days," Scholem writes, "has the belief gained ground that there is such a thing as an abstract mystical religion" (cited by Biale on p. 122). He objected, in other words, to the dislocation of this poetry from its Jewish cultural and ritual context. Biale's most recent work picks up where Scholem left off and sees Scholem himself—along with Kafka and Hayyim Nahman Bialik—as "secular Kabbalists." See Biale, *Not in the Heavens: The Tradition of Jewish Secular Thought* (Princeton, 2011), pp. 15 and 46–56, and below, "The Seeds of Secular Mysticism." My thanks to Robert Schine for translation and extensive discussion of Scholem's early review.

41. Joseph Dan writes: "Eight hundred years of intense and dynamic Kabbalistic creativity did not produce a genre that can be called 'Kabbalistic literature'" (Dan, *Kabbalah: A Very Short Introduction*, p. 38). In other words, just as Kabbalistic religious prose—commentary, homily, philosophy, and other genres—was absorbed into the modes of a given day, so too when the Kabbalist-poets sat down or got up to write poems, they wrote into the forms and manners that were available to them from the liturgical and philosophical poetry of the time. So much for form; it goes without saying that Kabbalah introduced radical innovation into the matrix of Jewish thought and life, and that this found potent expression in the poetry that emerged from the Kabbalistic context.

42. Scholem, *Kabbalah*, p. 3.

43. Translation of the sacred element of a tradition is among the steeper challenges facing a translator. In the conventional view, it is— theoretically—impossible, as is all literary translation, let alone the translation of the unsayable. Taking up a historical perspective, however, we see that it has been done with tremendous success, if success is to be measured by the ability of a sacred text to communicate or convey a sense of religious power beyond its own linguistic and even cultural matrix. For those intent on finding loss in translation, and seeing that loss as a defining quality, it might help to recall Benjamin's own "Kabbalistic" notion

of translation as transformation, put forth in "On Language as Such" (see the notes to the section on Avraham Abulafia, below), as well as the fact that translation at its historical root is overwhelmingly associated with religious texts. One is also aiming for another, older definition of the term: transmission to an afterworld without causing death—the poem's or the translator's (*Oxford English Dictionary*, s.v. "translation," definition c).

That said, when it comes to the translation of the esoteric aspect of those religious traditions, certain problems inevitably arise: How, for instance, does one acknowledge and account for the magical properties of a given sacred tongue (e.g., the names of God in Hebrew) in English translation? What about numerology, which figures so prominently in this work? In many cases these phenomena have to be relegated to notes (as they must for most readers of Hebrew today). Still, while translation connot account for certain powerful resonances of the semantic and aesthetic fields that surround given Hebrew words like halos, the translator must believe in the possibility of creating powerful and, in their own way, magical English force fields in the form of new constellations of English sounds (per Abulafia's view cited in note 18, above). These English constellations should conduct the gist and maybe even the *geist* of this poetry and bring it off the page and into the reading spirit.

Poems of the Palaces and Early Liturgical Hymns

Poems of the Palaces

Information for the headnote is drawn from the following sources: Ithamar Gruenwald, *Apocalyptic and Merkavah Mysticism* (Leiden, 1980), pp. 127–73 and chap. 2, sect. B; Gershom Scholem, *Jewish Gnosticism, Merkabah Mysticism, and Talmudic Tradition* (New York, 1965), esp. chaps. 1, 2, 4, 8, and 10, and Scholem, *Major Trends in Jewish Mysticism* (New York, 1941), chap. 2; Elliot R. Wolfson, *Through a Speculum That Shines: Vision and Imagination in Medieval Judaism* (Princeton, 1994), pp. 74ff., Wolfson, "*Yeridah la-Merkavah*: Typology of Ecstasy and Enthronement in Ancient Jewish Mysticism," in *Mystics of the Books*, ed. R. Herrara (New York, 1993), pp. 13–44, and Wolfson, "Mysticism and the Poetic-Liturgical Compositions from Qumran: A Response to Bilhah Nitzan," *Jewish Quarterly Review* 85:1–2 (1999), pp. 185–202; Peter Schäfer, *Hidden and Manifest God* (Albany, 1992), chaps. 1, 2, 3, and 7, and Schäfer, *The Origins of Jewish Mysticism* (Tübingen, 2009), pp. 32 and chap. 8; Moshe Idel, *Ascensions on High in Jewish Mysticism: Pillars, Lines, Ladders* (Budapest, N.Y., 2005), chap. 1; Joseph Dan, *The Ancient Jewish Mysticism* (Tel Aviv, 1993), pp. 7–107; Ronit Meroz, "The Middle Eastern Origins of Kabbalah," *Journal for the Study of Sephardic and Mizrahi Jewry* 1 (2007), pp. 39–56; David Halperin, *The Faces of the Chariot* (Tübingen, 1988), pp. 11–37, 370–72, and 439–46; Rachel Elior, *The Three Temples: On the Emergence of Jewish Mysticism* (Oxford, 2004), pp. 2–38, and 232–65, Elior, "Early Forms of Jewish Mysticism," in *The Cambridge History of Judaism: The Late Roman-Rabbinic Period*, ed. Steven Katz (Cambridge, 2008), pp. 749–90, and Elior, *Jewish Mysticism: The Infinite Expression of Freedom*, trans. Yudith Nave and Arthur B. Millman (Oxford, 2007); Moshe Halbertal, *Concealment and Revelation: Esotericism in Jewish Thought and Its Philosophical Implications*, trans. J. Feldman (Princeton, 2002), pp. 18–27; and Michael Swartz, "Jewish Visionary Tradition in Rabbinic Literature," in *The Cambridge Companion to the Talmud and Rabbinic Literature*, ed. Charlotte Elisheve Fonrobert and Martin Jaffe (Cambridge, 2007), pp. 198–220. The "Work of the Chariot" is discussed, for instance, in *Hagigah* 2:1 and 14b. Halbertal stresses the remarkable combination of sublime remoteness and intimacy in this literature, and God's desire for experience of His glory to be shared.

Quotations are from the following sources: *meter-making argument*: Ralph Waldo Emerson, "The Poet," in *Selections from Ralph Waldo Emerson*, ed. Stephen E. Whicher (Boston, 1950), p. 225 (and see also Yeats, *Selected Criticism*, ed. A. Norman Jefferies [London, 1964], p. 170); *No man shall see Me*: Exodus 33:20, cited in Halbertal, *Concealment and Revelation*; *to go before the ark*: Scholem, *Jewish Gnosticism*, p. 20; *those who reach down*: Scholem, *Kabbalah* (New York, 1974), p. 6; *practices that fell under the immediate spell*: Gruenwald, *Apocalyptic and Merkavah Mysticism*, p. 133; *ministering angels*: Elior, *Three Temples*, p. 14; *revolutionary manifesto*: Halperin, *Faces of the Chariot*, p. 443 (but see also pp. 37, 434–37, and 445); *constitutes anew the communion*: Schäfer, *Hidden and Manifest God*, pp. 157–58; *physically or psychically*: Schäfer, *Hidden and Manifest God*, p. 149; *a grandiose literary effort*: Schäfer, *Hidden and Manifest God*, p. 161; *immense solemnity*: Scholem, *Jewish Gnosticism*, p. 21; *Open Sesame of religion*: Scholem, *Major Trends*, p. 57.

The Heikhalot poems are found in a number of texts, including *Heikhalot Rabbati, Heikhalot Zutarti, Merkavah Shelemah*, and others. The textual situation is chaotic and there is no single reader-friendly edition. A synoptic edition of all the textual variants has been prepared by Peter Schäfer (*Synopse zur Hekhalot-Literatur* [Tübingen, 1981]). See also *Beit HaMidrash*, ed. A. Jellinek (1853–77; Jerusalem, 1967), and *Battei Midrashot*, ed. Shelomoh Wertheimer (Jerusalem, 1953–55).

The term *yordei hamerkavah*, it should be noted, remains elusive. We find something similar to Scholem's explanation of the term as an expression of interiority at the opening of *Heikhalot Zutarti*, which combines the warning of *Hagigah* 2:1 and an interior mystical approach: "If you want . . . the secrets of the world and the mysteries of wisdom to be revealed to you, you should study this mishnah . . . and neither try to understand what is behind you nor inquire into the sayings of your lips. Just understand what is in your heart and keep quiet, so that you will be worthy of the Beauties of the Chariot" (Gruenwald, *Apocalyptic and Merkavah Mysticism*, p. 142). Along the same lines, Hai Gaon, among the most prominent early-eleventh-century Jewish religious leaders, observes: "It is not that [the merkavah mystics] ascend to heaven, but that they look and see within their heart . . . and they hear and say and speak as those who see through the holy spirit" (in Elior, *Jewish Mysticism*, p. 66). And David Halperin conjures Freud to help us understand the merkavah mystics' imagery: noting that Freud in *The Interpretation of Dreams* wrote of the way in which a dream has a "navel, the spot where it reaches down into the unknown," he proposes that "for the rabbis [of this mystical tradition], Ezekiel's *merkavah* was such a navel. Through it, their dreaming was nourished" (*Faces of the Chariot*, p. 455). Halperin understands the literary experience of these hymns (in their composition and their recitation by readers) as participation in an empowering fantasy—though he acknowledges that some of the writers may have had actual "experience" (i.e., hallucinations) of the heavenly ascent (p. 451). For a thorough discussion of the term *yored la-merkavah* in the Heikhalot and related literature, see Wolfson, *Through a Speculum*, pp. 82ff., and Wolfson, *"Yeridah la-Merkavah*," pp. 13–15, 26. Wolfson suggests that the term means "to go before, or enter, the chariot" and indicates the last stage of the heavenly ascent that involves entry into the throne room or throne world. The true mystical experience, he argues, consists of the aspirant's enthronement beside God, and not merely his participation in the heavenly liturgy (*"Yeridah la-Merkavah*," p. 15).

Once within that throne world, notes Peter Schäfer, human beings can do more than the angels who guard it as they praise God; for through their knowledge of traditional texts in combination with His esoteric knowledge, men can affect God through the manipulation of the letters of the Divine Name and other magical means (Schäfer, *Hidden and Manifest God*, pp. 9, 23–34, 141–42). For an excellent survey of the scholarship in the field, see Wolfson, *Through a Speculum*, pp. 74ff., and in relation to the connection between the Heikhalot hymns and the Dead Sea Scrolls, see Wolfson, "Mysticism and the Poetic-Liturgical Compositions from Qumran," p. 85. For more on the background to the Merkavah literature, see Schäfer, *Origins of Jewish Mysticism*.

Hymn to the Heavens

Text: Scholem, *Jewish Gnosticism*, pp. 21–22; *Heikhalot Rabbati* 8:1, in *Beit HaMidrash*, vol. 3, p. 89; *Battei Midrashot*, vol. 1, pp. 82–83; Schäfer, *Synopse zur Hekhalot-Literatur*, no. 158 (B238), pp. 68–69. On the graphic arrangement of the Heikhalot texts (and *Sefer Yetzirah*), see Daniel Abrams, *Kabbalistic Manuscripts and Textual Theory: Methodologies of Textual Scholarship and Editorial Practice in the Study of Jewish Mysticism* (Jerusalem and Los Angeles, 2010), pp. 69–70.

The poem, and with it this book, begins in the direct address of the mystic-poet to the angels encountered during his ascent to the throne of God. With its structural symmetries and simplicity—descriptive apostrophe or turn to the angels, followed by a series of questions relating to the nature of their behavior and then the angels' answer—the hymn conveys at once a sense of intimacy and awe. Above all, it embodies an experience of contact with the divine as an overwhelming mystery. This is the aspect of the numinous that invokes fear and trembling, even as it entrances, attracts, and intoxicates. (Borrowing from Rudolf Otto's *The Idea of the Holy* and Mircea Eliade's *The Sacred and the Profane*, we might say that it combines the *mysterium tremendum* with the *mysterium fascinans*.) Tightly woven and resonant with assonance and both internal and near rhyme, the poem reflects the solemnity of that encounter in its cadence and sound.

Most modern Jews, and certainly English-speaking non-Orthodox Jews, are surprised to find that the heavens and history of Judaism are swarming with angels—benevolent and malign, soaring or fallen—sometimes ambiguous but always busy. The messengers from the divine realm (which is what the term *malakh* originally meant in Hebrew) also serve as courtier-like attendants in the divine retinue. They are quite common in the Bible and also in the Talmud, the midrash, and the liturgy. Angels are perhaps even more conspicuous in the Jewish mystical tradition, where we find them male and female, merciful and severe, ministering and corrupting (e.g., *Zohar* 1:119b, 1:159a, and 1:195b–196a [trans. Daniel C. Matt, 5 vols. (Stanford, Calif., 2004–9), vol. 2, p. 191, vol. 2, pp. 384–87, and vol. 3, p. 195; see also *Wisdom of the Zohar*, arranged and rendered into Hebrew by Fischel Lachower and Isaiah Tishby; introductions and annotations by Isaiah Tishby, trans. David Goldstein, 3 vols. (Oxford, 1997), vol. 2, pp. 623–52]). In some accounts they consist of fire and water, in others of "four heavenly elements: mercy, strength, beauty, and dominions." As in the Bible, they can take on human form—Borges describes them as, on occasion, "brawny as farmhands"—but mostly they populate the divine realm (the Heikhalot), where, as these poems make clear, they sing continuously in praise of God. Angels have also been understood in the history of Jewish philosophy as thoughts, and even as letters. See *Encyclopedia Judaica* (Jerusalem, 1972), vol. 2, pp. 956–77, and Moshe Idel, *The Angelic World: Apotheosis and Theophany* [Heb]

(Tel Aviv, 2008), pp. 7–73. See also Jorge Luis Borges, "A History of Angels," trans. Esther Allen, in *Selected Non-Fictions*, ed. Eliot Weinberger (New York, 1999), pp. 16–19.

This poem introduces key motifs that will appear in much of the Heikhalot literature. These include the transcendent God before whom the angels on high sing (He is both terrible in His judgment and merciful in His benevolence) and the angels as intercessors of sorts between the worshipper and the deity (Schäfer, *Hidden and Manifest God*, p. 34). The sudden shift between fear and delight testify to the precariousness of the ongoing enterprise and the need for constant vigilance (Arthur Green, "Religion and Mysticism: The Case of Judaism," in *Take Judaism, for Example: Studies Toward the Comparison of Religions*, ed. Jacob Neusner [Chicago, 1983], p. 78). This polarity is characteristic of much of the literature that derives from Ezekiel's vision of the Merkavah, where the creatures "run and return" (Ezekiel 1:14), both drawn and driven back by what they find. My thanks to Haviva Pedaya, who shared her unpublished analysis of this hymn with me.

It should be noted that the Presence of God, or Shekhinah, in the final stanza is not the feminine aspect of the Divine Presence that it would become in later Kabbalah, with the *Bahir* (see below, "The Kabbalah in Spain"; Gershom Scholem, *On the Mystical Shape of the Godhead: Basic Concepts in the Kabbalah* [New York, 1991, pp. 140–96]; and Peter Schäfer, *Mirror of His Beauty: Feminine Images of God from the Bible to the Early Kabbalah* [Princeton, 2002], pp. 8–9, 19–38, 79–102, and 118ff.).

Line 3: Other manuscripts read, "knowledge's array." Haviva Pedaya notes that, here and in other poems like this one, invocation and arrangement—the recollection and ordering of poesis—are the means by which the aspirant copes before the sublime and capricious powers of heaven (unpublished ms.).

9: There are numerous variations for this line in the extant manuscripts. Several others read, "When the wheels of the chariot of power [*gevurah*] darken." Cf. Ezekiel 1:4 and the vision of the chariot as "a great cloud with brightness about it." When that brightness dims, the angels grow sad.

A Measure of Holiness

Text: *Heikhalot Rabbati* 3:4, in *Beit HaMidrash*, vol. 3, pp. 85–86; Scholem, *Jewish Gnosticism*, pp. 59–60; Schäfer, *Synopse zur Hekhalot-Literatur*, no. 102, pp. 48–49; Schäfer, *Hidden and Manifest God*, pp. 19–20.

Like many of the Heikhalot hymns, "A Measure of Holiness" demonstrates what Scholem has described as "a mechanism comparable to the motion of an enormous fly-wheel" (*Major Trends*, p. 59)—which is to say, a device designed to regulate the rotational speed and motion of a machine to which it is attached. The flywheel stabilizes the part of the machine that is turning at a high velocity. In this case, the machine is the human spirit. Like the "Hymn to the Heavens," this poem records an experience of ecstatic revelation, though the vision here is face-to-face, and life-threatening.

This poem too begins in an identification and enumeration of elements that are part of the vision of the chariot. In this case the hymn highlights—almost talismanically—emotions that the worshipper who "descends to the chariot" (or ascends to the palaces) will undergo.

The body of the poem focuses on the robe of God (who here is called Zoharariel—a name implying splendor or light—*zohar*). This divine robe or garment of light is as close as one can come to a direct vision of God, and proximity to it is perilous. The robe constitutes not only a kind of border or limit of human experience but is in itself a powerful presence, like the Gnostic Pleroma or Fullness, says Scholem (*Jewish Gnosticism*, pp. 56ff., and *Origins of the Kabbalah*, ed. R. J. Zwi Werblowsky, trans. Allan Arkush [Princeton, 1987], p. 68, and see also *Major Trends*, pp. 40–79; others have challenged his linking this tradition to Gnosticism—see *The Early Kabbalah*, ed. and introduced Joseph Dan, texts trans. Ronald C. Keiner [New York, 1986], p. 5). In this way it is like the cosmic raiment or *pargod* of several other Heikhalot hymns—which, like language, both reflects the divine and separates the aspirant from the full force of its unmediated power. At the same time it is an embodiment of that power. Again, my annotation is, in part, based on Haviva Pedaya's reading, along with commentaries by Scholem, Schäfer, and others. See Scholem,

Jewish Gnosticism, pp. 58ff., and Schäfer, *Hidden and Manifest God*, p. 19; also 3 Enoch, trans. P. Alexander, in *The Old Testament Pseudepigrapha: Apocalyptic Literature and Testaments*, ed. James H. Charlesworth, 2 vols. (New York, 1983), vol. 1, pp. 223–302.

The very notion of "seeing" is at the heart of this poem, and the Hebrew explicitly mentions three sorts of sightings, each of which has historical associations in biblical and rabbinic literature: *ro'eh* (to see or behold directly) alludes to Exodus 33:20ff. — "For man may not see Me and live"; *metziz* (to look, glimpse, or cast a glance) alludes to *Hagigah* 14b and the Talmud's story of the four who entered the Garden or Orchard (of mystical interpretation or, some would say, heaven); and *mistakel* (to reflect, speculate, or consider) recalls the Mishnaic notion that "whoever reflects upon four things would be better off had he not been born: What is above, what is beneath, what is before, and what is after" (*Hagigah* 2:1 — where the discussion is of esoteric subjects, including "the chariot," that are forbidden to study under certain circumstances). A similar caution is found in the Book of Ben Sira 3:21–22: "Seek not things that are too hard for thee, and search not things that are hidden from thee." The order of the English translation here departs from the Hebrew, in the interest of texture and sound, but the meaning remains much the same. In lines 24–28 the fire that issues forth from man is the fire reflected from the divine; he is, literally, burned by the experience. I have followed Scholem's Hebrew text, but line 29 in most manuscripts reads, "Because of the image of the eyes of the robe of Zoharariel" — which might be understood as meaning either "because of the eye's image of Zoharariel's robe" or "because of the image of the eyes in the robe," which would suddenly introduce a new and confusing element into the poem at its climax. In some manuscripts the poem concludes with an additional three lines: "pleasing and sweet in its beauty / like the beauty, glory, and splendor of the eyes of the holy creatures, / as it is said: Holy, holy, holy is the Lord of hosts."

Awe and Adornment

Text: *Heikhalot Rabbati* 16, in *Beit HaMidrash*, vol. 3, pp. 103–4; *Battei Midrashot*, vol. 1, pp. 101–11; Schäfer, *Synopse zur Hekhalot-Literatur* no. 275, pp. 120–21; M. Bar-Ilan, *Sitrei Tefilah veHeikhalot* (Ramat Gan, 1987), p. 16; Ephraim Hazan, *Poems and Prayers from the Siddur* [Heb] (Jerusalem, 1979), pp. 82ff.

As it enumerates God's attributes in alliterative and alphabetically acrostic pairs, this poem propels the worshipper or reader into the recurrent epithet, *lehay* (pronounced *lehī*) *olamim*, which can be translated in any number of ways, including, literally, "for one who lives eternally" or "appertain to Him who lives eternally." The term appears in a slightly different form in Daniel 12:7 (*hay ha'olam*—"Him that liveth forever" or "the Ever-Living One"), and in the Talmud it is one of the names of God. (For more on the later esoteric use of this term, which comes to mean "the Life of the Universe," see Scholem, *On the Mystical Shape of the Godhead*, pp. 96ff.) In this way the epithet becomes a mantra-like, transformative object of meditation. The translation here—"for Life Everlasting"—is designed to reflect the compactness of the Hebrew and maintain the pulse and pace of the poem as well as its binary structure: two terms in the first half of the line, two terms in the second half. Sometimes the pairs involve synonyms, and sometimes the relation between them is more dynamic (e.g., cause and effect). The English rearranges the elements of the Hebrew in order to maintain the alphabetical acrostic, and in a few instances it adds images from the related literature to account for the four additional letters of the English alphabet.

Throughout the poem, the divine attributes are extended by implication to the human realm. The medieval commentator Eleazar of Worms (see below, in connection with the "Hymn of Divine Glory") called the hymn the "Song of the Angels," and indeed in its original context in *Heikhalot Rabbati* (chap. 28), it is sung by the angels (though recited by the aspirant). The principle of repetition is central not only to the structure of the poem but to its content, situation, and desired effect as the hosts of angels loudly and hypnotically repeat their praise of God in heaven and in the earthly liturgy: "Holy, holy, holy is the Lord of hosts" (Isaiah 6:3).

While there is nothing conspicuously mystical about this Merkavah composition, Scholem, who notes the "numinous character" of all the Heikhalot hymns, calls it "a classic example of an alphabetical litany which fills the imagination of the devotee with splendid concepts clothed in magnificent expression; the particular words do not matter" (*Major Trends*, p. 59; see also the commentary to 3 Enoch by P. Alexander in *Old Testament Pseudepigrapha*, vol. 1, pp. 251–53). At the other end of the temperamental scale, the ever-rational, sometimes cranky, and decidedly anti-mystical Ismar Elbogen, in his classic work *Jewish Liturgy: A Comprehensive History* (1913; trans. Raymond P. Scheindlin [Philadelphia, 1993], p. 287), notes that this poem appears at the end of *Heikhalot Rabbati*, where "hymns intended for the highest level of ecstasy" are found, though he adds somewhat unfairly that it "is composed of that abundance of half-intelligible words [which are] typical of the prayers of these mystics . . . and do not advance the train of thought." He bitingly compares them to what he considers the more dignified sobriety of the Psalms, which observe: "To You, silence is praise."

The poem has been included in the Ashkenazic rite for the Day of Atonement probably since the tenth century; its force and attraction are such that in some Hasidic circles it is recited weekly as part of the Sabbath morning prayers after Psalm 136. Some Sephardic communities recite it on Rosh HaShanah. The hymn might also be seen as a kind of midrash or commentary on the verses from Chronicles 29:11–12, which became a prominent part of the daily liturgy: "Thine, O Lord, is the greatness, and the power, and the glory, and the victory, and the majesty." See Joseph Dan, "Ashkenazi Hasidic Commentaries in the Hymn *Ha-Aderet we-ha-Emunah*," *Tarbiz* 50 (1981), pp. 396–404.

Each Day

Text: *Heikhalot Rabbati* 11, in *Beit HaMidrash*, vol. 3, p. 92; Poem 1: Schäfer, *Synopse zur Hekhalot-Literatur*, no. 173, pp. 76–77; Poem 2: Schäfer, *Synopse zur Hekhalot-Literatur*, no. 189, pp. 60–61.

The two hymns gathered here under this title appear consecutively in *Heikhalot Rabbati*. Both concern the prayer or song of the heavenly creatures before the throne, and commentators have noted the striking physicality of the poems and their likeness to intimate rituals of courtship. Some have argued for an explicitly sexual interpretation of the ritual choreography depicted there. During the morning prayer God reveals His face while the creatures cover theirs; in the afternoon prayer the dynamic is reversed: God covers His countenance while the faces of the angels are exposed in their longing. Thus "the erotic play of gazing and hiding," as Elliot Wolfson calls it (*Through a Speculum*, pp. 101–3), is central to the effect of this hymn, which presents a kind of cosmic "sexual drama" or at least "a very intimate scene" (Schäfer, *Hidden and Manifest God*, p. 24; see also pp. 46, 119). See also Halperin, *Faces of the Chariot*, pp. 394–95. For more on the "theoerotic" aspect of these poems generally and the angels' declaration at the end of this poem—"Kadosh, Kadosh, Kadosh" (Holy, holy, holy)—see Moshe Idel, *Kabbalah and Eros* (New Haven, 2005), pp. 35–37, where he discusses the secondary meaning of *kadosh* (and *kiddushin*) as a wedding, in this case one that brings together "God and the supernal representation of Israel." Also striking is the fact that, as Schäfer notes (*Origins of Jewish Mysticism*, pp. 263–66), despite the angels' loyalty and continual labor (of bearing His throne), God silences the holy creatures so that He can hear the morning prayers of the People of Israel (in synagogues).

From Whose Beauty the Depths Are Lit

Text: Scholem, *Jewish Gnosticism*, pp. 61ff.; *Heikhalot Rabbati* 24, in *Beit HaMidrash*, vol. 3, p. 101; Schäfer, *Synopse zur Hekhalot-Literatur*, no. 253, pp. 112–13.

One of many "royal hymns" in *Heikhalot Rabbati*, the poem has as its central image God's crown, or wreath, the circle of which spirals out into a depiction of cosmic forces and of what Scholem called "the wonders of creation stemming from God's majesty, His beauty, His stature, His crown, and His garment" (*Jewish Gnosticism*, p. 62). Haviva Pedaya reads it as a coronation hymn in which God's crown or wreath widens into a circular cosmic dance of nature's powers. So the poem moves from the Godhead down through the radiant heavens to the lower natural world, where the divine word and presence (as fire) take hold of all things. In this scheme, the act of writing itself (and certainly of composing these hymns) participates in the ongoing rite that diffuses the divine glory through the universe. My thanks to Haviva Pedaya for her discussion of this poem with me. There are very different versions of the final lines of the hymn. My reading is based on Scholem. An alternative translation of the last two lines might read, "giving to those who encircle it, / and sending them back to their places."

To Rise on High

Text: Scholem, *Jewish Gnosticism*, p. 78; Rachel Elior, *Heikhalot Zutarti: Ms. Ny 8128* (Jerusalem, 1982), p. 24 (Supplement 1 to *Mehkerei Yerushalayim beMahshevet Yisrael*, 1982); Schäfer, *Synopse zur Hekhalot-Literatur*, nos. 349 and 361, pp. 146–47 and 152–53.

As with many of the Heikhalot poems, it isn't hard to find analogues between the poesis on high and the poesis below. This might be seen, then, as a "writer's hymn." It is inserted into a later medieval narrative about Rabbi Akiva, which tells a story about his ascent to Paradise (or that same Garden of Esoteric Interpretation mentioned above in note 7 to the Introduction). The poem is in Aramaic, not Hebrew.

Line 3: "To ride the [chariot's] wheels": to engage in esoteric speculation or mystical activity.

7: The meaning of the Aramaic (*ishra'ah*) is uncertain here. Schäfer (*Origins of Jewish Mysticism*, pp. 287–88) and Scholem (*Jewish Gnosticism*, p. 78) understand it as "to dwell with the Crown," though the former notes it might also mean "to make [magical] use of the crown" (i.e., to draw on its powers). It is also possible to understand it as the reflexive form of the root "to bless." See M. Sokoloff, *Dictionary of Jewish Babylonian Aramaic of the Talmudic and the Geonic Periods* (Baltimore, 2003), p. 1180b. My thanks to Uri Melammed and his colleagues at the Academy of Hebrew Language for help with this. In the narrative about Akiva's ascent, God says to the angels that would destroy Akiva: "Leave this elder alone, for he is worthy to contemplate my glory" (Scholem, *Jewish Gnosticism*, p. 77).

9: To "sound Glory": Schäfer (*Origins of Jewish Mysticism*, pp. 287–88) reads this as "to be transformed by his glory" or "to investigate glory," and Scholem (*Jewish Gnosticism*, p. 78) has "to praise the glory"; *sound* combines that sense of probing and also of extolling or praising (the other meaning attributed to the line).

11: To "link letters" alludes to the activity of Bezalel, whose name means "in the shadow of God"; he was entrusted with the building of the Tabernacle—which the midrash understands as itself being "in the shadow of the Almighty" (Exodus 31:3 and *Exodus Rabbah* 34:1; *Numbers Rabbah* 12:3; *Midrash Tehillim* 91:1)—and, the Talmud tells us, "knew to combine the letters by which heaven and earth were created" (*Berakhot* 55a). The implication is that the initiate can manipulate the letters of the Names of God to magical effect, but the exoteric or plain sense of the text is particularly resonant on its own.

19: "Rivers of fire" alludes to Daniel 7:10, where rivers of fire flow forth from God's throne.

20: "Lightning" alludes to Ezekiel 1:13 and 1:28; it issues from the fire identified with the holy creatures. Schäfer refers to the "highly individualistic" mystic of this poem as a "new Ezekiel" (*Origins of Jewish Mysticism*, pp. 287–88).

Blessed Is the Eye

Text: *Merkavah Shelemah* 4a, in M. Bar-Ilan, *Sitrei Tefilah veHeikhalot* (Ramat Gan, 1987), pp. 65–66.

A hymn in praise of one who has been granted a vision of both the trials of Israel and its treasuries of consolation and salvation. Among the latter the aspirant beholds "groups of angels sitting and weaving garments of salvation, fashioning crowns of life . . . smelling fragrant spices, and sweetening wine for the righteous" (*Merkavah Shelemah* 3b–4a, in Green, "Religion and Mysticism," pp. 76–77). Then he sees David himself at the head of a procession of Israel's kings who, in response to the heavens and the angels on high, praise God, saying, "The Lord shall be King over all the earth [Zechariah 14:9]." Arthur Green describes the concluding hymn attached to this possibly messianic passage as a kind of deceleration out of the ecstasy of the vision itself (p. 77). The experience of the divine world is, in the hymn, traced back to its constituent elements, and Green notes that many of these Heikhalot lyrics are remarkable for the way in which they preserve the intensity of the experience they depict: "Here we have no mystic's complaint about the inadequacy of language or the impossibility of true communication. We are confronted rather with a skillful writer, one who has been able to recreate in his narrative the dramatic excitement and intense pace of ecstatic experience" (pp. 77–78). There are direct parallels between the poem's formulations and a passage in the Talmud. *Hagigah* 14b (which also contains the story of the four who entered "Pardes"—the Garden) reports that, while listening to R. Eliezer b. Arak hold forth on the "Work of the Chariot" as fire came from heaven and took hold of all the trees in the field (which began to sing), "R. Johanan b. Zakkai rose and kissed [R. Eliezer] on his head and said: . . . Happy art thou, O Abraham our father, that R. Eliezer b. Arak hath come forth from thy loins." And in the same passage he says to R. Yose, who had just witnessed the assembly of angels on the day of the summer solstice: "Happy are ye, and happy is she that bore you; happy are my eyes that have seen thus." Rabbi Ishmael, in the penultimate line of the poem, is one of the two principal sages who experience the Heikhalot visions.

Early Liturgical Hymns

Information for the headnote is drawn from the following sources: *Mahzor Yannai: A Liturgical Work from the Seventh Century, Edited from Genizah Fragments*, notes and introduction by Israel Davidson, additional notes by Louis Ginzberg (New York, 1919); *The Liturgical Poems of R. Yannai, according to the Triennial Cycle of the Pentateuch and the Holidays* [Heb], ed. Zvi Rabinovitz (Jerusalem, 1985–87); Shulamit Elizur, *A Poem for Every Parashah* [Heb] (Jerusalem, 1999), pp. 166–70; Ithamar Gruenwald, "Yannai's Liturgical Poetry and the Literature of the Descenders to the Chariot" [Heb], *Tarbiz* 36 (1967), pp. 257–77, and Zvi Rabinovitz's response on pp. 402–5; *Hagigah* 14a: "Every day, ministering angels are created from the fiery stream, and utter song, and cease to be, for it is said: 'They are new every morning: great is Thy faithfulness'" (Lam 3:23); Ezra Fleischer, "Eliezer biRibbi Kallir: The Question of Provenance" [Heb], *Tarbiz* 54 (1985), pp. 383–427, and Fleischer, "Studies in the Problems Relating to the Liturgical Function of Types of Early Piyyut" [Heb], *Tarbiz* 40 (1971), pp. 41–63; Idel, *Ascensions on High in Jewish Mysticism*, p. 36. On the recovery of Yannai's work, see Adina Hoffman and Peter Cole, *Sacred Trash: The Lost and Found World of the Cairo Geniza* (New York, 2011), chap. 6.

It remains an open question whether the payyetanic tradition was directly influenced by the Heikhalot poetry; some scholars have suggested that the two traditions simply drew on a common set of rabbinic sources that contained Merkavah material—with the piyyutim presenting the more public or popular face of a rarefied sort of mystical doctrine. More provocative is the notion that the Heikhalot material evolved as an advanced form of mysticism *from* the ordinary mysticism embodied in poems composed by poets such as Yannai. The comparative question is considered in the exchange between Gruenwald and Rabinovitz (above); in Laura Lieber, *Yannai on Genesis: An Invitation to Piyyut* (Cincinnati, 2010), pp. 226–41, and 296–98; and in Jodi Magness, "Heaven on Earth: Helios and the Zodiac Cycle in Ancient Palestinian Synagogues," *Dumbarton Oaks Papers* 59 (2005), pp. 1–52. Lieber also discusses the relevant scholarly literature pertaining to the synagogue architecture of the day and its bearing on this question. The fact that angels appear in the mosaic floors and ceilings of synagogues in Byzantine Palestine, for example, may be directly related to the conspicuous presence of the heavenly creatures in these communities' hymns, where they play a central, sanctifying role.

Quotations are from the following sources: *there is a* kedushah: *The Zohar* 2:129b, trans. Daniel C. Matt, 5 vols. (Stanford, Calif., 2004–9), vol. 5, p. 207; *God dons ten garments*: Wolfson, *Through a Speculum*, p. 93; *ascended to heaven and question[ed] the archangel*: Idel, *Ascensions on High in Jewish Mysticism*, p. 36.

The Priest's Appearance

Text: Daniel Goldschmidt, *Mahzor for the Days of Awe* [Heb] (Jerusalem, 1970), pp. 483–84; *Avodah: An Anthology of Ancient Poems for Yom Kippur*, ed. and trans. Michael D. Swartz and Joseph Yahalom (University Park, Pa., 2005), pp. 343–47; Yosef [Joseph] Yahalom, *Poetry and Society in Late Antiquity* [Heb] (Tel Aviv, 1999), pp. 15–16.

The Glory of God (*kavod*), or Shekhinah, is the subject of other poems in this anthology, including the Ashkenazic "Hymn of Divine Glory" and several poems by Yehudah HaLevi. As in the Heikhalot hymns, the Shekhinah here is not the feminine aspect of the Divine Presence that it would become in later Kabbalah.

This hymn constitutes the final section of a Seder Avodah, or "order of worship." The Seder Avodah is a liturgical genre that consists of a series of liturgical poems that describe the high priest's service at the Temple on Yom Kippur. The first part of the Seder Avodah rehearses the creation of the world, its history, and the history of Israel up through the Exodus and the erection of the Tabernacle. The second part describes in minute detail the Yom Kippur ritual sacrifice. In the alphabetical acrostic of this section, the priest emerging from the holy of holies on Yom Kippur is likened to elements of the classical Jewish tradition, most of which are "artificial" or "cultic" and embody cosmic forces in a human setting—a trope suggesting the influence of the "jeweled style" of the Byzantine context in which this tradition developed. As such, the phenomenon reflects, says Yosef Yahalom, the "divine mysterium" (Yahalom, *Poetry and Society*, pp. 15–16).

The images are drawn from both biblical and rabbinic sources, and their order has been shuffled here for the sake of the English acrostic. In a few instances liberties have been taken to account for the four additional letters of the English alphabet (Hebrew has twenty-two). In these cases, the translation draws additional material from the inventory of images used in the rest of the series. Some of the allusions the poet employs include Numbers 22:22–31 and the story of Balaam for the image of the "Angel alighted"; Exodus 28:34 and its description of the high priest for the "Bells of gold"; Isaiah 40:22 for the image of the "Tent stretched taut"; Ezekiel 1:28 for "the Rainbow's ascent through clouds in the sky"; and Ezekiel 1:13 for the image of the "Shine flashing" forth. Additional material relates to the new moon (*Exodus Rabbah* 15:24), the questions posed to the sages (alluding generally to the Talmud), the Urim and Thummim

(Exodus 28:13), the lily among the thistles or thorns (Song of Songs 2:2), and the image of Zion (e.g., Isaiah 55:5, 57, 60:1).

On the whole the language of the hymn recalls passages from Ezekiel that are associated with Merkavah mysticism: e.g., Ezekiel 1:13: "the living creatures . . . their appearance like . . . out of the fire went forth lightning." See also Ezekiel 1:28, in relation to the appearance or likeness of the Glory of the Lord. It also echoes elements of the protomystical passage in the Book of Ben Sira (50:1–14), which depicts the high priest emerging from the holy of holies: "How glorious he was when the people gathered round him / as he came out of the inner sanctuary! / Like the morning star among the clouds, / like the moon when it is full." The poem is followed by a prose passage that recalls the joy taken in these things when they existed. In other words, by implication it returns the worshipper to the present, from which the Temple and its cult are absent.

Windows of Worship

Text: Bar-Ilan, *Sitrei Tefilah veHeikhalot*, p. 27.

This is hardly a well-known hymn, but its gentle clarity and progression of both sound and sense are compelling, and it resembles numerous other hymns that employ a similar structure: "Gates of light / gates of blessing / gates of gladness / gates of rejoicing . . ." (from the prayers for the Havdalah ritual, or "separation" from the Sabbath that marks a border between sacred and profane parts of the week). The Merkavah text 3 Enoch is more explicit in its literary application: It tells us that when Rabbi Ishmael ascended toward the vision of the chariot and entered into the seventh palace, he was overcome with fear of the power of Prince Qatzpiel, the angel of destruction—whose name derives from the Hebrew for "anger." To Ishmael's aid God sends the angel Metatron, prince of the Divine Presence, whose function is to disclose secrets (see the commentary by P. Alexander in *Old Testament Pseudepigrapha*, vol. 1, p. 292). Metatron guides him into the palace and "the presence of the high and exalted King to behold the likeness of the chariot . . . before the throne of glory." But the princes of the chariot (the fiery seraphim and cherubim and ophanim) turn their gaze on Ishmael, and he recoils, trembling, and falls. Metatron rebukes the heavenly host and Ishmael revives, but as he puts it: "I still had not strength enough to sing a hymn before the glorious throne of the glorious King." Finally, after an hour passes, he says that "the Holy One, blessed be He, opened to me

> *Gates of Presence Gates of Peace Gates of Wisdom Gates of Strength*
> *Gates of Power Gates of Speech Gates of Song Gates of Praise*
> *and Gates of Incantation."*

In other words, the aspirant must pass through the various trials of the ascent, the final hurdles of which involve overcoming both fear of the Angel of Anger and awe before the heavenly powers. See *Old Testament Pseudepigrapha*, vol. 1, pp. 254–57.

The far quieter "Windows of Worship" is also explicitly about visionary ascent, but it might be read as well in relation to the more normal "vision" of a continually constructed consciousness. And in fact, in a parallel midrash (see Wertheimer, *Battei Midrashot*, vol. 1, p. 278) it becomes clear that the twelve windows of this hymn correspond to the twelve hours of the day (as continual trial). In their endless permutations they can be understood as "infinite." Seen along these lines the poem intensifies awareness—in semi-talismanic fashion—of precariousness and possibility, which is to say, of multiple perspectives and flux. It also recalls Nadia Boulanger's response to Leonard Bernstein's asking her, on her deathbed, if she heard music in her head: "One music," she said, then added after a long pause, "with no beginning, no end" (Bruno Monsaingeon, *Mademoiselle: Conversations with Nadia Boulanger*, trans. Robyn Marsack [Manchester, U.K., 1985], p. 119).

Angel of Fire

Text: *The Liturgical Poems of Yannai* [Heb], ed. Menahem Zulay (Berlin, 1938), poem 33, part 7; *Liturgical Poems of R. Yannai* [Heb], ed. Rabinovitz, poem 46, part 7, pp. 271–72. See also commentary in Elizur, *Poem for Every Parashah* [Heb], pp. 166–70, and Nahum M. Bronznik, *The Liturgical Poems of Yannai: A Commentary* [Heb] (Jerusalem, 2000), vol. 1, notes to poem 46.

The "seder" or biblical portion that Yannai is treating here begins at Exodus 3:1. In their original context, many of these hymns were intended either to invite the participation of the congregation or simply to arouse its awe. The cadenza-like seventh unit of the kerovah, for instance—known as the *rahit*, or "runner," because of the striking way in which it employs speed and density of ornament as an embodiment of virtuosity, racing from the past of Scripture to the present of the listener—showcased the poet's musical talents in order to draw in or wake up members of the congregation. This poem is a particularly stunning example of the rahit. The comment in the headnotes about the poem's carrying down with it the entire alphabet is by Shulamit Elizur in *A Poem for Every Parashah* [Heb]. It is perhaps relevant in this context to note that according to the biblical commentators the name of God—YHVH—is revealed by the burning bush, and that Jewish mysticism from early on sees that name as the source of all language (Scholem, "The Name of God and the Linguistic Theory of the Kabbalah," *Diogenes* 79 [1972], pp. 62–63, and see also the Introduction to this volume).

The translation departs in several places from the literal Hebrew in order to preserve the spirit of the poem. As Ezra Fleischer has noted with regard to the Hebrew liturgical poetry of late antiquity, "Sometimes what the poet is saying is not important; what's important is how he says it and the intensity of the magic and the wizardry of the words" (*Yediot aharonot*, March 20, 1987).

The annotation below follows that of Elizur and Rabinovitz.

Line 1: The fire from on high can devour angels, which are made of fire.

5: Cf. Ezekiel 1:27–28: "as the appearance of fire . . . as the appearance of the bow that is in the cloud.," i.e., with all its shades.

13: See *Tanhuma* Exodus, 15: "The upper fire sends out fronds and burns and does not consume and is black." See also *Midrash Rabbah* Exodus, 2:5.

15: Cf. Isaiah 66:15: "For, behold, the Lord will come in fire, and His chariots shall be like the whirlwind."

17: The Shekhinah is revealed within the fire and the mist.

20: See note to line 13, and *Song of Songs Rabbah* 5:11: "His head is fine gold, his locks are wavy and black as a raven's." The midrash mentions the Torah as black fire (of the words) being written on white fire (of the parchment). In the mystical context, the white fire is also said to refer to the spaces between the letters.

21: Cf. Ezekiel 1:28: "As the appearance of the bow that is in the cloud." As in the Merkavah vision, the rainbow bridges "the terrible gulf between [the worshipper] and God" (Halperin, *Faces of the Chariot*, p. 449).

From the Sky to the Heavens' Heavens

Text: *Liturgical Poems of R. Yannai* [Heb], ed. Rabinovitz, poem 9, part 8, pp. 118–20.

There are numerous allusions in the poem to the same Talmudic tractate we've already encountered several times: see *Hagigah* (12b and 13a) for the seven heavens and their qualities, as reflected in the translation here; the poem is also saturated with other rabbinic citations (drawn from *Midrash Rabbah* and other collections). And there are of course numerous allusions to biblical texts, including Psalms 18:11, 77:20, 104:3; Ezekiel 1:7, 14; Nahum 1:3; and Daniel 7:10. The poem constitutes the eighth part of the kerovah (there are up to nine parts in a full kerovah), which is known as a *siluk*—a term implying "removal." The form of the siluk varies, but it usually consists of a kind of elevated (and in this case ecstatic) and highly cadenced "prose"—which is actually much closer to modern notions of free verse than to anything resembling expository writing or even prose poetry. The ziggurat-like arrangement of the verse is mine, based on the rhythmic units of the original, but the amassed nature of the imagery of ascension is of course Yannai's. It is of interest here that David Halperin, in his analysis of the Heikhalot ascension literature, suggests that "one of the functions of the grandiose heavenly structures in the Heikhalot may have been to provide a Jewish answer . . . to the splendid religious buildings erected by the Christian Roman emperors as advertisements for their faith" (*Faces of the Chariot*, p. 443).

For a detailed analysis of Yannai's "commentary" to the Babel story, and of his contrasting the abuse of language (and its subsequent loss) with the proper use of its serious powers (in worship and — by extension — in poems) "to close the gap between earth and heaven," see Laura Lieber, "The Generation That Built the Tower: Yannai on Genesis 11," *Review of Rabbinic Literature* 8 (2006), pp. 161–88, and Lieber, *Yannai on Genesis*, pp. 369–91. Lieber notes that the larger kerovah this poem is drawn from is one of Yannai's best.

King Girded with Might

Text: Goldschmidt, *Mahzor for the Days of Awe* [Heb], vol. 1, p. 43.

A *yotzer* for Rosh HaShanah, attributed to Eliezer beRibbi Kallir. A yotzer is one of the earliest and most important kinds of poems composed to ornament the liturgy; it was inserted before the blessings of the Shema that praise God as the creator (*yotzer*) of light. In addition to the spine-like anaphoric structure (the repetition at the start of each line), the poem in Hebrew maintains an alphabetical acrostic at the start of the second word of each of its stanzas. (Another acrostic spelling out the names Isaac and Rebecca is embedded in the epigraph-like liturgical prelude as well.) The final six lines of the English (as in the Hebrew) enfold an acrostic that spells out a different pronunciation of the poet's name: Elazar. The stanzas are rhymed or repeat the same word at the end of each line. This repetition of word and sound along the generally short lines and compact stanzas creates a mounting and pounding percussive effect, one that reaches its peak toward stanzas 9–13, though the intensity is maintained almost to the end.

As with all of Kallir's work, the poem is saturated with rabbinic and biblical allusions. In particular we find allusions to *Pesikta deRav Kahanah* 22:5; *Pirkei deRabbi Eliezer*; *Song of Songs Rabbah* 4:10; *Yalkut Shimoni* 2:506, 988; *Deuteronomy Rabbah* 2:37; and more. Biblical allusions include Psalms (47:8–9, 65:7, 76:13, 89:8, 89:14, 93:1, 104:1–2, 37:6), Isaiah (5:16, 13:11, 21:11, 24:21–22, 34:8, 44:7, 57:15, 59:17, 61:2, 63:1), and Daniel (2:22, 7:9), to single out just a few.

As Goldschmidt and Wolfson note, the key fourth stanza (which breaks the acrostic and so is printed in prayer books in a smaller font and indented—here it is italicized) alludes to the midrashic tradition according to which God puts on ten garments, corresponding to the ten scriptural instances where Israel is called His bride. Wolfson singles out *Devarim Rabbah* 2:37, according to which "Israel is said to crown God with ten garments corresponding to the ten times that God refers to Israel as a bride," and he describes this poem ("King Girded with Might") as "a poetic reworking of this aggadic motif." See Wolfson, *Through a Speculum*, p. 93. See also Ezra Fleischer, *The Yotzer: Its Emergence and Development* [Heb] (Jerusalem, 1984), p. 214. In line 59, "Dumah's burden" alludes to Isaiah 21:11.

On the whole, the poem recalls elements of certain Heikhalot hymns found in *Heikhalot Rabbati*. See Morton Smith's translation, chapters 25 and 26: "King beloved and lovely and clean,/Exalted beyond all the haughty,/Haughty, clothed in majesty beyond the majestic,/Majestic, lifted up beyond the mighty,/Mighty, upraised beyond the powerful. . . . King true and only, King who liveth forever,/King who killeth and maketh alive, King who sayeth and doeth,/King who formeth every disease, and createth every cure . . ." (http://www.digital-brilliance.com/kab/karr/HekRab/HekRab.pdf).

Creatures Four-Square About the Throne

Text: Goldschmidt, *Mahzor for the Days of Awe* [Heb], vol. 1, pp. 216–17. See also Bar Ilan, *Sitrei Tefilah veHeikhalot*, p. 45.

An alphabetical acrostic in which the final stanza contains the letters of the poet's first name, this is an ofan (the second section of a yotzer), which takes as its subject the angels. Its content, notes Moshe Idel, is closely related to Ezekiel's vision (*Ascensions on High in Jewish Mysticism*, p. 63; on the circumstances of the composition of the poem and their resonance for later Kabbalists see p. 36). For more on the ofan as a genre, see Shelomoh Ibn Gabirol, "Angels Amassing," below, and the commentary to that poem.

Line 1: Cf. Ezekiel 1 and the image of "the four living creatures." The Throne is God's throne of glory. The poet immediately creates the sensation of mounting movement and tremendous excitement, even frenzy, much like the agitation of the creatures and the wheels of Ezekiel 1, which informs the poem throughout.

2: The figure of 256 wings is derived from Ezekiel 1:6ff. and its Targum: there were four creatures, with four faces or aspects each, and four wings to each aspect, and these faces or aspects and wings were repeated on the four sides of each creature. The math yields 256.

11: Ezekiel 1:7: "And their feet were straight feet."

22: The line alludes to Genesis 25:27 and the image of Jacob—"an upright (or pure) man"—cut into the throne.

23: The angels both bear and are borne by the Throne. The same image appears at the end of Yehudah HaLevi's "Where Will I Find You," below.

Release, Please

Text: *Otzar HaTefillot* [Heb] (Jerusalem, 1970), vol. 1, p. 159; Hazan, *Poems and Prayers* [Heb], pp. 38–41; *My People's Prayer Book: Traditional Prayers, Modern Commentaries*, ed. Lawrence A. Hoffman, 10 vols. (Woodstock, Vt., 1997–2007), vol. 8, pp. 109–14.

The forty-two-letter Name of God is mentioned in the Talmud (*Kiddushin* 71a), and at least one scholar has associated the poem thematically with the Heikhalot hymn "Heteir heteir yotzer bereshit" (Release, release, O You who fashioned the world), where the notion of release is, as here, related to Israel's salvation (Bar-Ilan, *Sitrei Tefilah veHeikhalot*, p. 31). See also S. Tal, "Ana baKo'ah" [Heb], *Sinai* 92 (1983), pp. 287–88. Scholars have differed markedly in determining the provenance of the poem, with some suggesting that it emerges from German Pietist circles and others saying that it was composed much later, most likely in a Palestinian Kabbalistic context. Current scholarship dates the poem to the Gaonic period (before 1038) and places it in the East. My thanks to Shulamit Elizur for referring me to *New Gaonic Responsa* [Heb], ed. Simha Emmanuel (Jerusalem, 1995), p. 135. Thanks too to Uri Melammed for supplying information from the Academy of Hebrew Language in Jerusalem regarding the dating of the poem.

God in the Jewish tradition has many names—some of the more common ones being YHVH, Elohim, El Shaddai, and Ehyeh Asher Ehyeh (I Will Be That I Will Be). In the mystical tradition, the names proliferate in sometimes bizarre fashion. According to rabbinic tradition, the powerful forty-two-letter Name mentioned in this poem "played an active part in the creation" (Scholem, "Name of God, p. 69); for this and other reasons it was "passed along only to mature, discreet, and modest people, fully in charge of their emotions and not likely to use it for personal gain" (Hoffman, *My People's Prayer Book*, vol. 8, p. 114, and see generally 108–14).

The poem is sometimes recited in bed as, according to the *Zohar*, the soul returns to its source while we sleep ("When a person climbs into bed, his soul leaves him and ascends on high," 1:83a [trans. Matt, vol. 2, pp. 29–30]); and sometimes it is recited just before death, when the soul returns to its source beneath the divine throne. In prayer books it is often printed after the passage recalling the Temple sacrifices—again, presumably because the deep theme of the poem is an offering (of words and intention) that will ascend on high. In other communities it is recited as part of the Friday evening Kabbalat Shabbat service (just before the hymn "Lekhah Dodi"; see Alkabetz, "Hymn to the Sabbath," below), which "welcomes" the Sabbath and ushers in the sacred aspect of the week. And in still other communities it is said as part of the additional service for the High Holy Days. Each of these ritual instances involves a connection of the lower world with the upper world, and also of gentleness with strength—hence the placement of this poem of borders within them.

Line 1: The opening lines of the poem involve several compelling allusions: Exodus 15:6 establishes the link between the right hand and power ("Thy right hand, O Lord, glorious in power"), while the mystical Jewish tradition associates the right side with mercy and kindness. The result is the equation of power with mercy and gentleness. The "bound one" at the end of the line in the English is the grammatically feminine Knesset Israel, "Congregation of Israel," which is bound in exile like the forlorn women of 2 Samuel 20:3, who were locked away by David, "shut

up unto the day of their death, in widowhood, with their husband alive."
The Hebrew for this term (*tzrurah*) also implies that the speaker is refer-
ring to the soul bound or held captive and limited in the body.

4: The Hebrew contains an epithet for God here—"Awesome one"—
rather than "Lord."

6: One phrase in the original is left out of the English translation.
The sixth line of the English (line 3 of the Hebrew) might be rendered
literally as "protect those who seek your oneness like the apple of your
eye" (Psalms 17:8)—the implication being that the People of Israel invoke
God's oneness through, among other things, the daily recitation of the
Shema, and they should be protected accordingly by God's love.

11–12: Literally, "Turn . . . to your people, those who remember your
sanctity."

14: In liturgical contexts the poem usually appears with an additional
line at the end: "Blessed be the glorious name of the Lord, His Kingdom
is for eternity."

The Book of Creation

Information for the headnote is drawn from the following sources: Ger-
shom Scholem, *Origins of the Kabbalah*, ed. R. J. Zwi Werblowsky, trans.
Allan Arkush (Princeton, 1987), pp. 24–35; Joseph Dan, *Kabbalah: A Very
Short Introduction* (Oxford, 2007), pp. 17–20, and Dan, *The Ancient Jew-
ish Mysticism* (Tel Aviv, 1993), pp. 198–211; Yehudah Liebes, *Ars Poetica
in Sefer Yetzirah* [Heb] (Tel Aviv, 2000), esp. pp. 16ff., 141ff., and 244ff.;
3 Enoch, trans. P. Alexander, in *The Old Testament Pseudepigrapha*,
ed. James Charlesworth, 2 vols. (New York, 1983), vol. 1, p. 292; Ithamar
Gruenwald, "A Preliminary Critical Edition of *Sefer Yetzirah*," *Israel Ori-
ental Studies* 1 (1971), pp. 132–77; Ezra Fleischer, "On the Antiquity of
Sefer Yetzirah: The Question of the Kallirian Evidence" [Heb], *Tarbiz*
71:3–4 (2002), pp. 405–32; Steven Wasserstrom, "*Sefer Yetzirah* and Early
Islam: A Reappraisal," *Journal of Jewish Thought and Philosophy* 3 (1993),
pp. 1–30, and Wasserstrom, "Further Thoughts on the Origins of *Sefer
Yetsira*," *Aleph* 2 (2002), pp. 201–21; Elliot R. Wolfson, "Text, Context, and

Pretext, Review Essay of Yehudah Liebes's Ars Poetica in *Sefer Yetsira*," *Philonica Annual* 16 (2004), pp. 218–28; and Y. Tzvi Langermann, "On the Beginnings of Hebrew Scientific Literature and on Studying History Through '*Maqbilot*' (Parallels)," *Aleph* 2 (2002), pp. 169–89.

With regard to the question of dating, Liebes is an outlier, as he argues for a Second Temple dating of the text; Ezra Fleischer suggests that an eighth-century dating makes more sense, and Wasserstrom in his rich 2002 article proposes the likelihood of a ninth-century origin in the "Shi'i-influenced gnostic intellectualism" of the day. Liebes's mention of the Indian influence is in *Ars Poetica* [Heb], pp. 83, 118, 236–39; his discussion of Bialik and the book is on pp. 153ff. Scholem argues for an earlier (second- or third-century C.E.) dating ("The Name of God and the Linguistic Theory of the Kabbalah," *Diogenes* 79 [1972], p. 72). The scholar who identifies the book as a kind of Wisdom literature is Ronit Meroz, in "Between *Sefer Yezirah* and Wisdom Literature: Three Binitarian Approaches in *Sefer Yezirah*," *Journal for the Study of Religions and Ideologies* 6:18 (Winter 2007), pp. 101–42. On the question of Indian influence, see also David Shulman, "Is There an Indian Connection to *Sefer Yetzirah*?" *Aleph* 2 (2002), pp. 191–98. Shulman makes a highly suggestive case for Indian influence on the linguistic theory of *Sefer Yetzirah*, especially for the generative qualities of language: "That creation is a matter of sound and vibration and hence of language, broadly conceived, is axiomatic already in the *Rig Veda*. . . . Three-quarters of language is hidden and potentially generative of reality; only the final quarter is manifest in human speech." The *Zohar* will repeatedly take up and develop *Sefer Yetzirah*'s treatment of the letters, expanding into the erotic realm and that of the later book's conception of the *sefirot* (e.g., see *The Zohar* 1:159a–b, trans. Daniel C. Matt, 5 vols. [Stanford, Calif., 2004–9], vol. 2, pp. 385–89).

Quotations are from the following sources: *a poem that is always a poem*: a slightly altered version of Harold Bloom's formulation: see Introduction to this volume, note 38; *a vade mecum for the Kabbalah*: Scholem, *Origins of the Kabbalah*, p. 33; *earliest extant speculative text*: Scholem, *Major Trends in Jewish Mysticism* (New York, 1941), p. 75; *a greater influence on the Jewish mind*: Louis Ginzberg, "Yetzirah, Sefer," *Jewish*

Encyclopedia (New York, 1925), 12:603; *at once pompous and laconic*: Scholem, *Major Trends*, 75; *The author undoubtedly wished*: Scholem, *Origins of the Kabbalah*, p. 25; *to enter the mind of Abraham*: Wasserstrom, "*Sefer Yetzirah* and Early Islam," p. 220; *The Kabbalah didn't give birth*: Liebes, *Ars Poetica* [Heb], p. 244; *a question of ordinary numbers*: Scholem, *Origins of the Kabbalah*, p. 27; [*The angel*] *Metatron said to me*: 3 Enoch 41:1, 2, in *Old Testament Pseudepigrapha*, p. 292; *to build a world*: Ezra Pound, *Selected Prose, 1909–1965* (New Directions, 1975), p. 7 ("the essential thing in a poet . . . that he builds us his world").

One of the leading historians of Jewish mysticism, Joseph Dan, describes *Sefer Yetzirah* as "a brief treatise" that is "one of the most important texts that ancient Judaism gave to Jewish mysticism in the Middle Ages and in the modern era." Almost in the same breath, however, he adds that because of its compact style and "unique terminology . . . the majority of the book cannot be understood by us. . . . The writer felt that he had the right to completely reexamine some of the most basic assumptions of Jewish thought, . . . and to follow his own individual path" (*Ancient Jewish Mysticism*, pp. 198–201). Others, such as Yehudah Liebes, have gone into great and sometimes sublime detail in an effort to comprehend even the most obscure elements of the book. The commentary below seeks to present an elementary sort of gloss that might help the uninitiated reader follow along and see both how this text develops elements from earlier Jewish mystical traditions and why it is taken up again and again in later work. An excellent discussion of the linguistic dynamics present in the book can be found in Scholem, "Name of God," pp. 72ff., and Scholem, *Kabbalah* (New York, 1974), p. 25–26; and in Liebes, *Ars Poetica* [Heb], pp. 16ff.

Text: The layout of the poem is modeled on that of *Sefer Yetzirah* [Heb], ed. A. Lieder and T. Ziskind (Ra'anana, 2007). On the effectiveness and importance of this arrangement, see Abrams, *Kabbalistic Manuscripts*, p. 70. The sections translated according to the traditional division of the text are 1:1–8, 2:2–6, 4:16.

Line 1: "Thirty-two hidden paths": The opening sentence announces the enigma and can be understood in any number of ways, as the textual situation regarding (the originally unvocalized) *Sefer Yetzirah* is anything but stable. There are two principal versions—one long and one short—and numerous variant readings exist for each. Scholars now assume that two distinct lines of thought came together in the work: one that was preoccupied with the question of the ten sefirot, and the other which took up the question of the twenty-two letters. The thirty-two paths combine these lines of inquiry. See A. Peter Hayman, *Sefer Yesira: Edition, Translation and Text-Critical Commentary* (Tübingen, 2004); and also his "*Sefer Yetzirah* and the Heikhalot literature," *Jerusalem Studies in Jewish Thought* 6:1–2 (1987), pp. 71–85 (English section); Gruenwald, "A Preliminary Critical Edition." One version reads, "In [with/by means of/through] thirty-two wondrous/hidden paths of wisdom God . . . carved out." What God carved out isn't grammatically clear, but it would seem to be the universe. How did He carve it out? "With three groups of letters [*sefarim*]." Another text reads more along the following and somewhat clearer lines: "YAH, the Lord of hosts . . . carved out thirty-two wondrous/hidden paths of wisdom. He created His universe with three groups of letters [*sefarim*]." In the first version God carves out the universe by means of the thirty-two paths; in the second God carves out the thirty-two paths, and then with three "groups of letters" (or words) creates the universe. In keeping with biblical usage, most scholars and translators understand *netivot pela'ot* as "wondrous paths," but Ronit Meroz points out that in rabbinic literature (e.g., *Hagigah* 13a) and in work more closely related to *Sefer Yetzirah*, *pela'ot* more often indicates concealment (Meroz, "Between *Sefer Yezirah* and Wisdom Literature," pp. 101–42).

10: "Three words": These three words are perhaps as potent as any in the history of Hebrew mysticism. But since the original manuscripts are unvocalized, we can't be sure how the words were to be pronounced and what they actually were. Most scholars today believe they should be read as *sefer, sfar, sippur* (all from the *s-f-r* root—the letter *peh* becomes hard in *sippur*, changing the "f" sound to a "p"): literally, "book," "number," "speech" (or "recounting," as in a story). Others understand *sfar* to mean "border." Still others understand the three words to refer to the three dimensions the text treats: world (space), year (time), and soul (person).

For subsequent permutations of the imagery of *Sefer Yetzirah*, see also Ibn
Gabirol's "He Dwells Forever," below. *Sefer Yetzirah* also exerted a strong
influence on Yehudah HaLevi in his prose work, *The Kuzari* (see the
headnotes to the section on Yehudah HaLevi), and on Avraham Abulafia,
about whom see the section below and also Idel, *Messianic Mystics* (New
Haven, 1998), pp. 59, 82, and 121. Whatever the words are and mean, the
universe emerges from them. "Letter, limit, and tale" try to account for
the linguistic, spatial, and narrative aspects of these elusive terms and at
the same time preserve something of an acoustic connection through the
"l" and "t" sounds.

13: "Ten": A key number in so many mystical traditions (the six direc-
tions plus the four elements; the ten fingers and the ten toes). Here at the
outset we find ten ciphers (or numbers): the ten sefirot posited as one of
the constituent units of the thirty-two paths of wisdom, and the ten digits
of the hand. Normative rabbinic literature mentions the ten sayings with
which the world was created—i.e., the ten times in Genesis 1 where the
text states, "and God said . . ." (*Pirkei Avot* 5:1, in Joseph Dan, *Ancient
Jewish Mysticism*, p. 201).

13–14: "Spheres/ciphers": The Hebrew reads "ten sefirot," and at
this point all who treat Kabbalistic material in English face a formidable
problem. There is no English word that begins to account for the unique
Hebrew term *sefirot* (singular, *sefirah*). Most scholars, understandably,
choose not to translate the term at all. But in a book of poetry it seems crit-
ical to try. Despite Scholem's caution that the word's derivation is Semitic
and not Greek (that is, from a root implying number or a word implying
brightness or radiance—as in "sapphire"), I have chosen to translate the
word in this context as "spheres" (as in fact Scholem himself does in
Major Trends, p. 206), in part for the sound, but primarily because I want
to emphasize the spatial metaphor of the figure and the concept. To that
end, the notion of the sefirot is first introduced here with a kind of double
exposure: "Ten spheres of restraint" (for *eser sefirot belimah*) is followed
by "ten ciphers of Nothing"—that is, ten numbers involved (in a codelike
way) in divine action through which creation takes place. Liebes suggests
that the meaning here is "ten counted things," though the substance of

those counted things is not yet defined (*Ars Poetica* [Heb], pp. 13–15). El-
liot Wolfson has a particularly compelling idea of the sefirot, one which
emphasizes the centrality of the "imaginative capacity . . . not only of
the mystic visionary but of human beings in general." Wolfson sees the
sefirot as both "realities that constitute the divine realm and the psycho-
logical paradigms by means of which the mystic visualizes these realities"
(*Through a Speculum That Shines: Vision and Imagination in Medieval
Judaism* [Princeton, 1994], pp. 72–73). The notion of *eser sefirot belimah*
is, then, elusive in the extreme, and as Dan points out (*Ancient Jewish
Mysticism*, pp. 203ff.), *Sefer Yetzirah* itself spends a good deal of time at
the start trying to explain what it might mean. A working definition for
our purposes might be that these sefirot are "cosmic principles" or "divine
vehicles" or "receptacles" that come in units of ten and through which
the world is constructed. They are not, however, the ten named sefirot of
later Kabbalah.

13–14: "Restraint/Nothing": The Hebrew here—*belimah*—is particu-
larly obscure (and critical). In Job 26:7 the word is construed to mean "noth-
ing" or "nothingness": "He hangs the world on nothingness." That reading
derives from separating the word into two words: *bli* (without) *mah* (any-
thing). The word *belimah* also means "restraint," "blockage." Some schol-
ars understand it in the context of *Sefer Yetzirah* in a more positive fashion,
as "foundation" (Hayman, *Sefer Yesira*, p. 64; Ronit Meroz, "Between *Se-
fer Yezirah* and Wisdom Literature," *Journal for the Study of Religions and
Ideologies* 6:18 [Winter 2007], p. 103). Again, the English introduces the
concept by doubling the translation to capture the resonance of the word,
the point being that it is only through limitation and definition (as an in-
strument or receptacle of encoding) that creation can take place, and that
the sefirot are themselves the belimah. That restraint on thought and ex-
pression (i.e., the practice of modesty and the avoidance of hubris) might
lead to contemplation and understanding of cosmic principles. Liebes
points out the analogues or precedents in rabbinic literature, including
Hulin 89a: "R. Ila'a said, The world exists only on account of [the merit
of] him who restrains himself [*bolem et etzmo*] in strife, for it is written,
'He hangeth the earth upon *belimah*' [nothing/restraint] (Job 26:7)." And

in *Sotah* 12b we read: "R. Johanan said, Words of Torah only remain with him who makes himself like one who is *nothing*, as it is said, Wisdom shall be found from *nothing* [*me'ayin*]" (Job 28:12) — usually translated as "Where [*me'ayin*] shall wisdom be found?" (Liebes, *Ars Poetica* [Heb], pp. 60–62). Liebes also finds a parallel in the world of English poetry, and in this context of the cancellation or suspension of ego he quotes Shelley's "A Defence of Poetry": "Poetry and the principle of self . . . are the God and Mammon of the world" (Liebes, *Ars Poetica* [Heb], p. 153). Shelley's passage continues in still more relevant fashion: "The functions of the poetical faculty are twofold: by one it creates new materials of knowledge, and power, and pleasure; by the other it engenders in the mind a desire to reproduce and arrange them according to a certain rhythm and order which may be called the beautiful and the good. The cultivation of poetry is never more to be desired than at periods when, from an excess of the selfish and calculating principle, the accumulation of the materials of external life exceed the quantity of the power of assimilating them to the internal laws of human nature. . . . Poetry is indeed something divine. It is at once the centre and circumference of knowledge; it is that which comprehends all science, and that to which all science must be referred. It is at the same time the root and blossom of all other systems of thought" (*The Selected Poetry and Prose of Shelley*, ed. Harold Bloom [New York, 1966], p. 442). Liebes also sends us to another poet — the modern Hebrew writer Hayyim Nahman Bialik and his classic essay "Revealment and Concealment in Language" (see below in this volume, and Bialik, *Revealment and Concealment: Five Essays*, with an afterword by Zali Gurevitch [Jerusalem, 2000]), which identifies "the eternal 'what' frozen on man's lips" for which there is no reply, only "nothingness" and "closed lips."

16–17: "Mothers/doubles": These are technical terms referring to the Hebrew letters (the letters that can be doubled, and the letters that serve as "mothers"). The important element here is the descent into the tangibility of the letters and their possible combinations (morphology, sound, syntax, and grammar) as instruments of creation. Briefly, the mothers are *alef, mem,* and *shin* — the first letter in the alphabet, the middle letter, and the last letter (excluding *tav*, which is one of the doubles). We will see below and in what follows that this structural principle—the right, the left, and what is between them—is critical to much of later kabbalistic thought. The doubles are the seven letters that (originally) express different sounds (hard and soft) when a dot (*dagesh*) is added to them: *bet, gimmel, dalet, kaf, peh, resh, tav*. The elementals are the other twelve letters, which have a single sound.

20: "Digits," etc.: The fundamental structure of things is now seen (imagined) in relation to the human embodiment of them. Think of Blake's "human form divine": "For Mercy has a human heart, / Pity a human face, / And Love, the human form divine, / And Peace, the human dress. // Then every man, of every clime, / That prays in his distress, / Prays to the human form divine, // Love, Mercy, Pity, Peace" ("The Divine Image"). In the world of Kabbalah, however, the human form, including its sexuality, will also be projected or imagined upward and applied to God. As Dan writes: "There are five fingers on each hand and in the middle is the tongue, the source of the 'word,' and there are five toes opposite five, with the circumcision between them" (Dan, *Ancient Jewish Mysticism*, pp. 203–4). The author puns on the word *milah*, which can mean both "word" and also "circumcision," and to a lesser extent on the word *brit*—which means "covenant" but is also part of the term *brit milah*, "circumcision" (cf. Exodus 6:12, Deuteronomy 30:6, and elsewhere). Here *brit* is translated as "bond" and "pact." Hayman understands *brit yahid* as an epithet for God—the Unique One. It can also be read as "a single (unique) *brit*." This pun is unpacked into two English lines. We have already seen sexual imagery in the Jewish mystical tradition (beginning with the Song of Songs, and in places in the Heikhalot literature); this passage hints at the erotic dimension of language. Later Kabbalah will extensively develop other erotic aspects of the tradition.

32: "Restore the Creator": or "set the Creator in His place" (Wolfson, *Through a Speculum*, p. 70), or "seat the Creator on His base." The meaning is elusive, but its thrust seems to be in the alignment between upper worlds and lower worlds: there is a movement down from above and also an establishment of fundamentals—i.e., what is what and where. The process of "drawing down" from the divine realm on high will also be key in later Kabbalah, as will the elevation of human thought and imagination to the plane of the heavens.

54: "Runs and returns": As we've seen in the Heikhalot poetry, the image of running and returning derives from Ezekiel 1:14 ("and the living creatures ran and returned as the appearance of the flash of lightning"), and it is taken up in numerous places in the later mystical literature, including the *Zohar* (2:136a–b [trans. Matt, vol. 5, pp. 257–58]). It generally indicates mystical activity itself. Wolfson comments, "There is an inherent danger in this process of visualization, especially if it is communicated in a public forum; hence the continuation of the text warns one to stop one's heart from meditation on, and to close one's mouth from speaking about, the sefirot. If one's heart runs, that is, if one gets carried away, one must return to one's point of departure, just as the celestial beasts run to and from the realm of the chariot. It is thus the process of forming an image of the sefirot that allows one to gain gnosis of the divine anthropos, but that process must be carefully monitored. The way is marked by a double movement of advance and retreat" (*Through a Speculum*, p. 73).

65–67: "Bridle your mouth . . . and if it wanders": The rarefied abstraction and proliferation of imagery that will attend to the contemplation of the throne and the mysteries of the universe are potentially overwhelming (to the spirit, to one's language, to the imagination).

71: "A pact": The implication is, or might be, that a covenant was made between God and the spiritual aspirant regarding the activity of mystical speculation and inquiry. "Bridle your mouth" and "return to the place" and all will be well. The notion of a meeting in the middle is also key to the worldview of this text. That central or mediating dimension is embodied in the tongue, the phallus (or, less exclusively, the genitals), and in a vision of language (and worship) in which upper and lower worlds are joined.

82: "Certain sounds": The translation skips now from chapter 1 to chapter 2 (verses 2–6). *Sefer Yetzirah* and Kabbalah generally involve extensive engagement with the magical properties of letters—numerologically, anagrammatically, and in terms of their sound. This section offers just the briefest sense of it, but it should be familiar to anyone who lives intensely with literature (and certainly with poetry). Instead of "certain," the Hebrew specifies which letters are associated with each site in the mouth.

93–94: "*Oneg/neg'a*": These words are made up of three letters: *ayin, nun,* and *gimmel.* When their order is shuffled, the world is turned on its head and "pleasure" becomes "plague."

98: "Aleph with all": Aleph is associated with the throat and thorax. The implication is that each letter can be combined with all of the others in a dizzying array of permutations. Some commentators work out that math.

106: "Issuing from a single Name": The unutterable four-letter Name of God.

118: "Longed-for things": In Hebrew, *hafatzim*—literally, "things," but it is also derived from the verb "to long for" or "desire."

120: "From here on in consider": The translation jumps here to 4:16. The "scientific" understanding of the verse might be, "calculate all these permutations of the letters, which can't be pronounced or heard" (see *Rosh HaShanah* 27a), but the phrase resonates more generally across the entire work and into the tradition of Jewish mysticism.

Al-Andalus and Ashkenaz

Al-Andalus

Information for the headnote is drawn from the following sources: Gershom Scholem, *Kabbalah* (New York, 1974), p. 93, Scholem, *Major Trends in Jewish Mysticism* (New York, 1941), p. 33, and Scholem, "Traces of Ibn Gabirol in the Kabbalah," in *Studies in Kabbalah*, ed. ben Shelomo and Moshe Idel [Heb] (Tel Aviv, 1998), pp. 39ff.; Moshe Idel, "The *Sefirot* Above the *Sefirot*" [Heb], *Tarbiz* 51 (1982), pp. 239–80, and Idel, *Kabbalah: New Perspectives* (New Haven, 1988), p. 9; Peter Cole, *Selected Poems of Solomon Ibn Gabirol* (Princeton, 2001), pp. 3–37, and Cole, *The Dream of the Poem: Hebrew Poetry from Muslim and Christian Spain, 950–1492* (Princeton, 2007), pp. 74–110; *The Heart and the Fountain: An Anthology of Jewish Mystical Experiences*, ed. Joseph Dan (Oxford, 2001), p. 81. Ibn Gabirol's two influential prose works are *Tikkun Middot haNefesh* (On the Correction of the Moral Qualities) and *Mekor Hayyim*

(The Fountain of Life). The latter is a major Neoplatonic work that went on to have a marked impact on the development of Scholastic philosophy in Europe, though Ibn Gabirol was identified as its author only in the late nineteenth century. Translations of "The Palace Garden" and "I Am the Man" appear in Cole, *Selected Poems of Ibn Gabirol*. Information on HaLevi is drawn from Judah Halevi, *The Kuzari: An Argument for the Faith of Israel*, trans. Hartwig Hirschfeld, introduction by Henry Slonimsky (New York, 1964), 4:25, 4:1–3, 2:36ff., 5:22, 1:103ff.; Cole, *Dream of the Poem*, pp. 143–70; Ross Brann, "Judah Halevi," in *The Literature of al-Andalus*, ed. María Rosa Menocal, Raymond P. Scheindlin, and Michael Sells (Cambridge, 2006), pp. 265–81; Raymond P. Scheindlin, *The Song of the Distant Dove: Judah Halevi's Pilgrimmage* (Oxford, 2008) and *The Gazelle: Medieval Hebrew Poems on God, Israel, and the Soul* (Oxford, 1991); Diana Lobel, *Between Mysticism and Philosophy: Sufi Language of Religious Experience in Judah Ha-Levi's Kuzari* (Albany, N.Y., 2000). Detailed discussion of both poets can be found in Hayyim Schirmann, *The History of Hebrew Poetry in Muslim Spain* [Heb], ed. Ezra Fleischer (Jerusalem, 1995). See also Joseph Yahalom, *Yehudah HaLevi: Poetry and Pilgrimage*, trans. Gabriel Levin (Jerusalem, 2009). On HaLevi's thought in the *Zohar*, see Isaac Broydè, "Judah Halevi: As Philosopher," *Jewish Encyclopedia* (New York, 1925), and *Zohar* 3:221b. For a more detailed treatment of the influence of both Ibn Gabirol and HaLevi on Zoharic thought, see *Wisdom of the Zohar*, arranged and rendered into Hebrew by Fischel Lachower and Isaiah Tishby; introductions and annotations by Isaiah Tishby, trans. David Goldstein, 3 vols. (Oxford, 1997), vol. 1, pp. 76–77.

Quotations are from the following sources: *mystical spirituality*: Scholem, *Kabbalah* (New York, 1974), p. 36; *motivated in the last resort by mystical leanings*: Scholem, *Major Trends*, p. 33; *acquainted with mystical concepts*: Moshe Idel, *The Kabbalah in Italy, 1280–1510: A Survey* (New Haven, 2011), p. 29—Idel also notes the clear-cut influence of "Jewish mystical sources such as the Heikhalot literature and Sefer Yetzirah on both Ibn Gabirol and HaLevi"; *quintessence and embodiment of our country*: Brann, "Judah Halevi," p. 265; *the language created by God*: Halevi,

Kuzari, trans. Hirschfeld, p. 229. On the notion of Jewish spiritual superiority in HaLevi, see Cole, *Dream of the Poem*, p. 438, and sources there. In later Kabbalah as well, the Jewish soul was considered to be metaphysically superior to that of the non-Jew. See Jody Myers, "Kabbalah for the Gentiles," in *Kabbalah and Contemporary Spiritual Revival*, ed. Boaz Huss (Beer Sheva, 2011), pp. 183–87.

He Dwells Forever

Text: *Liturgical Poems of Shelomoh Ibn Gabirol* [Heb], ed. Dov Yarden (Jerusalem, 1971–72), no. 6. The original involves an acrostic containing a version of the poet's name, with each line of each stanza beginning with a letter of that name: Shelomoh haKatan bar Yehudah.

This majestic poem in praise of God opens with a verse from Psalms that—like a kind of tuning fork—sets both the thematic and prosodic tone for the poem as a whole. In the original, the end of each strophe rhymes with that epigraph-like verse or ends with the same word. The poem itself offers up a commanding view of the entire cosmos, which is described in striking metaphysical and physical detail. The garment of God, the *sefirot*, the twenty-two letters, creation from Nothing and Chaos, the directions and elements, earth, the heavens and their constellations, human history, the life of nature and human growth, and death—all are presented in terms of the vision of *Sefer Yetzirah*. If *Sefer Yetzirah* is a chaotic book about the creation of cosmic order (a cosmic *ars poetica*), Ibn Gabirol's poetry (and this poem in particular, along with *Kingdom's Crown* and numerous other works by the poet) presents a masterful and orderly embodiment of what seems to be a chaotic reality but is in fact a world miraculously fashioned by God. "He Dwells Forever" might, in other words, best be thought of as the literary realization of *Sefer Yetzirah*'s poetics. Not surprisingly, Ibn Gabirol's poem drew the interest of early-thirteenth-century Kabbalists in Girona (Scholem, "Traces of Ibn Gabirol," p. 42).

The poem is recited during the service for the New Year in the Sephardic liturgy. The Psalmic verse it opens with is 145:13: "Your kingdom is the kingdom of eternity" (or, in the NJPS: "Your kingship is kingship for eternity"). In addition to the dense web of allusions to the *Sefer Yetzirah*, the poem weaves together numerous motifs drawn from apocalyptic midrashim such as *Pirkei deRabbi Eliezer*. In what follows, only the allusions to the esoteric tradition are cited; it goes without saying that the poem also makes extensive use of the biblical register.

Lines 1–5: *Sefer Yetzirah* 1:1 and 5, (long version) 6:1; *Pirkei deRabbi Eliezer* 3. The three words with the *s-f-r* root are *sefer, sfar, sippur*—see the annotation for line 10 of *Sefer Yetzirah*, above. "The light of his garment" appears in the Heikhalot poetry (see especially "A Measure of Holiness, above).

6–10: The teacher's counsel here is the Torah. The ten spheres are the sefirot. Five against five—literally, "are aligned" or "in agreement." Idel argues that this refers to the Kabbalistic notion of the existence of ten additional, supernal sefirot above the standard ten—an existence acknowledged by all the important Kabbalistic schools of the thirteenth century. Idel traces the tradition to various pre-Kabbalistic texts, including this poem. With this, in part, he challenges Gershom Scholem's argument vis-à-vis the evidence for Kabbalistic knowledge in Ibn Gabirol (Idel, "The Sefirot Above the Sefirot" [Heb], and Scholem, "Traces of Ibn Gabirol" [Heb]; see also Wolfson, *Through a Speculum That Shines: Vision and Imagination in Medieval Judaism* [Princeton, 1994], p. 139). Cf. *Pirkei deRabbi Eliezer* 3: "The Holy One, blessed be He, consulted the Torah . . . to create the world"; *Sefer Yetzirah* 1:1–2.

11–15: See above, ll. 1–5, for allusions to *Sefer Yetzirah*. For a fuller development of the mathematical aspect of God's uniqueness, see *Kingdom's Crown*, canto 2, in Cole, *Selected Poems of Ibn Gabirol*.

16–20: "Caught in a siege"—cf. *Sefer Yetzirah* 1:5: "Their end is contained in their beginning, their beginning in their end"; see also *Sefer Yetzirah* 1:5, which is translated in this volume as ll. 11–15, above. One editor understands this to refer to their impenetrability, or obscurity. *Sefer Yetzirah* 6:3.

21–25: *Sefer Yetzirah* 2:1: "Twenty-two foundational letters"; *Sefer Yetzirah* 3:3; *Sefer Yetzirah* 5:3.

26–30: *Sefer Yetzirah* 2:5; *Sefer Yetzirah* 1:12: "Chaos is an azure line that surrounds all the world; Void consists of the spongy rocks that are established in the abyss, between which water emanates."

31–35: Up and down, in addition to East, West, etc. *Sefer Yetzirah* 1:14: "He selected three letters from among the Elementals, and fixed them in His great Name, YHVH; with them He sealed the six directions"; *Sefer Yetzirah* 1:13.

36–40: *Sefer HaRazim* 7:29: "He hung the world like a cluster of grapes." The notion that God creates out of desire (or will) is central to Ibn Gabirol's philosophical masterwork, *The Fountain of Life*. For an extensive poetic development of this notion, see *Kingdom's Crown*, canto 9, and "I Love You" (both in this volume).

41–45: "Life beyond time"—literally, "eternal life." *Sefer Yetzirah* 1:9. For more on God's throne see the first section of this anthology ("A Measure of Holiness," "Each Day," "From the Sky to the Heavens' Heavens," and "Creatures Four-Square About the Throne"), as well as *Kingdom's Crown*, cantos 26 and 27 (in this volume).

46–50: *Sefer Yetzirah* 6:1.

56–60: The vision of the constellations and heavenly spheres as part of this cosmic ordering and divine making is sublimely presented in *Kingdom's Crown*, cantos 10–25 (see Cole, *Selected Poems of Ibn Gabirol*).

Angels Amassing

Text: *Liturgical Poems of Shelomoh Ibn Gabirol* [Heb], no. 28.

An *ofan* for the Day of Atonement. Acrostic: "Shelomoh."

Ibn Gabirol wrought major changes on most of the liturgical modes of his day, introducing an Andalusian or Arabized sense of deep order and beauty to these inherited liturgical genres. So with the ofan. The ofan is a piyyut that is incorporated into the liturgy to accompany the prayer that blesses the "Creator of the holy ones . . . whose ministering angels all stand in the heights of the universe and proclaim loudly and together with awe the words of the living God and King of the universe. . . . And the ofanim and holy creatures with a great noise raise themselves towards the seraphim. Facing them they give praise, saying: 'Blessed is the glory of the Lord from His place' (Ezekiel 3:12)." The term *ofan* literally means "wheels," as in Ezekiel's vision of the wheels within wheels, and in the first hymn in this anthology; in the biblical verse cited, however, it means a kind of angel. The literary ofanim employ various and often complex strophic structures. Normally, says Hayyim Schirmann, they describe the holiness of the angels and sometimes the world of creation (*Hebrew Poetry in Spain and Provence* [Heb], 2 vols. [Jerusalem, 1960], vol. 2, p. 701). Formally the ofan relies on considerable (Hopkinsesque) internal rhyme and rhythmic turbulence to mirror the rush and noise of the heavenly creatures. Along these lines, and given that angels were sometimes understood as thoughts, it might help to think of this poem as the Vision of a Loud Mind.

To see how the form evolved, compare Kallir's scrumlike ofan of Late Antiquity ("Creatures Four-Square About the Throne") and Ibn Gabirol's far more refined and ordered aesthetic of the eleventh century.

Lines 1–6: The English opening to a certain extent reflects the heavy alliterative effect of the Hebrew, which is characteristic of the genre and, as it were, imitates the sound the angels make. It is drawn from Psalms 68:18: "The chariots of God are myriad, even thousands upon thousands." Also Ezekiel 3:13: "Then a spirit lifted me up, and I heard behind me a great rushing: . . . also the noise of the wings of the living creatures as they touched one another, and the noise of the wheels beside them, even the noise of a great rushing." The translation of the refrain incorporates elements of Psalms 29:1, which refers to the angelic retinue around God and would have resonated for the Hebrew reader in full: "Give unto the Lord, O ye mighty, give unto the Lord glory and strength" (KJV). The 1917 JPS version has "sons of might." More recent versions translate literally: "O divine beings" or "sons of God [or gods]." A literal translation of the refrain might be: "Give to the Lord, sons of gods/divine beings, give."

7–12: The Hebrew specifies certain kinds of angels in these lines (*erelim* and *hashamlim*)—which are drawn from Ezekiel 1:4: "Behold . . . a great cloud with a fire flashing up, so that a brightness was round about it . . . as the color of electrum [*hashmal*]," and *Hagigah* 13b: "What does

[the word] *hashmal* mean?—Rab Judah said: Creatures of fire speaking."
Also Ezekiel 1:14: "And the living creatures ran and returned as the appearance of a flash of lightning"—a phrasing that figures in *Sefer Yetzirah*, chapter 1, where it refers to the heart's (or mind's) activity and risks.
"The angels consist of fire and water, or according to another account, of four heavenly elements: mercy, strength, beauty, and dominion, corresponding to the four earthly elements: water, fire, earth, and air" ("Angels and Angelology," *Encyclopedia Judaica* [Jerusalem, 1972]). Avraham Ibn Ezra recalls the intellectual aspect of the angels as well, in his biblical commentary to Genesis 28:12 (Jacob's ladder): "And R. Shelomoh the Spaniard [Ibn Gabirol] said that the ladder alludes to the upper soul, and the angels of god to wisdom's thought."

13–18: "Partition" is the word used for the cover or curtain before the Holy Ark in the synagogue, *pargod*. *Pirkei deRabbi Eliezer* 4: "Seven angels created in the beginning serve Him before the veil which is called *pargod*." See "A Measure of Holiness," above, and the notes there.

31–36: *Hagigah* 13b: "Sandalfon . . . stands behind the chariot and wreathes crowns for his Maker"; Job 31:36; *Sefer Yetzirah* 3:7: "He made the letter *alef* king over breath and bound a crown to it."

37–42: *Pirkei deRabbi Eliezer* 4: "And the creatures stand in fear and terror"; for "will set strong," literally, "their feet were straight" (Ezekiel 1:7). In the Kedushah prayer the word *Holy* is repeated three times, as in Isaiah 6:3. "Holy" in Hebrew denotes separation.

I Love You

Text: *Secular Poems of Shelomoh Ibn Gabirol* [Heb], ed. Dov Yarden (Jerusalem, 1984), no. 74.

This ostensibly secular poem is suffused with an intensely visionary metaphysics that brings it into "mystical" territory, and it has generated considerable discussion. (The classification of a poem in the Hebrew-Andalusian context as "secular," it should be pointed out, meant only that it wasn't intended for liturgical use; "nonliturgical" might be a more appropriate designation, awkward as it is.)

Essentially the debate around the work concerns the nature of the poem and its philosophical or theological implications. According to the Arabic heading it is "an answer to a student who has asked about the nature of existence." In another medieval source it is described as a poem about "the mysteries of creation." Also relevant in this context is the legend according to which Ibn Gabirol created a female golem, a "Frankenstein-like creature energized by the power of the Divine Name" (Steven Katz, "Mystical Speech and Mystical Meaning," in *Mysticism and Language,* ed. Steven Katz [Oxford, 1992], p. 18): "And they said of R. Shelomoh Ben Gabirol that he created a woman, and she waited on him. When he was denounced to the authorities, he showed them that she was not a perfect creature, and [then] he turned her to her original [state]—to the pieces and hinges of wood, out of which she was built up" (from Shelomoh del Medigo, *Matzref leHokhmah,* in Moshe Idel, *Golem* [Albany, N.Y., 1990], p. 233). Reading this poem in light of the foundational esoteric text, *Sefer Yetzirah,* and the philosophical treatise *The Fountain of Life,* Yehudah Liebes notes that "in the relationship between the teacher and the pupil the secret of creation is given expression" ("Book of Creation and R. Shelomoh Ibn Gabirol" [Heb], p. 117).

Lines 1–2: Genesis 22:2: "Take now thy son, thine only son, whom thou lovest, even Isaac, and get thee into the land of Moriah."

3: Deuteronomy 6:5, from which the Shema is taken: "And you shalt love the Lord thy God with all thy heart and with all thy soul and with all thy might."

5–7: Liebes points out that Sa'adia Gaon in his introduction to the *Sefer Yetzirah* also describes the first principle and the secret of creation as "far off and deep."

9: The Hebrew for "something" in this line is *davar,* one of the more complex and overloaded words in the language; from the same root we derive "commandments," "thing," "a matter of importance," and the verb "speak." It appears three times in this poem—as "the issue" (line 7), "something" (line 9), and "words" (line 19).

11–13: The Hebrew is particularly difficult to paraphrase, and the English is woven accordingly. Liebes suggests that the "sages" of the poem are in fact the sages of the Neoplatonic Gnostic gospels, in particular the *Gospel of Truth* ("Book of Creation and R. Shelomoh Ibn Gabirol" [Heb], pp. 120–23); Jacques Schlanger also suggests that the lines refer to thinkers "with gnostic tendencies" (Schlanger, *Shelomoh Ibn Gabirol's Philosophy* [Heb], translated from the French by Y. Ur [Jerusalem, 1979]). "Owes all" in line 12 is based on a reading by E. Zemach (*As the Root of the Tree* [Heb] [Tel Aviv, 1973]), but is usually understood to mean "for the sake of." See also *Fountain of Life* 410: "Unity [oneness] overcomes (the) all and extends through (the) all, and sustains (the) all." Line 13 might also be understood as saying that the secret, or mystery, of all creation resides in each person (in all), in their power to create. This individual aspect of "all" is used in Isaiah 43 (v. 7), a chapter Ibn Gabirol alludes to several times in the course of the poem.

14: Literally, "He longs to establish there-is as there-is," or "being as near-being." Hayyim Nahman Bialik and Yehudah Ravnitzky comment in their early edition of Ibn Gabirol's poetry: "'Primary matter,' which in *The Fountain of Life* is called 'foundation,' has no true existence of its own, but is 'like-existence,' and longs to couple with 'form,' so that the Creator will give it true existence; and this desire of matter to take on form is very great . . . and according to the ancients is the reason for the eternal movement in creation" (*The Poems of Shelomoh ben Yehuda Ibn Gabirol* [Heb] [Tel Aviv, 1927], vol. 2, p. 48). Yarden glosses: "All things long for God to establish them in being that resembles the true being, which is the Lord" (*Secular Poems*, no. 74). See *Sefer Yetzirah*, line 109.

Liebes locates the source of the view of creation presented in the poem first of all in the best-known of Plato's works in the Arab world of the Middle Ages, the *Timaeus* (29–30). The second link in Liebes's background probe takes him to Pseudo-Aristotle and the Neoplatonic *Theology of Aristotle*: "All intellectual things possessing any sort of desire are after (or one step below) that which is intelligence alone and lacks desire. And when the intelligence gains possession of some desire, it goes out on account of that desire in any way it can, and does not remain in its initial position, for it longs to act and to ornament the things it has seen with the mind. As a pregnant woman upon whom pain has come in order to give birth to that which is in her womb—so is intelligence when drawn by the form of desire—its desire is to bring into action the form within it, and it craves and strives to attain this with great effort, while toil and pain take hold of it, and bring forth the form into action as a result of its desire for the concrete world" ("Book of Creation and R. Shelomoh Ibn Gabirol" [Heb], p. 119). Liebes further comments on the notion of "ornament"— *kosmein*—in the passage, from which English derives "cosmetic" and "cosmos." This becomes central to understanding the so-called ornamental poetics of the age, in which ornament is not a decorative accessory but a necessary element for the completion of the poem as a poem, and a vital constituent of the order and energy it embodies.

The third pivot on which Liebes turns his study of the poem is the term "all." The background to this complex of images he traces to the Valentinian *Gospel of Truth*, which refers to "the Father, the perfect one, the one who made the all, while the all is within him and the all has need of him. . . . He went into the midst of the schools (and) he spoke the word as a teacher. . . . Since the perfection of the all is in the Father, it is necessary for the all to ascend to him" (*Nag Hammadi*, 38–40). This "all" Liebes identifies with "light," as in the "Light of the World" (John 1:3–4). For Ibn Gabirol, Liebes claims, the "all" is God's wisdom out of which the world was shaped. Liebes ("Book of Creation and R. Shelomoh Ibn Gabirol" [Heb], pp. 122–23) finds other parallel uses of the term as well, and then concludes with a poem by Ibn Arabi, the great Andalusian Islamic philosopher-poet (1165 1240): "And all is in need, not what is satisfied, / This is the truth, and we've spoken plainly. / If I've mentioned the rich, I mean those who lack nothing. / And here now you know what I mean. / All is linked with all—nothing exists without it. / Accept this matter which I have told you."

from Kingdom's Crown

Text: Both the graphic arrangement of the poem on the page and the commentary below are drawn from the excellent and still unsurpassed edition of *Kingdom's Crown* by Yisrael Zeidman, *Keter Malkhut* (Jerusalem, 1950).

In many ways a reprise of the poet's entire *diwan*, or collected writings, *Kingdom's Crown* is a highly musical and even symphonic poem that attempts nothing less than a map of "what is"—lower-limit world, upper-limit Lord. While it is framed by its magnificent hymn to the Creator and the magisterial concluding confession, the bulk of the work consists of a cosmography based on the Ptolemaic universe: it ascends from earth's four elements to the Throne of Glory, as it takes one up through the spheres and the planets before returning, not merely to earth but to the heart of man as he confesses his lowliness and comes to an understanding of his place in the universe. For all its ingenious use of biblical quotation and diverse sources including the Talmud, midrash, and early Hebrew liturgical verse from Palestine and Babylonia, the bulk of the poem is universal in its vision. It should be taken in, or offered up, quite literally as a music of the spheres. (Ibn Gabirol's spheres, or *galgalim*, are not to be confused with the sefirot of the previous poem or of *Sefer Yetzirah*, nor are the names of the Kabbalistic sefirot—Keter, Malkhut, Gedulah, etc.—to be identified with Ibn Gabirol's use of these words in a much freer and wholly unrelated manner.)

Technically, *Kingdom's Crown* is a *bakkashah*, or poem of petition, though its hybrid composition renders it in many ways unique in Hebrew literature. While it is doubtful that the poem was originally intended for synagogue use, its powerful religious emphases have led to its incorporation into the rite for the Day of Atonement, when it is uttered quietly by individual worshippers. More detailed discussion of its fascinating and Qur'anic prosody—a kind of highly cadenced free verse known in Arabic as *saj'*, suffused with internal and irregular rhyme, virtuoso percussive effects, and a stunningly sustained music—can be found in Cole, *Selected Poems of Ibn Gabirol*, pp. 22–23 and 290 The commentary that follows ignores most of the poet's scriptural allusions (except in key places) and focuses instead on the dimension of the text that is most relevant to the Kabbalistic tradition. The excerpts themselves highlight passages relevant to that tradition—though along the same line of thinking the entire poem could easily have been included here.

Canto 9: This is the final and most potent section of the "prelude" to *Kingdom's Crown*, which attempts to list God's indescribable qualities.

The entire section reverberates against the "autobiography of wisdom" as it is set forth in Proverbs 8, esp. 22–31: "The Lord made me as the beginning of His way, the first of His works of old." But it also develops the notion of divine making, as we have encountered it in *Sefer Yetzirah* and "He Dwells Forever."

Lines 11–13: Cf. *Genesis Rabbah* 1:1, on "artist": "I was an instrument of the artistry of the Holy One, blessed be He"; Zeidman adds: "like a workman and artist [or artisan] with whose help the Holy One, blessed be He, created the world"

14–15: This is the prevalent medieval theory of vision. Israel Davidson notes: "According to Empedocles, vision was occasioned by particles continually flying off the surface of bodies which met with others proceeding from the eye" (*Selected Religious Poems of Solomon Ibn Gabirol*, ed. Israel Davidson, trans. Israel Zangwill [Philadelphia, 1923], p. 178).

16–19: Cf. *The Epistles of the Brethren of Purity*, part 1, letter 8: "And know, my brother! Every flesh-and-blood artist has need of six things in order to complete his work . . . Primary matter, place, time, tool, vessel and movement. . . . ; whereas the exalted Lord has no need of any of these, all of which are his creations and works" (Zeidman).

20–22: In the Hebrew the active agency and grammatical subject of these lines is God's desire (line 12) or will. Emanating from God, this desire works like an artist, or artisan, to give shape to the world. The sequence of pronouns in the original is complicated and rich in overtones, and shifts from the second person to the third—which might be understood either as "it" (the Divine Will) or "He"—God. In line 24 the agency is extended to the third-person "hand of desire." These lines have drawn extensive commentary for their relevance to the study of early Kabbalah. In particular, see Shlomo Pines, "And He Called to Nothing Which Split: On Keter Malkhut" [Heb], *Tarbiz* 50 (1980): 339–47; Scholem, "Traces of Ibn Gabirol in the Kabbalah" [Heb]; and Yehudah Liebes, "The Book of Creation [*Sefer Yetzirah*] and R. Shelomoh Ibn Gabirol and a Commentary on His Poem 'I Love You'" [Heb], *The Proceedings of the Second International Congress on the History of Jewish Mysticism*

(1987), pp. 73–123. Moshe Idel points out another close parallel in Kabbalistic literature, namely, in *Sefer HaYihud*, which speaks of the sefirah Keter (crown) as follows: "It is called a . . . light that is made like a crack changing from matter to matter until it splits and in that splitting the powers of all the sefirot are drawn from it" (cited in Pines, "And He Called to Nothing Which Split" [Heb], p. 339). Liebes proposes a provocative and compelling interpretation—namely, that the image contains residues of an early myth, deriving perhaps from Persian Manichaeism and Greek Gnosticism. The line, he offers, holds a conscious (or semi-conscious) echo of the Orphic creation myth of the egg and the god Phanes, who shines out of the egg as it cracks. Going even further, though with some reservation, he notes the similarity between the Greek word *oion* (egg) and the Hebrew word *ayin* (nothing, or nothingness). The latter, he says, is a nothingness of plenitude. See also Daniel C. Matt, "*Ayin*: The Concept of Nothingness in Jewish Mysticism," in *Essential Papers in Kabbalah*, ed. Lawrence Fine (New York, 1995), pp. 74–75. Matt writes: "Gabirol's cryptic and pregnant words in *Keter Malkhut* seem to endow *ayin* with a new dimension of meaning: Ontological essence. Since we know that the Kabbalists were indebted to Gabirol for a number of images and terms, it is not surprising that the mystical career of *ayin* is linked to his poetry." For more on this concept in the Kabbalistic poetry, see, in this volume, *Sefer Yetzirah*; Ibn Gabirol, "He Dwells Forever"; Moshe ben Nahman, "Before the World Ever Was"; Avraham ben Maimon, "Hidden God"; the Shabbatian hymn "Secret Pleasure"; and the selection from Shneur Zalman, *The Tanya*. A modern embodiment of the notion can be found in Paul Celan's "Mandorla": "what stands in the almond? / The Nothing. //. . . In Nothing—who stands there? The King," and also his "Psalm": "A Nothing we were, are now, and ever / shall be, blooming: / the Nothing-, the / No One's-Rose" (trans. John Felstiner, in Felstiner, *Paul Celan: Poet, Survivor, Jew* [New Haven, 1995], pp. 180, 167). As Felstiner notes, Celan's concept of Nothing most likely derives from his reading of Scholem (especially on Lurianic Kabbalah).

23–26: The imagery here is taken from the description of the wilderness sanctuary in Exodus and, as is the case with the final line of each of the poem's cantos, presented with a twist that in some cases radically alters the meaning of the biblical verse. Cf. Exodus 26:4: "And thou shalt make loops of blue upon the edge of the one curtain that is at the edge of the first coupling"; also Exodus 36:17: "And he made fifty loops upon the edge of the curtain that was outmost in the first coupling [set]," where "coupling" is understood, by Zeidman, as referring to the system of the spheres. In the scheme laid out here, God's desire or will, literally "the power [of His/its hand]," reaches from the highest "innermost chamber" of the tenth sphere to the "outermost edge" of the lower creation, with earth at its center. Elsewhere Ibn Gabirol identifies God's will as "the power of unification." As is often the case with Ibn Gabirol, the ornamental or cosmetic becomes the cosmic. For more on this notion, see notes to "I Love You," above. The ellipsis at the end of the canto is mine (as are the ellipses in the cantos translated here). All cantos included are translated in full.

Canto 24: With canto 24 we jump ahead to the tenth sphere of intelligence (or intellect), which is an innovation of Ibn Gabirol's (beyond the ninth "all-encompassing sphere" or the sphere of the prime mover in the Ptolemaic scheme).

Line 4: 1 Kings 6:17: "The house, that is the Temple, before [the Sanctuary] . . ."—where the Hebrew for "Temple" is *heikhal*, and might, as we've seen, also be translated as "palace" or "chamber."

5: Leviticus 27:32: "Every tenth . . . shall be holy to the Lord." Cf. *Sefer Yetzirah* and the note to line 13 regarding the use of "ten."

15–16: Genesis 4:7: "unto thee is its desire," where the phrase is spoken by God to Cain, who is angry and about to kill his brother, Abel. In the biblical context, "its" refers to the sin that "crouches at the door" when one behaves unjustly. Here the phrase takes on a wholly different import, timbre, and tone, as "its" refers to the reality and matter of the tenth sphere (intellect or mind)—or the sphere itself. Again Zeidman notes the parallel to the poet's *Fountain of Life*, where we hear that "Primary matter longs to take on primary form in order to achieve the good, which is being/existence/reality. The same goes for all that is created from matter and form. All that is imperfect or incomplete moves to take on the form of completion and perfection. . . . [the basic principle being that] the desire for the First Agent, sometimes referred to as 'the Author of All,' and the movement toward him is common to all." Cf. "I Love You," above. In a subtle and clever employment of scriptural echoes and overtones, Ibn Gabirol no doubt also has in mind Song of Songs 7:11, which sounds similar in the Hebrew but employs a different preposition. The meaning of that verse is much closer to the poet's use: "And his [my beloved's] desire is toward me" (Ibn Gabirol, *Fountain of Life*, translated from the Arabic by Ya'akov Blobstein [Heb] [Tel Aviv, 1964], pp. 408–9).

Canto 25: This canto's sphere of intelligence is the sphere of the angels.

Line 2: The circle of mind doesn't participate in the rotation of the other spheres.

4: "Spirits on high" are angels: Avraham Ibn Ezra on Exodus 3:15: "Know that there are three worlds: . . . the lower world . . . and the intermediary world . . . and the upper world which is the world of the holy angels . . . and the soul of humankind." Zeidman notes that both souls and angels were created from the glow of the circle of mind.

11–14: Cf. *Fountain of Life* 5:4: "The soul resembles clear glass"; Ezekiel 1:1ff. on the "living creatures," esp. 1:22: "And over the heads of the living creatures there was the likeness of a firmament like the color of the terrible ice"; also *Pirkei deRabbi Eliezer* 4.

15–19: See "Angels Amassing," above, for similar imagery and source material on the angelic camps.

24–25: Cf. *Pirkei deRabbi Eliezer* 4: "The angels are created on the second day, and when they are sent (as messengers) by His word they are changed into winds, and when they minister before Him they are changed into fire, as it is said, 'Who makest winds Thy messengers, the flaming fire Thy ministers'" (Psalms 104:14).

29–45: Cf. Daniel 7:10: "A fiery stream issued and came forth from before him; Thousands upon thousands ministered unto him, and ten thousand times ten thousand stood before him."

46: Psalms 100:3, Isaiah 64:7: "But now, O Lord, Thou art our Father; we are the clay, and Thou our potter, and we are the work of Thy hand."

Canto 26: The location of the Throne of Glory, beyond the outermost sphere. See Raphael Loewe, *Ibn Gabirol* (New York, 1991), p. 109.

Lines 3–6: On the "Throne of Glory" see *Pesahim* 54a: "Seven things were created before the world was created, and these are they: The Torah, repentance, the Garden of Eden, Gehenna, the Throne of Glory, the Temple, and the name of the Messiah. . . . The Throne of Glory and the Temple, for it is written, 'Thou Throne of Glory, on high from the beginning, Thou place of our Sanctuary' (Jeremiah 27:12)"; see also notes to Canto 24.

9: Cf. Exodus 34:3: "And no man shall come up with thee [. . . onto the mount]." Again, Ibn Gabirol jolts the phrase into a new orbit, as it were, so that instead of referring to God's prohibiting any man from joining Moses on Sinai to receive the commandments, it now refers to God's place on the Throne of His power, where "no man might ascend."

Canto 27: This canto treats the place of righteous souls beneath the Throne.

Lines 1–3: *Shabbat* 152b: "R. Eliezer said: The souls of the righteous are hidden under the Throne of Glory."

9: The verse involves a play on Genesis 9:19: "The sons of Noah"; *noah* also means "rest" in Esther 9:16.

16–20: Descriptions of the world to come and its pleasures abound in rabbinic literature. See, for an elaborate example, *Yalkut Shim'oni* to Genesis (in Zeidman). A more concise description is found in *Berakhot* 17a: "In the future world there is no eating nor drinking nor propagation nor business nor jealousy nor hatred nor competition, but the righteous sit with their crowns on their heads feasting on the brightness of the divine presence, as it says, *And they beheld God, and did eat and drink* (Exodus 24:11)."

21–24: Cf. Numbers 13:27: "A land [that]. . . . floweth with milk and honey, and this is the fruit of it." In the book of Numbers the phrase "flowing with milk and honey, and this is the fruit of it" refers to what Moses' spies saw when they went ahead to scout out the land of Canaan. Here Ibn Gabirol has it refer to the rewards of the afterworld.

Canto 29: The formation of the soul from radiance of the divine glory.

Lines 15–17: Cf. Exodus 19:18: "Now Mount Sinai was altogether in smoke, because the Lord descended on it in fire."

True Life

Text: *Diwan Yehudah HaLevi* [Heb], ed. H. Brody (Berlin, 1894–1930), vol. 2, p. 296.

The transparency of this poem is representative of the transparency at the heart of HaLevi's mystical vision, which involves the aspirant's surrender to the divine and his passive reception of God's presence. Along these lines the poem takes up the language and imagery of both Islamic and Jewish mysticism, as Raymond Scheindlin points out in a characteristically astute reading (*Song of the Distant Dove*, p. 86). The experience at the heart of this poem, notes Scheindlin, is the desire for a concrete vision of God, though the Bible warns that no one can survive such an experience. (See "A Measure of Holiness," above, and the Heikhalot writers' aspiration toward direct vision of the deity. Elliot Wolfson argues that the Heikhalot literature was more influential for HaLevi's work than has been previously acknowledged. See *Through a Speculum*, pp. 174, 180–81.) Here the implication is that, since death is in fact bliss—in which the desire for vision will be realized by the soul released from the body—the poet would be willing to die for his vision (see also "Lord, [All My Desire]," below). The language employed is that of the Sufi martyrdom of love.

The image of God appearing in a dream recalls the night visitation of the lover in Arabic secular love poetry (see, for instance, Yosef Ibn Hasdai's poem on pp. 70–73 of Cole, *Dream of the Poem*), and this adds a measure of passion and vulnerability to the poem. The poem's final image recalls Rabi'a, the mystical eighth-century Arabic poet who was known to shut the windows of her home in spring, since, as Rumi put it in his version of her story, "the gardens and the fruits are inside, in the heart" (Annemarie Schimmel, *Calligraphy and Islamic Culture* [New York, 1990], p. 39, and Scheindlin, *Gazelle*, p. 200). As HaLevi writes in the *Kuzari*, 4:3: "Our intellect . . . cannot penetrate to the true knowledge of things, except by the grace of God, by special faculties which He has placed in the senses. . . . To the chosen among His creatures He has given an inner eye which sees things as they really are, without any alteration. . . . [The] prophets without doubt saw the divine world with the inner eye. . . . His sight reaches up to the heavenly host direct, he sees the dwellers in heaven, and the spiritual beings which are near God, and others in human form" (trans. Hirschfeld, pp. 206–9). True vision occurs here with the eyes shut, just as in other poems spiritual awakening occurs in physical sleep, during a dream. As Scheindlin understands it (in relation to another HaLevi poem), "sleep, a simulacrum of death, affords [the soul] a glimpse . . . of its own redemption"—though that glimpse proves unsatisfactory (Song of the Distant Dove, p. 48). In both cases HaLevi effectively blurs the border between inner and outer, dream vision and the waking state.

At the heart of HaLevi's poetry and philosophical writing lies a deeply "antimetaphysical" outlook. While Ibn Gabirol, heavily influenced by certain strains of Arabic philosophy, presents the possibility of communion between man and God through what was called the "Active Intellect" of the cosmos, HaLevi is influenced by other strains of Islamic and Jewish thinking (such as that represented by the Sufi al-Ghazali) and denies the power of the intellect to effect a communion of this sort. Only prophetic revelation and devotional surrender to God's presence and power can bring about this experience of the divine presence. For more on HaLevi's religious philosophy see Isaac Husik, History of Medieval Jewish Philosophy (Philadelphia, 1941), pp. 150ff., and, in relation to his poetry, Wolfson, Through a Speculum, pp. 160–87.

Where Will I Find You

Text: The Liturgical Poems of Yehudah HaLevi [Heb], ed. Dov Yarden (Jerusalem, 1978–86), no. 97.

This poem is part of a longer ofan for the festival of Simhat Torah, and it involves what might be thought of as a more intimate and meditative development of that genre (see Kallir's "Creatures Four-Square About the Throne" and Ibn Gabirol's "Angels Amassing," above). The poem contains some of HaLevi's most powerful devotional lines, especially the opening five lines and ll. 28–31. Like "True Life," it is constructed around a series of paradoxes; instead of blindness offering vision, sleep producing true wakefulness, and death providing access to true life, this poem reveals a powerful tension between immanence and transcendence (Scheindlin, *Song of a Distant Dove*, p. 44). On the one hand, God is so wholly transcendent that it is hopeless to dream of encountering Him directly; on the other hand, the soul in HaLevi's still Neoplatonic scheme comes from the divine realm beneath the Throne of Glory (see Ibn Gabirol's *Kingdom's Crown* and the Heikhalot poems) and so contains a spark of divinity and is itself divine. Yet that sense of the divine is distant in its nearness and somehow available in its awe-inspiring transcendence. In seeking Him without, one finds Him within. In looking within, one discovers He is everywhere. The situation is at once reassuring and disturbing. For more on this poem, which Scheindlin calls an anxious "mystical testimony," see *Song of a Distant Dove*, pp. 42–47.

Lines 1–5: The presence of God once lay on the cherubim's wings in the Temple in Jerusalem. Solomon's prayer in 2 Chronicles 6:18: "But will God in very truth dwell with me on the earth? Behold, heaven and the heaven of heavens cannot contain Thee; how much less this house which I have builded."

10: Again, God's presence would lie on the cherubim over the ark of the Temple.

12: The hosts are of course the angels praising God on high. Mention of them at a certain point in the liturgy provides the occasion for this poem, which is ostensibly a meditation on these hosts. In fact, the poem focuses on humankind, whose relation to God is contrasted with that of the angels. Moshe Idel discusses HaLevi's depiction of angels as men in the *Kuzari* in *The Angelic World: Apotheosis and Theophany* [Heb] (Tel Aviv, 2008), pp. 30–33.

13–16: Scheindlin notes that the chamber here also refers in traditional Jewish terms to the Temple (as above, in 2 Chronicles), but in this context it might also suggest the chambers of the heart. See, for instance,

"True Life," above, line 7: "If I could see His face in my heart's chamber." Wolfson understands this inner seeing (or eye of the heart) as an imaginative faculty, the precedent for which he believes to be in the Heikhalot literature and the work of those who comment on it. It is this literature that may have provided "the basis to appropriate and transpose the Sufi notions that parallel ideas found in the Jewish texts" (*Through a Speculum*, pp. 172–74). Along the same lines, notes Wolfson, "the basic themes of the mystical experience described in the Heikhalot are all appropriated by HaLevi . . . in order to describe his own experience in the moment of ecstasy induced by poetic composition (*Through a Speculum*, p. 181).

28–31: Exodus 19:17: "And Moses brought forth the people out of the camp to meet God." Rashi comments on this verse: "This (the word *likrat*, 'to meet,' which is used when two persons are approaching one another) tells us that the Shekhinah was going forth to meet them, as a bridegroom who goes forth to meet his bride" (*Pentateuch with Targum Onkelos, Haphtaroth and Rashi's Commentary*, trans. and annot. M. Rosenbaum and A. M. Silbermann [Jerusalem, 1930], p. 100); see also Rashi to Deuteronomy 33:2: "He (God) was Himself going forth facing them" (see also Lobel, *Between Mysticism and Philosophy*, p. 150). On the whole, as Scheindlin points out, the poem blends mystical testimony regarding God's presence with a subtle uncertainty or anxiety about that presence.

Lord, [All My Desire]

Text: *Liturgical Poems of Yehudah HaLevi* [Heb], no. 32.

A *bakkashah* (poem of petition) for Yom Kippur. This is perhaps the most philosophical of the four HaLevi poems included in this anthology, but it takes up many of the themes and strategies we've already seen, including the centrality to his worldview of surrender and paradox. The poem begins and ends with a confession of inadequacy: the poet is a burden to himself—"the little I am weighs on me"—and sees himself as "desire's prisoner" who lives in lies; moreover, he is acutely aware of the inadequacy of speech itself before God's omniscience.

The deep theme of the poem is the need for surrender of the self and ego to God's will and the difficulty of doing so while one is in the prime of life. This is a central tenet of medieval Sufi thought, where it is known as *tawakkul* (the placement of absolute trust in God, complete surrender to Him). Scheindlin notes that there are other elements of the Sufi approach at work here, including *kunu'*, or satisfaction with one's state, and *ridhaa*, or "loving acceptance of God's will," regardless of what that entails (Scheindlin, *Song of a Distant Dove*, pp. 22, 40). Diana Lobel (*Between Mysticism and Philosophy*, pp. 147–54) points out the parallel treatment of all this in HaLevi's *Kuzari*, where the Arabic religious term *ittisal*—"union," "connection," "mutual engagement"—is key, as in the "Jewish covenantal ideal." She highlights the paradoxical formulation of ll. 7–8 ("I wander from you—and die alive;/the closer I cling—I live to die"), observing that, as HaLevi sees it, "True connection with God is available in this life, and guarantees life in the world to come." The *Kuzari* puts it as follows: "For one whose soul is attached [*ittasalat nafsuhu*] to the *amr ilahi* [the divine thing, order, or command—like the Logos] while he is [still] busy with the accidents of the body, it stands to reason that he will join [*yattasilu*] [the *amr ilahi*] when he withdraws and leaves this unclean vessel" [3:20, trans. Lobel]. Lobel goes on to point out the connection between HaLevi's use of "cling" (*edbak*) in line 8 and the Jewish mystical category of *devekut*, which is for HaLevi associated with the Arabic *ittisal*.

The other conspicuous element of this poem is, once again, its paradoxical formulations. We have already seen this at work—and intensified by their rhetorical figuration, assonance, and rhyme scheme—in ll. 7 and 8 (which allude to *Berakhot* 18a–b, where wicked men are called dead while alive, and the righteous are called alive when they die). But there is the larger paradox within which the person who truly trusts in God wouldn't even need to pray, at least not to pray for anything specific, or to observe the petitionary prayers of the standard liturgy. The true believer's prayer would constitute both an expression of surrender and perhaps a request for God's help to perfect that surrender (Scheindlin, *Song of a Distant Dove*, pp. 40–41). Here too, as so often in HaLevi's poetry, reason is short-circuited or transcended. The circular structure of this poem (it returns to its opening formulation) reflects that larger paradox. It also points ahead to another poem about desire as an obstacle to the experience of the divine, that is, "Why, My Desire" (see below), which is attributed to the great Kabbalist of Safed, Yitzhak Luria.

A Dove in the Distance

Text: *Liturgical Poems of Yehudah HaLevi* [Heb], no. 357.

This is one of HaLevi's finest poems. Its genre isn't known; Hayyim Schirmann (*Hebrew Poetry in Spain and Provence* [Heb], vol. 1, p. 471) tentatively classifies it as a *selihah*, or penitential poem. Its Hebrew acrostic reads "Yehudah Levi." The dove in the Hebrew liturgical tradition is — by virtue of its tenderness and poignant cooing (which imply suffering) — associated with the congregation of Israel. (See Hosea 11:11 and Isaiah 39:14 and 60:8.) In the Andalusian context it also carries overtones of the spring garden and all that implied (and in the secular Hebrew realm it is, as in the Song of Songs 2:14, 5:12, and 6:9, associated with the beloved). The rhythm of the opening in Hebrew and English alike mimics the fluttering and flight of the dove. For all its involvement with God's distance, the poem registers a remarkably intense and even intimate sense of God's presence through absence. The image of powerlessness presented in the poem is also critical to HaLevi's philosophy of surrender to the divine. See Salo Baron, "Yehudah HaLevi: An Answer to a Historic Challenge," *Jewish Social Studies* 3:3 (1941), pp. 243–72, esp. p. 265, and HaLevi, *Kuzari* 1:113ff. and 4:21ff.: "The Rabbi: I see thee reproaching us with our degradation and poverty, but the best of other religions boast of both. Do they not glorify Him who said: He who smites thee on the right cheek, turn to him the left also; and he who takes away thy coat, let him have thy shirt also. He and his friends and followers, after hundreds of years of contumely, flogging and slaying, attained their well-known success, and just in these things they glorify. This is also the history of the founder of Islam and his friends, who eventually prevailed, and became powerful. The nations boast of these, but not of these kings whose power and might are great, whose walls are strong, and whose chariots are terrible. Yet our relation to God is a closer one than if we had reached greatness already on earth" (trans. Hirschfeld). See Scheindlin, *Gazelle*, pp. 73ff., for more detailed commentary.

Line 1: Psalms 56:1: "Upon the silenced dove, of those that are far away" (*The Hirsch Psalms* [Jerusalem and New York, 1997]). In the Targum, the community of Israel far from its cities is likened to a silent dove.

7: It was thought that the redemption would come a thousand years after the destruction of the Temple, i.e., 1068 (calculated in the Jewish calendar from 68 C.E. rather than 70).

12–13: Isaiah 53:12: "He bared his soul unto death."

14–17: Jeremiah 20:9: "And if I say: 'I will not make mention of Him, nor speak any more in His name,' then there is in my heart as it were a burning fire shut up in my bones."

24: Job 14:21.

27: Psalms 50:3.

Ashkenaz

Information for the headnote is drawn from the following sources: Scholem, *Major Trends*, chap. 3; Joseph Dan, *Kabbalah: A Very Short Introduction* (Oxford, 2007), pp. 20–22, *Shir HaYihud: The Hymn of Divine Unity, with the Kabbalistic commentary of R. Yom Tov Lipmann Muelhausen* [Heb], introduction by J. Dan (Jerusalem, 1981), Dan, *Heart and the Fountain*, pp. 23–27, and Dan, *Studies in the Literature of German Pietists* [Heb] (Tel Aviv, 1975), pp. 62ff.; Ivan Marcus, *Piety and Society: The Jewish Pietists of Medieval Germany* (Leiden, 1981), Marcus, "Shir HaKavod," in *My People's Prayer Book: Traditional Prayers, Modern Commentaries*, ed. Lawrence A. Hoffman (Woodstock, Vt., 1997–2007), vol. 10, pp. 180–93, and Marcus, "The Historical Meaning of Hasidei Ashkenaz," in *Jewish Spirituality*, ed. Arthur Green, 2 vols. (New York, 1986), vol. 2, pp. 103–14; Elliot R. Wolfson, *Along the Path: Studies in Kabbalistic Myth, Symbolism, and Hermeneutics* (Albany, N.Y. 1995), pp. 1–62, 111–87; Ismar Elbogen, *Jewish Liturgy: A Comprehensive History*, trans. Raymond P. Scheindlin (1913; Philadelphia, 1993), pp. 288–90; and Ephraim Hazan, *Poems and Prayers from the Siddur* [Heb] (Jerusalem, 1979), pp. 85–93.

Quotations are from the following sources: *to the consternation of neighbors in the synagogue*: Marcus, "Shir HaKavod," p. 180; *He maintains His silence*: Scholem, *Major Trends*, p. 112.

Hymn of Divine Glory

Text: A. M. Habermann, *Shirei HaYihud veHaKavod* [Heb] (Jerusalem, 1948), p. 46.

The hymn comprises a conclusion to the long Hymn of Unity and was at one point recited daily, despite the objections of prominent figures who considered it too exalted to risk becoming "hackneyed through overuse." Today it is largely read in Ashkenazi circles at the end of the Sabbath morning prayers, with the ark opened, out of respect for its message, which combines an expression of longing and awe, desire and fear, with anthropomorphic descriptions of God's glory (*kavod*).

The concept of glory around which the poem takes shape lies at the heart of German Hasidism, which saw it as the aspect of God that is revealed to humankind. Glory is not *entirely* or *exactly* identified in this Pietistic scheme with God as the Creator; it is, in a sense, His first creation, an aspect and extension of Him. The Creator Himself remains unknown and unknowable, but His glory, "the great radiance" which is called at times the Shekhinah (and at other times the *ru'ah hakodesh*, "holy spirit"), consists of a "primeval light" that is very much a part of God revealed variously to prophets and mystics through the ages. The tripartite division of the Godhead is perhaps best summed up by Ivan Marcus: "On the one hand, God, the pure Oneness, is *borei* . . . 'the creator.' On the other hand, there is indeed a *kavod*, but far from being a created entity separate from God, the *kavod* is part of God—and it has two aspects facing in different directions. The part that is turned away from humanity, 'God's face,' considered the upper *kavod*, is the inaccessible part of God that one cannot apprehend and is high up. The lower *kavod*, on the other hand, 'God's back,' is like a screen onto which God projects various images for the benefit of the prophets and other mortals. When one prays, it is either to the creator or . . . to the upper *kavod*. When the poet addresses a divine 'You,' this should be understood either as the *borei* ('creator') or as the upper *kavod*" (Marcus "Shir HaKavod," pp. 181–84; see also Wolfson, *Through a Speculum*, chap. 5).

"The Hymn of Divine Glory" subtly addresses the problem of how to imagine, address, know, and perhaps even see the invisible and unknowable God who is essentially beyond conception. The author cast his solution in the form of a fairly straightforward poem, because, for all its theosophic underpinnings, "The Hymn of Divine Glory" was intended for public recital and not for absorption by a select circle of initiates. Its plain and almost populist prosody is pitched accordingly. It climbs along a ladder of accessible, unmetered rhymed couplets—here set out as quatrains that echo the rhyme of the original. The lack of a regular meter notwithstanding, a pronounced cadence of four stresses (and four words) per line drives the poem on. An alphabetical acrostic is sandwiched between introductory and concluding verses. The following commentary is particularly indebted to the detailed and excellent annotations prepared by Arthur Green (*Keter* [Princeton, 1997], pp. 106–20), Ivan Marcus ("Shir HaKavod," pp. 180–93), and Ephraim Hazan (*Poems and Prayers*, pp. 85–93).

Lines 1–4: Literally, "I offer up sweet hymns or melodies." The line echoes two famous biblical verses relating to David: Psalms 42:2 introduces the erotic overtones of the longing involved ("As the hart longs for streams of water,/so my soul longs for You, O God"), and messianic overtones to the poem are established by the poem's opening—*an'im zemirot*—which alludes to 2 Samuel 23:1, where David is the *na'im zemirot*, or "sweet singer" (of Israel). The Hebrew also contains a play on the words for "weave" (*a'arog*—with an *aleph*) and "yearn" (*a'arog* with an *ayin*); while not translated directly, a similar slippage is hinted at between "hymns" and "yearns" in the English. The word "weave" may be alluding to Yehudah's notion of mystical prayer and also to that of his disciple, Eleazar of Worms; the former believes that the letters, words, and names of the prayers were woven together to create "a universal numerical harmony that extended to every realm of existence," and that a semiotic analysis of the text will reveal this harmony (Dan, *Heart and the Fountain*

p. 26; see also Scholem, *Major Trends*, pp. 100–103). The five introductory stanzas (ll. 1–20) make it clear that one praises God not because He needs to be praised but because one longs to be close to Him and, in that longing, to tell of His greatness.

5–8: The Hebrew here, *razei sodekha* (the mysteries or secrets of your secrets or councils), recalls Eleazar of Worms's writing in numerous places, especially his *Sefer HaHokhmah* (Book of Wisdom): "Whoever knows the secret of [the crown and the Shekhinah] has a place in the world to come" (Green, *Keter*, 127).

9–12: The term *kavod* is introduced and repeated numerous times in the following stanzas (ll. 9–24), with variations on its root (i.e., "glory" and "honor"). Marcus suggests that the repetition underscores the "frustration . . . of having to settle" for the lower, *visible* kavod, when the deeper desire is for a vision of the invisible upper glory ("Shir HaKavod," p. 187). The intimate aspect of German Pietism is also evident here—in contrast, for example, to what we find in *Sefer Yetzirah* or in the Heikhalot literature. Apart from the language of intense and ultimately unrequitable longing, one notes, for example, the absence in this poem of any angels whatsoever—that is, there are no intermediaries (Green, *Keter*, p. 118). All of which is to say that attachment and intimacy are key to the experience of prayer in its mystical aspect.

17–20: In the context of a discussion of German Pietism in *Major Trends*, Scholem writes: "A direct prayer to the Creator . . . is possible only in the world to come. In this life, prayer can be 'directed only towards the Shekhinah, the spirit of the living God,' i.e., His 'holiness,' which in spite of everything is almost defined as the Logos" (p. 116); the Shekhinah here is identified with the kavod. Marcus notes the allusion to Moses' close brush with the divine presence (*kavod*) in Exodus 33:22–23: "As my presence passes by, I will . . . shield you with my hand. . . . Then I will take my hand away and you will see my back; but my face must not be seen" ("Shir HaKavod," p. 187).

21–24: "Your prophets' . . . secrets" are the Torah and its secrets, which is to say, the word of God and the Logos-like aspect of the visible glory unfolded in images (as we'll see) that give God's glory form. Green notes the relevance of *Genesis Rabbah* 27:1: "Great is the power of the prophets, who liken the formed to its Former," i.e., they use the language of man to describe man's maker (*Keter*, p. 111). Scholem: "The finite word of man is aimed at the infinite word of God" (*Major Trends*, p. 116). The poet also begins to make repeated use of the *d-m-h* root, indicating "image," "imagination," "likeness," "form"—as once again the reflective or imaginative faculty is central to the mystical expression.

29–32: With this stanza and in the descriptions that follow we move into the heart of the poem's attempt to account for man's experience of God's visible and inner glory, His revealed and unknowable aspects. The key notion here is that God is not seen as either unknowably transcendent *or* palpably immanent. He is both at once. This somewhat startling sense of God is given expression in a passage from one of the hymns of Divine Unity (for Tuesday): "All is in You, and You are in all; You fill all things and encompass them." Scholem notes Augustine's parallel notion—which was popular with thirteenth-century mystics—that God is closer to His creatures than the latter are to themselves, or in Scholem's own formulation: "God is closer to the universe and to man than the soul is to the body" (*Major Trends*, p. 108; see also Dan's Hebrew introduction to *Shir HaYihud*; Wolfson, *Through a Speculum*, pp. 188ff., and esp. pp. 196ff.). See also Yehudah HaLevi, "Where Will I Find You," ll. 17–20, in this anthology.

33–36: Cf. *Sefer Yetzirah* and Ibn Gabirol's "He Dwells Forever," both above.

37–42: A series of anthropomorphic descriptions follow, instances of man's attempt to account for God's various aspects; all are taken from Scripture and the midrashic literature, where Rashi, for instance, notes in his commentary to Exodus 20:2 that God has been depicted as "a mighty man of war" (in this case implying youth) and an old man full of compassion (giving the Torah), "Thus the Divine Glory changed according to circumstances. . . . Do not say there are two divine beings" (*Pentateuch with Targum Onkelos*). Green (*Keter*, p. 111, relying on another midrash) reads this as also alluding to Israel in its youth (coming out of Egypt) and then, forty years later, in its old age (at Sinai). Cf. also Song of Songs 5:10ff. and Daniel 7:9: "And one that was ancient of days did sit: His raiment was as white snow, and the hair of his head like pure wool." The word "head" (*rosh*) and head imagery in general become dominant here and something of an obsession. *Rosh* appears twelve times, and the attendant imagery proliferates: hair, helmet, curls, the brow, and, above all, crowns. As though to bring the Hebrew reader's attention to this, the alphabetical acrostic doubles the letter *resh* (which begins *rosh* and sounds like it). Scholars have noted the importance of the image of the head in the mystical context—where in the history of Jewish mysticism it has connoted, among other things, the upper divine realm of existence (later on, the *sefirah* Keter, or crown), the first letter of the unknowable divine name (*yod*), and phallic masculinity (and sometimes masculine potency). "It is known that the human being is the most glorious of the creatures, and the head of a human the most glorious of all the limbs, and so it is above" (Eleazar of Worms, in Green, *Keter*, pp. 91ff.). See Elliot R. Wolfson, *Circle in the Square: Studies in the Use of Gender in Kabbalistic Symbolism* (Albany, N.Y., 1995), for numerous other instances and detailed discussion; see also Wolfson, *Through a Speculum*, p. 43, and Wolfson, "Images of God's Feet: Some Observations on the Divine Body in Judaism," in *People of the Body: Jews and Judaism from an Embodied Perspective*, ed. Howard Eilberg-Schwartz (Albany, N.Y., 1992), p. 157. Holiness in stanza 12 (ll. 45–48) is the third aspect of God's visible reality according to the Pietists (Scholem, *Major Trends*, p. 115). Also important here is that much of the anthropomorphic imagery emphasizes intimacy: lines 49–56 and 81–84 in particular.

45–48: The address shifts to the third person. It is possible to understand this simply as a distinct description of the warrior to which the poet likens God, but given the way the poem develops in subsequent stanzas, and the return to the intimate second-person address toward the end (ll. 97–100), it's more likely that the adoption of the third person is indicative both of the multiple facets of God (as the poet conceives Him) and the distance implied by this more majestic and awesome image. The image of the helmet and battle can be read against the historical background of the poem's composition: the Crusades and their decimation of Jewish communities in the Rhineland. Green notes that calls for vengeance are common in the literature of the day. That said, the "salvation" sought is general and goes beyond the historical circumstances (Green, *Keter*, p. 112).

49–52: The image of the dew in the hair is taken from Song of Songs 5:2, where its erotic dimension is clear: "Open to me, my sister, my love, my dove, my undefiled; for my head is filled with dew, my locks with the drops of the night." Green and others see this as explicitly relating to sexual arousal in the Song of Songs, and unconsciously so in the "Hymn of Divine Glory." The blurring of sexual borders is of interest. Even though the poem is written by a male poet using the first person, the poem is recited in the synagogue by the grammatically feminine Knesset Israel, or "Congregation of Israel," to the masculine deity. Dew is also an image of resurrection. See Isaiah 26:5 and the Talmudic/midrashic verse: "When God resurrects the dead, He shakes out His locks and the dew falls" (*Song of Songs Rabbah* 5:2). Joseph Dan (*Heart and the Fountain*, p. 109) cites a related passage from Eleazar of Worms's *Sodei Razayya* that is too striking not to quote at length:

> "The Root of Love [of God]: It is to love God when the soul is over-flowing with love and is bound with the bonds of love in great happiness. This happiness drives away from a person's heart the pleasures of the body and the enjoyment of worldly things. . . . The enjoyment of his children and wife become like nothing compared with the immense love of God. [What he feels is] more than like a young man who did not have sexual intercourse with a woman for a long time, and he craves her and desires her and his heart is burning to be with her, and because of his great love and desire when he has intercourse with her his semen shoots from him like an arrow and his enjoyment is supreme. All this is like nothing compared with the following of God's will, and making others worthy, and sanctifying himself and surrendering himself to God in his love. . . . and he . . . devotes all his energy to fulfilling the will of God and singing songs of praise expressing the joy of the love of God."

53–56: God is adorned or glorified by the delight He takes in the poet or congregation (the verb is reflexive in the Hebrew), and His splendor becomes a crown (or adornment) for them. See also lines 81–84, for the same structure of mutuality. The theme of coronation begins to dominate the poem here, again, in a much more intimate manner than it does in the Heikhalot literature.

57–64: Green, arguing for the importance of the Merkavah tradition to the German Pietists, notes that while the image of the warrior's head having the semblance of choice gold comes from Song of Songs 5:11 and Psalms 21:4, it also derives from the *Shi'ur Komah* literature. That strain of mystical literature concerns itself with, among other things, the measurements of the divine body: "The crown on His head is 500,000 [parasangs—one parasang is roughly three miles] by 500,000; Israel is its name. On the precious stone between its staves *Yisra'el ami* (Israel is my people) is inscribed. . . . 'His head is like finest gold'" (Green, *Keter*, pp. 52, 60).

65–68: The hair is thick, and the intended impression conjures Samson, in Judges 16:13 and 19, and the lover of Song of Songs 5:11. On the whole, says Green, the image of masculine virility in the poem is "rare in postbiblical and medieval Jewish descriptions of God (before Kabbalah)" (*Keter*, p. 116).

69–72: Literally, "The habitation of Righteousness," alluding to the Temple, per Jeremiah 31:23: "Abode of righteousness, O Holy Mountain." The Hebrew for "highest joy" is, literally, "the head of delights"—where the feminine congregation asks to be kept.

73–76: "Resplendence" here might also be translated as "crown." The Hebrew yields both. Cf. Isaiah 62:3.

81–84: See ll. 65–68. The "glory" of this stanza most likely also refers to the tefillin, or phylacteries, which are wrapped around the arm and the head in prayer. See stanza 23, where this is made explicit. God is at one and the same time indescribable and unknowable (ll. 17–20 and 39–36) and as close as can be (i.e., He is virtually wrapped around the worshipper). Cf. HaLevi's "Where Will I Find You" and "Lord, [All My Desire]," above.

85–88: Usually an image of messianic redemption—the Messiah as "ruddy." Here, as Green observes (*Keter*, p. 114), the figures of the lover and warrior come together in an image of vengeance. Edom stands in medieval Hebrew literature for Christianity.

89–92: "At the back of his head" refers to the back of God's head, which is all that Moses sees (Exodus 33:23), and it is also where the tefillin strap is tied. The overtone in the English is of course that it is also kept figuratively "at the back of his mind."

105–8: Marcus notes the allusion to *Hagigah* 13b and the notion that a crown for God can be made out of prayer. The comparison of prayer to sacrifice (and its rising incense) is begun here.

109–12: An untranslated play on words in the Hebrew associates "the poor" (*rash*) to the imagery relating to "head" (*rosh*); by way of compensation, the English weave tightens here to link "prayer" and "poor" and other related elements.

113–16: The allusion is, says Green, primarily to God, but it may also suggest the Messiah (*Keter*, p. 116). I am inclined to think it's the latter here.

117–20: In *Sodei Razayya*, Eleazar suggests that it is the *kavvanah*, or the intention of the worshipper and the direction of his heart, that enables the prayer to rise like incense (Green, *Keter*, 123). The nodding of the head to express acceptance is found in *Berakhot* 3a and 7a (where God indicates acceptance of Rabbi Ishmael's prayer amid the ruins of Jerusalem); Wolfson reads it in the context of erotic interplay. It also involves the culmination of the imagery relating to the head.

121–24: The poem ends with a very close echo of its opening, forming what would imply an endless loop of longing and praise.

The Kabbalah in Spain

Information for the headnote is drawn from the following sources: Joseph Dan, *Kabbalah: A Very Short Introduction* (Oxford, 2007), pp. 23–31 and 36–37, *The Heart and the Fountain: An Anthology of Jewish Mystical Experiences*, ed. Joseph Dan (Oxford, 2002), pp. 27–31, and *The Early Kabbalah*, ed. and introduced Joseph Dan, texts trans. Ronald C. Keiner (New York, 1986), pp. 28–37; Gershom Scholem, *Kabbalah* (New York,

1974), pp. 42–60, Scholem, *Origins of the Kabbalah*, ed. R. J. Zwi Werblowsky, trans. Allan Arkush (Princeton, 1987), pp. 365ff., and Scholem, "The Kabbalah of R. Ya'akov and R. Yitzhak HaKohen" [Heb], *Madda'ei HaYahadut* 2 (1927), pp. 165–290; Peter Schäfer, *Mirror of His Beauty: Feminine Images of God from the Bible to the Early Kabbalah* (Princeton, 2002), pp. 10–11, 118–34, and 169–72; Ezra Fleischer, "The Gerona School of Poetry," and Bernard Septimus, "'Open Rebuke and Concealed Love': Nahmanides and the Andalusian Tradition," both in *Nahmanides: Explorations in His Religious and Literary Virtuosity*, ed. Isadore Twersky (Cambridge, Mass., 1983); *The Bahir: An Ancient Kabbalistic Text Attributed to Rabbi Nehuniah ben HaKana, First Century, C.E.*, trans. and ed. Aryeh Kaplan (New York, 1979), pp. 22–23. See also *The Book Bahir: An Edition Based on the Earliest Manuscripts* [Heb], ed. Daniel Abrams with an introduction by Moshe Idel (Los Angeles, 1994), p. 141, Abrams, *Kabbalistic Manuscripts and Textual Theory: Methodologies of Textual Scholarship and Editorial Practice in the Study of Jewish Mysticism* (Jerusalem and Los Angeles, 2010), pp. 135ff., and Abrams, "Bahir, Sefer ha-," in *Encyclopedia Judaica* (2007), vol. 3, pp. 62–63. Abrams argues that the book emerged in its present form in Ashkenazic circles and may have been almost completely ignored in Provence. Furthermore, he notes that it was never really "a book" by a single author, so much as a midrash-like body of material that circulated. On the development of the Kabbalists' notion of the Shekhinah and its relation to the material in the *Bahir*, see Abrams, *Kabbalistic Manuscripts*, pp. 118–97.

Quotations are from the following sources: *"They asked him"*: the *Bahir*, sect. 43, in Abrams, *Book Bahir* [Heb] (part 1, sects. 62–63 in Kaplan, *Bahir*, and p. 212)—the translation is mine, based on Abrams, Kaplan, and Scholem, *Origins of the Kabbalah*, pp. 168–69, Scholem, *On the Mystical Shape of the Godhead* (New York, 1991), pp. 162–63, and Abrams, *Kabbalistic Manuscripts*. Schäfer calls this "one of the most important texts about the Shekhinah" (*Mirror of His Beauty*, p. 130); *counter poetics . . . poetry became poetry*: Fleischer, "Gerona School of Poetry," p. 167. *[In] the magnificient opening*: Septimus, "'Open Rebuke and Concealed Love,'" pp. 28–29; *a mystical hymn . . . streams forth*: Gershom Scholem,

Major Trends in Jewish Mysticism (New York, 1941), p. 239. Scholem also translated the poem into German; *mythic descriptions of evil . . . end-time: Early Kabbalah*, ed. and introduced Dan, p. 36; *a mysterious hymn*: Scholem, "Kabbalah of R. Ya'akov and R. Yitzhak HaKohen" [Heb], p. 173; *opening of the heart*: Scholem, "Kabbalah of R. Ya'akov and R. Yitzhak HaKohen" [Heb], p. 173; *with the Kohen brothers*: *Early Kabbalah*, ed. and introduced Dan, p. 37.

The Ramban's "Before the World Ever Was" may have been preceded by a poem by the Provençal philosopher Asher ben David that treats the *sefirot* in more explicit and specifically Kabbalistic fashion. Ben David places his poem at the front of his *Sefer HaYihud* (*R. Asher ben David: His Complete Works and Studies in His Kabbalistic Thought, Including the Commentaries to the Account of Creation by the Kabbalists of Provence and Gerona* [Heb], ed. Daniel Abrams [Los Angeles, 1996], pp. 25–32, 49ff). While ben David's poem isn't compelling as literature, it names the sefirot and demonstrates their dynamic nature as "vessels for the activity of God" (Scholem, *Kabbalah*, p. 101). This seems to be one of the earliest instances of the sefirot's names (*Sefer Yetzirah* does not employ this terminology), and as such it is one of the first explicitly Kabbalistic poems:

> Thirty-two paths in the book were cut.
> He counted and then recounted his spheres.
> Deeply furrowed are the ways He engraved,
> and as a garden they'll flourish and flower.
> Thirty-two they are in number.

Ben David goes on to list the ten sefirot (which are added to the twenty-two letters to get the thirty-two paths, as we saw in *Sefer Yetzirah*). The names of the sefirot will vary somewhat from school to school, but on the whole they are cast along the lines we find in ben David's poem: The first is unknowable (in later formulations it would be widely referred to as Keter, or crown). The second is Hokhmah (wisdom). The third is Binah (understanding). The fourth is Hesed (grace or love). The fifth is Gevurah (power, or judgment). The sixth is Tiferet (beauty). The seventh is Netzah (endurance). The eighth is Hod (splendor). The ninth is Yesod (foundation). And the tenth is the Shekhinah (the feminine presence or aspect of the divine—in later formulations this is known as Malkhut, or kingdom). My thanks to Daniel Abrams for bringing this poem to my attention and discussing it with me.

The doctrine of the sefirot, Scholem notes, "ultimately became the backbone of Spanish Kabbalistic teaching" (*Kabbalah*, p. 99; see also p. 104), and it would, as that system grew increasingly complex, saturate Kabbalistic writing from then on. In this full-fledged Kabbalistic scheme the ten sefirot constitute the manifestation of "the God *who expresses himself*. The God who 'called' His powers to reveal themselves named them, and, it could be said, called Himself also by appropriate names" (p. 99). They are "configurations of the divine power" (p. 36). In essence, the sefirot are identical with God, and unlike the Neoplatonic emanations, they never leave the divine realm (pp. 101ff.). Moshe Idel refers to them as "either part of the divine structure or directly related to the divine essence, serving as its vessels or instruments" (*Kabbalah: New Perspectives* [New Haven, 1988], p. 112). Of particular relevance to a consideration of the *poetry* of Kabbalah is Scholem's observation that "the process by which the power of emanation manifests itself from concealment into revelation is paralleled by the manifestation of divine speech from its inner essence in thought, through sound that as yet cannot be heard, into the articulation of speech" (*Kabbalah*, p. 99). As in the world of divine expression, so too in the world of human expression. For more on the sefirot and their names, their nature, and their presence in Kabbalistic poetry, see "The Safed Circle," and specifically the poem by Avraham ben Maimon, "Hidden God," below.

Before the World Ever Was

Text: *Kitvei Rabbeinu Moshe ben Nahman*, ed. H. Chavel (Jerusalem, 1963), vol. 1, p. 392. A *selihah* (penitential poem). Acrostic: Moshe ben Nahman Yerondi Hazak.

Nahmanides' poetic output was slim (only eighteen poems are extant), but it's clear that poetry was for him neither window dressing nor diversion. On the contrary, his poems give every indication that their author possessed considerable literary gifts. While there is some disagreement as to just how Kabbalistic this particular poem is, the vision it presents is undoubtedly the product of a mystical consciousness. Hayyim Schirmann writes that the link to mysticism and Kabbalah is palpable (*History of Hebrew Poetry in Christian Spain and Southern France* [Heb], ed. Ezra Fleischer [Jerusalem, 1997], pp. 326–27). Septimus adds (to the passage quoted in the headnote) that the poem "constitutes a kind of Kabbalistic *tikkun* (or correction) of the traditional Andalusian genre of soul-poems having a tripartite structure and progression: the soul's origin in the upper world; its earthly exile; and ultimate reunion with its heavenly source." Ezra Fleischer, on the other hand, argues that previous scholars have read the poem incorrectly, and that in fact its imagery and terminology are Neoplatonic and not Kabbalistic at all. Scholem's later writing contains a sentence that would seem to resolve the question—though it isn't clear what he's referring to exactly, and closer study would be needed to support his claim that "no matter how much he spoke of God, in his writings, Nahmanides managed extremely well without the [Kabbalistic] term *'en-sof* [the infinite], using a strictly orthodox language in spite of the fact that everything he had to say about God's actions really referred to his sefirotic manifestations only" (*Origins of the Kabbalah*, p. 433). Elsewhere Scholem distinguishes helpfully between Neoplatonic and Kabbalistic theories of Emanation: In the Neoplatonic system "the stages of emanation . . . are not conceived as processes within the Godhead. . . . In Kabbalah, emanation as an intermediate stage between God and creation was reassigned to the Divine" (*Kabbalah*, p. 98). One other tangential note here is something that the Ramban suggests in his commentary to *Sefer Yetzirah*, where he characterizes the sefirot as the interiority or innerness of the letters [*penimi'utam*]: "The [ten] sefirot [of *Sefer Yetzirah*] are invisible within the [twenty-two] letters and go out with them along a single path. . . . The [thirty-two] paths are narrow [subtle] trails, and from the head of the trail no man can see where he is going to go" (Gershom Scholem, "Chapters in the History of Kabbalistic Literature" [Heb], *Kiryat Sefer* 6 [1929–30], pp. 401–2). While the poem is about the emanation of the soul, not the sefirot or Neoplatonic levels of existence, these Kabbalistic and philosophical notions hover behind it. The poem was incorporated into the Rosh HaShanah rite in a number of communities and into the Yom Kippur rite in others (*Kitvei Rabeinu Moshe ben Nahman*, ed. H. Chavel [Jerusalem, 1963], pp. 382–84).

At least one other Nahmanides poem appears to allude to the esoteric tradition as well—the end of "One Hundred Verses," which pays tribute to the martyrdom and Pietistic ideal of Hasidei Ashkenaz, including the movement's mystical dimension. Another Hebrew poet of interest in this circle is Meshullem DePiera, who was either aligned with the new Spanish Kabbalists or a member of their circle. His poetry is accomplished but, it seems, only marginally related to anything explicitly Kabbalistic. See Peter Cole, *The Dream of the Poem: Hebrew Poetry from Muslim and Christian Spain, 950–1492* (Princeton, 2007), pp. 229–32 and notes.

Lines 1–4: The poem is preceded by the scriptural verse: "I say, My work is concerning a king"—or, in the NJPS version, "I speak my poem to a king" (Psalms 45:2), which is then sung as a refrain after each stanza. All subsequent quatrains of the poem end with the word *king*. The speaker in the poem at this point is the soul, which in both the Neoplatonic and early Kabbalistic worldviews was sent down from its source on high and will return to it at death. In that kabbalistic context *me'ayin* (from nothing) in line 3 might allude to the sefirah of Keter, something that would be entirely appropriate at this place in the poem. Nehemiah 13:6: "In the thirty-second year of Artaxerxes, king of Babylon, I went unto the king, and after certain days asked I leave of the king."

5–8: Esther 3:9: "to bring it into the king's treasuries." Just as the soul will be "withdrawn" at the end, so in the beginning it is drawn out and endowed with form from "heaven's foundation." The Hebrew verb here is *limshokh* (to draw), which in the thought of Nahmanides indicates creation through emanation (*atzilut*). Scholem writes: "This influx [of the sefirot] is given the name *hamshakhah* ('drawing out'), that is to say, the entity which is emanated is drawn out from its source. . . . According to Nahmanides (in his commentary to Numbers 11:17) and his school, the . . . term *atzilut* expresses the particular position of this emanation.

The term is understood as deriving from *etzel* ('nearby,' or 'with'), for even the things that are emanated remain 'by Him,' and act as potencies manifesting the unit of the Emanator" (*Kabbalah*, pp. 102–3).

10: Zechariah 4:3. Some commentators suggest that the image of left and right involves an allusion to Kabbalistic concepts, though it isn't clear what they stand for exactly. Traditionally in Kabbalistic theory, the left is the side of the feminine, strict justice, the nations, and darkness, while the right is associated with the masculine, mercy, Israel, and light.

11–12: With this stanza the drama of emanation begins in full force. Nehemiah 3:15: "and the wall of the pool of Siloam by the king's garden." This is sometimes understood to refer to Siloam's pool in Jerusalem or simply an "irrigation pool." Here too a Kabbalistic reading might be applied, if only retroactively: just as in the first stanza *me'ayin* (from nothing) might allude to Keter, so "the palace [or King's] garden" can be seen as the lowest sefirah of Malkhut.

13–16: Now the speaker seems to be both the soul and man. Nehemiah 2:6: "For the king said unto me . . . 'For how long shalt thy journey be? And when wilt thou return?'"

17–20: Proverbs 24:21: "My son, fear thou the Lord and the King."

21–24: 2 Samuel 3:37: "It was not of the king to slay Abner."

25–28: Nehemiah 2:9: "I gave them the king's letters"—i.e., what the King has recorded.

29–32: Ecclesiastes 8:2: "I counsel thee: Keep the king's command."

33–36: I.e., I'll be judged for sins I've committed that went unseen. Daniel 1:10: "I fear my Lord the king."

37–40: The subject is the now-penitent "heart" of line 33. Proverbs 25:5: "Take away the wicked from before the king."

41–44: *Avot* 4:22: "Despite your wishes you are going to give a full accounting before the king of kings, the Holy One, blessed be He."

49–52: Ezra 8:22: "For I was ashamed to ask of the king."

53–56: Literally, "the body in its prison" (i.e., the ground), as in Psalms 142:8. Proverbs 30:28: "Yet is she in the king's palace."

57–60: "She" refers to the soul. 1 Kings 3:28: "And all Israel heard of the judgment which the king had judged."

61–64: Scholem comments: "The will reverses its direction and brings all things back to their original essentiality, 'like someone who draws in his breath.' But this return of all things to their proprietor is also their return to the mystical pure Nothingness" (*Origins of the Kabbalah*, p. 449 and n. 201). Nehemiah 2:8: "Asaph the keeper of the King's park."

Prayers for the Protection and Opening of the Heart

Text: Scholem, "Kabbalah of R. Ya'akov and R. Yitzhak HaKohen" [Heb]: Poem 1: p. 224, ll. 9–10; Poem 2: p. 225, ll. 10–11; Poem 3: pp. 225–26, ll. 30–35.

The longer work from which these poems are excerpted has been attributed to Ya'akov HaKohen because it is copied out in manuscript as the continuation of a prayer clearly indicated as being by Ya'akov, but it is impossible to attribute the latter to him with any degree of certainty. The first poem translated here comprises the opening section of what Scholem printed in his 1927 monograph-length article containing the complete extant works of the brothers. The third poem is an excerpt from the final section of the prayer.

The poems are written out in lines of prose but there are clear prosodic markers that justify their being treated as poetry: full (if not always evenly deployed) rhyme, an almost regular cadence (generally four or five stresses and Hebrew words per unit), and a conspicuous structural integrity.

Poem 1: "May the Name send its hidden radiance": The prayer introduces the Name (of God) as the active power in the poem.

Poem 2: The Name of God in question is specified: Ehyeh Asher Ehyeh, which is usually translated as "I Am That I Am" or "I Will Be What [That] I Will Be." In Kabbalistic thought, the name Ehyeh is associated with Keter, the highest sefirah, which is a link to the Infinite and that which is beyond cognition. Keter is also identified with God's Will, through which the world is made. The dire historical circumstances of the prayer's composition, as well as the messianic dimension of the Kohen brothers' thought, are directly alluded to in the next and final two lines of this section of the prayer (not included here): "Strengthen your children—like lions in your name they call, and send us Elijah, [and] the Messiah of our righteousness, in whose shadow we [might] dwell."

Poem 3: The unpronounceable and utterly unknown Name of God (the Tetragrammaton) is given expression through other names, including Ehyeh.

Line 2: Literally, "will live forever" or "in eternity."

4: "All worlds hang": Discussing thirteenth- and fourteenth-century Kabbalistic thinking in another context (in relation to the Kohen brothers, among other things), Scholem writes that "we can trace the development of a unified doctrine of a series of worlds from above to below forming one basic vector along which creation passes from its primeval point to its finalization in the material world" (*Kabbalah*, pp. 118–19). The image of "grapes in a cluster" appears numerous times in the *Zohar*.

5–6: The Hebrew stanzas from here on involve a subtle play on the root *m-z-l*, which yields "pour forth" (*mezil*) and "fortune" (*mazal*). The English doesn't replicate this directly, but accounts for it tangentially, in acoustic fashion across and down the couplet, linking "blessing" and "dispensation" in the process.

7–8: "Husks" are the *kelippot*, which might also be translated as "shards" or "shells" that contain the forces of evil in the world and must be confronted in the restoration (*tikkun*) of that world. (See Moshe Hallamish, *An Introduction to Kabbalah* [Albany, N.Y., 1999], pp. 174ff., for a discussion of the term and the concept behind it, in relation to the Tree of Life and its kelippah, or bark. Also see R. J. Zwi Werblowsky, "R. Shelomoh Ibn Alkabetz's *Tikkun Tefilot*" [Heb], *Sefunot* 6 [1962], pp. 135–82.) See also Proverbs 3:1–4: "My son, do not forget my teaching. . . . For they bestow on you length of days. Let fidelity and steadfastness not leave you. . . . Write them on the tablet of your mind [heart], and you will find favor and approbation in the eyes of God and man."

10: From the Grace after meals and the Jerusalem Talmud 31, 4:1: "Do not make us reliant on the gifts of flesh and blood, or make us depend for food on men, for the gifts of men are small and their shame is great." In other words, do not make us dependent on charity.

The Zohar

The distinction drawn at the opening of the headnote to these excerpts from the *Zohar* is made by K. E. Grözinger in "Tradition and Innovation in the Concept of Song [the Poem] in the *Zohar*" [Heb], *Mehkerei Yerushalayim beMahshevet Yisrael* 8 (1989), pp. 347–55. The headnote as a whole takes up and builds on Grözinger's analysis. Lilith appears in the Talmud in *Shabbat* 151b, *Eruvin* 100b, and *Niddah* 24b. She appears in the *Zohar* in, among other places, 1:14b; 1:54b; 2:96a; 2:111a; 3:19a; 3:76b. See *Wisdom of the Zohar*, arranged and rendered into Hebrew by Fischel Lachower and Isaiah Tishby; introductions and annotations by Isaiah Tishby, trans. David Goldstein, 3 vols. (Oxford, 1997), vol. 2, pp. 538–43.

Other information for the headnote is drawn from Moshe Idel, "Music," in *Contemporary Jewish Religious Thought*, ed. Paul Mendes-Flohr and Arthur Cohen (New York, 1982), pp. 635–42. Idel notes that "for the Kabbalists . . . the purpose of music clearly transcended any aesthetic consideration. . . . This perspective holds true for all the art forms pertaining to the Jewish experience; aesthetics per se was of no relevance to Jewish theology." Andulsian Hebrew poetry is a notable exception. On the composition of the *Zohar*, see Scholem, *Major Trends*, pp. 157–204, and Scholem, *Kabbalah*, pp. 213–43; Yehudah Liebes, *Studies in the Zohar*, trans. Arnold Schwartz, Stephanie Nakash, and Penina Peli (Albany, N.Y., 1993), pp. 85–138; and Arthur Green, *A Guide to the Zohar* (Stanford, Calif., 2004), pp. 162–68. The position that de Leon was the *Zohar's* author was put forth before Scholem by Heinrich Graetz, among others. Excellent overviews of the reception of the *Zohar* can be found in Boaz Huss, "Admiration and Disgust: The Ambivalent Re-Canonization of the *Zohar* in the Modern Period," in *Study and Knowledge in Jewish Thought*, ed. H. Kreisel (Beer Sheva, 2006), pp. 203–37; Huss, "*Sefer haZohar* as a Canonical, Sacred and Holy Text: Changing Perspectives of the Book of Splendor Between the Thirteenth and Eighteenth Centuries," *Journal of Jewish Thought and Philosophy* 7 (1998), pp. 257–307; and Huss, *Like the Radiance of the Sky: Chapters in the Reception History of the Zohar and the Construction of its Symbolic Value* [Heb] (Jerusalem, 2008), esp. chaps. 1 and 6. (On the topic of antipathy toward Kabbalistic literature in general, see David N. Myers, "Philosophy and Kabbalah in *Wissenschaft des Judentums*: Rethinking the Narrative of Neglect," *Studia Judaica* [*Cluj-Napoca*] 16 [2008], pp. 56–71.) See also Ronit Meroz, "The Middle Eastern Origins of Kabbalah," *Journal for the Study of Sephardic and Mizrahi Jewry* 1 (2007), pp. 39–56. For more on the *matnitin*, see Melila Hellner-Eshed, *A River Flows from Eden: The Language of Mystical Experience in the Zohar* (Stanford, Calif., 2009), pp. 204–51, and Ephraim Gottlieb, "Matnitin and Tosefta in the *Zohar*," in *Studies in the Literature of Kabbalah*, ed. Joseph Hacker [Heb] (Tel Aviv, 1976), pp. 163–214. See also Scholem, *Kabbalah*, pp. 213–43, and Scholem, *On the Kabbalah and Its Symbolism*, trans. Ralph Manheim (New York, 1969), p. 157; Yehudah Liebes, "*Zohar* and Eros" [Heb], *Alpayyim* 9 (1994), pp. 67–119; and *Rabbinic Fantasies: Imaginative Narratives from Classical Hebrew Literature*, ed. David Stern and Mark Jay Mirsky, translations by Norman Bronznick (Philadelphia, 1990), pp. 183–84, for Ben Sira and Lilith's objection to having intercourse in the missionary position. Also see *The Zohar*, trans. Daniel C. Matt, 5 vols. (Stanford, Calif., 2004–9), vol. 1, p. 102, and *Wisdom of the Zohar*, introductions and annotations by Isaiah Tishby, vol. 1, pp. 23–39. For a thorough survey of the evolution of the study of the *Zohar* as a book, see Abrams, *Kabbalistic Manuscripts*, pp. 224ff. Abrams argues that the *Zohar* is not a book at all, but a gathering of fragments or literary units from disparate sources.

Scholem and Liebes both note that many of the matnitin, which are scattered throughout the book, contain a summary of the idea of emanation and other major principles of the *Zohar*, and as such embody "distinctive characteristics of Zoharic consciousness" (Scholem, *Kabbalah*, p. 216; Liebes, "*Zohar* and Eros" [Heb]). Their thrust reflects the book's overall attempt to "preserve the substance of naïve popular faith" (Scholem, *Major Trends*, p. 206) and the *Zohar* circle's desire to combat the elitist nature of earlier Kabbalistic thought in Spain (Huss, *Like the Radiance* [Heb], pp. 38–42).

Quotations are drawn from the following sources: *normal mysticism*: see Max Kadushin, *Worship and Ethics* (Evanston, Ill., 1964), pp. 13ff.; *King bedecked with robes of song . . . song is His Name*: Grözinger, "Tradition and Innovation in the Concept of Song in the *Zohar*," p. 349 (see also *Ma'aseh Merkavah*, in Peter Schäfer, *Synopse zur Hekhalot-Literatur* [Tübingen, 1981], p. 588, and Gershom Scholem, *Jewish Gnosticism, Merkabah Mysticism, and Talmudic Tradition* [New York, 1965], pp. 26, 104–6, 114, and 128); *man doesn't need new poetry*: Grözinger, "Tradition and Innovation in the Concept of Song in the *Zohar*," p. 355; *unbridled and hence baleful impact*: Idel, "Music," p. 638; *Now we must understand that the secret of the quality*: Idel, "Music," p. 639; *For centuries it stood out*: Scholem, *Major Trends*, p. 156; *the divine force cloaked in words*: Hellner-Eshed, *A River Flows*, p. 208; *do not "interpret" . . . they are aroused*: Hellner-Eshed, *A River Flows*, p. 215; *[The Torah] reveals herself to no one*: cited in Hellner-Eshed, *A River Flows*, p. 216, from *Zohar* 2:99a, trans. Daniel C. Matt (*Zohar*, vol. 5, p. 31); *Under the gaze of the Zohar's protagonists*: Hellner-Eshed, *A River Flows*, p. 221; *almost . . . in the form of a mystical novel*: Scholem, *Major Trends*, p. 157; *the actualization of divinity in the world*: Hellner-Eshed, *A River Flows*, p. 207, and see also pp. 222–23; *the Muse of masturbation*: Harold Bloom, *Kabbalah and Criticism* (New York, 1975), p. 46; *infringe on the domain of Eve*: Scholem, *On the Kabbalah and Its Symbolism*, p. 157; *in the hour . . . he should turn*: Scholem, *On the Kabbalah and Its Symbolism*, p. 157.

On Awakening and Drawing Near

Poem 1: **Text**: *Zohar* 1:161b in *Sefer HaZohar* [Heb], ed. Reuven Margaliot (Jerusalem, 1953). For another translation, see Hellner-Eshed, *A River Flows*, p. 212–13.

"And neither look nor see nor know": Hellner-Eshed points out the link to the language of Psalms 115:4–8 mocking idolaters. The same locution appears in the following three sections, and it is repeated numerous times throughout the *Zohar*. It also appears in a prose work identified as being by de León: "I looked at the ways of the people of the world and saw how in all that concerns these [theological] matters, they are enmeshed in foreign ideas and false, strange notions. One generation passes away and another generation comes, but the errors and falsehoods abide forever.

And no one sees and no one hears and no one awakens, for they are all asleep, . . . And when I saw all this I was forced to write and conceal and study so as to reveal [the matter] to every wise man" (cited in Hellner-Eshed, *A River Flows*, p. 222). The abrupt shifts of perspective are typical of the *Zohar*'s style. The first-person plural refers to the Masters of the *Zohar*, who hear the voice. The second- and third-person plurals refer to the sleepers who "do not know."

Poem 2: Text: *Zohar* 1:62b in *Sefer HaZohar* [Heb], ed. Margaliot. For other translations of this passage, see *Zohar*, trans. Matt, vol. 1, pp. 358–59, and Hellner-Eshed, *A River Flows*, p. 215.

"*Fabulous constellations*": A resonant description of the Kabbalists themselves. The three aspects of their souls (their *nefesh* [being/vitality], *ru'ah* [spirit], and *neshamah* [higher soul]) combine to make them what they are, and in turn their own souls are linked and tied to the life of the divine realm. All this is implied by the obscure word which has been rendered in various translations as "constellation" or "cluster." They are fabulous in the ordinary sense, but also in the sense that they are involved with pseudepigraphic or invented teachings and fablelike tales. The Aramaic supports both readings. Likewise the Kabbalists resemble fortifications that can't be breached, so strong is their faith (and so obscure their teaching). The *Zohar* is fond of arcane terms of this sort, the precise meaning of which remains elusive. "*A voice*": from heaven. The heavenly herald is speaking. "*who see without seeing*": Matt cites *Hagigah* 12b: "Rabbi Yose said, 'Woe to creatures, for they see but do not know what they see, they stand but do not know on what they stand.'" Again, Hellner-Eshed (*A River Flows*, p. 210) notes the allusion to the biblical language used to describe an idolater (Psalms 115:4–8). "*the one held by two within*": The "one" is the most profound or highest aspect of the soul, which is wrapped in spirit, which in turn is wrapped in animal vitality. "*While one—the master maker*": The people in question manage to subsist through the power of the lesser aspects of the soul, and—as Matt puts it—they make no effort to attain the deeper spirituality of the inner soul, which emanates from the Shekhinah and is the source of creativity. Matt has extensive Zoharic cross-references to all these points. "*memory's books*": According to Matt, these are "the celestial books in which all human actions are recorded."

Poem 3: Text: *Zohar* 1:121a in *Sefer HaZohar* [Heb], ed. Margaliot. For another translation, see Hellner-Eshed, *A River Flows*, p. 213.

Those who hear the voice are the mystics. All others—those who slumber, including, presumably, the readers—will have to encounter the voice only through the mediation of the text. The penalty for failing to awaken, notes Hellner-Eshed, is erasure from the Book of Life.

Poem 4: Text: *Zohar* 1:4a in *Sefer HaZohar* [Heb], ed. Margaliot. For other translations, see *Zohar*, trans. Matt, 1:4a, vol. 1, pp. 21–22, and Hellner-Eshed, *A River Flows*, p. 214.

"*High, hidden ones*": Probably the angels, or the souls of the righteous. "*You below . . . drowsing*": Humanity. "*Turn darkness to light*": Act righteously. "*The Doe*": The Shekhinah. The King is united each day with the Shekhinah (the lowest *sefirah*) and returns her from exile.

Many other Zoharic passages treat the erotic-hermeneutical penetration of the text mentioned in the headnote. Cf. *Zohar* 2:99a: "Come and see! This is the way of the Torah: At first, when she begins to reveal herself to a human, she beckons him with a hint. If he knows, good; if not, she sends him a message, calling him a fool. Torah says to her messenger: 'Tell that fool to come closer, so I can talk with him!' as it is written: Who is the fool without a heart? Have him turn in here! [Proverbs 9:4] He approaches. She begins to speak with him from behind a curtain she has drawn, words he can follow [i.e., words suitable to his level of understanding], until he reflects a little at a time. . . . Once he has grown accustomed to her, she reveals herself face to face and tells him all her hidden secrets" (cited in *Zohar*, trans. Matt, vol. 5, p. 34 [see also pp. 31ff.], and in Hellner-Eshed, *A River Flows*, p. 216). On Zoharic interpretation, see also *Wisdom of the Zohar*, introductions and annotations by Tishby, pp. 1077ff. Hellner-Eshed summarizes the erotic dynamic as follows: "Beyond the specific purpose of the kabbalists' endeavor (namely, to awaken themselves or to arouse themselves with Torah) lies the ultimate objective: to arouse the feminine dimension of the divine so that the masculine dimension of this reality will in turn be aroused toward her. The arousal of both of these aspects reaches its climax with their union, and the ensuing pleasure of this union prompts the flow of divine plenty into the world" (p. 222).

Incantation Against Lilith

Text: The incantation appears in the *Zohar* to Leviticus 3:19a in *Sefer HaZohar* [Heb], ed. Margaliot.

The passage in Leviticus treats the sin (as in "error") and purification of the priest who is to perform a sacrifice. The discussion of Lilith emerges at a characteristically oblique angle to the scriptural text. The poem is preceded and followed by a discussion of man's original and perfect androgynous state, "the female affixed to his side, and the holy spirit in him spread to each side, thus perfecting itself. Afterwards God sawed the man in two and fashioned his female and brought her to him like a bride. . . . When Lilith saw this she fled, and she is still in the cities of the seacoast trying to snare mankind. . . . She is the ruin of the world. . . . The remedy is this: When a man unites with his wife, he should sanctify his heart to his Master and say, . . ." The incantation follows, and further instructions are offered: "Then for a time he should wrap his head and his wife's head in cloths, and afterward sprinkle his bed with fresh water" (*The Zohar*, trans. Maurice Simon and Dr. Paul P. Levertoff [London, 1934/1973], vol. 4, p. 361). The expectation is that Lilith might approach the marriage bed and seek to cling to the spirits of the couple having intercourse. Various commentators note Lilith's habit of entering into the sheets of the speaker (the husband) in order to gather up the spilled seed or semen of the union, from which she would produce demons. See Yehudah Liebes, "Sefer Tzadik Yesod Olam—A Shabbatian Myth" [Heb], *Da'at* 1 (1978), pp. 105–6, and *Gershom Scholem's Zohar* [Heb], facsimile edition (Jerusalem, 1992), pp. 244–45. Tishby comments on *Zohar* 1:148a–b in *Wisdom of the Zohar*, vol. 1, p. 538: "[This is] the finery that she uses to seduce mankind: her hair is long, red like a lily; her face is white and pink; six pendants hang at her ears; her bed is made of Egyptian flax; all the ornaments of the east encircle her neck: her mouth is shaped like a tiny door . . . she is dressed in purple. . . . The fool turns aside after her." My thanks to Daniel Matt for help with this poem and the Aramaic text.

Line 1: "Veiled in velvet" is Ralph Manheim's rendering of the first words of Scholem's German translation of the poem (in *On the Kabbalah and Its Symbolism*, p. 157). Matt translates, "One wrapped in a bedspread is looming" (in a private communication to me). The Aramaic would seem to refer to a blanket, bedspread, sheet, or even cloak.

2: Manheim and Matt (in a private communication to me) translate, "Loosened, loosened!"—and note that it refers either to Lilith's wrap or the spell she would cast on the couple.

5: "It" refers to the semen that is spilled.

7–8: Lilith dwells at the bottom of the sea. See other Zoharic passages for the connection of Lilith and her host to the seaside, e.g., 3:19a–b: "Now in the depth of the great abyss [the realm of husks] there is a certain hot fiery female spirit named Lilith, who at first cohabited with man. . . . She is in the cities of the sea." Also 3:76b.

9–10: Matt notes that the "holy portion" here may refer to the higher aspects of the soul.

Scholem (*Jewish Gnosticism*, pp. 72–74) also cites the following fourteenth-century charm against Lilith:

> Black sorceress, blackness of darkness,
> blood will you eat and blood will you swallow.
> And like a bull will she bellow.
> And like a bear will she roar.
> And like a wolf she will trample.

As Liebes notes, the harmony of masculine and feminine is a supreme value in the Kabbalah, and its disruption a supreme violation, as severe as the spilling of seed ("*Zohar* and Eros" [Heb], p. 100).

Abulafia and Gikatilla

Information for the headnote is drawn from the following sources: Moshe Idel, *The Mystical Experience in Abraham Abulafia* (Albany, N.Y., 1988), esp. pp. 74, 95–105, 140, and 157–58, Idel, *Language, Torah and Hermeneutics in Abraham Abulafia* (Albany, N.Y., 1989), esp. pp. 1–28, Idel, "The Contribution of Abraham Abulafia's Kabbalah to the Under-

standing of Jewish Mysticism," from *"Major Trends in Jewish Mysticism"*
Fifty Years After, ed. Peter Schäfer and Joseph Dan (Tübingen, 1993),
pp. 117–43, Idel, *Absorbing Perfections: Kabbalah and Interpretation* (New
Haven, 2002), pp. 438–48, Idel, *Messianic Mystics* (New Haven, 1998),
pp. 58–100, and Idel, *Kabbalah in Italy, 1280–1510: A Survey* (New Ha-
ven, 2011), chaps. 1–7; Gershom Scholem, *Major Trends*, pp. 119–55; and
Boaz Huss, "The Formation of Jewish Mysticism and Its Impact on the
Reception of Rabbi Abraham Abulafia in Contemporary Kabbalah," in
*Religion and Its Other: Secular and Sacral Concepts and Practices in In-
teraction*, ed. Heicke Bock, Jörg Feuchter, and Michi Knechts (Frankfurt,
2008), pp. 142–62. See also Colette Sirat, *A History of Jewish Philosophy
in the Middle Ages* (Cambridge, 1990). Information on Gikatilla is drawn
from Scholem, *Kabbalah*, pp. 409–11; Dan, *Heart and the Fountain*, p. 30
(where Dan says that Gikatilla may have contributed to the composition
of the *Zohar*); and Gikatilla, *Gates of Light*, trans. Avi Weinstein, intro-
duction by Moshe Idel (San Francisco, 1994), pp. xvii–xxxiv. See also
Liebes, *Studies in the Zohar*, pp. 99ff.

Quotations are from the following sources: *the sefirot are worse than
the Trinity*: Idel, *Messianic Mystics*, p. 60; *the inner road that emphasizes
. . . the transformation*: Idel, "Contribution of Abraham Abulafia's Kab-
balah," p. 129; *The main message of his Kabbalah*: Idel, "Contribution of
Abraham Abulafia's Kabbalah," p. 139; *Life is the life of the world to come*:
Idel, *Language, Torah, and Hermeneutics*, p. 6, where Idel is quoting
from Abulafia's *Sefer Otzar Eden HaGanuz*; *the Messiah is the human
intellect*: Idel, "Contribution of Abraham Abulafia's Kabbalah," p. 139;
*the arrival of the time of the end . . . arousal of the soul . . . to a spiritual
life*: Idel, *Kabbalah in Italy*, p. 62; *the Messiah is dormant in every person*:
Idel, *Messianic Mystics*, p. 70; *a charlatan: The Essential Kabbalah: The
Heart of Jewish Mysticism*, comp. and trans. Daniel C. Matt (Edison,
N.J., 1997), p. 12; *one of the most interesting apocalypses*: Idel, *Kabbalah
in Italy*, p. 45; *to unseal the soul*: Scholem, *Major Trends*, p. 131 (he notes
the parallel to certain Buddhist theosophical notions); *the natural and
normal borders*: Scholem, *Major Trends*, p. 131; *The principle of language
is not its meanings*: Idel, *Old Worlds, New Mirrors: On Jewish Mysticism
and Twentieth-Century Thought* (Philadelphia, 2010), p. 172; *Translation*

is removal: Walter Benjamin, *Selected Writings*, ed. Marcus Bullock and Michael Jennings, 4 vols. (Cambridge, Mass., 1996–2003), vol. 1, p. 70; *widening of the [initiate's] consciousness . . . divine sphere*: Scholem, *Major Trends*, pp. 135–37 (for more on consciousness skipping, see Scholem, "Chapters from Rabbi Yehudah Albotini's *Sefer Sulam HaAliyya*" [Heb], *Kiryat Sefer* 22 [1945], pp. 161–72; Albotini was one of Abulafia's students, and the single quotation marks inside Scholem's citations set off Albotini's formulations [p. 163]).

from the Book of the Sign

Text: *Sefer haOt: Apokalypse des Pseudo-Propheten und Pseudo-Messias Abraham Abulafia*, ed. A. D. Jellinek, in *Jubelschrift zum Sibzigsten Geburtstage des Prof. Dr. H. Graetz* (Breslau, 1897), sect. 4, p. 70. The Hebrew version printed here is courtesy of Moshe Idel. Its layout replicates that of Idel's text, which was transcribed from the Rome-Angelica Ms.

In making these selections from the some 1,400 lines of verse in the *Book of the Sign* I have tried to give a sense of the poem's various modes (lyrical, narrative, apocalyptic) as well as its shifting rhythms and moods. I have not, however, included any of the most obscure language-centered passages, which are composed entirely of numerologically significant neologisms. Apart from the first section, the excerpts here are taken from the final 350 lines of the poem. My commentary is based in large part on the work of Moshe Idel. The speaker in this poem is one Zekharyahu, whose name is numerologically equivalent to "Avraham," and the book has also been called *Sefer Zekharyahu*. The role of the first person in Abulafia's work is also highly unusual in the context of the Kabbalistic thought of the day. Kabbalah, for Abulafia, was a "path to individual redemption," and his thought was more personal than the national and public doctrine of so many other Kabbalists (Idel, "Contribution of Abraham Abulafia's Kabbalah," p. 138).

Lines 1–14: "And the sign sings": The Hebrew involves anagrammatic play on "the letter" *(ha'ot: hey, aleph, vuv, tav)* and "desire" *(ta'avah: tav, aleph, vuv, hey)*, both of which are formed from four letters:

hey, aleph, vuv, tav; in the same way the poem plays with "sky" (*veha-shahak*) and "desire" (*hahoshek*: "the one who desires"), both of which employ *hey, het, vuv, shin, kuf*. Emphasizing the semantic rather than the transformational aspect of the verses, one might also translate the opening as, "And the letter is longing, / and sky desire / to know the will . . ."

15–30: "And YHVH spoke": Jellinek, sect. 6, p. 81; Idel's manuscript, p. 17a. "The letter" (or "sign") in Abulafia's thought indicates Active Intellect. Kingdom and Law are among the several conflicting forces that appear in the poem, and in Abulafia's thought generally. "Your father and mother" here are most likely Adam and Eve. Throughout his work Abulafia makes extensive use of Hebrew numerology: here, for instance, "my father and mother" = 70 = Blood and Ink = Adam and Eve; "And Ink" = 26 = YHVH; while the full form of the Divine Name (*Yod Hey Vuv Hey*) = 44 = blood. The Sabbath's triumph over the days of the week is the triumph of the sacred over the profane, but also of intellect over imagination, and life over death. In *Sefer HaMelitz*, Abulafia writes: "A line of life, a line of ink; and a line of death, a line of blood." Elsewhere he states plainly: "'Adam and Eve' in numerology equals 'my father and my mother,' and their secret is blood and ink, and this latter is proven by this name, YHVH, and one who merits it will have engraved upon his forehead a *tav* [the Hebrew letter]—for one a *tav* of blood, for the other a *tav* of ink." He goes on to derive the significance of that *tav* from its combination, when it is written out, with ink (*dyo*) in the word *yoledet* (she gives birth), as opposed to that of blood (*dam*) in *muledet* (she is born). In the former (*yoledet*) the letters *yod, lamed*, and *dalet* are combined with the *tav*; in the latter, the same three letters are combined with *mem* (as in blood). A follower of Abulafia's thought, Isaac of Acre (in the thirteenth to mid-fourteenth century) writes: "The blood alludes to the secret of the sacrifices and the prayers, while ink is like the writing of the Torah in ink upon a book." Taking this even further, Abulafia associates "blood" with the Satanic aspect of *demut*, "image" or "imaginary faculty" (e.g., narrative), which had to be destroyed in order to break through to the visionary plane of consciousness. For more details, see Idel, *Mystical Experience*, pp. 96, 99, 155, and 158, and Idel, *Absorbing*

Perfections, appendix 2: "Abraham Abulafia's Torah of Blood and Ink," pp. 438–48.

31–112: "The Lord revealed to me": Jellinek, sect. 7, p. 81; Idel manuscript, pp. 18a–b. The vision of the man and his army is met with fear on the part of the poet-seer, which, as Idel notes, might be taken as either a Jungian fear of encounter with the inner self or a Rudolph Otto-like dread and awe before the "wholly Other." Referring to another of Abulafia's works (*Sitrei Torah*) in which the poet-seer cites *Sefer Yetzirah* 5:2—"the heart in the soul [i.e., within man] is like the king in a battle"—Idel is convinced of the internal nature of the events described. The man himself is an external product of the "intellectual flow." The sign or letter on the man's forehead, which stands for the letters of the Divine Name, becomes the fount of seventy tongues, that is, the Active Intellect. "The Active Intellect is the potion of life for those who are able to receive its flux, while for those who are unable to do so it is the potion of death" (Idel, *Mystical Experience*, p. 97). Likewise, the transformation of the colors here—black to red and vice versa—is indicative of the dual potential of the letter. *Shabbat* 55a: "The Holy One, blessed be He, said to Gabriel: Go and record upon the forehead of the righteous a line of ink, that the angels of destruction may not rule over them; and upon the foreheads of the wicked a line of blood, so that the angels of destruction may rule over them." In this section, at line 58 the phrase "I'd turned into another man" alludes to 1 Samuel 10:7, where prophecy itself transforms Saul. Idel observes that the combination of *mo'ah* (brain), *lev* (heart), and *kaved* (liver) yields, acrostically, *melekh*, or king.

60: The number seventy here alludes to the rabbinic notion that seventy is the symbolic number of the nations and languages of the world (e.g., according to the Talmud, *Sukkah* 55b; and see, for instance, "Nations and Languages, The Seventy," *Jewish Encyclopedia* [New York, 1925]). The "faces of Torah"—or ways of interpreting the Torah—are also seventy (*Numbers Rabbah* 13:15), which is to say, numerous.

84–85: The unabridged poem contains many permutations of the divine name, an extremely elusive if also central Kabbalistic phenomenon. One might think of this incessant permutation as an engagement with constant recalibration of the aspirant's consciousness. It exposes, as it were, both the cybernetic pathways of the divine power that courses through existence and the ultimately unfathomable source of that power.

98–99: "And from the bow of knowing": Jellinek, sect. 7, pp. 82–83; Idel manuscript, pp. 20a–b.

113ff.: "And I lifted my eyes": Jellinek, sect. 7, p. 83; Idel manuscript, pp. 22a–23b.

120: The "stone that drew it" is in Hebrew *even zohelet* (the stone of Zohelet—literally, "a creeping stone") from 1 Kings 1:9, where Adonijah slays sheep and oxen; here Abulafia seems to be describing a magnet. Later in the poem Abulafia says that the arrows are words that pierce the heart; the stone in question (of Zohelet) is the mind disturbed with terror and fear: "And the stone you saw is really a disturbing, shocking thought/mind that draws the word as a stone drags iron along with force."

146: "V.i.s.i.o.n" is marked (in the Hebrew) to indicate an acronym, most likely for *meshalim, remazim, aggadot, halakhot* (parables, symbols, legends, and laws) = *mareh* (vision). Idel notes that *bemareh* (in a vision) is an anagram of the poet's first name—Abraham (*Messianic Mystics*, p. 90, and notes there). The old man in that vision, according to Idel, is Metatron (Prince of the Face or Presence), again, the Active Intellect. What is central is that in this case, as with the previous vision, the encounter is between two men, in (Blakean) human form—not between disembodied intellectual capacities. The Throne of Judgment involves the "two attributes by which the word is led": judgment and mercy.

164ff.: "The name of the first is Kadri'el": Jellinek, sect. 7, p. 84; Idel manuscript, pp. 24b–25a. The names of the kings would seem to reflect the powers they embody and might be understood as the East of God, the Word of God, the Rule of God, and the Era of God. Magdi'el has been identified with Rome and Christianity. Isaac of Acre describes the "four worlds" as emanation, creation, formation, and action. Yaho'el means "God is willing" (Idel, *Mystical Experience*, p. 105). Elliot Wolfson also identifies Yaho'el as Metatron (Wolfson, *Abraham Abulafia, Kabbalist and Prophet* [Los Angeles, 2000], p. 101).

171: Ro'i'el (God sees me) has the same numerological value as Abraham.

177: Idel: "There can be no doubt that the fifth king is the Messiah" (*Messianic Mystics*, p. 90). The word "fifth" (*hamishi*) is an anagram of Messiah (*mashiah*).

197: "The year of mind" (or "spirit": *shnat hamo'ah*) is the numerological shorthand (48) for the Hebrew year 5048, or 1288 C.E., when Abulafia wrote the poem.

The Nut Garden

Text: The poem serves as a motto to *Sefer Ginat Egoz leRabbi Yosef Gikatilla* [Heb] (Jerusalem, 1989), p. 1.

Zohar 1:19b: "The blessed Holy One had to create everything in the world, arraying the world. All consists of a kernel within, with several shells covering the kernel. The entire world is like this, above and below, from the head of the mystery of the primordial point to the end of all rungs: all is this within that, that within this, so that one is the shell of another, which itself is the shell of another." Daniel Matt notes that "the ultimate kernel" in this Zoharic picture is Ein-Sof (the infinite), and he adds: "The human being, fashioned in the image of God (Genesis 1:27), manifests the structure of kernel and shell" (*Zohar*, trans. Matt, vol. 1, p. 151).

8–10: The anagrammatic permutation of "East" to "eats" here is not in the Hebrew, but it represents the kind of transformation one finds frequently in this tradition and throughout Gikatilla's book.

The Safed Circle (Galilean Kabbalah)

Information for the headnote is drawn from the following sources: Zvi Werblowsky, "The Safed Revival and Its Aftermath," in *Jewish Spirituality*, ed. Arthur Green, 2 vols. (New York, 1989), vol. 2, Werblowsky, "Mystical and Magical Contemplation: The Kabbalists in Sixteenth-Century Safed," *History of Religions* 1 (1961), p. 35, and Werblowsky, *Joseph Karo: Lawyer and Mystic*, 2nd ed. (Philadelphia, 1977); Lawrence Fine, *Safed Spiritual-*

ity: *Rules of Mystical Piety, the Beginning of Wisdom* (Ramsey, N.J., 1984), p. 23, and Fine, *Physician of the Soul, Healer of the Cosmos: Isaac Luria and His Kabbalistic Fellowship* (Stanford, Calif., 2003), esp. pp. 13, 41–49, 66, 167–86, 259 ff., 266, and 347; Gershom Scholem, *Kabbalah* (New York 1974), pp. 67–79 and 401–44, Scholem, *On the Kabbalah and Its Symbolism*, trans. Ralph Manheim (New York, 1969), pp. 139–41, and Scholem, *Major Trends in Jewish Mysticism* (New York, 1941), pp. 244–86; Solomon Schechter, "Safed," in his *Studies in Judaism*, second series (Philadelphia, 1908), pp. 202–86; *Jewish Mystical Autobiographies: Book of Visions and Book of Secrets*, trans. and introduced by Morris M. Feierstien, preface by Moshe Idel (Mahwah, N.J., 1999); Idel, *Old Worlds, New Mirrors: On Jewish Mysticism and Twentieth-Century Thought* (Philadelphia, 2010), pp. 95ff., Idel, *Absorbing Perfections: Kabbalah and Interpretation* (New Haven, 2002), pp. 26–44, and Idel, "On the Concept of 'Tzimtzum' in the Kabbalah and Its Research" [Heb], *Mehkerei Yerushalayim beMahshevet Yisrael* 10 (1992), pp. 91ff.; *My People's Prayer Book: Traditional Prayers, Modern Commentaries*, ed. Lawrence A. Hoffman, 10 vols. (Woodstock, Vt., 1997–2007), vol. 7, pp. 26–28, and, in vol. 8, Sharon Koren, "The Mystical Spirituality of Safed," pp. 33–42; Mordechai Pachter, "Alkabetz, Solomon" and "Azikri, Eliezer," both in *Encyclopedia Judaica*, 2nd ed. (Detroit, 2007), vol. 1, pp. 662–63, and vol. 2, pp. 768–69, and Pachter, "The Life and Personality of R. Eliezer Azikri in Light of His Mystical Diary and *Sefer Haredim*" [Heb], *Shalem* 3 (1981), pp. 127–47; Joseph ben Shelomo, "Moses Cordovero," *Encyclopedia Judaica*, 2nd ed. (Detroit, 2007), vol. 5, pp. 220–22; Elliot R. Wolfson, *Luminal Darkness: Imaginal Gleanings from Zoharic Literature* (Oxford, 2007), p. 169; B. Gezundheit, "Yedid Nefesh: Its Author, His Sources, and the Meaning of the Piyyut" [Heb] *Da'at* (2004), http://www.daat.ac.il/daat/sifrut/maamarim/nefesh-2 .htm; and Paul Fenton, "Sufi Influence on the Kabbalah in Safed" [Heb], *Mahanayyim* 6 (1993), pp. 170–79. Fenton notes that there is clear evidence of Sufi activity in the Galilee in the thirteenth and fourteenth centuries; in the mid-seventeenth century—when Kabbalistic activity was still flourishing—one Muslim traveler counted seven Sufi *zawiyyas* (chapels) in the town, and he observed that Muslim musical rites were conducted on Mondays and Saturdays; the influence of this Sufi musical tradition upon the Jewish rite was probably direct, either here or from other parts of the Ottoman Empire ("Les Bakkashot d'orient et d'occident," *Revue des études juives* 134:1–2 [1975], pp. 101–21).

Quotations are drawn from the following sources: *Victorious march through the world*: Scholem, *Major Trends*, p. 251; *celestial mentor*: Werblowsky, "Safed Revival," p. 13; *mystical peregrinations*: Werblowsky, "Safed Revival," p. 15; *new ideas would come to us*: Werblowsky, "Safed Revival," p. 16; *So it was quiet*: Celan, "Conversation in the Mountains," from *Collected Prose*, trans. Rosmarie Waldrop (Manchester, U.K., 1986), p. 18; *it is the custom*: Werblowsky, "Mystical and Magical Contemplation," p. 16; *while God has given man a wife*: Fine, *Safed Spirituality*, p. 13; "*the soul is a seat [or throne] for the Shekhinah*: Pachter, "Life and Personality of R. Eliezer Azikri" [Heb] p. 141; *all the consequences of violent love*: Werblowsky, "Safed Revival," p. 17; *a Sufi-like abandon*: Werblowsky, "Mystical and Magical Contemplation," p. 35; *the royal road to [it] was solitary contemplation*: Werblowsky, "Safed Revival," p. 19; *his eyes focused on God*: "The Diary of Eliezer Azikri," in Mordechai Pachter, *From the Safed's Hidden Treasures: Studies and Texts Concerning the History of Safed and Its Sages in the Sixteenth Century* [Heb] (Jerusalem, 1994), p. 125 (the entry is from 1571, when Azikri was thirty-eight); *a petition for union and the desire for love*: *Sefer Haredim* (Venice, 1591), pp. 42–43, Pachter, "Azikri, Eliezer."

Hymn to the Sabbath

The four-square (if not quite Isaac Watts–like) aspect of this hymn is most obviously evident in its stanzaic structure: quatrains framed fore and aft by the two-line refrain. Metrically the Hebrew is constructed according to the syllabic system of the day; while the Hebrew does not count stresses per se, there are four per line. The four-line English stanzas follow suit. The English refrain has four stresses in the first line and a truncated three in the second, in order to propel the reader forward. The English doesn't maintain the Hebrew signature acrostic consisting of part of the poet's name, Shelomoh HaLevi.

Thematically the fourfold nature and elaborate coding of the poem has been worked out in exhaustive fashion by Reuven Kimelman (in *The Mystical Meaning of Lekhah Dodi and Kabbalat Shabbat* [Heb] [Los Angeles and Jerusalem, 2003]). He notes the poem's preoccupation with four planes: the Sabbath (time), Jerusalem (space), the People of Israel (the human plane), and the world of the *sefirot* (the heavenly plane). The function of the poem is to bring about the unification of these four realms, and more generally of the lower and upper worlds. The nine stanzas correspond to the nine lower sefirot, and the tenth sefirah (Keter, or crown) is represented by the refrain. The commentary that follows touches on all these elements and is largely based on Kimelman's analysis, which in turn is based on a close reading of the relevant mystical literature of the day by Alkabetz himself, his friend and disciple Moses Cordovero, and their predecessors, contemporaries, and students.

Text: Kimelman, *Mystical Meaning of Lekhah Dodi* [Heb]. See also Kimelman's commentary in *My People's Prayer Book*, vol. 8, pp. 128–32. Kimelman notes there that the poem is traditionally sung between Psalm 29 (which marks the end of the profane week) and Psalm 92 (which is "for the Sabbath day").

Refrain: The refrain might also (and more literally) be translated, "Go, my beloved, to meet the bride" or "Go forth, my love." In keeping with its direct biblical allusion to the Song of Songs 7:12 ("Come, let us go forth to the fields"—which perfectly suits the occasion of the sixteenth-century poem), I have translated it as "Come, my beloved." This also makes more sense in the context of the poem as a whole. It is, however, by no means clear who is speaking and whom the speaker is addressing. And here, too, everything is split-level, and multiple readings are possible. Is the poet speaking? The prayer leader (*hazan*)? Or the masculine People of Israel? Or the feminine Congregation of Israel? Or is God Himself addressing His beloved people and instructing them to meet the bride? But who is the bride? And who is being addressed? God, or Alkabetz's fellow Kabbalists and companions (collectively)? Or could he be addressing himself or his soul, urging himself on? Or perhaps the first line of the refrain is directed toward one addressee and the second line is directed toward that addressee along with another?

Evidence for each of these readings can be found in the religious literature of the day. Whoever they are, the addressees—the first line is a singular imperative, and the second line is cast in the first-person plural—are urged to go welcome the Sabbath. (It appears from the literature that Alkabetz himself did not walk out into the fields as part of the Kabbalat Shabbat ritual; in fact, he may not have recited the poem as part of a ritual at all. Moreover, Yitzhak Luria probably didn't recite the poem either; we first find it in a Moroccan document from 1577 and in a prayer book from 1584. See Kimelman, *Mystical Meaning* [Heb], p. 23.) Line 2 of the refrain is literally: "We'll receive the face of the Sabbath," which idiomatically means simply "to welcome" or "to greet." The lines are also based on *Shabbat* 119a (and *Baba Kama* 32b), where R. Haninah is depicted as wrapping himself in a cloak near sunset as the Sabbath approaches and saying, "Come, let us go out to greet the Sabbath Queen." In *Genesis Rabbah* 11:8, the Nation of Israel is described as the Sabbath's partner or spouse.

Like the poem as a whole, the refrain can be read in straightforward devotional fashion and esoterically in Kabbalistic terms. In the straightforward reading the refrain gives expression to Israel's love for God and the Sabbath (and vice versa). In the Kabbalistic reading the refrain emphasizes the notion of a sacred wedding and the unification of the world of the sefirot through God-the-groom's love for His bride, the Sabbath—which is to say, the Shekhinah, or feminine aspect of Himself (Wolfson, *Luminal Darkness*, p. 169). Moshe Cordovero writes that the word for "my beloved," *dodi*, can also be read esoterically as a permutation of the four-letter Name of God, which is applied to the sefirah of Tiferet, the masculine principle in the sefirotic realm (Kimelman, *Mystical Meaning* [Heb], p. 59). In this erotic reading, God and Israel are urged to welcome their brides: and as man comes into sexual union with his wife on the Sabbath evening, so too God and His bride on high are made one in a sacred and erotic union of heavenly powers. Moreover, the erotic dynamic in the lower world *brings about* the union on high. Finally, through this union below and the union on high, Israel and God will also be brought together.

All this theory is embodied in earthly consciousness and practice: according to the *Zohar* 1:50a, "When a man is in his home, the essence of the home is his wife, because the Shekhinah does not depart from the house on account of his wife" (trans. Daniel C. Matt, 5 vols. [Stanford, Calif., 2004–9], vol. 1, p. 277). See also *Wisdom of the Zohar*, arranged and rendered into Hebrew by Fischel Lachower and Isaiah Tishby; introductions and annotations by Isaiah Tishby, trans. David Goldstein, 3 vols. (Oxford, 1997), vol. 3, p. 992. Alkabetz's close friend Moses Cordovero wrote: "One who doesn't know desire for his wife cannot experience love and desire for God . . . for devekut [attachment to God] is exactly like the desire of a man for his bride" (Kimelman, *Mystical Meaning* [Heb], p. 64). See also Elliot R. Wolfson, *The Book of the Pomegranate: Moses De León's Sefer Ha-Rimmon*, (Atlanta, 1988), p. 223: "There is no male, when married, who does not stand between two females, one secret and invisible, and one, his wife, who is visible. . . . You will hence find that the Shekhinah does not rest upon an unmarried man." Taking that one step further Elijah de Vidas of Safed noted: "A love [that] involves rising at night in order to study Torah . . . may be compared to that of a man for his wife. For at night when he awakens with strong feelings of love, he will hasten to satisfy his longing with deep affection, particularly when he knows that she whom he loves loves him as well. So it is with Torah scholars. . . . It is proper for them to make haste in their desire for Torah; for through its study they cleave to the life of the upper realm as well as to the Shekhinah" (Fine, *Safed Spirituality*, p. 139).

In addition to this mythic picture, the refrain encodes an arcane numerological mechanism, through which its recitation mathematically composes the four-letter Name of God. The translation aims for a sonorous simplicity and at least a faint echo of the wordplay in the elusive Hebrew. The first word of the refrain is *lekhah* (come, go), and the last word of the first line is an anagram of that—*kalah* (bride). The English reversal of the *l-v* of "beloved" and "arrival" quietly echoes that play of the Hebrew. The internal rhymes of "greet" and "meet" along with the assonance of "bride" and "arrival" echo the full rhyme of the Hebrew. (One also notes the presence of the word *kabbalah* in the Hebrew refrain—*penei shabbat nekabbalah* [we'll welcome, or receive].)

3–6: The Talmud, in *Rosh HaShanah* 27a, comments on the notion of observing and remembering and the fact that in Exodus 20:8 the commandment is to "remember" the Sabbath, while in Deuteronomy 5:12 it is to "observe" the Sabbath: "Can two distinct sounds be caught at once? Has it not been taught: 'Remember' and 'observe' were spoken in a single utterance [by God], a thing which transcends the capacity of the [human] mouth to utter and of the [human] ear to hear?" The terms also build on a network of earlier Kabbalistic references and associations, which give one a sense of just how freighted Kabbalistic reading can be. The poet, Kimelman notes, reverses the biblical "remember" and "observe" not only because it suits the acrostic, but because in the *Zohar* (2:92a), *observe* is associated with the evening and *remember* with the day, and in the *Bahir, observe* is associated with the feminine principle and *remember* with the masculine. As the evening in the Jewish calendar precedes the day, and in this case begins the Sabbath, so the feminine principle comes first in the mystical scheme and marks that beginning. "Arousal begins from below," says one seventeenth-century Kabbalistic commentary, and the lowest sefirah is the feminine Malkhut, or Shekhinah. The *Zohar* also states explicitly that *remember* and *observe* are the Holy One, blessed be He and His Shekhinah (*Tikkunei HaZohar*, 6:21b). On *zakhor* (remember), see *The Zohar* 2:92a, trans. Matt, vol. 4, pp. 526–28. See Kimelman, *Mystical Meaning* [Heb], pp. 36–45.

9–12: "Creation's end, though first in conception": Endlessness and existence are united, as the lowest sefirah, Malkhut, is the object of the highest, Keter (Kimelman, *Mystical Meaning* [Heb], p. 48). The poem will move symbolically from one to the other, in the process uniting them in the mind of the worshipper. Cf. 1 Samuel 9:9, Isaiah 2:5, and Proverbs 8:23.

15–18: "The valley of weeping" (Psalms 84:7) is the Exile. The first two stanzas treated a sacred temporal aspect of existence, the Sabbath. The next six treat a sacred spatial aspect, the city of Jerusalem and its restoration as part of the unification of the cosmic order. The two aspects— the Sabbath and Jerusalem—are analogous and identified with each other here (Kimelman, *Mystical Meaning* [Heb], pp. 55–57). The exile of the Shekhinah, who must be welcomed back each Friday at dusk, is parallel to her exile from the ruined city (which in turn stands for the People of Israel, awaiting redemption and seeking to bring it about through the observance of rituals in which hymns such as "Lekhah Dodi" were sung). In one of his descriptions of the midnight vigils that took place at Yosef Karo's house, Alkabetz describes the celestial voice that came into the room, lamenting the sufferings of the Shekhinah and praising the companions for "raising her up" through their devotions (Fine, "Safed Revival," p. 13—but see also Fine, *Joseph Karo: Lawyer and Mystic*, pp. 99, 108, and 110). As ruin and exile were brought about through the desecration of the Sabbath, so observance of the Sabbath and the sacralization of time will produce the restoration of the holy city and its sense of sacred space (*Shabbat* 118a–19b). Once again, arousal begins from below—with awakening having to take place on the earthly plane in order to bring it about on high. That said, the end of this stanza acknowledges the mutual dynamic, in which movement from below will be answered with compassion from above. See also Amos 7:13; Jeremiah 15:5.

21–24: The messianic implications of this stanza are evident in the reference to ben Yishai of Bethlehem (the line of David, which will culminate in the Messiah King) and the direct call for redemption. Both are reminiscent of a sermon Alkabetz gave in Salonika before he left for Palestine, on which occasion he made it clear that the principal motivation for his immigration was his concern for the state of the Temple, which was in ruins, and his desire to serve as a model to others in the Salonika community. The reparative and therefore redemptive cast of his pilgrimage (and his presence thereafter in Safed) becomes clear from this talk, and it finds powerful expression in this and the following stanzas of the poem. See Pachter, "R. Shelomoh Alkabetz's Aliyyah to Eretz Israel" [Heb], *Shalem* 7 (2001), pp. 251–63. See also Isaiah 52:2; Psalms 69:19. Line 24 is spoken by the feminine Knesset Israel to God.

27–30: Structurally this fifth stanza contains the center of the poem: While it develops the theme of redemption that the poem has been working out (the restoration of Jerusalem, the observance of the Sabbath, the unification of the sefirotic realm, and so forth), light itself has not been part of the poem's vocabulary, and commentators have wondered about the sudden introduction of this motif and looked to the plane of esoteric interpretation for guidance. To begin with, the Hebrew contains a homonymic play with "light" (*aleph, vuv, resh*) and "awake" (*ayin, vuv, resh*)—*or* and *hit'orer*; the roots sound the same, though they are formed from different letters. That linguistic slippage slides one down the rabbit hole of Kabbalistic hermeneutics, where we find a network of commentaries around what becomes a triple homonym. The gist of that discussion concerns the original, pre-Fall state of man, in which no clothes were worn and man's skin gave off light (*or*, with an *aleph*). (One might say that the poem is picking up on the mention of "robes of splendor" in the previous stanza.) After Adam's sin, garments of leather (*or*, with an *ayin*) were required. Now the poem is calling for awakening (*hit'orerrut*) within that fallen state because a light (*or*) has been revealed from on high. (Alkabetz treats this subject directly in his Salonika sermon—see Pachter, "R. Shelomoh Alkabetz's Aliyyah" [Heb].) On the Sabbath, and in the world to come, white garments, of holiness and light, are worn, not the leather skin of the profane world. The Hebrew for "awake, arise" in line 29 is in this context understood not just as "awaken," but as "strip off your clothes of leather," again, through a pun on the root *or*; i.e., return to innocence. (While spiritual arousal in the Kabbalistic scheme generally begins from below, Redemption itself must be initiated on high, and so the Congregation of Israel—the sefirah Malkhut—is urged to respond with song to the light and revelation of God—or Tiferet, beauty.) See Kimelman, *Mystical Meaning* [Heb], pp. 134ff., and note in *My People's Prayer Book*, vol. 8. See also Isaiah 51:17 and 60:1; Judges 5:12.

33–36: See Isaiah 45:17; Psalms 42:6; Jeremiah 30:18.

39–42: Restoration of Jerusalem is tantamount to restoration of the soul, and by extension of the Shekhinah to her place in the cosmic scheme. While both Alkabetz and Azikri after him (see "Soul's Beloved," below) were drawn to immigrate to Palestine for messianic reasons, and while they write or speak of the Temple along these lines in their work, it's also evident in their poems that the imagery associated with the Temple is first and foremost spiritual in its import. As Moshe Idel writes: "Someone who feels the unmediated presence of the divine no longer needs any other sort of *aliyyah* [ascent or immigration] . . . [and] pilgrimage is not likely to be the essence of the matter" (Idel, "Eretz Yisrael and the Kabbalah in the Thirteenth Century" [Heb], *Shalem* 3 [1981], pp. 125–26). With line 42 the poem now begins to move back toward the theme of the sacred wedding and the more overtly erotic dimensions of the ritual. In the Kabbalistic scheme, just as man was created male and female, so an androgynous God split into male and female aspects—King and Bride (Kimelman's commentary in *My People's Prayer Book*, vol. 8, p. 130). See also Jeremiah 30:16; Isaiah 49:19 and 62:5.

45–48: Kimelman (*Mystical Meaning* [Heb], p. 82ff.) rightly asks what or who the subject of "you'll spread" is, noting that it appears at this point to be more than merely the People of Israel or Jerusalem, as in the preceding several stanzas. He argues convincingly that it should be understood polyvalently here as combining all four levels the poem has been treating. The Hebrew verb, he says—which also implies a kind of breakthrough or bursting forth—stands for a comprehensive sense and presence of holiness that includes the Sabbath, the Congregation of Israel, Jerusalem, and the sefirah of Malkhut (all grammatically feminine). Each will move from a position on the periphery to the center, and from the center to the outermost edge. The (messianic) movement toward holiness will, in other words, be total, in a restoration of a pre-Adamic world or Eden. The erotic and sefirotic joy of line 42 now spreads, not only through the people but through the upper world of the sefirot. The unification sought by the poem extends from the lower feminine sefirah of Malkhut (the Shekhinah, a figure of receptivity) below, up through the masculine and phallic sefirah of Yesod (stanza 8, ll. 45–48, which deals with dissemination), Tiferet (stanza 5, ll. 27–30, the center of the poem, which treats light and awakening), Binah (stanza 2, ll. 9–12, which focuses on the Sabbath's approach), and Keter (the refrain, which embodies the cyclical reunion of all these elements).

Lawrence Fine notes that "unlike Hokhmah and Binah, whose love is described as harmonious and perfect, the relationship between Tiferet and Malkhut is one of tension. Under the proper conditions they are in perfect union, while at other times this union is rent asunder. They express the intuition that all life, patterned after the model of divine life, is constituted of male and female. And they reveal the eternal dialectic between male and female" (*Safed Spirituality*, p. 162). When Tiferet (everlasting beauty) and Malkhut (kingdom/the Shekhinah) are aligned, or united (in consummation), divine energy is created and flows into the world. But when that union is interrupted, the flow of divine energy is blocked and diverted toward the sustenance of the dark forces of the universe. The arcane aspect of all this apart, what we have here is a carefully calibrated visionary system that seeks to account for the most minute, elusive, complex, and continually dynamic dimension of spiritual experience. (And where the Kabbalists have sefirot, the poet might understand "words well arrayed.")

In line 47, Peretz is David's ancestor and stands for the Messiah, who will, as Kimelman puts it, "repair the breach created by Adam and restore things to their original state" (commentary in *My People's Prayer Book*, vol. 8, p. 131). Kimelman also reads a political dimension into this Messianic image of spreading from the center to the right and left—in which the Jewish Sabbath embraces the sacred day of Christianity (Sunday, to the right) and of Islam (Friday, to the left), implying a triumphal absorption of these faiths into Judaism (*Mystical Meaning* [Heb], p. 89ff.). See also Isaiah 25:9 and 54:31; Ruth 4:18.

51–54: With this stanza the poem returns to its beginning, like the week coming round to its sacred aspect. At this point the sacred wedding is celebrated on all levels of existence—erotic and sefirotic, spiritual and national. "Treasured people" is *am segulah* in the Hebrew, as in Deuteronomy 7:6, 14:2, and 26:18. It might also be translated as "singular people" or "special." See also 2 Samuel 20:19. On the phrase "come, my bride," see *Shabbat* 119a and note to the refrain, above.

Peace Be upon You

This famous and quietly haunting hymn is based on the Talmudic tradition that two ministering angels—one good and one bad—accompany each individual home at the beginning of the Sabbath (*Shabbat* 119b), and if the home is properly prepared for the Sabbath the good angel says,

"May it be God's will that it be so for another Sabbath," and the other angel is compelled to answer, "Amen." If the house is not properly prepared, the situation is reversed. Earlier readings may have understood the hymn as being offered not to these two angels but to other angels who, riding aromatic myrtle branches carried by congregants returning home, accompany the super-soul, or extra soul that Jews receive on the Sabbath. On the whole, it can be seen as a hymn for the peace of the household.

Text: *My People's Prayer Book*, vol. 7, pp. 65ff.

Lines 1–10: The phrase *shalom aleikhem* derives from Psalms 125:5 and 128:6: "Peace be upon Israel." See also Psalms 91:11 ("For he shall give his angels charge over thee, to keep thee in all thy ways") and 121:8 ("The Lord will keep your going out and your coming in"). Biblical angelology (see, for instance, the stories of Abraham and Jacob, in Genesis 16–28, Balaam in Numbers 22; the Exodus story, chapters 14 and 23; Isaiah 6, Ezekiel 1 and 3, and Job 1 and 2; and Daniel 8 and 9) does not include "ministering angels" and "angels of heaven," and generally speaking twenty-first-century readers do not usually associate an active angelology with Judaism. We've already seen that the Judaism of the Heikhalot hymns had a developed angelology, however, and this was inherited by subsequent Judaisms and their poets (see the sections on Kallir and Ibn Gabirol, above). In fact, by the time of the Dead Sea Scrolls, angelic population had swelled. It is generally acknowledged that Christianity inherited its angels from ancient Judaism, and midrashic Hebrew literature also extensively developed that ancient legacy—with medieval Jews counting between "a few hundred thousand and 496,000 myriads" angels. As the Kabbalists saw them, angels were emanations of the divine light that does God's work in the world. Others have seen them as thoughts, or even as letters. See Idel, *The Angelic World: Apotheosis and Theophany* [Heb] (Tel Aviv, 2008), chap. 1.

11–20: There has been considerable objection to the recitation of the lines blessing the angels' departure, as it is considered inappropriate to ask the angels to leave. So the lines are understood as indicating that one should bless the angels when they decide to leave (per Deuteronomy 28:6: "Blessed are you in your coming in and blessed are you in your going out"). On the other hand, if the angels in question are understood to be those who accompany the Sabbath soul, then there is no difficulty in the line whatsoever. They would naturally depart with the departure of the Sabbath.

Soul's Beloved

The four stanzas of this poem begin in Hebrew with letters that spell out the four-letter Name of God. This is no mere trick or decorative embellishment. Azikri writes in his mystical diary (which he kept on and off for a period of some thirty-five years) that he would meditate on the acrostic until he saw the four letters rise up off the page and form a single flame of fire. And that is the subject of this poem: clinging to God's Presence and longing for union with that Presence. So the acrostic becomes a kind of tattooed embodiment of the poet's spiritual ambition. Charting the dynamic of this attachment to God, Azikri says, "I am my beloved's at first and then my beloved is mine [Song of Songs 6:3], . . . and one must awaken and fill the heart with the love of God, may He be blessed always with His four letters of fear, compassion, modesty, and joy . . . for the Lord has drawn His four letters in your face—*yod* in the mouth, *hey* on the right side of the face, the other *hey* on the left side of the face, and *vuv* is the nose, as it is written, so that the fear of God shall be on your faces [Exodus 20:17]" (Pachter, "Life and Personality of R. Eliezer of Azikri" [Heb], p. 145). Along the same lines Elijah de Vidas of Safed wrote: "A person who desires to gladden his soul ought to seclude himself for a portion of the day for the purposes of meditating upon the splendor of the letters YHVH" (Fine, *Safed Spirituality*, p. 154).

Text: The text and commentary are drawn from numerous sources, but are especially indebted to B. Gezundheit, "Yedid Nefesh," and *My People's Prayer Book*, vol. 7, pp. 135–46. See also Arthur Green, "Religion and Mysticism: The Case of Judaism," in *Take Judaism, for Example: Studies Toward the Comparison of Religions*, ed. Jacob Neusner (Chicago, 1983), which notes the poem's alternation between masculine and feminine subjects—the poet/servant of stanzas 1 and 3, and the feminine soul of stanza 2. "By the final stanza," Green notes, "father and son are no longer to be found, and the poem reveals itself to be one of passionate, sacred eros" (p. 81). The poem was originally written as a private meditation, and eventually incorporated into the liturgy.

Lines 1–6: The image of the speaker as a "servant" or "slave" (*eved* in the Hebrew) is common in Azikri's prose writings (especially his diary), where it surfaces in conjunction with silence, isolation, and an intense longing for and sense of God's presence. It draws, says Joseph Yahalom, on the Turkish slave-master relationship, which, in Ottoman society, allowed for a good deal of autonomy and opportunity for advancement, and "symbolized unwavering loyalty and a personal attachment that bordered on love" (Andreas Tietze and Joseph Yahalom, *Ottoman Melodies, Hebrew Hymns: A Sixteenth-Century Cross-Cultural Adventure* [Budapest, 1995], pp. 28ff.; Yahalom is drawing on Walter Andrews, *Poetry's Voice, Society's Song—Ottoman Lyric Poetry* [Washington, D.C., 1985], pp. 89–91).

The term "merciful father" in line 1 introduces one of the major motifs of the poem—God's mercy and compassion, attributes that are associated with the particular Name of God invoked by the acrostic. In his diary, either in 1575 or 1589 (the evidence suggests the latter, though it isn't entirely clear), Azikri also writes of a "proclamation of servitude" that he has issued and which he vows to read to himself at least once a day during one of the three prayer sessions or one of the four periods of "shifting times" during the day: dawn, midday, dusk, midnight. This is also when certain Sephardic communities recite the poem. At the height of his ecstatic state, he notes, "the light of the fire's flame envelops me with four hues, white—love, red—awe, green—humility, black—joy." (For all quotations from the diary and *Sefer Haredim*, see Pachter, "Life and Personality of R. Eliezer Azikri" [Heb].) The fourfold division and description of the flame is reminiscent of his meditation on the four letters of God's Name and their presence in this poem.

The intimate tone of the poem and the imagery of the opening lines recalls that of Psalms 42:2–3: "As the hart panteth after the water brooks, so panteth my soul after thee, O God." Both the tone and the erotic tenderness of the poem, along with its subject—longing for mystical union with God—and its development, make it clear that the addressee in its opening (*yedid*, in the Hebrew, which is usually translated as "friend" or "companion") might also be rendered as "beloved." There are numerous scriptural parallels indicating that the term *yedid* assumes a special meaning with regard to the relationship between Israel and God vis-à-vis Jerusalem (2 Samuel 12, Jeremiah 11 and 12, Psalms 84, Isaiah 4); see especially Jeremiah 12:7: "I have given the dearly beloved of my soul into the hand of her enemies." See also Song of Songs 1:4 ("Draw me, we will run after thee") and 8:14; Psalms 19:11: "sweeter also than honey and the honeycomb."

7–12: The poem develops from an initial plea (a call to the self to awaken spiritually) to a description of God's magnificence (which is really a plea for a glimpse of that magnificence). The poet is lovesick, and only God's mercy can heal his soul, by granting the poet a vision of the divine brilliance and splendor. Here too there is a subtly coded Kabbalistic allusion, or play on words, in the Hebrew, where *titrafe* (be healed) and *tiferet* (the sefirah of God's splendor or beauty—the subject of this stanza and a word that appears explicitly in stanza 3) are anagrams of each other. Tiferet is also associated with compassion. The English doesn't try to replicate this play, though the weave of sound is intensified and numerous echoes are set up in these stanzas, joining the various terms. In the *Zohar*, "world's luster" and "your brilliance's pleasure" are associated with the giving of the Torah and devotion to its study. Lovesickness, or the state of the failing soul, is associated with being in a state of exile (*Zohar* 2:58b [trans. Matt, vol. 4, p. 306]). See also Isaiah 63:1; Numbers 12:13.

13–18: At this point the call widens by association with other elements of the liturgy and its scriptural background—both of which suggest that the imagery here relates to Jerusalem and to the end of Exile. See Genesis 31:30; Isaiah 41:8; 2 Chronicles 20:7; Psalms 89:18, 70:2, and 6. Ancient of Days is an epithet for God. See also Luria's "Hymns for the Three Sabbath Meals," below.

19–24: The call for revelation and restitution becomes more explicitly general and reaches here to the world as a whole. The pursuit of peace, particularly peace within the People of Israel, was a central tenet of the groups that Azikri assembled around him in Safed—one of which was known as Sukkat Shalom (the Shelter of Peace). As in Alkabetz's "Hymn to the Sabbath," many of the scriptural allusions in this stanza refer to the restoration of Jerusalem. In Azikri's other writings, it's clear that the restoration or reintegration of the individual soul was insufficient, and that the individual's effort must extend to work on behalf of the people as a whole and out of concern for the Shekhinah's fate. At the same time, the inner mystical aspect is still intense in Azikri: "Be conscious," he writes, "that you are standing in the presence of your Creator. When you are studying Torah you are looking at the light of His garment, and when you are walking in the market or sitting in any place you encounter the light of the Shekhinah, for His glory fills the world." See also Ezekiel 43:2; Psalms 102:14; Malachi 3:4; Amos 9:11; Isaiah 25:9. The poem ends with a return to an allusion from Song of Songs 1:4, this time emphasizing the delight the lover takes in her beloved.

School of Luria

Information for the headnote is drawn from the following sources: Fine, *Physician of the Soul*, esp. chaps. 3–6 and 9; Scholem, *Kabbalah*, pp. 140–44, and 420–28, Scholem, *On the Kabbalah and Its Symbolism*, pp. 142–45, and Scholem, *Major Trends*, pp. 244–86; Tovah Be'eri, "Two New Poems by Yitzhak Luria Ashkenazi (HaAri) and an Examination of the Poems Attributed to Him," *Pe'amim* 128 (2011), pp. 9–34; S. Bernstein, "A Hymn Mistakenly Attributed to the Ari" [Heb], *Sefer Yovel shel haDo'ar* (New York, 1957), pp. 83–85; Naftali ben Menahem, *Zemirot shel Shabbat* (Jerusalem, 1949), pp. 34–36, 144–45; Meir Benayahu, "R. Yisrael Najara" [Heb], *Asufot* 4 (1990), pp. 203–84; Moshe Idel, "On the Concept of 'Tzimtzum' in the Kabbalah" [Heb], pp. 59–112; Tietze and Yahalom, *Ottoman Melodies, Hebrew Hymns*, pp. 9–41; Yosef Yahalom, "R. Yisrael Najara and the Renewal of Hebrew Poetry in the East after the Expulsion from Spain" [Heb], *Pe'amim* 13 (1982), pp. 96–124, Yahalom, "Mystical Hebrew Poetry and Its Turkish Background" [Heb], *Tarbiz* 60 (1991), pp. 625–48, and Yahalom, "The Poetry of Kabbalah and Its Turkish Background," *Dimui* 5–6 (1993), pp. 88–96; Aharon Mirsky, "Yisrael Najara, *Zemirot Yisrael*," *Kiryat Sefer* 25 (1949), pp. 39ff., Mirsky,

"Poems of Redemption by R. Yisrael Najara" [Heb], *Sefunot* 5 (1961), pp. 209–34, and Mirsky, "New Poems of R. Yisrael Najara" [Heb], *Sefunot* 6 (1962), pp. 259–302; Tovah Be'eri, "*Olat Hodesh* by R. Yisrael Najara: Themes and Contents" [Heb], *Asufot* 4 (1990), pp. 311–24, and Be'eri, "The Sephardic Foundations in the Poetry of R. Yisrael Najara" [Heb], *Pe'amim* 49 (1991), pp. 54–67; Fenton, "Sufi Influence" [Heb], Fenton, "Shabbatai Tzvi and His Muslim Contemporary Muhammad an-Niyazi," in *Approaches to Judaism in Medieval Times,* ed. David R. Blumenthal (Atlanta, 1988), vol. 3, pp. 81–88, and Fenton, "Bakkashot d'orient et d'occident"; Amnon Shiloah, "The Influence of the World of Kabbalah on the Development of the Singing of Piyyut" [Heb], *Mekedem umiyam* 2 (1986), pp. 209–15; and Edwin Seroussi, "On the Beginnings of the Singing of *Bakkashot* in Nineteenth-Century Jerusalem" [Heb], *Pe'amim* 56 (1993), pp. 106–24.

Quotations are drawn from the following sources: *seems to have lacked the literary faculty*: Scholem, *Major Trends,* p. 253; *because all things are interrelated*: Fine, *Physician of the Soul,* p. 113, as recorded by Hayyim Vital; *the process of cosmic restoration and reintegration*: Scholem, *Kabbalah,* p. 140; *suffused all of existence*: Vital in Fine, *Physician of the Soul,* p. 126; *Ein-Sof then withdrew*: Vital in Fine, *Physician of the Soul,* p. 128; *one of the most amazing and far-reaching conceptions*: Scholem, *Major Trends,* p. 260; *Luria had the originality*: Bloom, *Kabbalah and Criticism* (New York, 1975), p. 39; *a protagonist in the great process of restitution*: Scholem, *Major Trends,* 289; *the preparation of men's hearts*: Scholem, *Major Trends,* 306; *Eliot suggests: Selected Essays of T. S. Eliot* (New York, 1960, 1964), p. 199; *the magnificent sweep of mind which visualizes*: Scholem, *Major Trends,* 271; *the solemn drapery of their Zoharic Aramaic . . . of a mystery religion*: Scholem, *On the Kabbalah and Its Symbolism,* pp. 142–43; *master, of blessed memory*: Vital in Fine, *Physician of the Soul,* pp. 253–54; *a somewhat strange address*: A. M. Habermann, "Shirat HaAri," in his *Kevutzei Yahad* [Heb] (Jerusalem, 1980), p. 111; *the great Kabbalist*: Scholem, "A Poem of R. Yisrael Najara Among the Shabbatians," in *Ignace Goldziher Memorial Volume,* ed. S. Loewinger and S. Somogyi (Budapest, 1948–58), pp. 41–44; *an examination of Najara's poetry in light of Kabbalistic inquiry*: Mirsky, "Yisrael Najara,

Zemirot Yisrael," p. 41; spiritual concerts: Fenton, "Sufi Influence" [Heb],
p. 171; In the middle of the night on every Sabbath: Shiloah, "Influence of
the World of Kabbalah" [Heb], p. 211, and also in Meir Benayahu, Sefer
Toldot HaAri [Heb] (Jerusalem, 1967), pp. 227–28; between sanctity and
sacrilege: Tietze and Yahalom, Ottoman Melodies, p. 10; what the Ital-
ian Don Juan: in Shiloah, "Influence of the World of Kabbalah" [Heb],
p. 212, originally from Bialik's essay "Our Young Poetry" [Heb]; to raise
the sparks of holiness: Yosef Yahalom, "Najara and the Renewal of Po-
etry" [Heb], Pe'amim 13 (1982), p. 119; He who has never desired a woman:
Tietze and Yahalom, Ottoman Melodies, p. 24, quoting Elijah de Vidas in
Reshit Hokhmah; Hocus pocus . . . defiled . . . like adulterers: de Lonzano
from Shtei Yadot [Heb] (Brooklyn, N.Y., 1993), p. 142, and in Benayahu,
"R. Yisrael Najara" [Heb], pp. 224–25; a frenzy of food and drink: Tietze
and Yahalom, Ottoman Melodies, p. 13; The truth is that his hymns: Vital,
Sefer HaHezyonot [Heb] (Jerusalem, 1954), p. 34. For another translation
of this passage, see Jewish Mystical Autobiographies, pp. 71–72; My mouth
will condemn me: Aharon Mirsky, "The Poems of Nagar ubar Nagar"
[Heb], Sefunot 6 (1962), p. 263; all he took from the foreign poetry: Bena-
yahu, "R. Yisrael Najara" [Heb], p. 221. See also Be'eri, "Olat Hodesh by
R. Yisrael Najara" [Heb], p. 324; aura of Kabbalism: Tietze and Yahalom,
Ottoman Melodies, p. 24.

Hymns for the Three Sabbath Meals

These three hymns are among the handful of works that can be confi-
dently identified as being by Luria and not merely by his school. Each
of them bears his acrostic signature, and various disciples attest to his
authorship and to his recitation or singing of the poems after the meals
in question. Vital, for instance, writes that Luria "composed three special
poems based upon esoteric knowledge (hokhmat ha-emet) consisting of
all the detailed contemplative intentions associated with the Sabbath, one
song for the evening meal, one for the late-morning meal, and one for the
afternoon" (Fine, Physician of the Soul, pp. 253–54). The hymns were
first printed in Venice, just a few years after Luria's death (Habermann,
"Shirat HaAri" [Heb], pp. 106–19). Scholem classifies them as "among

the most remarkable products of Kabbalistic poetry," and he notes their presence in "almost every prayer-book of Eastern Jewry" (*Major Trends*, p. 254). They have also given rise to many imitations. Their origin derives from numerous statements in *Shabbat* 118a, including: "He who observes [the practice of] three meals on the Sabbath is saved from three evils: the travails of the Messiah, the retribution of Gehinnom, and the wars of Gog and Magog."

(The well-known hymn "Yom Zeh LeYisrael" [This day belongs to Israel], which is traditionally attributed to Luria, in part because it bears an acrostic with the name "Yitzhak L.," has been attributed by modern scholarship to an obscure Crimean hymnist named Yitzhak Handali, and more recently, and convincingly, to a poet named Yitzhak Salameh. The stanza beginning with the letter *lamed* [L] seems to have been added, perhaps to strengthen the attribution to Luria. Later versions of "Yom Zeh LeYisrael" contain additional stanzas, so that the full acrostic—Yitzhak Luria Hazak—is spelled out. See Bernstein, "Hymn Mistakenly Attributed to the Ari" [Heb] pp. 83–85; Habermann, *Kevutzei Yahad* [Heb], p. 106; ben Menahem, *Zemirot*, pp. 34–36, 144–45; and Be'eri, "Two New Hymns by Luria," pp. 27–28.)

Text: The text and commentary that follow are based on Yehudah Liebes's comprehensive article, "Songs for the Sabbath Meals Composed by the Holy Ari" [Heb], *Molad* 23:4 (1972), pp. 540–55. Liebes also produced an excellent Hebrew translation of the poems, which for the most part I've followed. See also Gershom Scholem, *On the Kabbalah and Its Symbolism*, pp. 142–45; and Lawrence Fine, *Physician of the Soul*, esp. pp. 124–49 and 248–58, and *Safed Spirituality*, pp. 61–80.

Hymn for the First Meal: Acrostic: "I [am] Yitzhak Luria ben Shelomoh." The poem in the original is rhymed (AAAB/CCCB, along with a good deal of internal rhyme), and it maintains a fixed and simple quantitative meter. "In the eyes of the Kabbalists," writes Scholem, "this hymn was in a class apart. Unlike other table songs for the eve of the Sabbath, which could be sung or not, as one pleased, it was an indispensable part of the ritual. In Luria's hymn new meaning was not injected into an old prayer by means of mystical exegesis or *kavvanah*; rather, an esoteric conception creates its own liturgical language and form" (*On the Kabbalah and Its Symbolism*, p. 145). For a detailed treatment of the mystical nature of the Sabbath meals and their power, see *Wisdom of the Zohar*, introductions and annotations by Tishby, vol. 3, pp. 1234–38. E.g., "It is through these meals that Israel are recognized as sons of the King, as belonging to the royal palace, and as the songs of faith" (*Zohar* 2:88a–b, trans. Matt, vol. 4, pp. 497–503). Tishby notes that this first meal is the most important of the three, as it concerns the lowest *sefirah*, Malkhut. "On Sabbath even the Shekhinah prepares herself for intercourse by 'arranging a table for the King,' and on the night of the Sabbath there takes place 'the joy of the consort with the King and their union.' Therefore 'a man must arrange his table on the night of the Sabbath, because blessings descend upon it from above, and a blessing cannot exist on an empty table.' . . . On the night of the Sabbath one must taste everything in order to demonstrate that 'the tabernacle of peace' comprises everything" (p. 1235). The passages in single quotation marks are from the *Zohar* (2:92a, 2:63b, and 1:48b).

Prelude: Each of the hymns is preceded by a prelude (though some sources state that only the first hymn received the prelude). According to the *Zohar* 2:88b, R. Shimon Bar Yohai and his companions would recite these words before the Sabbath meals: "When Rabbi Abba was sitting at a Sabbath meal, he would rejoice in each one. He would say, 'This is the holy meal of the Holy Ancient One, concealed of all.' At another meal he would say, 'This is the meal of the blessed Holy One!' . . . When he completed the meals, he would say, 'The meals of faith are complete.' Rabbi Shim'on would say as follows: 'Prepare the meal of faith! Prepare the meal of the King!'" (*The Zohar*, trans. Daniel C. Matt, 5 vols. [Stanford, Calif., 2004–9], vol. 4, pp. 499–500; the *Zohar* aligns the three meals and aspects of the divinity differently from the way Luria does [p. 500]). Luria makes use of key concepts relating to the Sabbath that had been developed in the *Zohar*, where, for example, the Field of the Holy Apples stands for the Shekhinah. In this context generally, "Field," says Scholem, stands for "the feminine principle of the cosmos, while the apple trees define the Shekhinah as the expression of all the other sefirot or holy orchards, which flow into her and exert their influence through her. During the night before the Sabbath the King is joined with the Sabbath-Bride; the holy field is fertilized, and from their sacred union the souls of the righteous are produced" (*On the Kabbalah and Its Symbolism*, p. 140). According to Fine, the trees signify the masculine aspect of the divine and correspond to the male adept who goes out into the feminine field (*Physician of the Soul*, p. 251).

The Shekhinah—which is called in the *Zohar* "the Sabbath of the Sabbath Eve"—is the explicit subject of this first hymn. She is joined at the meal by the Ancient Eminence or Holy One, and by the Impatient One or the Lesser Presence (Countenance). These are three of the five principal *partzufim* (divine physiognomies) in the Lurianic cosmic scheme, and each of the three hymns is associated with one of them. Luria's notion of the partzufim is particularly complicated. They are designed as configurations meant to aid in the reintegration of the shattered cosmos, and as such they might be thought of as post-catastrophic constellations of psychic and cosmic power. As Scholem depicts it, "in each of them newly emanated forces are bonded together with others that were damaged in the breaking of the vessels; thus, each *partzuf* represents a specific stage in the process of catharsis and reconstruction" (*Kabbalah*, p. 140). The five partzufim are: Arikh Anpin (the Long-Faced or Forbearing One), who is also known as Attika Kaddisha or Attik Yomin (the Holy Ancient One, or Ancient Eminence); Abba (Father); Imma (Mother); Ze'ir Anpin (the Lesser Countenance or Impatient One); and the Nukba de-Ze'ir (the feminine aspect of Ze'ir). Each of these contains all the sefirot but is in particular associated with one or a group of sefirot: Arikh Anpin is associated with Keter (or with the upper three sefirot), Abba with Hokhmah, Imma with Binah, Ze'ir Anpin with the six sefirot beneath them, and Nukba de-Ze'ir with Malkhut or the Shekhinah. The ultimate success of these partzufim depends, says Scholem, "on a long, almost endless series of developments." See Fine, *Physician of the Soul*, pp. 138ff., and Scholem, *Kabbalah*, pp. 140–44.

Lines 1–4: "I sing" in the Aramaic is *azamer*, a word that can also mean "to cut the shoots." One of Luria's principal disciples (Yisrael Sarug) understood it here to suggest, in addition to singing, cutting off the powers of evil—presumably with the song about to be sung. This association of song and the eradication of evil became common in Kabbalistic interpretation.

5–8: "Her" refers to the Shekhinah. The candles are part of the Sabbath ritual, as is the celebratory nature of the meal and the sumptuously set table. See Isaiah 58:13–14. *Zohar* 2:88b speaks of the delight that accompanies all the Sabbath meals. E.g., "Of Sabbath eve is written and I will cause you to ride upon the heights of the earth—that very night Matronita [the Queen, or Shekhinah] is blessed along with the entire Apple Orchard, and a person's table is blessed and a soul added. That night is joy of Matronita, and one should revel in joy and partake in the meal of Matronita" (trans. Matt, vol. 4, p. 500).

9–12: The Bride (the Sabbath, the Shekhinah) approaches through the sefirah Hesed (grace) on the right and the sefirah Din (judgment, an alternative name for the sefirah of Gevurah) on the left. Others understand "left and right" as referring to the three days of the week preceding the Sabbath and the three days that follow it.

13–16: The Shekhinah's husband in this scheme is Ze'ir Anpin (the Impatient One or Lesser Presence). The sphere of foundation is Yesod, the ninth sefirah, which is associated with the genitals. The scene depicts the union of cosmic forces on the sefirotic plane, but it clearly reflects the sexual union that will take place on the earthly plane on the Sabbath eve as well. The image of "pressing" is intentionally ambiguous; it also connotes the pressing of oil. (See below, ll. 69–72, where the image returns explicitly.) Choice oil in the vocabulary of the *Zohar* is drawn from the upper sefirot and symbolizes the divine effulgence, which is likened to the coat of sperm cast by Yesod within Shekhinah. In the Aramaic, the image recalls the union of the sefirot of Yesod and Malkhut (associated with the Shekhinah). See *Zohar* 3:247a–b, and *Wisdom of the Zohar*, arranged and rendered into Hebrew by Fischel Lachower and Isaiah Tishby; introductions and annotations by Isaiah Tishby, trans. David Goldstein, 3 vols. (Oxford, 1997), vol. 3, p. 1222, on the spiritual influence of the Sabbath as a unifying force.

17–20: The cries and vexation emerge from the Sitra Ahra, the Other (Dark) Side, the forces of which the hymn cuts down. According to the

Zohar, they have no right to be active on the Sabbath. See note to ll. 29–32 on the acquisition of an extra soul on the Sabbath. See also HaLevi on the Jewish soul in the headnote to "Andalus and Ashkenaz," above.

21–24: Joy is redoubled. The light shines from the Shekhinah's husband, or their union.

25–28: Fish symbolize fertility, and it was customary to eat them on Friday evening. "Meat" here is, literally, "fowl."

29–32: The idea that Jews received "an additional soul" on the Sabbath is found in the *Zohar* (e.g., 2:88b and 2:135b–136a): "Now—when they are all adorned with new, additional holy souls and spirits—is the time of their conjugal union, for the flow to that union is a flow of holiness of supernal tranquility, and holy children will issue fittingly" (*Zohar*, trans. Matt, vol. 5, p. 255). It is also found in the Talmud (*Beitzah* 16a, where it says that the additional soul is taken away after the Sabbath ends). The thirty-two paths are those of wisdom—the ten sefirot and the twenty-two letters of the Hebrew alphabet. This is the source of the additional soul. The notion of the thirty-two paths is introduced in *Sefer Yetzirah* (see the note to line 1 of "The Book of Creation," above). The three branches (or paths) are the three sefirot of grace, judgment, and compassion (others say Malkhut, Gevurah, and Binah—kingdom, power, and understanding) through which the additional soul descends.

33–36: The image of the seventy crowns comes from the *Zohar* 1:4b (trans. Matt, vol. 1, p. 25) and is associated by the Kabbalists with the version of the Friday night Kiddush they recited, which, in addition to the thirty-five words of the standard Kiddush (prayer of sanctification), contains another thirty-five words, making seventy in all. Moreover, seventy is the numerological value of *yayyin* (wine). The Zoharic passage mentioning the crowns is worth citing at length, because of its power and its direct relation to so much of what happens in these three hymns (see, for instance, "Hymn for the Second Meal," ll. 33–36). "The moment a new word of Torah originates from the mouth of a human being, that word ascends and presents herself before the blessed Holy One, who lifts that word, kisses her, and adorns her with seventy crowns—engraved and inscribed." For the continuation of this passage and its treatment of an "innovative word of wisdom," see "Hymn for the Second Meal," note to ll. 33–36.

37–40: All the lower worlds are spiritually impressed or carved in the Shekhinah. These worlds are brought forth in an active sense by the action of the upper visage, the Ancient Eminence (or Ancient of Days), who strikes or kicks, setting into motion a stream of emanations that sends forth the stored-up powers within a given realm. See, for example, *Zohar* 1:15a, which glosses in startling fashion the opening of Genesis: "Radiance! Concealed of concealed struck its aura. . . . Then this beginning expanded, building itself a palace worthy of glorious praise. Then it sowed seed to give birth, availing worlds. . . . With this beginning, the unknown, concealed one created the palace. This palace is called Elohim (God). The secret is: *Bereshit bara elohim*. With beginning, _____ created God" (*Zohar*, trans. Matt, vol. 1, pp. 109–10)—where the subject of the sentence is ambiguous, and where God *was created*.

41–44: Literally, "that She spread about His people." Sweet things are traditionally eaten on the Sabbath; and some understand this to refer to the words of Torah.

45–48: Some versions of the poem have for the fourth line of the stanza, "on the north I fatten," per Job 36:16: "Thy table should be full of fatness." The symbolism is based on that of the Temple, where the lamp was placed to the south and the table with the showbread was set on the north side. It also draws from *Baba Batra* 25b: "One who would grow wise should go to south, and one who would grow rich should go north—and your signs of this are that the table is set to the north and the lamp to the south." The *Zohar* develops these symbols in terms of the sefirot: The lamp is Hokhmah, which exerts an influence on Malkhut through the sefirah of Hesed (which is called south); and while Malkhut is under the influence of Hokhmah, it is called "the lamp."

49–52: The wine for the Kiddush. Traditionally there are two bundles of myrtle: one for "observe" (Shekhinah) and one for "remember" (Ze'ir Anpin—the Lesser Countenance). See note to "Hymn to the Sabbath," ll. 3–6, above. They are also associated with the groom and bride—God and His Shekhinah. Liebes notes: "By means of the myrtle the Kabbalists drew down the effulgence from on high and strengthened these two *partzufim*, which would grow weak during the six ordinary days between Sabbaths" ("Songs for the Sabbath Meals" [Heb], p. 546).

53–56: The "well-chosen" or choice words are those of the Kiddush and Torah, which will be read and uttered. Again, "seventy" refers to the number of words in the Kiddush. Wisdom's gates are, in the Hebrew, "the fifty gates"—i.e., the fifty gates of understanding (Binah). The line might also allude to the fifty blessings with which the forefathers were blessed (and which employ the word *kol* [all], as do both parts of the Kiddush).

57–60: This stanza doubles the letter *shin* in the acrostic. (There are a number of theories as to how to understand this; see Liebes, "Songs for the Sabbath Meals" [Heb], p. 547.) In the sanctuary, twelve loaves would be set out in two groups of six (see Leviticus 24:5–8). The Kabbalists would array all twelve on Friday night, and serve up four at each of the three meals, associating two with the upper sefirot (and *zakhor*, "remember") and two with the lower sefirot (*shamor*, "observe"). (At times, twelve were set out for each meal.) All told, six of the loaves would be associated with the Shekhinah. The symbolism is freighted further by the specific arrangement of the loaves, and in their associations. See *Zohar* 3:245a and *Wisdom of the Zohar*, introductions and annotations by Tishby, vol. 3, p. 1236. "Linked all around" is a loose rendering of the Aramaic *bevuvin titkatar*, literally, "she will be linked by vuvs"—the sixth letter of the He-brew alphabet, *vuv*, which also means "hook" and "and." *Vuv* is also part of the Tetragrammaton—*yud, hey, vuv, hey*. In this verse, it appears that the primary meaning is the hooks of the pillars in the sanctuary (Exo-dus 27:10 and elsewhere). The Kabbalists see the letter *hey* (ה) as being composed of three lines, which they take to be three *vuvs*. As *hey* is the Shekhinah in the Kabbalistic scheme, the Shekhinah is held together or linked by *vuvs*. The final line of the stanza is obscure: it plays on the word for the seventh letter, ז (*zayin*), which has been understood as the seven "minds" or aspects of consciousness that enter the Lesser Presence (which is associated with "six" and *vuv*). Scholem (*On the Kabbalah and Its Symbolism*, p. 144) renders the lines "connected on every side / with the Heavenly Sanctuary." See Fine, *Physician of the Soul*, p. 140.

61–64: The impure powers of the Other Side.

65–68: Lines 65–80 are detached from the hymn in most prayer books and recited along with the blessing over the bread. But as Liebes points out, they continue the acrostic — "I [am] Yitzhak Luria ben Shelomoh" — and are an integral part of the poem. "Like an olive or egg" refers to the argument in the Mishnah and Gemarah over what size meal requires *zimun*, or a summoning to recite the grace after meals (see *Berakhot* 7:1 and 49b). See *Zohar* 3:245a and Liebes, "Songs for the Sabbath Meals" [Heb], p. 548. One of the *yods* is for Hokhmah (which is mysterious and obscure) and the other for Malkhut (which is evident or clear).

69–72: "The purest oil" is the divine effulgence. Cf. ll. 13–16. The stones that press the oil are the sefirot of Netzah (endurance) and Hod (splendor or glory). The rivers that are drawn in a whisper are the six sefirot immediately above the Shekhinah. In the *Bahir* (178) the scriptural verse "All the rivers run into the sea, but the sea is never full" (Ecclesiastes 1:7) is understood as referring to these sefirot, while the sea is the Shekhinah.

73–76: The "secret things" are the teachings of the Kabbalah and the esoteric meaning of the Torah. Liebes is of the opinion that "in mystery dressed" alludes to *Hagigah* 13a, which interprets Proverbs 27:26 esoterically and understands it to say that things relating to the mystery of the world should be under your clothing—i.e., close to your skin.

77–80: There appears to be a superfluous letter to the acrostic here; it's also possible that this was the beginning of another part of the acrostic. Or that the stanza was omitted. The "supernal secrets" are the words of the esoteric Kabbalistic teachings, which adorn the Shekhinah. See *Zohar* 2:204b (*Wisdom of the Zohar*, introductions and annotations by Tishby, pp. 1290–95). On the notion of the "feast," see *Zohar* 3:94b. In the Talmud the Aramaic of the original (*hilulah*) means "wedding." The holy messengers are angels (Daniel 4:10), possibly those which accompany an individual home on the Sabbath (see "Peace Be upon You"). They might also be understood as the King and the Matronita, the Holy One, blessed Be He, and His Shekhinah.

The first hymn is followed by a prose prayer, asking that the supernal dew continue to be drawn down from the most hidden and concealed

Ancient Eminence, so that it fills the locks [head] of the Lesser Presence and waters the Field of Holy Apples with the light of His face, for the pleasure of all; and that compassion and grace continue to flow from on high for one's household and companions, and for the People of Israel, and deliver them from trials and tribulations in the world, and sustain them in every way and protect them from the evil eye and the angel of death and the judgment of Gehinnom.

Hymn for the Second Meal: This hymn is recited at the second meal, after the additional prayers of the morning service. Acrostic: "I [am] Yitzhak Luria."

Prelude: The hymn for this meal is dedicated to the Attika Kaddisha (the Ancient Holy One, or as it has been translated here, the Ancient Eminence). Friday evening is associated with the Shekhinah and the moon, as the Shekhinah-bride reflects the light of Her groom; Shabbat is associated with the source of the light itself. Its pleasure is transcendent and partakes directly of the source of all pleasure (Adin Steinsaltz, *A Song for the Sabbath Day* [Jerusalem, 1999], p. 78). That divine visage is accompanied at the feast by the Impatient One (Ze'ir Anpin) and the Field of Holy Apples (Hakal Tapuhin Kaddishin).

Lines 5–8: Literally, the Great Kiddush (Sanctification), as the Kiddush of the morning blessings (*Pesahim* 106a). The wine of the Sabbath is associated with Hesed (grace), whereas wine is usually associated with Din (judgment).

9–12: Traditionally, the esoteric teachings are passed on from mouth to mouth in a whisper. One commentator associates the goodness of this stanza with the smell of the good things that have been cooked and prepared for the Sabbath meal. See *Shabbat* 119a, where an emperor asks a rabbi why a Sabbath dish has such a fragrant odor. "We have a certain seasoning," says the sage, "called the Sabbath, which we put into it, and that gives it a fragrant odor." The emperor asks for the seasoning, but the rabbi explains that it is effective only for one who keeps the Sabbath.

13–16: The letter of His Name is the *vuv* (in the Tetragrammaton), which is the thinnest of all the letters and whose value when doubled is twelve, as the number of loaves.

17–20: The bundle of life, as in 1 Samuel 25:29: "The soul of my lord shall be bound in the bundle of life with the Lord thy God." The Kabbalists associated that bundle with, variously, the sefirot of Binah, Tiferet, and Malkhut. "She" in the final line of the stanza appears to be the Shekhinah, whose power is increased on the Sabbath so that She grows to the height of the Ze'ir Anpin.

21–24: "You reapers" are the Kabbalists who "work the field" (the Shekhinah), weeding it of thistles and weeds—the powers of the Other Side. See also Isaiah 9:2: "They joy before thee according to the joy in the harvest." They "give voice" to the words of Scripture through the Kabbalistic teachings, which are sweet.

25–28: "The Lord of all worlds" is the Ancient Eminence, and the "veiled words" are those of the esoteric teaching.

29–32: The table is identified with the Shekhinah; both will be adorned on the Sabbath with the effulgence from the Ancient Eminence. The mystery's treasure—the divine effulgence—does not descend below the level of the Shekhinah, so as not to be made known more widely.

33–36: New heavens are made from words of Scripture and their study. See *Zohar* 1:4b (and the note to the first hymn, ll. 33–36, above): "An innovative word of wisdom ascends and settles on the head of a Tzaddik, Righteous One—Vitality of the Worlds. From there it flies and soars through seventy-thousand worlds, ascending to the Ancient of Days. [Eventually] the Ancient of Days inhales the aroma of that word and it pleases him more than anything. Lifting that word, He adorns it with 37,000 crowns [a multiple of the three higher and the seven lower sefirot]. The word flies, ascending and descending, and is transformed into a [new] heaven" (*Zohar*, trans. Matt, vol. 1, p. 25). "That sun" is Ze'ir Anpin.

37–40: The "oil of anointing" is the divine effulgence, which pours from the Ancient Eminence to the Lesser Countenance with greater intensity on the Sabbath. His partner here is the Shekhinah, who is alone during the week.

41–48: As with the final stanzas of the first hymn, the concluding verses here were also detached in many prayer books and attached to the prayer for the washing of hands. According to Luria, the Sitra Ahra, or

Other Side, has no substantiality on its own; it is animated by the divine sparks. Three people are needed for the blessing after the meal with a glass of wine (*Zohar* 3:246a and 2:157b): "The cup of blessing pertains only with three, because from the mystery of three patriarchs it is blessed, so a cup is required only with three. The cup of blessing should be given with the right and left hands, and received between both of them, so that it will be placed between right and left. Afterward, it should be left in the right, since from there it is blessed" (*Zohar*, trans. Matt, vol. 5, p. 422). Matt notes that the cup symbolizes the Shekhinah, "blessed by the sefirotic triad of Hesed, Gevurah, and Tiferet (symbolized by the three patriarchs)."

Hymn for the Third Meal: The third and final hymn is dedicated to the Lesser Countenance (Ze'ir Anpin) and recited at the meal around the time of the afternoon prayer. Its acrostic begins at the second stanza after the prelude (ll. 5–8), and spells out "Yitzhak Luria."

Lines 1–4: The sons of the Palace are the Kabbalists who attend the three meals. The Palace itself is the Shekhinah. See *Zohar* 2:98b.

5–8: The figure of the King, Ze'ir Anpin, is worked into the shape of the Sabbath table itself, embedded or hidden in its spiritual (and invisible) ornamentation. The table is associated with the sefirah of Malkhut. Over time, with the development of Hasidic ritual, the Aramaic term for this ornamentation or carving (*gilufin*) became synonymous with mild inebriation.

9–12: During the week, the afternoon prayer is a time of judgment (the sefirah Din); but on Shabbat the power of judgment does not hold sway, and the afternoon meal and prayer becomes "a time of favor" (Psalms 69:14, which has become part of the afternoon prayer: "But as for me, my prayer is unto Thee, in an acceptable time: O God, in the multitude of thy mercy hear me"). See *Zohar* 2:88b (trans. Matt, vol. 4, pp. 499–503) and *Wisdom of the Zohar*, introductions and annotations by Tishby, vol. 3, p. 1281.

17–20: Ze'ir Anpin is speaking in this stanza and continues to speak for at least the following stanza, and possibly through the tenth. The dramatic situation is ambiguous, and as Liebes notes, Luria may well be identifying with Ze'ir Anpin here—calling to the disciples to gather and witness his power and the power of the ritual.

21–24: "Those without" refers to people outside the area of sanctity, which is the Sabbath. In the *Zohar* and other Kabbalistic literature, the Sitra Ahra, or evil forces, are often referred to as "dogs."

25–28: As Scholem sees it, these final stanzas constitute an exorcism of the forces of the Other Side (*On the Kabbalah and its Symbolism*, p. 145). Presumably the speaker is still Ze'ir Anpin, but again, Luria is speaking through these lines as well. In the *Zohar*, the prayers of Israel rise up and brighten the brow of the Ze'ir Anpin, which is usually associated with judgment, and so the forces of darkness are annulled.

29–32: The husks are the *kelippot*, or "shells," which contain sparks of holiness. (See Ya'akov HaKohen, "Prayers for the Protection and Opening of the Heart," above.) There are four dark powers—based on Ezekiel's vision before the chariot (1:4): a whirlwind, a great cloud, a fire infolding itself, and a great brightness about it. For more on the daemonic powers that threaten as the power of holiness wanes with the departure of the Sabbath, see *Wisdom of the Zohar*, introductions and annotations by Tishby, vol. 3, pp. 1236–37.

33–36: The powers of darkness and evil are forced to retreat to their natural dwelling place in the ground. See *Zohar* 2:203b. See also *Wisdom of the Zohar*, introductions and annotations by Tishby, vol. 3, pp. 1236–38.

41–44: Appended to the third hymn is a quote from the *Zohar* 2:88b. Some versions of the hymns—including the one translated here—use a somewhat longer closing line.

Why, My Desire

Text: Habermann, "Shirat HaAri" [Heb], pp. 106–19, where it is attributed to Luria, and Be'eri, "Two New Poems by Luria," pp. 30–31. The rhyme scheme of the Hebrew is AAA, BAA, CAA. Acrostic: "Yitzhak."

It is interesting to compare the poem to Yehudah HaLevi's "Lord, [All My Desire]" (above), for both poems take desire as their subject and are circular in structure. We have, though, no evidence of influence, and unlike Eliezer Azikri, who recommended the recitation of poems by Yehudah HaLevi and Avraham Ibn Ezra, Luria (as his student Hayyim Vital reports) "never recited any hymn, liturgical poem, or prayer composed by the later Sages, such as Rabbi Shelomoh Ibn Gabirol and the like. This is because these Sages were not familiar with the Kabbalah, made mistakes, and did not know what they were saying. He did recite, however, all the liturgical poetry and hymns composed by Rabbi Eliezar Kallir found in the prayer book of the Ashkenazim, since all the early Sages wrote in accordance with the Kabbalah" (Fine, *Safed Spirituality*, p. 74). See also Scholem, *Major Trends*, p. 255; Tietze and Yahalom, *Ottoman Melodies*, p. 31; and Hayyim Vital, *Sha'ar HaKavvanot: Nosah haTefillah* [Heb] (Tel Aviv, 1962), p. 328.

Lines 1–3: Job 13:23–24: "Make me to know my transgression and my sin. Wherefore hidest thou thy face, and holdest me for thine enemy?"

4–6: Joshua 24:13: "[These nations] shall be snares and traps unto you."

7–9: Lamentations 2:16: "All mine enemies have opened their mouth against thee: they hiss and gnash the teeth."

10–12: Isaiah 49:2: "In the shadow of his hand hath he hid me."

13–15: Psalms 119:148: "Mine eyes are awake before the watches of the night"; Lamentations 3:43: "Thou hast covered with anger, and persecuted us."

19–21: Proverbs 16:24: "Pleasant words are as a honeycomb"; Job 40:25: "Canst thou draw out leviathan with an hook? Or his tongue with a cord which thou lettest down?"

Hidden God

This poem is by Avraham ben Maimon, one of Moshe Cordovero's students, who has signed the poem with an acrostic: "Avraham Maimon, Hazak [be strengthened]." (Tovah Be'eri is of the opinion that the name should be Maimin: see Seroussi, "On the Beginnings of the Singing of *Bakkashot* in Nineteenth-Century Jerusalem," pp. 106–24 [note 12].) It progresses through a description of the ten sefirot, mentioning each by name and enumerating its qualities. The most common version of the sefirotic tree has Keter (crown) at the top of a triangle of which Hokhmah (wisdom) and Binah (understanding) form the base. An inverted triangle directly beneath them has Hesed (love or grace) and Gevurah (power) as the two bases and Tiferet (beauty, splendor, or glory) beneath them. The inverted triad beneath that has Netzah (endurance, triumph, or strength) and Hod (splendor or majesty) as the bases and Yesod (foundation) as the inverted apex. At the bottom of this sefirotic tree is Malkhut (kingdom). As the poem proceeds, it integrates a number of philosophical and mystical concepts, as it also weaves together more familiar scriptural passages (e.g., "the beginning of wisdom is fear of the Lord") and a number of *hapax legomena*, or Hebrew words that appear only once in Scripture. It is an extremely popular hymn, sung at the beginning of the winter sessions of *bakkashot* (poems of petition) in Syrian-Jewish (Aleppo) communities and as part of the third Sabbath meal in Hasidic communities.

Text: See www.piyut.org.il/textual/34.html and its thorough commentary, on which the notes below in large part rely. See also Seroussi, "On the Beginnings of the Singing of *Bakkashot* in Nineteenth-Century Jerusalem" [Heb].

Lines 1–4: "*Crown*" — Keter. The opening of the poem is taken from Isaiah 45:15, "You are a God who hides himself," and the stanza also weaves in allusions to Habakkuk 3:4 ("there is the concealment [veiling] of his power") and Jeremiah 43:10. The highest sefirah, Keter, is associated with the invisible, the infinite, and Nothingness. This is the mind of God which is beyond anything that the human mind can grasp. See Matt, "*Ayin*: The Concept of Nothingness in Jewish Mysticism," in *Essential Papers in Kabbalah*, ed. Lawrence Fine (New York, 1995), esp. pp. 76–77: "The other sefirot portray God in personal, anthropomorphic terms. . . . The highest sefirah, however, is characterized by undifferentiation and impersonality." Matt also cites Moshe de León's *Shekel HaKodesh*: "Keter Elyon . . . is called the pure ether that cannot be grasped. It is the totality of all existence, . . . the secret of the Cause of Causes and brings all into being." Cf. Ibn Gabirol's *Kingdom's Crown*, above, and the notes to canto 9, ll. 20–22. Line 4 is drawn from the Kedushah, the part of the Sabbath and festival liturgy that speaks of the angels that surround God.

5–8: "*Wisdom*" — Hokhmah. The sefirah of wisdom involves the beginning of divine manifestation or revelation. It is regarded as the "primordial point" or beginning of the revelation of God in the world, a flash or spark of an idea, which remains to be unfurled. Wisdom is associated with the Torah (the beginning of revelation) and with the letter *yod* in the Tetragrammaton. Traditionally, the Torah is thought to have preceded the creation of the world (*Tanna debe Eliyahu* 31). Job 28:12: "Where shall wisdom be found? And where is the place of understanding?" While line 7 is a play on Job's Hebrew (*me'ayin timatzei*—where *me'ayin* is understood not as "where" but as "from nothing"), it also reflects the Kabbalistic understanding that wisdom emerges from Keter, the sefirah above it, which is associated with Nothingness. The verse from Job also leads into stanza 3, which treats the sefirah of Binah, or understanding.

9–12: Understanding (*"Discernment"*)—Binah. The sefirah of understanding is associated with the heart, which takes up the flash of insight presented by wisdom and develops it in a further externalization or manifestation of the divine in the world. The river is traditionally associated with Binah. Proverbs 20:5: "Counsel in the heart of man is like deep water; but a man of understanding will draw it out." *Rosh HaShanah* 21b: "Fifty gates of understanding were created in the world and all were given to Moses except one." One remains always beyond mankind. The final line of the stanza quotes Psalms 31:24: "The Lord preserves the faithful."

13–16: Grace—Hesed, which is often translated as *"Mercy,"* the sefirah of influence and greatness, as in generosity. It is a greatness that fills the world. Gedulah—the quality of greatness (here "potency")—is commonly associated with, or another name for, Hesed. See Exodus 34:6; Psalms 108:5 and 119:49; Isaiah 63:7. Abraham (through his hospitality, for instance) is associated with this sefirah.

17–20: *"Power"* (or Strength)—Gevurah, which is the sefirah associated with judgment and limitation. Exodus 15:6: "Thy right hand, O Lord, is become glorious in power." The process of differentiation is intensified with this sefirah, which is associated with Isaac and with fear. Unlike Abraham, Isaac does not go back and forth between lands, does not cross borders. The "fear of Isaac" is Isaac's awe before the Lord; see Genesis 31:42.

21–24: *"Glory* of Israel"—Tiferet, which takes up a key position in the middle of the sefirotic tree, aligned with Keter on high and both Yesod (foundation) and Malkhut (kingdom) below. It is associated with Jacob, who combines attributes of Abraham and Isaac, and evokes harmony—perhaps a kind of repose within the borders of self-definition and definition in contrast to the divine.

25–28: The accent in line 25 is to indicate that line begins trochaically and the word *May* should be stressed. *"Endurance"*—Netzah, which is also translated as "eternity" or "victory" (*lenatze'ah* as a verb is "to triumph" or "oversee"; *netzah* as a noun is "eternity"). The phrase *"Endurance of Israel"* (line 26, as well as the sefirah itself) suggests, among other things, the ability to triumph over obstacles, including "darkness" of all sorts and "exile." See Ezra 3:8: "to set forward [supervise] the work of the house of the Lord." See 1 Samuel 15:29.

29–32: Splendor (*"Triumph," "Majesty"*)—Hod. Netzah on the right and Hod on the left constitute the sefirot of prophecy, like two pillars; hence the image of Yakhin and Boaz (1 Kings 7:21). Through these pillars spirit will move. Isaiah 54:13: "And thy children shall be taught of the Lord." The same scriptural reference appears in "Bar Yohai," by Shimon bar Lavi, and Boaz Huss has proposed (in a communication to me) that these two poems may well be the first whose architecture is determined by the sefirot; subsequently, numerous poems (especially in North Africa) will take up this structure.

33–36: *"Foundation"*—Yesod. Yesod is "hidden" in the seven lower sefirot (Hesed through Malkhut), absorbing into it the lights of the sefirot above it and passing them on to Malkhut, which is directly below it. It is associated with the covenant between God and man, and with the pure bond between man and wife. It is also associated with the phallus, with circumcision (as a sign), with the biblical Joseph—who is considered "righteous"—and generally with righteousness and the figure of the Tzaddik. See Proverbs 10:25: "The righteous is an everlasting foundation" and Psalms 119:137: "Righteous art thou, O Lord."

37–40: *"Kingdom"*—Malkhut. The tenth and lowest sefirah, Malkhut, receives the influence of all the sefirot above it and then, in its way, passes that influence on to the world. This sefirah is associated with absorption (like the moon and also like the earth) and with realization in the world. Song of Songs 3:11: "Go forth, ye daughters of Zion, and behold King

Solomon with the crown with which his mother crowned him in the day of his espousals." Isaiah 63:2: "Thou shalt also be a crown of glory in the hand of the Lord, a royal diadem in the hand of God."

41–44: The Kabbalist sees the sefirotic array as a unified force field, a single entity. God is one, and these are His aspects. It is also the task of the aspirant to contribute toward the unification of these aspects, which are dynamic and always in flux. The biblical verse "A whisperer separates close friends" (Proverbs 16:28) was and is understood by the Kabbalists to refer to the unity of the sefirot and the need for strength and purity in approaching them. The "whisperer" in this scheme is someone full of anger or resentment, a slanderer—someone, in short, who does not work toward righteousness or holiness—i.e., the godless individual, or a heretic, whose words cut one off from God and the light of His sefirot. The gemstone is, in the original, a *sapir* (sapphire), which some take to be the origin of the term *sefirah*. Lamentations 4:7: "The beauty of their form was like sapphire." Psalms 119:169: "Let my cry come near before thee, O Lord."

To the Shekhinah

Text: Yisrael Najara, *Zemirot Yisrael*, ed. Yehudah Preis-Horev (Tel Aviv, 1946), p. 139.

As with a number of these poems, the identity of the speaker is ambiguous: it might be the poet, the people (of Israel), or any devotee who longs for the radiant divine (feminine) aspect and is denied the experience of its or her presence (Tietze and Yahalom, *Ottoman Melodies*, pp. 24–27). The addressee is a female beloved who closely resembles the cruel beloved of classical Arabic and Hebrew poetry, and the sensual dimension is palpable. Yahalom notes the intentional blurring of boundaries between the symptoms of profane and sacred love: "Sorrow and pain, sleeplessness and awe—[all were] attributes . . . of the yearning, fervent mystics. This was the spirit in which the Early Risers sang their songs at the rim of dawn, while performing their special holy vigils. And just as these were songs to which the Kabbalists were wont to cleave, so did the aura of Kabbalism cleave to the circumstances of their composition" (Tietze and Yahalom, *Ottoman Melodies*, p. 25). The commentary below shows how Najara intensifies this blurring of borders through the use of scriptural verses that seem to "go both ways." This luminous aspect of the Shekhinah stands in stark contrast to, for instance, "Lekhah Dodi," where the Shekhinah is treated explicitly in terms of her exile and abjection. In Najara's poetry for the annual cycle of holidays, there is almost no mention whatsoever of this dimension of the Shekhinah (Tovah Be'eri, "*Olat Hodesh*, by R. Yisrael Najara" [Heb], p. 324, and Benayahu, "R. Yisrael Najara" [Heb]); on the contrary, in that body of work the Shekhinah (like other Kabbalistic concepts and symbols) is treated in integrated, implied, and often erotic fashion. While this poem is perhaps an extreme example of that erotic figuration, it is very much part of a continuum that defines Najara's oeuvre. The translation here consists of the first half of the poem: the entire poem embeds a signature acrostic: "I-S-R-AEL," a further indication of its devotional character, as in the Hebrew tradition, only liturgical or sacred poems bore acrostic signatures. (The second half of the poem is more generic in its imagery.) In the original the two lines about Venus are repeated as a refrain. The poet has, therefore, clearly placed the poems in a religious context (Benayahu, "R. Yisrael Najara" [Heb] p. 227), and—as with so many of Najara's devotional poems, the hymn is followed in the text by the scriptural verse that prompted it—in this case a citation from Isaiah 60:1–2: "Arise, shine, for thy light is come, and the glory of the Lord is risen upon thee. For, behold, the darkness shall cover over the earth, and gross darkness the people, but the Lord shall arise upon thee, and his glory shall be seen upon thee." Yahalom (Tietze and Yahalom, *Ottoman Melodies*, p. 23) points out the similarity between Najara's eroticized devotion and that of Indian devotional (or Bhakti) poetry. See Lee Siegel, *Sacred and Profane Dimensions of Love in Indian Traditions* (Oxford, 1978), pp. 9ff. As Tovah Be'eri observes, the words *poem* and *prayer* were virtually interchangeable for Najara, for whom the worshipper was himself, as it were, the sacrifice offered on the altar (Be'eri, "*Olat Hodesh* by R. Yisrael Najara" [Heb], pp. 319–20).

Lines 1–8: Psalms 64:8–10: "But God shoots his arrow at them: sud-
denly . . . all that see them shake their heads. And all men are afraid."
Isaiah 58:2: "They desire that God should be near."
9–16: Exodus 34:30: "Behold the skin of his face shone and they were
afraid to come near him."

Your Kingdom's Glory

Text: Najara, *Zemirot Yisrael*, p. 8.

This is one of Najara's most widely known poems. One senses in it
something one feels in much of Najara's work—namely, that the poems
rely heavily on their melodies and musical settings (which Najara him-
self sometimes composed), and that it is hard to separate the lyrics from
the song. Scholem's discussion of the poem in the Shabbatian context
was first published as "A Poem of R. Yisrael Najara Among the Shab-
batians," in *Ignace Goldziher Memorial Volume*, ed. S. Loewinger and
S. Somogyi (Budapest, 1948–58), pp. 41–44, and in *Behinot* 8 (1955), p. 85.
See also the appendix to the Hebrew edition of Scholem's *Sabbatai Sevi:
The Mystical Messiah* (Tel Aviv, 1957), and in G. Scholem, *Shabbatian
Studies* [Heb] (Tel Aviv, 1991), pp. 737–41. (The material is treated in
cursory fashion on p. 355 of the English edition [Princeton, 1973], which
notes that the hymn "was circulated from Gaza to the Diaspora . . . [and]
was considered a prophecy foretelling Sabbatai Sevi's coming. . . . In
due course [it] became a kind of signature which [Sabbatian] believers
used for over a century. Authors with Sabbatian sympathies would copy
it in their notebooks, and print it in their tracts and books.") See, too,
Edwin Seroussi, "Your Kingdom's Glory: A Piyyut by R. Yisrael Najara
Sung by the Shabbatians and Its Melodies" [Heb], *Tarbiz* 62 (1992–93),
pp. 361–79, and *The Kronika: On Jacob Frank and the Frankist Move-
ment* [Heb], ed. H. Levine (Jerusalem, 1984), pp. 44–45, 60–63. There is
a measure of odd poetic justice, or strange coincidence, to the phenom-
enon of the poem's embrace by the Shabbatians, as Najara's grandson
Yaakov, who eventually inherited his father and grandfather's position as
rabbi in Gaza, hosted Shabbatai Tzvi at his home and—convinced that

Tzvi was the Messiah—became one of his followers (Benayahu, "R. Yis-rael Najara," p. 216). See also Tietze and Yahalom, *Ottoman Melodies,* p. 30.

Lines 1–4: Psalms 145:11: "They shall speak of the glory of thy king-dom, and talk of thy power"; Jeremiah 23:5: "Behold the days come, saith the Lord, that I will raise unto David a righteous Branch, and a King shall reign and prosper"; 1 Chronicles 1:43.

5–8: Genesis 32:28; Proverbs 24:21.

9–12: Psalms 5:13; Isaiah 56:8.

13–16: Habakkuk 2:3: "Though it tarry, wait for it"; 1 Samuel 8:5: "make us a king."

17–20: Psalms 27:13: "I had fainted, unless I had believed to see the goodness of the Lord in the land of the living."

21–24: Psalms 147:13, 40:2–3; Job 33:30: "To bring back his soul from the pit, to be enlightened with the light of the living."

25–28: Psalms 26:6; Zechariah 9:17.

Extensions East and West

Information for the headnote is drawn from the following sources: *The Hebrew Poetry of Yemen* [Heb], ed. Yehuda Ratzhaby (Tel Aviv, 1988), Ratzhaby, "R. Shalem Shabazi and His Poetry" [Heb], *Sefunot* 9 (1965), Ratzhaby, "A Messianic Poem by Shalem Shabazi from the Shabbatian Period" [Heb], *Pe'amim* 44 (1990), and Zakharya al-Dhahari, *Sefer Ha-Musar,* ed. Yehuda Ratzhaby (Jerusalem, 1965), pp. 31 and 43, and in *Se-fer HaMusar,* bk. 6, ll. 1–19ff.; Yosef Tobi, "Two Poems Concerning Shab-batian Events in Yemen" [Heb], *Pe'amim* 44 (1990); Adena Tannenbaum, "Kabbalah in a Literary Key: Mystical Motifs in Zechariah al-Dhahari's *Sefer HaMusar," Journal of Jewish Thought and Philosophy* 17:1 (2009), pp. 47–99; Amnon Shiloah, "The Influence of the World of Kabbalah on the Development of the Singing of Liturgical Poetry" [Heb], *Mekedem umiyam,* 2 (1986), pp. 209–15; *The Poetry of Yemen* (Cincinnati, 1930); *Jewish Poetry in Yemen* [Heb], ed. Ratzon Halevi, 2 vols. (Kiryat Ono, 1997–2003); Hayyim Zafrani, *Hebrew Poetry in Morocco* [Heb] (Jerusalem

1984), pp. 12ff. and 72ff.; Efraim Hazan, *Hebrew Poetry in North Africa* [Heb] (Jerusalem, 1995), *Tehilah leDavid: The Poetry of David ben Hasin* [Heb], ed. Hazan (Lod, 1999), *The Poems of Fraji Shawat*, ed. Hazan (Jerusalem, 1976), and Hazan, "Praise of Saints in the Song and Poetry of the Jews of North Africa" [Heb], *Mehkerei Yerushalayim beFoklor* 2 (1982); Moshe Hallamish, *The Kabbalah in North Africa: A Historical and Cultural Survey* (Tel Aviv, 2001), Hallamish, "On the Genres of Kabbalistic Creation in Morocco" [Heb], *Pe'amim* 15 (1983), pp. 29–46, Hallamish, "Some Words on the Status of the Kabbalah and the Genres of Kabbalistic Creation in Morocco" [Heb], in *Misgav Yerushalayim: Studies in the Literature of the Jewish People* [Heb], ed. Efraim Hazan (Jerusalem, 1987), pp. 99–142, and Hallamish, "R. Yaakov Ifargan and His Work" [Heb], *Pe'amim* 43 (1990), pp. 85–110; and Moshe Ibn Tzur, *Tziltzelei Shema* (Alexandria, 1892), pp. 1–6.

Quotations are from the following sources: *If I hadn't held onto this [hidden] wisdom*: al-Dhahari, *Sefer HaMusar*, bk. 23, p. 266 (the allusion is to Blanchot's saying that one writes so as not to die; Zafrani refers to Blanchot in relation to Moroccan rather than Yemenite poetry in *Hebrew Poetry in Morocco* [Heb], p. 12, and cites Blanchot's *Space of Literature*, trans. Ann Smock [Lincoln, Neb., 1982]); *The lovely doe: Jewish Poetry in Yemen*, poem 25, vol. 1, p. 56.

Who Kissed Me

Text: *Hebrew Poetry of Yemen* [Heb], ed. Ratzhaby, p. 85; *Jewish Poetry in Yemen*, ed. Halevi, poem 220, vol. 1, p. 321; and at www.piyut.org.il. See also Ratzhaby, "R. Shalem Shabazi and His Poetry," pp. 135–66. Ratzhaby quotes the poet as expressing pride in the fact that he was not tempted to write love poems in the secular Arabic modes. "I did not sully my poems by writing of love affairs." Acrostic: "Shalem ben Yosef." Mishael Maswari Caspi takes this one step further and observes that "the genre of [these] 'who kissed me' [poems] transfers the Hebrew poetry of Yemen from the category of philosophical poetry to the category of Kabbalistic poetry" (*Hebrew Poetry in Yemen* [Heb] [Ramat Gan, 1991], pp. xvi–xvii).

Line 1: The situation the poet describes is both personal and collective. The soul's daily return to the body at dawn is described in the first prayer uttered on waking: "I offer thanks before you, O King who lives eternally, for you have restored my soul to me with mercy, great is your faith." The rest of the poem develops the body-soul relationship. In medieval Jewish thought, the divine kiss is often associated with death—which releases the soul from the body to which it had been bound. True life is found in that release, and so the kiss in fact brings deliverance. Shabazi seems to be reversing the polarity of this image: the mystical kiss is the miracle of waking daily—ideally to a life of perfection and elevation through study (see below, ll. 11–12). There are numerous additional elements embodying the interlinked Kabbalistic vocabulary in the poem. Other commentators have understood the kiss in midrashic terms as the descent of the Torah at Sinai. Cf. *Song of Songs Rabbah*, where the giving of the Torah is likened to a kiss, and, more centrally, Song of Songs 1:2–4: "Let him kiss me with the kisses of his mouth. . . . The king hath brought me into his chambers."

2: The king's chambers in this case can be identified as the presence of God (the beloved), or the space of spiritual immersion in the study of Scripture and its mysteries.

3–4: At dawn, upon waking. The sigh is both the sound of the body stirring and an expression of being moved.

5–6: Only God's mercy returns the soul to the body each day. Elsewhere the *Zohar* notes, "The soul of man in this world departs from him each night and is returned to him each morning." See *Zohar* 1:83a–b, trans. Daniel C. Matt, 5 vols. (Stanford, Calif., 2004–9), vol. 2, pp. 29ff. ("When a person climbs into bed, his soul leaves him and ascends on high. . . . The soul departs, and in the body remains nothing but a trace of a pint of the heart's vitality"); and see also *Zohar* 3:120b: "When night falls the lower tree [the Shekhinah], upon which death is dependent, spreads its branches and covers everything, and so it becomes dark. And everyone in the world has a taste of death. But man first entrusts his soul to it as a surety, and since it has taken it on trust, the surety returns to its original owner at the break of day. When morning comes, and his surety has been returned to him, a man must praise the Holy One, blessed be He" (*Wisdom of the Zohar,* arranged and rendered into Hebrew by Fischel Lachower and Isaiah Tishby; introductions and annotations by Isaiah Tishby, trans. David Goldstein, 3 vols. [Oxford, 1997], vol. 3, p. 1033).

7–8: The soul in the medieval understanding combines the various elements that make up a person's temperament or character, holding them together as one.

9–10: "You who have fathomed fate's trials" refers to the People of Israel, and especially to Yemenite Jewry and the trials it was then undergoing.

11–12: Literally, the secret (or mystery) of the Torah and the commandments. The soul in the body guides a person toward perfection through immersion in the mysteries of Scripture (in the broadest sense). While it's unlikely that Shabazi was familiar with Abulafia's teachings, an interesting parallel does present itself in the latter's ecstatic Kabbalah, where the kiss is associated with the descent of the Active Intellect upon the mind. Idel writes of Abulafia's belief that "intense spiritual apprehension may itself attenuate the connection between body and soul and bring about death. Elsewhere in Abulafia, we read: 'For he will kiss him with the kisses of his mouth: immediately he will awaken from his slumber and know the day of his death and understand the great difference between his soul and his body.' The voluntaristic aspect of the process here is striking: when the Active Intellect pours its 'kisses' upon the soul, the soul understands that it must acquire its eternity by means of study" (*The Mystical Experience in Abraham Abulafia* [Albany, N.Y., 1988], pp. 181–82).

13–14: I.e., upon death, when the soul returns to its source on high. Metatron, the highest angel, prince of the world, and heavenly scribe (*Avodah Zarah* 3b, *Hagigah* 15a, *Sanhedrin* 38b), figures prominently in mystical literature. He is identified with the Active Intellect, among other things, and often defends the People of Israel. He is also the prince of Torah and Wisdom (*Oti'ot deR. Akiva,* 1). According to de Vidas, he represents "the grade of spirit" (Lawrence Fine, *Safed Spirituality: Rules of Mystical Piety, the Beginning of Wisdom* [Ramsey, N.J., 1984], p. 140).

15–16: Ratzhaby comments that these lines indicate the poem may have been composed for one of the ten days of *teshuvah*, or repentance, between the Jewish New Year and the Day of Atonement, a time when God's presence might be more keenly felt.

17–18: At this point the poem takes a decidedly personal turn and speaks of the poet's children and their predicament—though once again, the personal and collective situations were virtually identical at this point and merge in powerful fashion.

The Myrtle's Scent

Text: *Jewish Poetry in Yemen*, ed. Halevi, poem 8, p. 44.

Lines 1–4: This poem seems to relate to the end of the Sabbath and the start of the profane week. This liminal time is perilous, as the *Zohar* makes clear: "As soon as Sabbath departs, a specter, an evil officer, ascends from Hell, intent on seizing power. . . . But Israel takes action with myrtle and wine, reciting Havdalah [the ritual marking the departure of the Sabbath and reentry into profane time, and] . . . that specter sinks into his place in Sheol. . . . Separation is always on the . . . left" (*Zohar* 1:17b, trans. Matt, vol. 1, p. 132). Myrtle (with wine) is used in the Havdalah (separation) ritual marking the end of the Sabbath. Its scent—like the prayers one recites at the time—is intended to ward off the daemonic powers and fires that had been in abeyance during the Sabbath and now return with a vengeance. See also *Zohar* 2:20a, 2:208b–209a, and *Wisdom of the Zohar*, introductions and annotations by Isaiah Tishby, vol. 3, p. 1237: "Myrtle sustains the holy place from which the souls come." Elsewhere the *Zohar* says that when the extra soul (or oversoul) of the Sabbath is removed, the soul and spirit would separate if the scent of the myrtle did not bind them (3:35a–b)—a theme we've already encountered in Shabazi's work ("Who Kissed Me"). Myrtle is, in the scheme of Kabbalistic commentary, the shrub on which souls grow—something noted in two Kabbalistic works, *Tola'at Ya'akov* and *Shenei Luhot haBerit*. See "Myrtle," *The Jewish Encyclopedia* (New York, 1925). The myrtle's scent, then, is associated with the Sabbath and the Shekhinah's presence, and also with spiritual awakening; it rises over the night of Israel's exile (analogous to the profane days of the week). Zechariah 1:8–11 talks of "the myrtle trees that were in the bottom"—which commentators understand as referring to Israel in the depths of exile. (See also Isaiah 55:13.) Kabbalistically, the myrtle is associated with the *sefirah* of Tiferet (beauty). Midnight is also the preferred time for study and song in the Kabbalistic context. The beloved is God and His presence, who guides the Congregation of Israel in its exile but has not yet brought it redemption. See *Rosh Hashanah* 23a: "R. Johanan further said: One who studies the Torah but does not teach it is like the myrtle in the wilderness. Others report [the saying thus]: One who studies the Torah and teaches it in a place where there is no [other] *talmid hakham* is like the myrtle in the wilderness, which is precious."

5–8: The desert is the desert of exile. The Congregation of Israel is speaking, though it seems as though she is also speaking for the Shekhinah, which is forced to wander abjectly. She and the feminine Congregation of Israel (Knesset Israel) are in similar positions.

9–12: The partner who wanders is the Shekhinah. See *Zohar* 1:250a, trans. Matt, vol. 3, p. 538.

13–16: Cf. Zechariah 1:10–11: "And the man that stood among the myrtle trees answered and said, These are they whom the Lord hath sent to walk to and fro through the earth. . . . And the angel of the Lord answered and said, O Lord of hosts, how long wilt thou not have mercy on Jerusalem and on the cities of Judah?"

17–20: The invisible soul dwells on high, in the sefirah of Wisdom.

21–24: The soul is inextricably involved with the ten sefirot and the three supernal worlds: Creation, Formation, and Action. (Ten times three equals thirty.) According to Moshe Cordovero, there are four spiritual worlds—the three just mentioned, and Emanation, which pertains only to the highest sefirah.

25–28: "The sinister aspect" is the evil impulse (which is identified with the left side). See notes to ll. 1–4.

29–32: The impulse toward good is identified with the right.

33–36: The palace is the upper world of the spirit.

41–44: The rivers of Eden, which cleanse souls.

45–48: The light of Creation, which stretched from one end of the universe to the other. The poem is followed by a verse from the liturgy: "Please, Lord, save us."

Bar Yohai

Shimon Lavi was born near the end of the fifteenth century and came to Fez with other Iberian refugees. In 1549 he set out for Palestine, but he was waylaid in Tripoli and settled there, where he found a community in need of religious leadership. He was the leading Kabbalist of the time in North Africa and was also known as a poet. His most famous prose work, *Ketem Paz*, is a commentary on the parts of the *Zohar* dealing with the days of creation and Exodus. (Recently, Yehudah Liebes has proposed that there is compelling evidence to conclude that the author of the poem translated here is not the author of the famous commentary on the *Zohar* but another Spanish refugee by the same name—Shimon Lavi. Moreover, he argues, the poem is primarily linked with Palestine, where it was probably written. See "Bar Yohai, Shiro Shel Shimon Lavi" [Heb], *Keshet HaHadashah* 5 [2003], pp. 126–42.) The principal work on Shimon Lavi and his *Zohar* commentary is by Boaz Huss: *Al adne paz: The Kabbalah of R. Shimon Lavi* [Heb] (Jerusalem, 2000) and "The Theory of the Sefirot in R. Shimon Lavi's *Ketem Paz*" [Heb], *Pe'amim* 43 (1990), pp. 51–84. Liebes agrees with Huss that prose work of Lavi offers no evidence whatsoever that would shed light on the poem in question.

It seems that the poem was originally intended to be sung as part of the Kabbalat Shabbat or after the Shabbat evening service in the synagogue, or perhaps as part of the late-night *bakkashot* or *tikkun Shabbat* gathering; in time it also became part of the Lag BaOmer rituals celebrated near Safed, at Mount Meron, the site of Shimon Bar Yohai's grave. Today it is regularly sung at the table before the Friday evening meal, and also on a variety of other occasions. Some objected to its recitation, citing the depth of its mystery and the strength of its Kabbalistic secrets. All the more interesting, then, is the fact that this is one of the most popular

Kabbalist hymns in the repertoire. See Hallamish, "Shir Bar Yohai," in *The Book of the Zohar and Its Generation: Proceedings of the Third International Conference on the History of Jewish Mysticism* [Heb], ed. Joseph Dan (Jerusalem, 1989), pp. 357–85; Hazan, "Praise of Saints" [Heb].

Bar Yohai figures prominently in the history of Jewish mysticism because he is the principal figure of the *Zohar*. In that book and in the Kabbalah generally, and even more intensively in North Africa, the figure of the Jewish sage, or saint, was regarded as symbolically linked to the powers and aspects of the sefirot. This sense of their holiness in part derives from the pronounced folk tradition in Moroccan Judaism but also from Islamic influence. With the saint's death, he returns to the world of truth, where his proximity to God strengthens his ability to exert an influence on the dynamics of the divine world. See Hazan, "Praise of Saints," p. 82; Isaiah Tishby, *Mishnat HaZohar* [Heb] (Jerusalem, 1961), pp. 655–734. As part of the general veneration of these saints, pilgrimages were regularly made by ordinary people—men, women, and children—to their graves and tombs (as in Safed), and especially in North Africa scores of hymns were composed on the occasion of these pilgrimages. Lavi's poem is, as mentioned, the prototype for such hymns. It is saturated with allusions to the *Zohar*.

Text: The text and commentary that follow draw primarily on Yehudah Liebes's article "Bar Yohai beShiro shel Shimon Lavi" [Heb] and the remarks at: www.piyut.org.il/articles/418.html#13. The poem's structure appears to be straightforward—ten stanzas that follow Rabbi Shimon Bar Yohai's ascent up through the ten sefirot—but Liebes presents a reading of the poem that departs from traditional interpretations in certain key ways. The poem embeds a signature acrostic, "Shimon Lavi," which Liebes believes sets up a compelling identification of the two men named Shimon—Bar Yohai and Lavi. (*Lavi* also means "lion," which is one of Bar Yohai's epithets in the *Zohar* and the Talmud. See especially the note to ll. 36–40 below.) As Liebes sees it, Lavi views himself as an incarnation of Bar Yohai, and the reader or worshipper who sings the hymn with the proper *kavvanah* (intention and concentration) himself becomes part of this legacy.

Refrain: Bar Yohai was one of seven students of the great Rabbi Akiva. His selection as leader of the rabbinical court after Akiva's martyrdom and under extremely dangerous conditions, as the Romans had forbidden gatherings of a political sort, is depicted in the Jerusalem Talmud, *Hagigah* 14b. Cf. Psalms 45:8: "Therefore God, thy God, hath anointed thee with the oil of gladness above thy fellows"; and *Zohar* 3:212b, where *sasson* (joy) is associated with God — so that the *"oil of joy"* here is anointment by God. In Liebes's reading the refrain corresponds to the sefirah of Malkhut (kingdom). Coming at the head of the poem and then after every stanza, like Malkhut it receives the influence of all the other stanzas (and all the other sefirot) and grows with their power. See also H. Kolitz, *Ben HaAliyyah* [Heb] (Jerusalem, 1986), pp. 42–49. Bar Yohai thus becomes identified with the Presence of God in the world (the Shekhinah). In this sense, the poem is not only about Bar Yohai's ascent through the sefirot, but the ascent of Malkhut, which reverses the flow that had come from on high. See Liebes, *"Zohar* and Eros" [Heb], *Alpayyim* 9 (1994), pp. 104–6, for extensive discussion.

Lines 4–8: Liebes associates this stanza with Yesod (foundation), as it treats the quality of holiness which draws oil through it; oil, like sperm, is in the Kabbalistic framework associated with abundance and is channeled through Yesod. (The standard reading associates the stanza with Malkhut.) Cf. Exodus 30:25, where the sacred oil was prepared for the utensils in the desert sanctuary. Here Bar Yohai is likened to the high priest wearing sanctity like a miter (cf. Exodus 39:30). In the *Zohar*, the priest's miter is evidence of connection to the divine. See also Ezekiel 24:17. The image here links Bar Yohai's wearing of tefillin to the biblical high priest Aaron's wearing a miter. In short, Bar Yohai and Yesod both draw down holiness from on high. See for example, *Zohar* 3:247a–b.

12–16: This stanza Liebes associates with Hod (majesty or glory), which is mentioned explicitly toward the end of the stanza. (The traditional reading links it to Yesod.) Bar Yohai fled the Roman authorities and hid in a cave with R. Eliezer. According to *Shabbat* 33b, he stayed in the cave for thirteen years, studying Torah and developing his powers. Cf. Isaiah 2:19: "And they shall go into the holes of the rocks, and into the caves of the earth, for fear of the Lord, and for the glory of his majesty." The cave or cleft in the rock traditionally marks the meeting of man (Moses and Elijah) and God. See also Psalms 45:4: "Gird thy sword upon thy thigh, O most mighty, with thy glory and thy majesty." Liebes also raises the possibility that the stanza encodes an allusion to the author's own flight and retreat to a sanctuary—his fleeing Iberia and finding refuge in North Africa (or Palestine).

18–22: In Liebes's reading this stanza corresponds to Netzah (endurance), as the *Zohar* associates divine study with this sefirah (e.g., *Zohar* 3:61a). (Traditionally it is associated with Netzah and Hod.) The acacias refer to the wooden columns of the sanctuary (Exodus 26:15), which in this context stand for the sefirot of endurance (and to an extent also Hod). These are likened to students immersed in sacred study, drawing from the sefirah of Tiferet (beauty). The columns hold up the sanctuary, to which the presence of God (the Shekhinah) attends; so too the students in their study. Both burn with a wondrous and enduring light. The Hebrew alludes to Isaiah 54:13, which has "disciples of the Lord" (spelled out YHVH—hence the translation of "the Name").

24–28: The Field of Apples is the space of Eden and Malkhut (Bar Yohai) reaching up to the sefirah of Tiferet. (Here and in the following stanzas, Liebes's reading coincides with the traditional view.) Tiferet is linked with the Torah and with the image of man. Bar Yohai's perfection was such that God had him in mind when He said, "Let us create man in our image" (Genesis 1:26). (See also Yitzhak Luria's "Hymns for the Three Sabbath Meals," above, where the field is associated in more standard fashion with Malkhut and the Shekhinah.)

30–34: This stanza treats the sefirah of Gevurah (power), which is associated with fire and rigor—the setting of boundaries and the eradication of evil. See Psalms 65:7. Bar Yohai is known in the Talmud as a fierce and fearless warrior on behalf of the People of Israel and its faith. See also Isaiah 28:5–6, Deuteronomy 33:2, and Ezekiel 21:10.

36–40: This stanza corresponds to Hesed (grace). The Palace of Marble is associated in the Talmud and the post-Talmudic tradition with mystical inquiry. It goes back to the famous story of Rabbi Akiva and the three other sages who ascend into the upper world of esoteric exploration, with its palace where the marble floors look like water. All except Akiva are struck down (*Hagigah* 14b; see note 7 to the Introduction, above). The lion is one of the four creatures of Ezekiel's chariot (*merkavah*), which is also associated with mystical speculation. See Ezekiel 1:10. "Stood . . . before the Lion" can also be understood in terms of the sefirot, as the lion is associated with Gevurah (power). Counting from the highest to the lowest sefirah, Hesed comes before Gevurah, i.e., before the lion — where Bar Yohai stands in this stanza, bearing witness to the heights of creation and its secrets (literally, the bowls on the capitals [of creation's pillars]). See 1 Kings 7:41.

42–46: The green region alludes to *Hagigah* 12a: "Tohu is a green line that encompasses the whole world, out of which darkness proceeds, for it is said: He made darkness His hiding-place round about Him . . . And he shall stretch over it the line of confusion." I.e., he has arrived at the place from which the universe and time come forth, where the line is drawn between chaos and order. "The green line" is associated with insight and understanding in the mystical literature, and the stanza is aligned with Binah. (See also Ibn Gabirol, "He Dwells Forever," ll. 26–30, above, for similar imagery.) The seven Sabbaths (and fifty days) are those between Passover and Shavu'ot (Pentecost), which marks the giving of the Torah. The "fifty's mystery" is, in the Talmudic and Kabbalistic tradition, the fifty gates of the sefirah Binah (understanding), to which this stanza corresponds. *Rosh Hashanah* 21b: "Fifty gates of understanding were created in the world, and all were given to Moses save one, as it says, Yet thou hast made him but little lower than a God." The implication here is that Bar Yohai is in a sense superior even to Moses, as he has access to all fifty, and that he was able to combine all the secrets involved (i.e., those of sacred time and knowledge) in the bond of the letter *shin*, which is engraved on, and stands for, the phylacteries tied and bound to the hand and the head. The letters spelled out (*shin, nun*) have the numerological value of three hundred and fifty, which is to say the seven Sabbaths multiplied by the fifty gates. The *shin* of the knot has been read as standing for Shaddai (the Almighty), one of the names of God. *Berakhot* 7a: "The Holy One, blessed be He, showed Moses the knot of the phylacteries."

48–52: This stanza is associated with the sefirah of wisdom (Hokhmah). "The point of wisdom's emergence" is, literally in the Hebrew, "the *yod* of ancient (primordial) wisdom"—i.e., its first sign, and also the first letter of the Tetragrammaton. "The depths of His resplendence" in the Hebrew alludes to Psalms 45:14: "All glorious is the King's daughter within her chamber." The thirty-two channels are those we first encountered in *Sefer Yetzirah*—the ten sefirot and the twenty-two letters of the Hebrew alphabet (see "Book of Creation," note to line 1, above). See also Ezekiel 28:14: "I created you, a cherub with outstretched shielding wings. . . . And you resided on God's holy mountain; You walked among stones of fire."

54–58: This stanza corresponds to the sefirah of Keter (crown), which is beyond comprehension and knowing, and is therefore often called "Nothing" or "Nothingness." The wondrous light, overwhelming fullness, and mystery allude to *Hagigah* 13a, which also resonates with the poem's previous stanzas: "Behold it is written: He revealeth the deep and secret things; He knoweth, what is in the darkness, and the light dwelleth with Him. There is no contradiction: the one [verse] refers to the inner chambers, the other to the outer chambers. And R. Aha b. Jacob said: There is still another Heaven above the heads of the living creatures, for it is written: And over the heads of the living creatures there was a likeness of a firmament, like the color of the terrible ice, stretched forth over their heads above. Thus far you have permission to speak, thenceforward you have not permission to speak, for so it is written in the Book of Ben Sira: 'Seek not things that are too hard for thee, and search not things that are hidden from thee.'" See Daniel C. Matt, "*Ayin*: The Concept of Nothingness," in *Essential Papers in Kabbalah*, ed. Lawrence Fine (New York, 1995), and notes to *Kingdom's Crown*, canto 9, ll. 20ff., above.

60–64: This stanza seems to refer to the secrets of the *Zohar* and also sums up the mysteries and wonders of the mystical doctrine embodied in the previous verses, which together constitute "the Work of the Chariot," as in *Hagigah* 14a. That Talmudic passage concludes with images that the poet incorporates into his poem: "R. Joshua and R. Jose the priest were going on a journey. They said: Let us also expound the 'Work of the Chariot' . . . and a kind of rainbow appeared in the cloud, and the ministering angels assembled and came to listen like people who assemble and come to watch the entertainments of a bridegroom and bride. [Thereupon] R. Jose the priest went and related what happened before R. Johanan

b. Zakkai; and [the latter] said: Happy are ye, and happy is she that bore you; happy are my eyes that have seen thus." The image of the first stanza has evolved. Bar Yohai is no longer wearing the miter of the priest; the *people* are like priests before him, and the Urim and Thummim (like Bar Yohai's teachings) are on their breastplates. Bar Yohai now assumes a Godlike presence.

In Praise of the Name and Its Mystery

Text: Moshe Hallamish, "R. Yaakov Ifargan and His Work" [Heb].

Ifargan was born ca. 1581 in Morocco. While he was an important transmitter of the Kabbalah there, he left behind only two books (one mystical) and three poems. In one of the poems—a rhymed-prose composition that is essentially a Kabbalistic reworking of Ibn Gabirol's *Kingdom's Crown*—the poet notes that God, in the sublime mystery of His great Name, sent out a second light (of the second sefirah, Hokhmah). That light contains the secret of the first letter of His Name (in this case, the *yod* of YAH), and from it all the letters of the alphabet emerged. Souls are nourished and given delight by this light. The poem translated here is among the most obscure in this volume, and elements of it resist decoding. At the same time, it casts a strong sonic spell and conveys as well as any Kabbalistic verse the sense of mystery that attends to the Name of God and the permutation of letters. It is presented here then, despite the fact that parts of it remain impenetrable. Hallamish's 1990 article provides background information but little in the way of explication; my commentary here is, in part, indebted to Dvora Bregman.

Lines 1–4: "The upper tip of the *yod* denotes the first and highest sefirah" (*The Early Kabbalah*, ed. and introduced Joseph Dan, texts trans. Ronald C. Keiner [New York, 1986], p. 131, n. 13). According to the thirteenth-century mystical work *Ma'ayan haHokhmah* (The Spring of Wisdom), the *yod* is—as Scholem puts it—"precisely the original source of language. . . . The *yod* is the 'purling well' of all linguistic movement, which ramifies and is differentiated in the infinite" (Scholem, "The Name of God and the Linguistic Theory of the Kabbalah," part 2, *Diogenes* 80 [1972], p. 170). For Moshe de León it is the first intellect emanated from God (Elliot R. Wolfson, "Letter Symbolism and Merkavah Imagery in the Zohar," in *Alei Shefer: Studies in the Literature of Jewish Thought, Presented to Rabbi Dr. Alexandre Safran*, ed. Moshe Hallamish [Ramat Gan, 1990], p. 204). The name of God in question appears to be the Tetragrammaton—the four-letter name: YHVH, though the final *hey* is never mentioned. The letter *yod* is understood to have three "crowns"—one pointing upward, one downward, and the third connecting the upper world and the lower world. This middle crown is hidden in the letter itself. On the mystery of the *yod* and the letters that follow it in the Tetragrammaton, see *Zohar* 2:133b–34a, trans. Matt, vol. 5, pp. 239ff.: "YHVH—inscription of the letter *yod*, supernal head of the Holy Name. (*Eloheinu*) Our God—mysterious inscription of the supernal letter *hey*, second letter in the Holy Name. YHVH—a flow conducted below by a mysterious inscription of the letter *vuv*, for those two letters are drawn here, and it is one. All these three are one in one unity." See also vol. 5, p. 158, and the notes there for more on the sefirotic symbolism of the Tetragrammaton.

5–8: These lines are difficult, and might be paraphrased as follows: The word *yod*—spelled out in Hebrew as *yod, vuv, dalet*—has the numerological equivalent of twenty and so is understood to contain the ten sefirot, descended and then ascended. The three crowns that the *yod* contains might also be seen as the first three sefirot—Keter, Hokhmah, Binah—all of which pertain to "knowing." The first *hey* in the Tetragrammaton is associated with Binah. The second *hey* of the Tetragrammaton is associated with the lowest sefirah, Malkhut—the link to the world.

9–12: *Vuv* is the connector, linking what is above and below and drawing down the holiness from on high, and raising the sparks of holiness from below. It is possible that it stands for the six intermediate sefirot (Hesed, Gevurah, Tiferet, Netzah, Hod, and Yesod). The *vuv* then links the upper and lower worlds through Binah to "its end that follows," which is to say, the lowest sefirah, Malkhut (the Shekhinah). See Fine, *Safed Spirituality*, pp. 187–88 (notes to de Vidas's *The Beginning of Wisdom*).

13–16: "Four" as in the four letters of God's Name, or the four Kabbalistic worlds, or the four stages or rings of emanation of which Ifargan writes in his prose—one linked or subordinated to the other. "Ten" as in the number of sefirot. In his prose Ifargan writes that the ten sefirot cling with ardor to the Infinite from which they spring (Hallamish, "R. Yaakov Ifargan and His Work" [Heb], p. 95).

17–20: *Nun* is the Hebrew letter whose numerological equivalent is fifty, and which is in turn associated with the fifty gates of Binah (knowing; see ll. 5–8). It may also be associated with *nefilah*, or falling. In other Kabbalistic poetry, the Shekhinah falls (associated with the fall of Jerusalem) and is sent into exile (see Moshe Zacut, "I rise in the middle of the night," in *I Raise My Heart: Poems by Moses Zacut* [Heb], ed. Dvora Bregman [Jerusalem, 2009], pp. 442ff.). The letter *ayin*, whose numerological value is seventy (as in the seventy faces of Torah or the seventy archetypal languages), is associated with the Infinite mystery, a fountain (or spring—*ayin*) of wisdom. In this light one might begin to make sense of this obscure stanza as follows: With the falling of *nun* (the descent of God's presence into the world as Binah, or knowing), or with the stumbling (transgression or error) of man, which paradoxically allows him to rise, "being in the Name comes to be." And the secret *at the end* of the mystery (or of the Infinite) turns out to be there *at its heart* all along. There may also be a play on the word *ayin* as "eye." In his other (Ibn Gabirol–like) poem, Ifargan writes, echoing canto 9 of *Kingdom's Crown*: "He illumines the seven branches with the secret of the fifty gates [of Binah], and draws light from Nothingness, in extending light from the eye."

21–26: De Vidas writes, "Our soul issues forth from the name Y-H-V-H, and it is said, 'Ye are the children of the Lord [Y-H-V-H] your God [Deuteronomy 14:1]'" (Fine, *Safed Spirituality*, p. 154). The secret of sacrifice is contained in the letters; and the laws of sacrifice are found in the Mishnah (the book that contains the laws pertaining to all varieties of ritual practice and behavior).

Jewish Muslims/Muslim Jews

Information for the headnote is drawn from the following sources: Gershom Scholem, *Sabbatai Sevi: The Mystical Messiah*, trans. R. J. Zwi Werblowsky (Princeton, 1973), esp. pp. 148–63, 400ff., 836ff., and 872ff., and Scholem, "Redemption Through Sin" and "The Crypto-Jewish Sect of the Dönmeh," both in his *The Messianic Idea in Judaism* (New York, 1971); Paul Fenton, "A New Collection of Shabbatian Hymns" [Heb], in *The Shabbatian Movement and Its Aftermath: Messianism, Shabbatianism and Frankism* [Heb], ed. Rachel Elior (Jerusalem, 2001), pp. 346–47; Shmuel Werses, "Meliselda Coming up from the River: The Transformation of a Spanish Romancero" [Heb], *Pe'amim* 88 (2001), pp. 75–97; Gad Nassi, "Meliselda: The Sabbatean Metamorphosis of a Medieval Romance," http://www.gadnassi.com/files/publications/Meliselda_-_The _Sabbatean_Metamorphosis_of_a_Medieval_Romance.pdf; Royce W. Miller, "Meliselda: Mystical Song of Sabbatai Zebi," *Judaica* 37:3 (1981), pp. 154–60; Samuel G. Armistead, "Melisenda and the Chansons de Gestes," *La Coronica* 27:1 (1998), pp. 55–58; and on Shabbatai Tzvi's letters see Yehudah Liebes, "Shabbatai Tzvi's Relation to His Conversion" [Heb], *Sefunot* 17 (1983), pp. 267–307, and Avraham Elkayam, "Bury My Faith: A Letter by Shabbatai Tzvi in Exile" [Heb], *Pe'amim* 55 (1993), pp. 4–37. An excellent short introduction to Shabbatai Tzvi and his world can be found in David J. Halperin, *Sabbatai Zevi: Testimonies to a Fallen Messiah* (Oxford, 2007). Halperin explains the predicted resurrection in *Zohar* 1:139b, based on Leviticus 25:13. His characterizations of Tzvi are particularly vivid (e.g., "He is not an easy person to like, this flawed and fallen messiah. At times it is difficult not to detest him. . . . Thus did Shabbatai Tzvi habitually deal with the world: as a stage on which his private fantasies might turn into public performances" [p. 14]; and "What are we to make of this messiah? At times he seems a divided, tormented soul, split between the Judaism he could not leave behind and the Islam he could not cease to profess without forfeiting his life. More often he comes across as manipulative and duplicitous. . . . As always, he is utterly without empathy, oblivious to the needs or even the existence of any human being but himself" [p. 125]). On the Dönmeh and their hymns see, apart from Scholem's work, Avner Peretz, *Water, Fire, and Love: Ghazals and Other Mystical Poems by the Shabbatians* [Heb] (Ma'aleh Adumim, 2006), pp. 11–15; Marc David Baer, *The Dönme: Jewish Converts, Muslim Revolutionaries, and Secular Turks* (Stanford, Calif., 2010); Jacob Landau, "The Dönmehs: Crypto-Jews Under Turkish Rule," *Jewish Political Studies Review* 19:1–2 (2007), pp. 109–18; M. Avrum Ehrlich, "Sabbatean Messianism as Proto Secularism," *Turkish-Jewish Encounters: Studies on Turkish-Jewish Relations Through the Ages*, ed. Mehmet Tütüncü (Haarlem, 2001), pp. 273–306; and "Bektashiyya," *Encyclopedia of Islam*, 2nd ed. (Leiden, 1960–2009). Above all see *Shabbatian Hymns* [Heb], transcribed and translated by Moshe Attias, with notes and commentary by Gershom Scholem, introduction by Yitzhak Ben-Tzvi (Tel Aviv, 1947), from which many of the poems that follow are drawn.

Quotations are from the following sources: *to confound Satan*: Scholem, *Sabbatai Sevi*, p. 399; *cupped his hands*: Scholem, *Sabbatai Sevi*, p. 398; *time to work for the Lord*: Scholem, *Sabbatai Sevi*, p. 399; *a profound mystery*: Scholem, *Sabbatai Sevi*, p. 399; *a mystical allegory of himself*: Scholem, *Sabbatai Sevi*, p. 400; *the most lovely lady*: Scholem, *Sabbatai Sevi*, p. 160; *strange actions*: Scholem, *Sabbatai Sevi*, p. 159; *revealed himself . . . as the Anointed*: Scholem, *Sabbatai Sevi*, p. 401; *in a separate room in holiness . . . true prophecy*: Scholem, *Sabbatai Sevi*, p. 204; *in order to find peace for his soul*: Scholem, *Major Trends in Jewish Mysticism* (New York, 1941), p. 295; *worthy to be king*: Scholem, *Sabbatai Sevi*, p. 218; *the spirit of Shabbatai Tzvi*: Scholem, *Sabbatai Sevi*, p. 233 (where it is transliterated "Sabbatai Sevi"); *holy sinner*: Scholem, *Sabbatai Sevi*, p. 359; *the unhappy dualism of the Marranic mind*: Scholem, *Major Trends*, p. 310; *the melancholy messiah*: Idel, "Jupiter [Shabbatai] and Shabbatai Tzvi: A New Approach to Shabbatianism" [Heb], *Madda'ei HaYahadut* 37 (1997), p. 182; *the first serious revolt in Judaism since the Middle Ages*: Scholem, *Major Trends*, p. 299 (and see *Messianic Idea*, p. 143); *the fundamental doctrine of Shabbatianism*: Scholem, *Major Trends*, p. 321; *crooked ways*: Scholem, *Sabbatai Sevi*, p. 828; *Sometimes he prayed and behaved like a Jew*: Scholem, *Sabbatai Sevi*, p. 823; *The last ten years of his life can be understood*: Halperin, *Sabbatai Zevi*, p. 11; *We can easily imagine him*: Scholem, *Sabbatai Sevi*, p. 880; *voluntary Marranos*: Scholem, *Messianic Idea*, p. 147; *at the intersection of Kabbalah and Sufism*: Baer, *Dönme*, p. 4; *unprecedented theology of Judaism*: Scholem, "Redemption Through Sin," pp. 96–97; *folk poetry . . . spiritual shepherds*: *Shabbatian Hymns* [Heb], transcribed and trans. Attias, p. 15; *the extinguishing of the lights*: Scholem, *Messianic Idea*, pp. 113–14, 163–65; *a specifically Jewish phenomenon*: Scholem, *Messianic Idea*, p. 84. Apropos the Jewishness of the phenomenon, Scholem comments in *Sabbatai Sevi*, "The 'Jewishness' in the religiosity of any particular period is not measured by dogmatic criteria that are unrelated to actual historical circumstances, but solely by what sincere Jews do, in fact, believe, or — at least — consider to be legitimate possibilities" (p. 283). On the way in which Shabbatianism contains the "seeds of modern Jewish life," see also Halperin, *Sabbatai Zevi*, pp. 15–19, who notes that "the age of Sabbatai Zevi was also the age of Spinoza's *Theologico-Political Treatise*."

Meliselda

In a long 1665 letter to the leader of Egyptian Jewry and his circle, Nathan of Gaza attests to the ability of hymns and songs to effect change, and he describes how, "by [the power of] the hymns and praises which he [Shabbatai Tzvi] shall utter, all nations shall submit to his rule" in this new messianic age (Scholem, *Sabbatai Sevi*, p. 272). As Scholem put it, "everything would be achieved by means of hymns" (*Sabbatai Sevi*, p. 287). With significant variations and usually in a longer narrative form, the poem is found in a number of European traditions, where the heroine is known variously as Melisenda, Beliselda, Bellisten, Benisela, and Belisera, among other permutations on the name of Charlemagne's daughter. Among Ottoman Jews "Meliselda" was the name of choice. The oldest version of the poem probably goes back to a French ballad from the Carolingian period ("Melisenda insomne"), though some think its real roots lie in the Song of Songs, chapter 3.

Text: There is considerable difference of opinion regarding which version of the *romancero* Shabbatai Tzvi actually sang that day in the Izmir synagogue. Moshe Attias proposes one such version (among two that he translates in *Sephardic Romancero* [Heb] [Jerusalem, 1955], pp. 82–83), but Scholem (*Sabbatai Sevi*, pp. 400–401) cites the version that the Dutch Protestant minister Thomas Coenen offers in his account of what happened in the synagogue. That is the version presented here. It is most likely only part of what Tzvi recited, but it is all that Coenen quotes. (The version at the back of this volume is a Hebrew translation of Coenen's Dutch version: Thomas Coenen, *The Dashed Hopes of the Jews as Revealed in the Figure of Sabbatai Tzvi* [Heb], translated from the Dutch by Asher Lagawier and Efraim Shmueli [Jerusalem, 1998], p. 56.) Still other versions seem to have been sung by Shabbatian communities, including a Hebrew variation that thoroughly reworks the poem in the same way that Najara reworked some of the Turkish popular songs of the day. In one of these variations, for instance, Meliselda becomes the Hebrew *melitz el da* (literally, "the advocate of God is this" [i.e., Shabbatai Tzvi]). Whichever version was taken up, it "acquired great sanctity in the eyes of the Sabbatian believers, who sang it at their meetings" (Scholem, *Sabbatai Sevi*, p. 313). Other Hebrew and Ladino variations on this theme followed. The great modern poet Hayyim Nahman Bialik (see below) translated one of these, which takes up the Ashkenazic pronunciation of the Hebrew word *milat-* (the word of), and begins as follows:

> Meliselda, when I saw her,
> Milas-el—God's word I called her.
> Upon the mountain I beheld,
> as I rose, the daughter of God.
> I saw her face, aglow with pleasure,
> as she went down toward the river,
> her naked glory along the path
> as she came up from the bath . . .
> Meliselda, when I saw her,
> Milas-el—God's word I called her.
> Her face was like a sword that's drawn,
> her lips were red as coral's burn.
> Her eyes resembled sparks of light . . .
> Her milk- and snow-like flesh was white.

In the years following his apostasy, Shabbatai continued his practice of singing the Spanish or Ladino romanceros, along with Psalms. During what appears to be his final "great illumination," in 1676 he marched one night through the upper-class Turkish quarter of the Albanian town he'd been banished to and went up "the wall of the tower" (which may have been a minaret); there he sang "his songs and hymns" (Scholem, *Sabbatai Sevi*, p. 914).

I Have Found Bliss

Text: *Shabbatian Hymns* [Heb], transcribed and trans. Attias, poem 71.

All the poems from this collection are rhymed in the original and maintain a syllabic meter. Unless otherwise noted, they were translated from Moshe Attias's Hebrew versions, which appear alongside the original Ladino in *Shabbatian Hymns*.

Lines 5–8: Literally, "the place where *tet* fell": i.e., the letter *tet*, the ninth Hebrew letter, which is associated with life and vitality. For one, it is the first letter of the word *tov*, "good"—as in "He saw it was good." It is also associated with the ninth *sefirah*, Yesod (foundation), which in turn is associated with the phallus, vigor, the river of life. The image of the *tet* having "fallen" (i.e., where it reigns) is ambiguous and appears to allude to the *Zohar* 2:151b–152b: "There is a place in civilization where that Destroyer has no power . . . and all those who dwell there do not die until they leave the town. Why is this? . . . When the Holy One created the world, He created it by the mystery of letters, and letters revolved and created the world by engravings of the Holy Name. . . . When they were revolving and the world was expanding and being created and the letters were circling to create, the blessed Holy One said, 'Enough! Be completed with *yod*.' The letter *tet* remained in that place, suspended in the air. *Tet* is life . . . since it was suspended above that place, death has no dominion there. . . . Come and see: *Tet* is radiance of life everywhere, and therefore the verse '*ki tov*' (that it was good) . . . from this letter the Angel of Destruction flees." The same image of the fallen *tet* appears again in "The Valley of Ishmael," line 17, where it is more clearly associated with vitality through an inversion of norms. In this Zoharic passage, the "place" is the town of Luz (cf. Judges 1:22–26 and *Sotah* 46b, where the angel of death cannot enter and where old men go outside of the city walls to die). See *The Zohar*, trans. Daniel C. Matt, 5 vols. (Stanford, Calif., 2004–9), vol. 5., pp. 383ff., and also line 21 in "The Valley of Ishmael," below.

9–12: "Our teacher" in the original is *Mor* (which sounds like *moreh*, "teacher"), a common epithet in this body of work for Shabbatai Tzvi.

Scholem offers numerous interpretations of it. The name conjures associations with the mountain of myrrh (in Hebrew, *mor*—as in Song of Songs 4:6: "Until the day breaks and the shadows flee, I will go to the mountain of myrrh and to the hill of incense"), but also with the name of Shabbatai's father, Mordekhai, which itself is glossed esoterically in *Hullin* 139a. The name also alludes to Mount Moriah and the mystery or secret of Abraham, which is the quality of Hesed (grace), and which is associated as well with the Shabbatians and also with Islam—see *Shabbatian Hymns*, p. 38. The secret of Abraham is contrasted with the Torah of Truth, which is the law of Moses. See also *Zohar* 2:152a, and in *Shabbatian Hymns*, poem 16, p. 39, and poem 51, p. 71.

17–20: The original reads "Zikhri renews it." According to Scholem, Zikhri (literally, "my remembrance," but also "my trace") in the still opaque Shabbatian scheme is the Holy King, the God of Israel (*Shabbatian Hymns*, pp. 25 and 216).

25–28: Scholem notes that this last stanza is especially obscure. It contains three key symbolic aspects of the Shabbatian theological worldview. Love (Ahavah) appears to be used symbolically (like Zikhri) and stands for one of the three bonds (or knots) of faith in the Shabbatian trinity. The other two are Zikhri (see above) and Tovah (goodness). At times it seems that Ahavah is the "soul of all things," and at times it seems to be identified with the Shekhinah (Tovah). At other times it is divinity in general. Moshe Attias is of the opinion that these three "knots" are also epithets referring to specific people. "Tovah" here would then refer to the major Shabbatian hymn writer of the day, Yehudah Levi (Tovah)—see "On the Extinguishing of the Lights" and "The Ghazal of Goodness," below. "Goodness" here is a symbol of the Matronita, which is to say, the Shekhinah, the noble lady and wife of Tiferet. "The King" is *Zikhri* in the original, as in lines 17–20.

The Valley of Ishmael

Text: *Shabbatian Hymns* [Heb], transcribed and trans. Attias, poem 241.

Lines 1–4: The first line of this stanza is in Hebrew (not Ladino) and quotes Genesis 48:20: "Through you shall Israel invoke blessings: God make you like Ephraim and Manasseh"; "you" (*bekha*) refers both to

Shabbatai Tzvi and to the the word's numerological value—twenty-two, as in the twenty-two letters of the *aleph-bet*. Part of the second line of the stanza (which serves as the poem's refrain) is also in Hebrew and contains the word *gai* (valley), which Halperin notes may also be an acronym for *Gevul Edom [ve]Yishma'el*, or "the border of Christendom and Islam" (*Sabbatai Zevi*, p. 88). See also line 9. Poem 15 (*Shabbatian Hymns*, p. 38) contains the line "He turned the 'valley' into a garden of truth." Scholem comments, "the Messiah enters this valley [of Ishmael and of the *kelippah*], and turns it into a garden" (*Sabbatai Sevi*, p. 825); see Scholem's comment, "Sabbatai also commanded many of his followers 'to appear before him and he explained to them that everything had been ordained in Heaven, as it was written in the *Pirke deRabbi Eliezer* that the messiah would be swallowed among the Ishmaelites.'" Scholem notes that this is "a Sabbatian misrendering of the text in *Pirke deRabbi Eliezer*." See *Pirkei deRabbi Eliezer*, trans. G. Friedlander (London, 1916), p. 222. In time, and possibly during the period of the composition of this hymn, certain Dönmeh communities would replace the prayer "Shema Yisrael . . . [Hear, O Israel], the Lord is One" with "Hear, O Ishmael!" (Scholem, *Sabbatai Sevi*, p. 825). The name may also be associated with Tzvi's son, whom he named Ishmael (Mordekhai), and who was, as Scholem puts it, "the object of certain soteriological hopes" (*Sabbatai Sevi*, p. 885). Scholem adds that Ishmael was appointed by the inner circle of believers as "Lord" and heir to his father's throne. Shabbatai Tzvi also gave his son the name Israel on the occasion of his circumcision (at age three) (*Sabbatai Sevi*, p. 848–49). On the circumcision see Halperin, *Sabbatai Zevi*, p. 15, and also p. 135. The image of the valley appears numerous times in this literature. It is the place of the kelippot, and the allusion is to Shabbatai's conversion and violation of the Law, i.e., his sin for the sake of redemption.

5–8: Scholem comments that the gist of this stanza—that the Lord dwells within his servant—alludes to the theory of God's incarnation in Shabbatai Tzvi. The syntax is intentionally ambiguous. God dwells in Shabbatai; but Shabbatai Tzvi also dwells in Him (see, for instance, poem 51 in *Shabbatian Hymns*, "Secret Pleasure," translated below).

9–12: Literally, "the abbreviation is the Redeemer," referring, it seems, to the opening line of the poem, where "through you" equals twenty-two.

Elsewhere in the hymnbook, the jubilee year (the fiftieth) is equated with the sefirah of Binah (which has fifty gates): "Fifty gates of Binah which is the [secret] of the Jubilee." See *Shabbatian Hymns*, p. 135.

13–16: Literally, "he repaired the Tehiru." Scholem notes that the term *Tehiru* is taken from the *Zohar*, where it is understood as "the brightness/splendor on high" (the supernal splendor). According to Lurianic Kabbalah, this is the space created after God's withdrawal into Himself so as to create a place for all worlds to exist. (Again, see "Secret Pleasure.") In the Lurianic context, only half of this Tehiru was "repaired," and the Messiah's task is to repair the other half, where the shells (kelippot) remain. (See Chaim Wirshubsky, "In the Footsteps of the Messiah" [Heb], *Knesset* 8 [1944], pp. 217–18, 229–30.)

17–20: Literally, "In a certain town fell the letter *tet*." On the letter *tet* in this context, see above, "I Have Found Bliss," notes to ll. 5–8.

On the Extinguishing of the Lights

Text: *Shabbatian Hymns* [Heb], transcribed and trans. Attias, poems 95 (poem 1 here) and 136 (poem 2).

These two poems appear to have been composed for the Dönmeh Feast of the Lambs, which marked the beginning of spring and celebrated the consumption of the first lambs of the year. On the eve of that festival, the Dönmeh observed a rite known as the Extinguishing of the Lights, during which, at a certain point, the lights would be doused and the couples in attendance (the ritual was limited to married couples) would, it seems, exchange partners and make love. Scholem is of the opinion that the accusations of "ritual fornication and free love in [the Dönmeh's] secret gatherings" were based in truth. Dönmeh theories of "sexual anarchy and promiscuity," he says, were backed up by bizarre scriptural interpretations (the new Law): "The biblical report of Elisha's visit to the woman from Shunem is treated as a paradigm of ritual fornication (2 Kings 4:8ff.). . . . Even among the songs that we now know there are some which were manifestly intended for celebrations of this kind and which employ the symbolism of eating, the table, the opening of the rose, 'providing,' and 'lending.' In such table songs [the writer Yehudah Levi] Tovah employs a symbolism which in his prose writings leaves no doubt about its sexual character, as he celebrates the 'permission of the prohibited' which has now become a sacred activity" ("Crypto-Jewish Sect of the Dönmeh," pp. 162–64, and, with regard to the "sexual licentiousness" of the Dönmeh, see also *Kabbalah* [New York, 1974], pp. 331–32). See also Scholem, *Messianic Idea*, p. 114, on the Festival of the Lambs, which "probably came to Salonika from Izmir, as both its name and its contents were evidently borrowed from the pagan cult of 'the Great Mother' which flourished in antiquity and continued to be practiced after its general demise by a small sect of 'Light Extinguishers' in Asia Minor under the cover of Islam. There can be no question that the Dönmeh took over this ancient bacchanalia based on immemorial myths and adapted it to conform to their mystical belief in the sacramental value of exchanging wives."

The translation of poem 136 omits two stanzas from the poem, including the final one, which mentions the poet's name. See also poems 122 and 134 in *Shabbatian Hymns*, and possibly even 51 ("Secret Pleasure," translated here), which employ some of the same imagery as these poems and appear to be treating the same subject.

Poem 1: Lines 1–5: The poem would seem to operate on two levels at once, much like the Dönmeh themselves. Ostensibly it seems to celebrate a ritual, and possibly the holiday meal; but read in the context of the larger body of Shabbatian writings, images such as the table, the opening rose, eating (or partaking), and remaining pure make the sexual reading seem likely. One of the other hymns in the same collection (*Shabbatian Hymns*, poem 22) is more explicit: "Lamb, /Lamb, we have eaten of the Lamb. /The holy flesh, the mystery of the Lamb, /Through you will Israel invoke blessings, /The Lamb to us has come." Scholem's note there states that the Festival of the Lambs symbolizes the coupling of male and female.

11–15: Scholem comments that the first line of this stanza is entirely obscure to him, and he suspects that the problem might be in the transcription. He offers an alternative reading, which I've followed, with some liberty. "Generosity" or "giving" is also generally part of the lexicon of these rites (in poetry and in prose). "Our lord," in the original is

"AMIRAH"—an acronym for the Hebrew words meaning "Our Lord and King, may his majesty be exalted," and indicating Shabbatai Tzvi; see the headnote to this section and also "Secret Pleasure," below.

16–20: On "Goodness" here see notes to "I Have Found Bliss," above, ll. 25–28.

Poem 2: Lines 1–4: The first line refers to Nathan of Gaza, the prophet of Shabbatai Tzvi—something that is explicit the Ladino ("Rav Nathan announces"). Scholem comments that he cannot find the source of this symbol ("the mystery of the sanctity" as an image of the Messiah) in Nathan's writings. The opening rose appears in a number of the Shabbatian hymns; Scholem notes that its meaning is obscure and possibly sexual, especially in conjunction with the images of the table and the "appointed time" (l. 11). Normally the rose would be associated with the Shekhinah (as in the opening section of the *Zohar*). The final stanza of the poem (not translated here) returns to what appears to be another image of Nathan's, namely, "the light that lacks conception" (see "On the Destruction of the Law," below).

5–8: The first line of this stanza recalls the correction Scholem has proposed for lines 11–15 of poem 95 (see the note above). As in the poem above, "our lord" in the original is "AMIRAH," indicating Shabbatai Tzvi.

9–12: The time appointed for the rite, which would be the beginning of spring.

13–16: David Halperin writes: "The most striking theme of [the Dönmeh's] speculative, exegetical literature is the split they make between the 'Torah,' the divine essence of Judaism, and the 'commandments,' the negative and indeed demonic shell in which this essence has been encased. 'The commandments have been abolished,' runs the Dönmeh credo. 'But the Torah shall remain for ever and for all eternity'" (*Sabbatai Zevi*, pp. 18–19).

Secret Pleasure

Text: *Shabbatian Hymns* [Heb], transcribed and trans. Attias, poem 51.

Lines 1–4: Sama'el is an angel in Talmudic and post-Talmudic literature. He has both nefarious and benevolent powers. As a fallen angel he is sometimes identified with Satan (or the angel of death), and his duties are often grim and destructive. In the Kabbalistic scheme he is associated with severity and temptation. See Scholem, *Kabbalah*, pp. 385–88.

5–8: Lines 5 and 6 are reversed in the original, and Scholem thinks that the text is corrupt here and should read "through *yod-hey*" (YAH, the Name of God) instead of "through Let there be." See *Menahot* 29b: "For with *yod-hey* God fashions worlds." See also below, note to ll. 17–20. On "Our teacher"—which in the original is *Mor*—see "I Have Found Bliss," above, note to ll. 9–12. The altered action in the context of this poem is Shabbatai Tzvi's conversion, which confers life in the world to come.

9–12: Shabbatai Tzvi's soul was emanated both from the root of the divine contraction (*tzimtzum*) that gave rise to the creation of the universe and from the mystery of the Shekhinah (which was made manifest just after the contraction). Again, "our lord" in the original is "AMIRAH," Tzvi as the Messiah (see the headnotes to this section). In the final line of this stanza, "it" refers grammatically to "all that came to be." The implication is that Tzvi is equal to the power that created the universe, i.e., God. Scholem notes that the implication may be to the divine countenance of Attika Kadisha (the Ancient Eminence). See Scholem's notes to poems 13 and 237 in *Shabbatian Hymns*.

13–16: The stanza is describing that act of tzimtzum and the creation of the Tehiru—the space that remains after God's withdrawal into Himself. From that primordial space of the Tehiru, which is at once negative and generative, God made the *malbush*, the garment which is woven *within* the divine substance—"like the grasshopper whose clothing is part of itself" (Scholem, *Kabbalah*, p. 132). The garment is made from the alphabet through tremendous and elaborate permutations of the twenty-two letters. It occupies "twice the area necessary for the creation of all the worlds." This Primordial Torah, as it was known, "contained potentially all that could possibly be revealed through the Torah to be given on earth. In effect, it was a Kabbalistic version of the Platonic world of ideas" (p. 132).

17–20: The soul of Shabbatai Tzvi the redeemer is fashioned from this primordial space, which is also a place of ultimate negation, and so of absolute evil. (See Scholem's commentary in *Shabbatian Hymns*, pp. 35 and 139, and Wirshubsky, "In the Footsteps of the Messiah" [Heb], pp. 215–17.) In the original, "twenty-two" is identical to "in you," and the word *golem* is used to refer to the primordial space of the Tehiru after the withdrawal of God into Himself. See also *Zohar* 1:16b: "Here begins the discovery of hidden treasures: how the world was created in detail. . . . Till here, all was suspended in space, from the mystery of Ein Sof. . . . A voice was generated . . . *Let there be light!* All that emerged, emerged through this mystery. *Let there be*, alluding to the mystery of Father and Mother, namely *yod-hey*, afterward turning back to the primordial point, to begin expanding into something else: *light*. . . . It expanded, and seven letters of the alphabet shone within, not congealing, still fluid. Then darkness emerged, and seven other letters of the alphabet emerged within, not congealing, remaining fluid. An expanse emerged, dissipating the discord of two sides, and eight other letters emerged within, making twenty-two. . . . The expanse congealed, and the letters congealed, folding into shape, forming forms. Torah was engraved there, to shine forth" (trans. Matt, vol. 1, pp. 122–24). The "it" that would be blessed by Tzvi's soul appears to be — grammatically — "the primal space of the void," or the negative space in which spiritual birth and rebirth occur.

21–24: The Ladino mentions "Shabbatai" by name as the Redeemer. The vale is, again, the place of the kelippot. As Scholem reads the lines, the allusion is to Shabbatai's conversion and violation of the Law (as given), which is to say, to his sin for the sake of redemption. See "The Valley of Ishmael," above. Cf. Psalms 119:126 — "it is time for Thee, Lord, to work, [for] they have made void Thy law." Shabbatai Tzvi turned the verse around — "It is time to work for the Lord" — on the occasion of his first public appearance in Smyrna (see the headnote to this section), echoing a well-known rabbinic homiletic interpretation of the Psalmic verse. The rabbis used it to indicate the need for a return to intense Torah study after a period of neglect. So Shabbatai Tzvi twice subverts the tradition: first, like the rabbis, he scrambles the literal meaning of Scripture, and then he reshuffles the rabbinic deck, finding a very different meaning in the rearranged verse. (See Scholem, *Sabbatai Sevi*, p. 399.) On breaking away from the Law, see the note to ll. 13–16 of "On the Extinguishing of the Lights," poem 2.

On the Destruction of the Law

Text: Fenton, "New Collection of Shabbatian Hymns," pp. 346–47. Translated via Fenton's Hebrew rendering.

An excerpt from an elegy for one of the Dönmeh, who translated the *Zohar* into Spanish. Of the sixteen lines in the full version of the poem, only two refer to the deceased. Instead, the poem takes up the theme of the destruction of the kelippot, or husks. With the destruction of these husks (and the abolition of the Law), the path is paved to the final tikkun. This theme was central to the thought of Avraham Yakhini (1617–82), who was among the Shabbatian movement's leaders in Constantinople. In an attempt to explain Shabbatai's conversion, Yakhini wrote of the way in which the Messiah's soul is rooted in the mystery of the source of creation through the power of destruction. The author of the poem, however, seems to be Yehudah Levi.

Lines 1–8: "The light that lacks conception," or thought, is a central notion in Nathan of Gaza's theology. See Wirshubsky, "In the Footsteps of the Messiah" [Heb], 215–17. Liebes believes that it refers to Shabbatai Tzvi himself.

13: The fourth husk or shell is the shell of "brightness," which is what Ezekiel saw in the vision of the chariot (1:4: "a great cloud with brightness about it"), as the *Zohar* understands the passage. The light of this shell of brightness is the redeemer. (On the fourth kelippah, the destruction of the kelippot, and the destruction of the Law, see Scholem in *Shabbatian Hymns* [Heb], transcribed and trans. Attias, pp. 105, 124, 138, and 180.) Poem 136 contains the lines "He destroyed the commandments, / nullified the shells, / and restored the worlds. / The secret of Holiness [sanctity] / is sent out [into the world]." On the destruction of the kelippot, see *Shabbatian Hymns*, poem 180, and on the destruction of the Law see poem 136. Also see Scholem, *Messianic Idea*, p. 114, on the conversion to Islam of several hundred families in Salonika, again, "so as to conquer the *kelippah* from within."

16: The last line alludes more loosely to the same Psalmic verse discussed above (see note to ll. 21–24 of "Secret Pleasure"). The Frankists also took up the same call in what Scholem characterized as their "mystical theory of revolution." Scholem cites a Frankist epistle that begins the way this poem ends: "Know that 'it is time for the Lord to work, [for] they have made void Thy law' [Psalms 119:126] and in this connection the rabbis of blessed memory have said [Sanhedrin 97a] [that the Messiah will not come] 'until the kingdom is entirely given over to heresy'" (Scholem, "Redemption Through Sin," pp. 138–39).

The Ghazal of Goodness

Text: Peretz, *Water, Fire, and Love* [Heb], p. 90. Translated via Peretz's Hebrew rendering.

For all intents and purposes this is a Persian ghazal, of the sort one would hear at a Sufi *dhikr*—though it is written in Judeo-Spanish. Fenton notes that the refrain of the poem—*la ilahu ila hu* (there is no God but Him)—was regularly used during the *dhikr* ceremony and, writing about another Shabbatian hymn much like this one (poem 231 in *Shabbatian Hymns* [Heb], transcribed and trans. Attias), he adds, "There is no doubt that [it] was performed along the lines of a *sama'a* [or spiritual concert] of the Dervishes" (Fenton, "New Collection of Shabbatian Hymns," p. 344). On the sama'a, see the headnotes in this volume to the poems of Yisrael Najara. In the original of this poem, which mixes Ladino with numerous Hebrew phrases, the final line employs the Arabic at the beginning of the phrase and then Hebrew at the end. It isn't clear whether the ghazals served as preludes to the prayer rites or as intervals of a sort between the prayers; in general the more developed and finer literary style of the ghazals would attract interest among the worshippers (Peretz, *Water, Fire, and Love* [Heb], p. 22ff.). The repetitions and circular or cyclical nature of the form works powerfully with the theme in this poem: wherever one turns, the divine is there.

The author of the poem is, once again, Yehudah Levi, whose pen name was Tovah. He lived in the early eighteenth century, seems to have been the head of a yeshivah, and was an extremely learned, devout, and

ardent follower of Shabbatai Tzvi. Scholem called him "the last signifi-
cant religious figure of the Dönmeh" (*Messianic Idea in Judaism*, p. 165).
See Fenton, "New Collection of Shabbatian Hymns," pp. 329–51 on
Shabbatian poems and the dhikr ceremony.

Lines 1–2 and refrain: Cf. John 1:3. See Scholem, "Redemption
Through Sin," p. 124, on the doctrine of incarnation and the identifica-
tion of Shabbatai Tzvi with God: "According to one view, when the re-
demption began, the Holy One, blessed be He, removed Himself upward
and Shabbatai Tzvi ascended to be God in His place." Cf. *Shabbatian
Hymns*, poems 15 and 184, which contain the line: "He is the Messiah,
there is no other." The phrase "no other" appears numerous other times
in the hymnbook as well with explicit reference to Shabbatai Tzvi as the
Messiah or Redeemer (e.g., poems 12 and 132). Poems 43 and 46 make
use of the identical refrain as this ghazal: *ela hu*. In poem 46, however,
Shabbatai Tzvi as the Messiah is woven into the very fabric of God's be-
ing in the poem: "David son of Jesse has come / His name is Myrrh, Shab-
batai Tzvi, / There is no other—said he, / There is no God but Him." The
last line of the poem alludes to the Muslim credo: *La ilaha ila allah*.
Throughout, the poem develops a conspicuous overtone of incarnation,
and here too, we can locate syncretic—i.e., mystical Shi'ite and even
Christian—influences, along the lines of those found in Ottoman Islamic
orders of the Bektashi Sufi sects and elsewhere.

5: On Sama'el and Belial, see "Secret Pleasure," above, note to ll. 1–4.
Belial is a demon and angel of hostility.

Italian Kabbalah

Information for the headnote is drawn from the following sources: *I Raise
My Heart: Poems by Moses Zacut* [Heb], ed. Dvora Bregman (Jerusalem,
2009), esp. pp. 1–52, and Bregman, "Moses Zacuto: Poet of Kabbalah," in
Hebraic Aspects of the Renaissance: Sources and Encounters, ed. Illana
Zinguer, Abraham Melamed and Zur Shalev (Leiden, 2011), pp. 170–81;
Gershom Scholem, "Moses Zacuto," in *Kabbalah* (New York, 1974),
pp. 449–51, and Scholem, *Sabbatai Sevi: The Mystical Messiah*, trans.

R. J. Zwi Werblowsky (Princeton, 1973), p. 769; Paul Fenton, "A New Collection of Shabbatian Hymns," in *The Dream and Its Reading* [Heb], ed. Rachel Elior (Jerusalem, 2001), p. 335; Isaiah Tishby, *Studies in Kabbalah and Its Branches: Researches and Sources* [Heb], 3 vols. (Jerusalem, 1993), vol. 3, and Tishby, *Messianic Mysticism: Moses Hayim Luzzatto and the Padua School*, introduction by Joseph Dan, trans. Morris Hoffman (Oxford, 2008), esp. pp. xi–xxv, 1–12, 114–71, 190–222, and 254–88; Joseph Dan and Joelle Hansel, "Moses Hayyim Luzzatto" and "Messiah," *Encyclopedia Judaica*, 2nd ed. (Detroit, 2007), vol. 13, pp. 281–86, and vol. 14, p. 112; Simon Ginzburg, *The Life and Works of Moses Hayyim Luzzatto* (Philadelphia, 1931), esp. pp. 30, 34, 56, and 66–69; Moshe Idel, *Kabbalah in Italy, 1280–1510: A Survey* (New Haven, 2011), and Idel, "Major Currents in Italian Kabbalah Between 1560 and 1660," in *Essential Papers on Jewish Culture in Renaissance and Baroque Italy*, ed. David B. Ruderman (New York, 1992). On the Kabbalah during the Renaissance, and specifically on Yohanan Allemano and his student Pico della Mirandola, see Scholem, *Kabbalah*, p. 67.

Quotations are from the following sources: *massive direct importations*: Idel, *Kabbalah in Italy*, p. 14; *a strange fire*: Scholem, *Sabbatai Sevi*, p. 769, *while keeping in mind a Kabbalistic formula*: Ginzburg, *Life and Works of Luzzatto*, p. 34; *psychologically . . . elements of the mystic's unconscious*: Scholem, *Sabbatai Sevi*, p. 209; *a whole new philosophy of history*: Dan and Hansel, "Moses Hayyim Luzzatto," pp. 281–86; *This movement . . . achieved within the very core*: Dan and Hansel, "Moses Hayyim Luzzatto," p. 284; *The truth is for ever and ever the world-wheel turns*: Ginzburg, *Life and Works of Luzzatto*, p. 88; *a message of encouragement*: Tishby, *Messianic Mysticism*, p. 120.

The Light Concealed

Text: *I Raise My Heart* [Heb], p. 436.

A hymn for a *tikkun hatzot* (a midnight vigil intended to rectify cosmic imbalance) written by Moshe Zacut. Bregman writes: "This mysterious light, described here by oxymoron as both hidden and revealed at the same time, is the very theme of the poem, which goes on to portray how [the light] flows from an entity called Ein-Sof (no end) into the other vessels, successively, each specified by name: Keter, Hokhmah, Binah, Hesed, Gedulah, Gevurah, Tiferet, Yesod, Netzah, Hod, Malkhut. These are no doubt the ten *sefirot*, in their correct order, receiving, in turn, the holy grace flowing from the highest source of Ein-Sof and passing it on" (Bregman, "Moses Zacuto," p. 173). My thanks to Dvora Bregman for help with the translation of the two poems by Zacut in this collection.

Lines 1–4: Cf. *Hagigah* 12a: "The light that the Holy One Blessed Be He created on the first day could be seen from one end of the world to the other. Because the Holy One Blessed Be He looked ahead to the generation of the Flood and saw the twisted things they would do, he hid the light from them and stored it away, as it is said: 'And from the wicked the light is withholden' [or 'the light shall be hidden from the wicked' (Job 38:15)]. And for whom did he store it away? For the righteous in the world to come." The light, notes Bregman, is also unknowable and beyond conception. "In the clearing's whiteness" alludes to Genesis 30:37, and the whiteness of the wood that Jacob exposed when he peeled back the bark. According to Lurianic Kabbalah, the whiteness exposed as a "clearing" is that of the light that shines from Ein-Sof (the Infinite) toward the entities (the splendors—*tzahtzahot*) above the sefirot. "Each in his place" refers either to each aspirant in his given situation or perhaps to each instance of diffusion—i.e., to each of the sacred emanations (cf. Numbers 2:2). The final line of the stanza alludes to Joshua 2:18, "Thou shalt bind this line of scarlet thread," but takes the glow of the line to be that of the light from Ein-Sof. Hayyim Vital of Safed writes in *The Tree of Life*: "And after the *tzimtzum* there remains a place of space and vacancy in the midst of the light of Infinity . . . a space which could receive the emanations . . . and then a line of light from Infinity was sent out directly from on high downward and into this space." For detailed commentary on these lines, see Bregman, *I Raise My Heart* [Heb], p. 436. See also *Zohar* 1:31b–32a (trans. Daniel C. Matt, 5 vols. [Stanford, Calif., 2004–9], vol. 1, pp. 192–98); *Zohar Hadash*, Ruth 85a; and *Wisdom of the Zohar*, introductions and annotations by Tishby, vol. 3, p. 1502.

5–8: "Delight"—literally, "plant of delight—is an image of the sefirot, which are planted there. Proverbs 8:30. "The brightness" here is the system of lights (tzahtzahot) above the sefirot. (See Isaiah 51:11 and Scholem, *Kabbalah*, pp. 91, 96, and 114.) All worlds and creatures were formed in this brightness. "The first being which emanated from the light was Adam Kadmon, 'Primordial Man'" (Gershom Scholem, *Major Trends in Jewish Mysticism* [New York, 1941], p. 265).

9–12: Psalms 145:13: "Thy kingdom is an everlasting kingdom." Daniel 7:9: "Thrones were placed, and the Ancient of Days took his seat." *He set His pillars*: the ten sefirot. Exodus 26:19. *Three above, then seven were fixed*: i.e., the roots of the first three sefirot and the seven lower sefirot. *The throne*: *Zohar Hadash, Song of Songs* 68a: "'The throne rests on the four columns." This is the base of Keter. See also Psalms 145:12 and 132:13, and Daniel 7:9.

13–16: From here on the particular sefirah treated is italicized, beginning with Keter (crown), from which all the others flow. See Exodus 34:6–7 and 3:14.

17–20: Psalms 111:10; Genesis 2:7; Jeremiah 32:19; Job 41:24; Psalms 118:19.

21–24: Proverbs 8:5; "knowing" here is the sefirah Binah (understanding), which traditionally has fifty gates (*Rosh HaShanah* 21b); Psalms 71:16. The way to Binah is through the sefirah of Gevurah, or power.

25–28: The sefirah Hesed. See Psalms 98:3. Magnanimity is equivalent to Hesed, which is also identified with Abraham.

29–32: Genesis 31:42. Isaac is associated with the sefirah of Gevurah.

33–36: The sefirah in question is Tiferet (glory or beauty). See Genesis 28:2; Psalms 69:14; Genesis 49:24; Isaiah 49:26 and 60:16.

37–40: The stanza treats the two sefirot of Netzah and Hod (eternity or victory, and majesty). They are associated with Moses and Aaron, who are mentioned explicitly in the Hebrew of this stanza. See also Psalms 17:5, 65:6, 86:17, and 59:6.

41–44: Psalms 80:2. Joseph is associated with the sefirah of Yesod (foundation). See also Isaiah 28:16; Job 27:13.

45–48: David is associated with the sefirah of Malkhut (kingdom); Elijah is his herald. See Jeremiah 23:5; Psalms 21:11.

49–52: See Ezekiel 1; Psalms 16:11 and 19:15. The country in question is the Land of Israel, which is known as Eretz haTzvi—"the land of the deer," a name that also conjures associations with Shabbatai Tzvi.

You Readied a Light

Text: The text and commentary here, as above, are based almost entirely on that of Dvora Bregman in her edition of Zacut's poems, *I Raise My Heart* [Heb], pp. 448–53. For her description of the occasion of this poem, see pp. 11ff., and 448.

Lines 1–28: This light that God "readied" is the upper light that He sent out through the Infinite—in the space created after His contraction within Himself (tzimtzum). Particles of that primordial light with which God created the world were preserved in the Shekhinah (Presence) that attended to the curtain of the Ark of the Law and within the lamp above it in the Temple; that light also followed Israel into Exile (*Mekhilta deR. Ishmael*, "Wherever Israel was exiled, it is as if the Shekhinah was exiled with them"). As Bregman puts it: "After the destruction [of the Temple], remains of the holy light were carried by the Shekhinah to shine in the synagogues of the Diaspora" ("Moses Zacuto," p. 173). God in this scheme is called *yedid*—a friend. "For us now" refers to Zacut and the members of his group, in Mantua, on the occasion of the great tikkun enacted by Zacut's new circle. While the light at the start of the stanza is clearly the primordial light, by the end of the stanza it is the Torah. *Zohar Hadash*, Ruth 85a: "For it is the Torah, and it is the hidden light" (*ha'or haganuz*). See the note to line 1 of "The Light Concealed," above.

29–44: In line 2, the "nation's merit" is the Torah, which was prepared from eternity to guide Israel and raise it in glory. In this way it was set apart from the nations, as the light is divided from darkness and also in the Havdalah prayers marking the end of the Sabbath and the beginning of the profane week.

45–60: See Numbers 23:9: "The people shall dwell alone." Cf. Genesis 1:18: "a firmament of the heavens to give light . . . and . . . to divide the light from the darkness." See Exodus 15:17: "the Sanctuary, O Lord, which thy hands have established." God's "glory" here is the Torah or the Shekhinah—His Presence. The light was gathered into the space between the walls of the Ark of the Law. And as an extension of the light, candelabra were lit in the Temple itself. With the phrase "your light drawn in" there is also an overtone of God's withdrawal into Himself in the beginning, which made room for creation. In this image, God is withdrawing His light into the Temple. Exodus 35:19: "His lamps, with the oil for the light."

61–76: The "Splendor" is the light of creation. Cf. 2 Samuel 22:31: "As for God, His way is perfect"; Leviticus 26:44: "When they be in the land of their enemies, I will not cast them away." The stanza alludes to the midrash according to which wherever Israel goes into Exile, the Shekhinah is exiled with it. Psalms 61:4: "For thou hast been . . . a strong tower from the enemy." Daniel 11:31: "the sanctuary of strength." *Zohar, Re'aya Mehemna*, Ki Teitzei 282a: "And the Shekhinah glowed (as is said in Ezekiel 1:13) 'and the fire was bright.' . . . And so the synagogue is called a bright fire"—i.e., the abundance and creative divine energy flowed down from the sefirot. Job 38:19: "Where is the way where light dwelleth?"

77–92: I.e., in building this synagogue, which was finished in 1610, when the initial group of what might be called early risers was founded, in the month of Shevat. Zacut's group and the congregation gathered in the synagogue's courtyard—between its walls—for the vigil of light. Deuteronomy 33:11: "Bless, Lord, his substance and accept the work of his hands." Job 33:28: "His life shall see the light."

93–108: The keepers of the vigil would rise early to recite prayers, as it says to do in Psalms 119:148: "Mine eyes look forward to the night watches, that I might meditate on thy word." Psalms 119:62: "At midnight I will rise to give thanks unto thee because of thy righteous judgments." Genesis 1:15: "And let them be for lights in the firmament of the heaven to give light upon the earth." Psalms 37:4: "Delight thyself also in the Lord." Exodus 35:8: "and oil for the light."

109–24: In 1630 the Jews were expelled from Mantua and their property was plundered. A year later a decree was issued permitting their return to the city and its synagogue. The poem also alludes at this point to a return to the sefirah of Gedulah, or greatness—parallel to Gevurah (power)—and to the light of God's mercy.

125–40: In the original this stanza alludes directly—by name—to three of the principal figures in the Mantuan community. Psalms 74:21: "Let not the oppressed return ashamed." Psalms 52:10: "I was like a green olive." Exodus 27:20: "Pure olive oil beaten for the light."

141–60: The stanza predicts the messianic restoration of the Temple and priestly offerings, which will awaken the fullness of God's love. The original contains a pun on the town's name—Mantua—hence the translation here: "with goodness through *man to a* people appointed." Psalms 36:10: "In thy light shall we see the light."

Messiah

Text: The poems in the manuscript (Guenzburg 745) in Tishby's edition (*Studies in Kabbalah and Its Branches*, vol. 3 [Heb]) do not bear the name of any author, but their editor has attributed the work to Luzzatto with considerable certainty and his attribution has been widely accepted. For more on the Messiah ben Joseph see Tishby, *Messianic Mysticism* (esp. pp. 273–80, 286), where the author notes the overlap between Luzzatto's thought and that of the Shabbatians with regard to this rival Messiah. The commentary here is based largely on Tishby's in *Messianic Mysticism*, pp. 120–21, 158–60, and 207–11.

Lines 1–2: The poem is addressed to Ephraim, Joseph's son, who in this case is the Messiah ben Yosef. See Genesis 41:52: "And the name of the second called he Ephraim: For God hath caused me to be fruitful in the land of my affliction," and 49:22: "Joseph is a fruitful bough." Also Genesis 48:1. See also *Pesikta Rabbati* 36, which explains that the light of the verse "For with you is the fountain of life; in your light we see light" (Psalms 36:10; see also Zacut, "You Readied a Light," above, ll. 141–60) is the light of the Messiah. God then explains to Satan that the light under His throne is for one who will put him [Satan] to shame. "He is the Messiah, and his name is Ephraim, my true Messiah, who . . . will pull up straight his generation, and who will give light to the eyes of Israel and deliver his people."

3: Messiah ben Joseph is associated with the sefirah of Yesod, which in turn is associated with the Righteous One, who "when the time comes for the Redemption . . . will be avenged upon the Sitra Ahra, at whose hands he suffered torments when he descended to the husks" (Tishby, *Messianic Mysticism*, p. 158).

4: Literally, "the house of the barren woman." See Isaiah 31:2: "He will arise against the house of the evildoers." Tishby suggests that the barren woman is the Sitra Ahra, because of its infertility. Another possibility is that it refers to Gog, "against whom Messiah ben Joseph will fight." Elsewhere Luzzatto writes of the masculine equivalent—the (sterile) uprooter of the house, who must be fought and vanquished. Cf. Psalms 2:2: "The kings of the earth set themselves, and the rulers take counsel together, against the Lord, against His anointed."

6–7: See Genesis 49:25–26: "Even by the God of thy father, who shall help thee; and by the Almighty, who shall bless thee with blessings of heaven above, blessings of the deep that lieth under, blessings of the breasts, and of the womb: The blessings of thy father have prevailed above the blessings of my progenitors unto the utmost bound [bounty] of the everlasting hills: they shall be on the head of Joseph, and on the crown of the head of him that was separate from his brethren." This is, notes Tishby, "an esoteric reference to the divine flow which descends from the *sefirot*" (*Messianic Mysticism*, pp. 120–21 and 160). See *Zohar* 1:247b: "Jacob inherited the finest of all . . . and he gave all to Joseph. Why? Because this is fitting; for the Righteous One absorbs all as one, all blessings abiding in Him. He pours blessings from the head above. . . . 'As great as the bounty of eternal hills'—desire of those hills of the world [or eternity]" (*Zohar*, trans. Matt, vol. 3, p. 518). Matt notes that in the *Zohar* "the two hills of the world are the two females, Binah and Shekhinah, each one a divine world. The desire of all the sefirotic limbs is to suckle from Binah, or higher Mother, and join with Shekhinah, or lower Mother. All the limbs convey their flowing desire to Yesod the Righteous One—symbolized by Joseph—who links both hills of the world" (Matt, *Zohar*, vol. 3, p. 519). See also Luzzatto's mystical Ketubah (Tishby, *Messianic Mysticism*, pp. 214–15): "The king makes himself a servant to the field. And I will honor, through honoring the Shekhinah in every detail.

And I will feed: this is the mystery of the beast which ate a thousand hills every day, 'behemoth on a thousand hills,' [Psalms 50:10] . . . And I will provide: by drawing the flow of divine bounty from above and also from below to sustain the One on high."

9: The bullock is Messiah ben Joseph. Cf. Deuteronomy 33:17: "He has horns like the horns of the wild ox; With them he gores the peoples, the ends of the earth one and all." The lion is Messiah ben David. Cf. Genesis 49:9: "Judah is a lion's whelp."

11: The serpent is the Sitra Ahra. Elsewhere Luzzatto writes that "your tongue is the staff of God which split the sea of the Torah . . . and the staff by which the serpent was turned into a staff, so that in this way all the other sides were subjected to the holy side" (Tishby, *Messianic Mysticism*, p. 197, n. 30).

13: Cf. Psalms 73:12: "Behold, these are the wicked, always at ease in the world."

Hasidic Devotion

Information for the headnote is drawn from the following sources: Gershom Scholem, *Major Trends in Jewish Mysticism* (New York, 1941), pp. 325–50, and Scholem "*Devekut*, or Communion with God," in *The Messianic Idea in Judaism* (New York, 1971), pp. 203–27; Aryeh Kaplan, *Chasidic Masters* (New York, 1984), pp. 4, 69–102; Samuel Dresner, *The World of a Hasidic Master: Levi Yitzhak of Berditchev* (New York, 1986); Avraham Rubinstein, et al., "Hasidism," Avraham Rubinstein, "Levi Isaac ben Meir of Berdichev," and Avrum Strull, "Shneur Zalman of Lyady," *Encyclopedia Judaica*, 2nd ed. (Detroit, 2007), vol. 8, pp. 393–434, vol. 12, pp. 704–6, vol. 18, pp. 501–5; Adin Steinsaltz, *The Long Shorter Way: Discourses on Chasidic Thought*, trans. Yehuda Hanegbi (Northvale, N.J., 1988), and *Opening the Tanya: Discovering the Moral and Mystical Teachings of a Classic Work of Kabbalah*, 3 vols., ed. Adin Steinsaltz, trans. Yaacov Tauber (San Francisco, 2007), vol. 3, pp. 38–45 and 181–210; Moshe Idel, *Old Worlds, New Mirrors: On Jewish Mysticism and Twentieth-Century Thought* (Philadelphia, 2010), pp. 234–37, Idel, "Hermeneutics in Hasidism," *Journal for the Study of Religions and Ideologies* 9:25 (2010), pp. 3–16, and Idel, *Hasidim: Between Ecstasy and Magic* (Albany, N.Y.,

1995), pp. 214–18. Solomon Schechter's classic essay "The Chassidim" appeared in his *Studies in Judaism*, first series (Philadelphia, 1896), pp. 1–45.

Quotations are from the following sources: *The earlier Kabbalah*: Kaplan, *Chasidic Masters*, p. 4; *God surrounds everything*: Scholem, *Major Trends*, pp. 347–48; *It is the communion with God through* devekut: Scholem, "*Devekut*," pp. 209–11; *a little about learning, but nothing about prayer*: Kaplan *Chasidic Masters*, pp. 86–87; *Here the descent into the mystical realm*: Green, "Religion and Mysticism: The Case of Judaism," in *Take Judaism, for Example: Studies Toward the Comparison of Religions*, ed. Jacob Neusner (Chicago, 1983), p. 74.

Song of You

Text: *The Language of Faith: A Selection from the Most Expressive Jewish Prayers. Original Text and New English Verse Translations*, ed. Naham N. Glatzer (New York, 1967), p. 80. See also Dresner, *World of a Hasidic Master*, pp. 104–6.

In 1781, Levi Yitzhak of Berditchev was chosen to represent the Hasidic movement in a debate with its opponents in Warsaw. He was asked why the Hasids jump and leap about when praying "as if the fear of Heaven were not upon you. . . . Such conduct is not proper before even a human king." Levi Yitzhak replied: "Do not bring proofs from a human king. . . . He fills only the place where he sits. . . . The King of kings, the Holy One, blessed be He, whose glory fills the world . . . there is no place where He is not, and wherever we turn there He is. Therefore, it is proper to leap and jump after the master of the World, always searching for him. . . . The Lord is everywhere!" (Dresner, *World of a Hasidic Master*, p. 33). Scholem notes that Hasidism, as a popular, unsophisticated movement, reflects a "far more definite pantheistic image in the formulation of the thoughts of the first Hasidic thinkers than ever before"; "Solomon Schechter," he continues, "defined the doctrine of God's immanence in all things not only as the very root and core of Hasidism, but as its distinguishing characteristic" (*Major Trends*, p. 347; and see Schechter, "Chassidim," pp. 19–21).

Lines 6ff.: Cf. Psalms 139:7: "Whither shall I go from Thy spirit? Or wither shall I flee from Thy presence? If I ascend up into Heaven, Thou

art there; If I make my bed in the netherworld, behold, thou art there."
Levi Yitzhak is quoting directly from Yehudah HaLevi's poem "Where
Will I Find You," ll. 1–4 (see above). See also Kaplan, *Chasidic Masters*,
p. 80: "There are two aspects of [our understanding of] God, namely that
He is near and yet far. We see God as far off since we believe that the
blessed Infinite Light was the First of the First, and that nothing in cre-
ation can comprehend Him at all. . . . This is the concept of God as being
distant, where He is transcendental and far from our understanding. At
the same time, we also understand God to be near, since we believe that
He fills all worlds. He is contained in all worlds, surrounds all worlds,
and no place is empty of Him." See *Zohar* 3:225a ("He encompasses all
worlds. . . . He fills all worlds," in *Wisdom of the Zohar*, arranged and
rendered into Hebrew by Fischel Lachower and Isaiah Tishby; introduc-
tions and annotations by Isaiah Tishby, trans. David Goldstein, 3 vols.
[Oxford, 1997], vol. 1, p. 259) and *Berakhot* 10a. Scholem writes of the way
in which devekut (communion) involves constant awareness of the fact
that God pervades everything. In fact, says Scholem, "to be out of *deve-
kut* is not simply a state of estrangement from God, it rather implies the
negation of His oneness and all-pervading presence" (*Messianic Idea in
Judaism*, p. 209). He also writes of the Baal Shem Tov's habit of interpret-
ing Psalms 81:10 in literal fashion, as the Hebrew sequence of words has
it: "God shall not be a stranger among [to] you" (instead of "There shall
be no strange God among you"). Therefore one should always follow the
Psalmist's injunction to set the Lord before one.

from the Tanya

Text: Shneur Zalman, *Likkutei Amarim* (*Tanya*) (Brooklyn, 1982),
chap. 50. See also the Chabad edition: *Lessons in Tanya: The Tanya of
Rabbi Shneur Zalman of Liadi*, elucidated by Rabbi Yosef Wineberg,
trans. Levy Wineberg, ed. Uri Kaploun (Brooklyn, 1996), chap. 50. The
commentary below draws from that edition and from *Opening the Tanya*.

The *Tanya* is a work of Hebrew prose; and while we've have sought
to include only "poems that are poems" in this volume, the essentially
poetic content and *formulation* of these lines has led to their being ex-

cerpted here as poetry. Grateful acknowledgment is due to Haviva Pedaya for suggesting the inclusion of the passage in this form. The poem treats what the author says is the highest kind of love there is—the soul's longing not simply to experience the divine but to be annihilated in union with God. This is a dangerous love that comes not from Hesed (grace, and the right side of the sefirotic tree, which is headed by Binah, or understanding) but from Gevurah (strength and power, i.e., the left side of the sefirotic array). The writer recognizes, however, that God's love can be known only from within the body—that is, through the observance of His commandments. Fire provides the parable: Just as a flame seems to want to separate itself from the wick and wood, so too the soul longs to ascend and detach itself from the body. But in order to bring the light of the Shekhinah down into the world, the worshipper must use his strength to overcome his longing for release into union and rechannel his desire through the observance of the commandments. Paradoxically, in other words, this concentration on the physical plane will lead to elevation, if not complete separation, from it. (See *Zohar* Balak 187a, which states that a Jew should be aware of the Shekhinah above him and keep it supplied with oil [good deeds].) Elsewhere in the *Tanya* Zalman writes, "The Torah originates in God's Will and Wisdom, where 'the Torah and God are one,' and where 'no thought can grasp Him at all.' From there, it progressively descends through the mysterious gradations, step by step through the sequence of universes, until it is finally clothed in physical ideas and worldly concepts. The Torah thus enters the realm of the physical, which comprises the vast majority of its commandments and laws. . . . When the Torah and Commandments clothe . . . the soul and encompass all of its 613 parts, then the soul is literally 'bound up in the bond of life with God.' The light of God literally surrounds the soul, clothing it from head to toe. . . . The only time when it is possible to grasp the Divine Presence itself is when one grasps the Torah and Commandments and is clothed in them." Devekut, Scholem notes, indirectly linking our two Hasidic poems, was preached "as a contemplative realization of the immanence of God in the concrete" (*Messianic Idea in Judaism*, p. 216).

Lines 1–4: The soul recognizes the greatness of the Infinite God and understands its place ("as nothing") in the order He has created. This is the reverence and fear that precedes or attends to the great love to be described. In that combination of great love and fear, the soul desires to become, as the *Tanya* puts it elsewhere, a "vehicle" for the *heikhalot* (chambers) of holiness rather than of impurity. Therefore one will "reflect on these matters . . . in order to break down his [pride and coarseness of] heart within him," so that the Sitra Ahra will be wholly nullified (*Tanya*, chap. 35). Cf. Song of Songs 8:6: "For love is strong as death; jealousy as cruel as the grave. The coals thereof are coals of fire, which hath a most vehement flame." (See Idel, "Hermeneutics in Hasidism.")

5: The image of the flame is found in the *Zohar* 1:50b–51a (translated by Arthur Green in "Religion and Mysticism," pp. 82–84): "He who wants to understand the mystery of the holy union should come and look at the flame as it rises from a coal or a lighted candle. No flame can rise unless it is attached to some coarse matter. . . . The blue-black flame [at the bottom] is joined to that thing beneath it, binding it together with the white light [above it]. Sometimes the blue or black light turns red but the white light above it never changes; it is forever white. The lower light [changing] . . . holds fast to both ends, to the white light above and to the burning substance beneath, ever consuming what comes its way. . . . The white light above, however, neither consumes nor destroys, nor does it change its light. . . . Above the white light is . . . an invisible light that surrounds it. There is sublime mystery here, and you will find it all in the rising flame." See also *The Zohar* 1:83b, trans. Daniel C. Matt, 5 vols. (Stanford, Calif., 2004–9) vol. 2, p. 32.

6–7: Cf. *Tanya*, chap. 35 (and its discussion of the *Zohar* Balak 187a), where the body is likened to a wick, and the light that shines on it to the Shekhinah. In order for a person—the average person, as the *Tanya* calls him—to draw the effulgence of the Shekhinah down to his body, he must observe the commandments. This is the oil or fuel from which (or through which) the flame emerges and shines in the world as good deeds are performed. "No matter how great . . . one's love of God, it cannot end in self-immolation, unlike the oil that burns (thanks to the wick) and is consumed" (*Opening the Tanya*, vol. 3, pp. 182, 191–92). In chapter 29, Steinsaltz likens the dulled heart of the average person to "a wooden beam that will not catch fire"; in order to help it catch fire, it should be chopped up into smaller pieces. So too, notes the *Tanya*, alluding to the *Zohar*, "the body into which the light of the soul does not penetrate should be crushed"—i.e., one must "set aside appointed times for humbling oneself" (*Tanya*, chap. 35). As the *Zohar* itself puts it: "The body on which the light of the soul does not ascend—they strike it, and the light of the soul ascends" (*Wisdom of the Zohar*, introductions and annotations by Tishby, vol. 2, p. 784). Later in chapter 50 the *Tanya* comments, alluding to the *Zohar*, that "the unity which is hidden shall become an aspect of the world that is revealed." This, it adds, with a play on the Hebrew root *k-l-h*—which yields both "bride" and "consume"—is the meaning of the verse in Alkabetz's poem "Hymn to the Sabbath" (above), which says, *Lekhah dodi likrat kalah*. The literal meaning is "Come, my beloved, toward the bride," but the deeper meaning is "Come, my beloved, toward consumption [or fulfillment] of the soul." That is, one should bring out the fulfillment of the soul in unification with the divine by causing the Beloved (God in this reading) to bring down the Shekhinah and the light of God into the world. This in turn recalls Levi Yitzhak of Berditchev's saying that "a person must fear God so much that his ego is totally nullified. Only then can he attach himself to Nothingness [a level higher than all worlds]. Sustenance . . . then flows to all universes" (Kaplan, *Chasidic Masters*, p. 73). Also of interest is Levi Yitzhak's saying that when a man prays "with all his heart and his soul then his spirit delights because it is elevated from the material world and only the spirit remains" (Rubinstein, "Levi Isaac ben Meir," p. 705).

The Seeds of Secular Mysticism

Information for the headnote is drawn from the following sources: Gershom Scholem, *Major Trends in Jewish Mysticism* (New York, 1941), pp. 349–50; H. N. Bialik, *Poems* [Heb], ed. A. Holtzman (Or Yehudah, 2004), pp. 292–99 and 306–7, Bialik, *Collected Poems: A Critical Edition* [Heb], ed. Dan Miron (Tel Aviv, 1990), pp. 215–16, Bialik, *Selected Poems*, trans. Ruth Nevo (Jerusalem, 1981), introduction, and Bialik, "Revealment and Concealment," in Bialik, *Revealment and Concealment: Five Essays*, with an afterword by Zali Gurevitch (Jerusalem, 2000), esp. pp. 127–29 and 139; Yehuda Liebes, *Ars Poetica in Sefer Yetzirah* [Heb] (Tel Aviv, 2000), p. 153; David Aberbach, *Bialik* (New York, 1988); and Avraham Regelson, "'The Pool': A Poem of Perfection" [Heb], *Al HaMishmar* 19 (July 1952). Also of note here is the relation between secular and religious thought in Jewish culture (on which see David Biale, *Not in the Heavens: The Tradition of Jewish Secular Thought* [Princeton, 2011], esp. pp. 15–58), and the link between Bialik's turn to the vocabulary of mysticism and the work of the Russian Symbolist poets and theorists he was reading. For a detailed discussion of the latter see Hamutal Bar-Yosef, *Mysticism and Modern Hebrew Poetry* [Heb] (Tel Aviv, 2008), esp. pp. 74ff. and 174ff.

Quotations are from the following sources: *cut off from the world . . . this other world*: Bialik, *Collected Poems* [Heb], ed. Miron, pp. 205–9; Bialik, *Poems* [Heb], ed. Holtzman, pp. 292–99; *My soul dwells in exile*: Bialik, *Revealment and Concealment*, from Gurevitch's afterword, p. 107; *See, saw, see, saw*: Gurevitch quotes and discusses this poem in *Revealment and Concealment*, p. 138, noting that it contains (and perhaps conceals) an explicit allusion to the question of mystical inquiry as that is raised in the Mishnaic tractate *Hagigah* 2:1 (cited also in relation to the Heikhalot hymn "A Measure of Holiness," above): "Whoever reflects upon four things would be better off had he not been born: What is above, what is beneath, what is before, and what is after." The Hebrew original of "Seesaw" appears in H. N. Bialik, *Collected Poems: Yiddish Poetry, Nursery Rhymes, Dedicatory Verses, a Critical Edition*, ed. Dan Miron et al. [Heb] (Tel Aviv, 2000), pp. 197–98. The translation of the poem here is mine.

from The Pool

Text: Bialik, *Collected Poems* [Heb], ed. Miron, pp. 203–9; Bialik, *Poems* [Heb], ed. Holtzman, pp. 292–99.

Bialik composed the first two-thirds of "The Pool" in Warsaw in 1904 and finished it in Odessa the following summer, when he was thirty-two. The excerpt translated here, which brings the poem to a close, appears to have been composed in a single sitting in Odessa (Bialik, *Collected Poems* [Heb], pp. 203–4).

Bialik's obsession with dualities in tension (such as these two worlds) is not merely evident in this poem; it becomes an essential part of the poem's subject. For more on the centrality of "reflection" in the Zoharic worldview, see Joseph Dan, *The Kabbalah: A Very Short Introduction* (Oxford, 2007), pp. 33–34: "The Zoharic worldview is based on the concept of reflection: everything is the reflection of everything else. The verses of scriptures reflect the emanation and structure of the divine world; as does the human body, in the anthropomorphic conception of the *sefirot*, and the human soul, which originates from the divine realm and . . . reflects the functions and dynamism of the *sefirot*. [In its structure], the universe reflects the divine realms, and events in it . . . parallel the mythological processes of the divine powers."

Line 2: "Presence" in the Hebrew is *kenaf haShekhinah*—"the wing of the Shekhinah." (For more on this image in Bialik, see the notes to "Bring Me in Under Your Wing.")

22: "Pool" in the Hebrew is *breikhah*, which Bar-Yosef (*Mysticism and Modern Hebrew Poetry* [Heb], p. 162) notes is close to *brakhah* (blessing), a word that appears a few lines later.

42: Elijah the prophet is often linked with the beginnings of the mystical tradition. In 1 Kings 18:38 he draws fire down from God on Mount Carmel, and with it he defeats the prophet of Baal. When he dies, he is translated to heaven in a chariot of fire (2 Kings 2:11). He reveals himself to many Kabbalists and imparts the secrets of the *Zohar* to its pseudepigraphic author, Shimon Bar Yohai.

57: In a June 1905 letter to a close friend of his, Bialik states that the pool is, as he sees it, "a symbol of the spirit of artistic creation." See Bialik, *Poems*, ed. Holtzman, p. 292. The parallel between artistic and religious (sacred) creation is, throughout the poem, clear if complex.

Bring Me in Under Your Wing

Text: Bialik, *Collected Poems* [Heb], ed. Miron, pp. 215–16; Bialik, *Poems* [Heb], ed. Holtzman, pp. 306–7.

Lines 1–4: While "wing" here is intentionally ambiguous, the situation of the poem conjures immediate associations of phrases from Scripture and the liturgy. See especially the famous hymn for a burial "El Malei Rahamim" (God Full of Mercy): "God full of mercy, who dwells on high, bring rest beneath the wings of the Shekhinah . . . to the souls of our beloved." The "sister" of line 2 recalls Song of Songs 5:2: "Open to me, my sister, my love, my dove, my undefiled." See also Psalms 17:8: "Keep me as the apple of the eye, hide me under the shadow of thy wings." The verse from Psalms refers to God, though the poem makes it clear that the addressee is feminine, and so the dominant association is with an earthly beloved, with a mother figure, or with a philosophical-theological figure along the lines of Sophia or the Shekhinah. As Bar-Yosef sees it, the erotic overtones of the lines are brought out by the fact that the Hebrew for "place of rest" is *heik*, meaning "bosom" or "lap" (cf. Deuteronomy 13:7 and Micah 7:5). Bar-Yosef discusses this in more detail in *Mysticism and Modern Hebrew Poetry* [Heb], pp. 26off. She also points out the erotic connotations of the Hebrew for "wing," which can be read as "dress" or "clothing" (cf. Deuteronomy 23:1 and 27:20; Ezekiel 16:8; Ruth 3:9). Like his medieval precursor, Shelomoh Ibn Gabirol, Bialik was powerfully and even erotically drawn to Wisdom. For more on Ibn Gabirol's relation to Wisdom, see the section on him in this volume ("Al-Andalus and Ashkenaz") and Peter Cole, *Selected Poems of Solomon Ibn Gabirol* (Princeton, 2001). The "unwanted" prayers in line 4 (in Hebrew, literally, "rejected" or "neglected") establish the place of liminality—of religious longing that finds no answer.

Another of Bialik's well-known lyrics takes up similar imagery in a much more explicitly religious context. In "Alone" (*Levadi*), which was written in 1902, it is the Shekhinah herself who is left behind, abandoned by all who were carried off by the new and fresh song of the morning. All, that is, but the speaker, who—in a reverse of the situation of this poem—finds himself under her broken wing, the two of them forsaken by the world they had known. See Bialik, *Poems*, ed. Holtzman, p. 228. "Alone" demonstrates the people's ability to negatively affect the forces of heaven and to wound the Shekhinah with their behavior (a classic Kabbalistic trope). In "Bring Me in Under Your Wing" the dynamic is reversed, and the celestial powers can bring about change *in the world*, as the Shekhinah-like figure is asked to heal the wounded, vulnerable individual. Bialik alludes to both aspects of this dynamic in a letter to his friend and biographer Fischel Lachower, where he tells of his "solitary sitting in the Beit Midrash [as] one of the most important influences on [his] state of mind and inner world." He writes: "Sometimes it would seem to me that I am an only child of the Almighty and the beloved child of the Shekhinah, and she too is here with me, spreading her wings and protecting me like the apple of her eye." The letter is quoted in Tzahi Weiss, "The Shekhinah's Broken Wing" [Heb], *Eretz Aheret* 47 (2008), and appears in F. Lachower, *Bialik: His Life and Works* (Tel Aviv, 1956), vol. 1, pp. 36–41.

5–8: In the Kabbalistic context dusk is actually an hour of danger and severity, except on Shabbat, when favor and grace become manifest (see *The Zohar*, trans. Daniel C. Matt, 5 vols. [Stanford, Calif., 2004–9], vol. 4, p. 503). It's possible that Bialik here is intentionally, and ironically, reversing the polarity of the association — as his prayers have already been rejected.

13–16: In the Kabbalistic and the Bialikian contexts, *nothing* is a complex term, and the Hebrew for this line — *ein li davar* ("I have nothing," or "I have not a word") — is more complex still. For one, it recalls the verse from Psalms 19:3: "There is no speech, there are no words [*ein devarim*]." The phrase also echoes Bialik's essay "Revealment and Concealment," which describes the words we use in daily language as husks (a term that conjures associations with the Kabbalistic *kelippot*), the centers of which are empty. Though it is true that the speaker has "nothing," in the Kabbalistic context "nothing" is also the ultimate generative principle, and the poet has this poem and others like it to tell of his situation, just as the Hasidic story replaces the spot in the woods and the fire and the prayer. And as the Hasidic tale served to accomplish the task at hand, so too the poem in its way brings about a kind of fulfillment.

17–20: The circular structure returns us to the speaker's unwanted prayers and underscores his exile from oneness and, to an extent, from language and tradition. But at the same time the structure itself conveys a sense of rest and closure, even as the poem tells of a denial of consolation and a painful suspension between worlds. That state recalls the Kabbalistic situation of restless "outcast" or "naked souls" which have yet to experience rebirth in a body. As Scholem describes it, this is "the most terrible fate that could befall any soul. . . . Such absolute exile was the worst nightmare of the soul which envisaged its personal drama in terms of the tragic destiny of the whole people. Absolute homelessness was the sinister symbol of absolute Godlessness. . . . Union with God or utter banishment were the two poles between which a system had to be devised in which the Jews could live under the domination of Law, which seeks to destroy the forces of Exile" (*Major Trends*, p. 250). While this poem is clearly a personal lyric, its imagery—the wing, the covering (alluding to Ruth and Ezekiel and the concealment of nakedness), and the dramatic situation of the work—calls up a world of highly suggestive religious and Kabbalistic associations. Consciously or unconsciously, the poem becomes a statement about the state of the soul, and especially the Jewish soul, within a secular world.

Aminadav Dykman

"WHEN THEY SAY: 'ALEXANDRIA,'" wrote the Russian poet Mikhail Kuzmin in one of his poems, "I see the white walls of a house, /A small garden with a bed of gilly-flowers /the pallid sun of an autumn evening /And I hear the sound of distant flutes." At the words "anthology of mystical verse" what does the general reader hear? Most likely a chain of celebrated names from East and West: the great Arabic, Persian, Turkish, and Hindi poet-mystics Attar, Hallaj, Muhyaddin Ibn al-Arabi, Jalaladdin Rumi, Yunus Emre, and Kabir. Then the major figures of Western mystical poetry: Hildegard of Bingen, Saint John of the Cross, perhaps the more obscure yet utterly fascinating German baroque mystics Quirinus Kuhlmann and Catharina Regina von Greiffenberg, the French mystical poets Claude Hopil, Madame Guyon, and Antoine Favre, and, of course, in the domain closest to the English reader, Robert Southwell, Henry Vaughan, Thomas Traherne, and, in the New World, Edward Taylor.

The thirty-eighth koan in the *Gateless Gate* of the Zen master Ekai contains a clear admonition against the idea of expressing the mystical experience in words: "Words cannot describe everything. The heart's message cannot be delivered in words." If an individual receives words literally, he will be lost. If he tries to explain with words, he will not attain enlightenment in this life. And yet the very essence of poetry yields the expectation that the ineffable mystical moment be expressed by it alone. It is with good reason that William James quotes Tennyson, Whitman, and Swinburne when he discusses the mystical experience.[1]

Over the past few decades, thanks to the work of eminent scholars such as Gershom Scholem, Moshe Idel, Yehudah Liebes, and others, Kabbalah has ceased to be a solely esoteric domain and is now firmly present in the imagination of a wider reading public. The moment is more than ripe to acquaint readers with a lesser-known facet of Kabbalistic thought and practice—namely, the poetry that was folded into it and, directly or obliquely, influenced by it.

While the body of Hebrew poetry that might be classified as mystical in the broad and common sense of the term is large, that which is explicitly taken up with Kabbalistic speculation as it emerges in the late twelfth century is in fact restricted in both scope and breadth, in part because the bulk of the creative energy of the Kabbalists proper was invested in the fulfillment of the commandments and in engagement with various mystical techniques that required tremendous spiritual and physical effort.[2] Moreover, the most intensive periods of Kabbalistic speculation and experiment did not coincide with any major moment of Hebrew poetic activity (such as the Golden Age of Hebrew poetry in Spain). Nonetheless, powerful poems emerge from the proto-Kabbalistic period (including that of the Hebrew Golden Age) and from the classical Kabbalistic period — poetry that can take its place alongside the major mystical poetry of other literary traditions from around the world.

The group of poems at the head of this anthology, for instance, undoubtedly deserves to stand among the world's masterpieces of mystical hymnology. Anonymous, or almost anonymous (our biographical knowledge of Yannai and Eliezer Kallir scarcely goes beyond their names), these hymns strike the reader with their overpowering energy, propelled as they are by repetition and synonymic variation. The almost machinelike movement of these "Poems of the Palaces" brings to mind the same poetic qualities of passages in the Rigveda. Consider, for instance, the opening lines of this early Hebrew hymn:

> King of kings —
> God of gods
> and Lord of lords,
> encircled by braided branches of crowns —
> encompassed by branching commanders of radiance —
> who covers the heavens with wings of His splendor
> and in His majesty appears on high;
> from whose beauty the depths are lit,
> whose glory flashes across the sky — [3]

or that of the tenth-century Hebrew-Spanish poet Yosef Ibn Avitor, who continued the ancient traditions of Jewish poets from Byzantine Palestine:

> Who established the heights of heaven
> then set out glowing orbs?
> Who will tell of all He's done,
> and who is greater than the Lord? . . .

> Who instructed the billowing waves
> to swell above the deepest seas?
> Who between the peaks of each
> put three-hundred leagues?
> Who spoke and opened channels
> on high before the rushing streams?
> Who said no two drops from clouds
> would fall — cut from a single mold?
> Who has gathered the wind in His fist
> and bound the waters in His robe?[4]

and the following stanza from a Sanskrit hymn to Indra:

> Who made the widespread earth when quaking steadfast,
> Who set to rest the agitated mountains,
> Who measured out air's middle space more widely,
> Who gave the sky support: this, man, is Indra.[5]

Yet most of all, the Hebrew hymns and liturgical poems, with their almost unbearable bursts of fire, light, and glory, bring to

mind Dante's nearly speechless description of his vision at the
very end of his journey, in the last canto of the *Paradiso:*

> Ne la profonda e chiara sussistenza
>> De l'alto lume parvermi tre giri
>> di tre colori e d'una contenenza;
>
> . . . .
>
> O luce etterna, che sole in te sidi,
>> sola t'intendi, e da te intelletta
>> e intendente te ami e arridi!
>
> [Within the deep and luminous subsistence
>> Of the High Light appeared to me three circles,
>> Of threefold color and of one dimension,
>
> . . . .
>
> O Light Eterne, sole in thyself that dwellest,
>> Sole knowest thyself, and, known unto thyself
>> And knowing, lovest and smilest on thyself!][6]

The history of poetry sometimes shows strange leaps for-
ward, as well as curious returns to the past. Thus, many typical
traits of European baroque poetry can be found centuries ear-
lier in the Hebrew poetry of the Golden Age. Such ubiquitous
images as "womb-tomb" appeared in the poems of Hebrew Ibe-
rian poets long before one finds them in the poetry of Quevedo
or the Elizabethans. In the same vein, it is fascinating to read
the world-class poems of Shelomoh Ibn Gabirol and Yehudah
HaLevi as forerunners of the English metaphysical poets and

their European contemporaries. Many lines in Ibn Gabirol's magnificent meditation *Kingdom's Crown* can be juxtaposed with passages in the poems of baroque metaphysical poets. Take, for example, the following lines of the Andalusian poet's masterwork:

> You are Lord,
> all creation relies on your godliness;
> all is sustained by your oneness.
>
> You are Lord,
> and there is no distinction between
> Your being divine and one;
> between your past and the real,
>
> between what you were and will be.
>
> All is a single mystery. [7]

And the following lines from a poem by the Elizabethan poet Joshua Sylvester (1563–1618)

> Alpha and Omega, God alone:
> Eloi, My God, the Holy-One;
> Whose Power is Omnipotence:
> Whose Wisdome is Omni-science:
> Whose Beeing is All Soveraigne Blisse:
> Whose Worke Perfection's Fulnesse is;
>
> . . . .

> Above All, over All things raigning:
> Beneath All, All things aye sustayning:
> Without All, All conteyning sole

Likewise, just as Hebrew poets speak of the sweetness of the word and experience of God,[8] so do George Herbert ("O what sweetnesse from the bowl/Fills my soul") or Catharina Regina von Greiffenberg ("erfüllt mit Geistes-Thau/mit Himmel-Hönig-Must/der Seelen Kählen süß und fliest zu Gottes Ehre." ["Filled with Spirit's-dew, with the juice-of-heavenly-honey/The soul-throat, sweetness, soars to honor God."]). And the language and atmosphere of the Song of Songs inform Eliezer Azikri's "Soul's Beloved" and Shelomoh Alkabetz's "Hymn to the Sabbath"—two of the most famous and enduring poems in the entire Jewish tradition—much as they give shape to Saint John of the Cross's gentle mystical pastoral, "Songs Between the Soul and the Bridegroom," however different the subjects of these poems. A similar parallel exists, through a chain of direct influence, between Turkish love songs of the seventeenth century and both Sufi and Hebrew devotional poems.[9]

That said, for all Hebrew poetry has in common with the broader currents of mystical verse in the world republic of letters—the examples above are only a handful among hundreds—difference within that sameness isn't hard to find. In particular, the comparison with European metaphysical poetry may be helpful in order to elucidate the special nature of Hebrew mystical poetry. The English metaphysical poets, we remember, wrote in a variety of religious modes—devotional, meditative, and contemplative. Louis Martz has shown how Donne and his fellow poets were influenced by the meditative techniques of Ignatius of Loyola and others—taking, for instance, scenes from the life of Christ or of one of the saints of the church as an object of meditation in verse. In view of the important role of meditation in Kabbalah, one might expect to find considerable poetry in Hebrew that takes up Kabbalistic meditative techniques. And while one does encounter first-rate work of this sort (Azikri's "Soul's Beloved," for instance), it is by no means common, because whereas the Christian mystic had a visual subject to meditate upon, the Kabbalist's object was almost wholly abstract. At the same time, in part perhaps because Islamic poetry was not written for the liturgy but rather for individual expression, it displays greater freedom, offering us the marvelous lightness of Rumi: "What images does He play at, what tricks contrive! . . . Seek Him in the sky, and He shines from the water like the moon; enter the water, and He flees up to heaven."[10] (Only the eighteenth-century Hasid Levi Yitzhak of Berditchev comes close to this in his "Song of You," though Ibn Gabirol does sometimes engage in a subtly coded taunt of God.) Far more common in the Hebrew scheme are devotional poems expressing a desire for nearness to the divine. Some of these are masterpieces of the highest poetic order.[11]

Hard as it is to pinpoint the difference between Jewish mystical poetry and its Muslim, Christian, Hindu, and Buddhist counterparts, a tentative definition needs to be broached, though it sounds like a peculiar truism: Jewish mystical poetry is special in its being Jewish. That is, it is concerned with Jewish concerns (though these are sometimes worked out under the influence of Christian and Islamic practices). Rather than notions of, for instance, incarnation, transubstantiation, stigmata, or the extinction of consciousness, front and center in the consciousness of the poets in this volume are messianic longing; a desire to participate in the heavenly liturgy; the multiple and often bizarre Names of God; the system of divine influence known in Kabbalah as the *sefirot*; the history of the Jewish people and its role in human and even cosmic history; and the nature of Hebrew as a sacred language. No Hindu, Buddhist, or Catholic mystic bestowed upon his native language the overwhelming centrality or potency that the Jewish poets gave to Hebrew, the Holy tongue. Moreover, where the mystics of many traditions sought the silence of union beyond language, the Hebrew poets produced hundreds of language-centered poems that focused on the assorted values of Hebrew itself—numerological substitution, acronymic permutation, etymological slippage-and-exfoliation.

And last but not least, it seems that an essential notion is embedded in the last word of this anthology's subtitle— "Mystical Verse from the Jewish Tradition." It is hard to think of any other mystical poetry that might match this tradition for continuity. The line that extends back from Victorian England and Francis Thompson's "The Hound of Heaven" to the anonymous fourteenth-century English mystical poem "Quia amore langueo" is less direct and coherent than the one connecting Hayyim Nahman Bialik's "The Pool" or Levi Yitzhak of Berditchev's "Song of You" to the *Zohar* and the poems of Ibn Gabirol or *Sefer Yetzirah* (The Book of Creation). In this way the angels surrounding the throne of God in song—and as song—in the late-antique or early-medieval Heikhalot hymns are powerfully echoed and transformed in the chorus of this anthology by the seventh-century liturgical work of Kallir and the eleventh-century poetry of Yehudah HaLevi. Haunting and compelling harmonies are added to this mystical wall of sound by the poems composed in seventeenth-century Safed and, in Salonika, by the eighteenth-century Shabbatians of the Dönmeh sect.

That continuity, as we have seen, reaches beyond its own tradition. And nowhere is this reach more evident or exhilarating than in the strange echo established by the exceptional thirteenth-century figure of Avraham Abulafia—with his apocalyptic messianism and grand vision of the Divine Name inscribed in his heart, and with his psychomachia, or war for the soul, and allegory of blood and ink (imagination and intellect), all inextricably rooted in an immensely complex theory of language. Strange if wildly indirect parallels with Abulafia's vision and audition can be found in the poetry of William Blake, with his incorporation of the spirit of Milton and his mental fight for Jerusalem; and stranger still is the parallel with the Russian mystic-futurist Velimir Khlebnikov and his reality-transmuting "language of the stars" and war of letters. For the close reader of world literature and its mystical component, all this, and more, is almost magically summoned by the superbly rendered poems in this volume. As such, they confirm the essential and original understanding of the term *Kabbalah* as that which is received and passed on through the generations.

Notes

1. See William James, *The Varieties of Religious Experience: A Study in Human Nature* (New York, 1902), chaps. 4, 16, and 17.

2. This is Moshe Idel's thesis, as presented with regard to erotic mystical verse. See Idel, *Kabbalah and Eros* (New Haven, 2005), pp. 244–45.

3. See "From Whose Beauty the Depths Are Lit," in this volume.

4. See Peter Cole, *The Dream of the Poem: Hebrew Poetry from Muslim and Christian Spain, 950–1492* (Princeton, 2007), pp. 33–34.

5. See *Hymns from the Rigveda*, trans. A. A. Macdonell (London, n.d.), p. 49.

6. Dante, *Paradiso*, canto 33; trans. Henry Wadsworth Longfellow.

7. See *Selected Poems of Solomon Ibn Gabirol*, trans. Peter Cole (Princeton, 2001), pp. 147–48.

8. See, in this volume, Ibn Gabirol's *Kingdom's Crown*, canto 27; HaLevi's "Lord, [All My Desire]"; Abulafia's *Book of the Sign*; Azikri's "Soul's Beloved"; Luria's hymns; and Luzzatto's messianic sonnet.

9. See the poems of Yisrael Najara in this volume and the notes there.

10. *Mystical Poems of Rumi*, trans. A. J. Arberry (Chicago, 1968), poem 116.

11. Ibn Gabirol's taunting can be found, among other places, in "Before My Being" (Cole, *Dream of the Poem*, p. 90), and a similar sense of God's evasiveness is evident in Yehudah HaLevi's "Where Will I Find You," especially stanza 3, translated in this volume.

Poems in Hebrew and Other Languages

לִי נִדְמְתָה כְּאִלּוּ הִיא בַת-עַיִן פְּקוּחָה
שֶׁל שַׂר הַיַּעַר גְּדָל-הָאֲרָזִים
וְאֶרֶךְ הַשַּׂרְעַפּוֹת.

Page 249

הַכְנִיסִינִי תַּחַת כְּנָפֵךְ,
וַהֲיִי לִי אֵם וְאָחוֹת,
וִיהִי חֵיקֵךְ מִקְלַט רֹאשִׁי,
קַן-תְּפִלּוֹתַי הַנִּדָּחוֹת.

וּבְעֵת רַחֲמִים, בֵּין הַשְּׁמָשׁוֹת,
שְׁחִי וַאֲגַל לָךְ סוֹד יִסּוּרָי:
אוֹמְרִים, יֵשׁ בָּעוֹלָם נְעוּרִים —
הֵיכָן נְעוּרָי?

וְעוֹד רָז אֶחָד לָךְ אֶתְוַדֶּה:
נַפְשִׁי נִשְׂרְפָה בְלַהֲבָהּ;
אוֹמְרִים, אַהֲבָה יֵשׁ בָּעוֹלָם —
מַה-זֹּאת אַהֲבָה?

הַכּוֹכָבִים רִמּוּ אוֹתִי,
הָיָה חֲלוֹם — אַךְ גַּם הוּא עָבָר;
עַתָּה אֵין לִי כְלוּם בָּעוֹלָם —
אֵין לִי דָבָר.

הַכְנִיסִינִי תַּחַת כְּנָפֵךְ,
וַהֲיִי לִי אֵם וְאָחוֹת,
וִיהִי חֵיקֵךְ מִקְלַט רֹאשִׁי,
קַן תְּפִלּוֹתַי הַנִּדָּחוֹת.

אָז הוֹלֵךְ וּמִתְמַלֵּא דְּמִי תוֹחֶלֶת,
כְּאִלּוּ הוּא תוֹבֵעַ עוֹד וָעוֹד, וּמְצַפֶּה
לְגִלּוּי שְׁכִינָה קְרוֹבָה אוֹ לְגִלּוּי אֵלִיָּהוּ.
וּבְעוֹד קַשּׁוּבָה אָזְנִי וּמְיַחֶלֶת,
וּבְמַאֲוַיֵּי קָדְשׁוֹ לִבִּי יָחִיל, יִכְלֶה, יִגְוָע —
וּבַת-קוֹל אֵל מִסְתַּתֵּר
תִּתְפּוֹצֵץ פִּתְאֹם מִן הַדְּמָמָה:
"אַיֶּכָּה ?!"
וּמָלְאוּ נְאוֹת הַיַּעַר תְּמִיהָהּ גְּדוֹלָה,
וּבְרֹאשֵׁי אֵל, אֶזְרָחִים רַעֲנַנִּים,
יִסְתַּכְּלוּ בִּי בְּגַדְלוּת הוֹד, מִשְׁתָּאִים דּוּמָם,
כְּאוֹמְרִים: "מַה-לָּזֶה בֵּינֵינוּ ?"

שְׂפַת אֵלִים חֲרִישִׁית יֵשׁ, לְשׁוֹן חֲשָׁאִים,
לֹא קוֹל וְלֹא הֲבָרָה לָהּ, אַךְ גַּוְנֵי גְוָנִים ;
וּקְסָמִים לָהּ וּתְמוּנוֹת הוֹד וְצָבָא חֶזְיוֹנוֹת,
בְּלָשׁוֹן זוֹ יִתְוַדַּע אֵל לִבְחִירֵי רוּחוֹ,
וּבָהּ יְהַרְהֵר שַׂר הָעוֹלָם אֶת הִרְהוּרָיו,
וְיוֹצֵר אָמָּן יִגְלָם בָּהּ הֲגִיג לְבָבוֹ
וּמָצָא פִתְרוֹן בָּהּ לַחֲלוֹם לֹא חָגּוּי,
הֲלֹא הִיא לְשׁוֹן הַמַּרְאוֹת, שֶׁמִּתְגַּלָּה
בְּפַס רְקִיעַ תְּכֵלֶת וּבְמֶרְחָבָיו,
בְּזַךְ עֲבִיבֵי כֶסֶף וּבִשְׁחוֹר גַּלְמֵיהֶם,
בְּרֶטֶט קָמַת פָּז וּבְגַאֲוַת אֶרֶז אַדִּיר,
בְּרִפְרוּף כְּנַף צְחוֹרָה שֶׁל הַיּוֹנָה
וּבְמוּטוֹת כַּנְפֵי נָשֶׁר,
בִּיפִי גֵו אִישׁ וּבְזֹהַר מַבַּט עַיִן,
בְּזַעַף יָם, בִּמְשׁוּבַת גַּלָּיו וּבִשְׂחוֹקָם,
בְּשִׁפְעַת לֵיל, בִּדְמִי כּוֹכָבִים נוֹפְלִים
וּבְרַעַשׁ אוּרִים, נַהֲמַת יָם שַׁלְהָבוֹת
שֶׁל זְרִיחוֹת שֶׁמֶשׁ וּשְׁקִיעוֹתָיו —
בְּלָשׁוֹן זוֹ, לְשׁוֹן הַלְּשׁוֹנוֹת, גַּם הַבְּרֵכָה
לִי חָדָה אֶת חִידָתָהּ הָעוֹלָמִית.
וַחֲבוּיָה שָׁם בְּצֵל, בְּהִירָה, שְׁלֵוָה, מַחֲשָׁה,
בַּכֹּל צוֹפִיָּה וְהַכֹּל צָפוּי בָּהּ, וְעִם הַכֹּל מִשְׁתַּנָּה,

וּלְבָבִי יָדַע עוֹד עָרֹג וּכְלוֹת וּתְמֹהַּ דּוּמָם
וּלְבַקֵּשׁ מַחֲבֵא לִתְפִלָּתוֹ,
הָיִיתִי מַפְלִיג לִי כְּחֹם יוֹם קַיִץ
אֶל מַמְלְכוּת הַשַּׁלְוָה הַנֶּאְדָּרָה —
לַעֲבִי הַיַּעַר.
וְשָׁם, בֵּין עֲצֵי אֵל לֹא שָׁמְעוּ בַּת-קוֹל קַרְדֹּם,
בִּשְׁבִיל יָדְעוּ רַק הַזְּאֵב וְגִבּוֹר צַיִד,
הָיִיתִי תוֹעֶה לִי לְבַדִּי שָׁעוֹת שְׁלֵמוֹת,
מִתְיַחֵד עִם לְבָבִי וֵאלֹהַי עַד בֹּאִי,
פָּסוֹחַ וְעָבוֹר בֵּין מוֹקְשֵׁי זָהָב,
אֶל קֹדֶשׁ הַקֳּדָשִׁים שֶׁבַּיַּעַר — אֶל בַּת עֵינוֹ:

מִבַּיִת לַפָּרֹכֶת שֶׁל הֶעָלִים,
שָׁם יֵשׁ אִי קָטֹן יָרֹק, רָפוּד דֶּשֶׁא,
אִי בּוֹדֵד לוֹ, כְּעֵין עוֹלָם קָטֹן בִּפְנֵי עַצְמוֹ,
דְּבִיר קֹדֶשׁ שַׁאֲנָן, מִצְנָע בֵּין צֶאֱלִים
שֶׁל זִקְנֵי יַעַר רַחֲבֵי נוֹף וּמְסֻרְבְּלֵי צֶמֶר:
תִּקְרָתוֹ — כִּפַּת תְּכֵלֶת קְטַנָּה,
הַכְּפוּיָה וּמֻנַּחַת עַל הָעֵצִים מַמָּשׁ,
רִצְפָּתוֹ — זְכוּכִית: בְּרֵכַת מַיִם זַכִּים,
רְאִי כֶסֶף בְּתוֹךְ מִסְגֶּרֶת דֶּשֶׁא רָטֹב,
וּבוֹ עוֹד עוֹלָם קָטֹן, עוֹלָם שֵׁנִי,
וּבְאֶמְצַע כִּפָּה זוֹ וּבְאֶמְצַע אוֹתָהּ בְּרֵכָה,
זוֹ נֶגֶד זוֹ, שְׁתֵּי אַבְנֵי כַדְכֹּד קְבוּעוֹת,
כַּדְכֻּדִּים גְּדוֹלִים וּמַבְהִיקִים —
שְׁנֵי שְׁמָשׁוֹת.

וּבְשִׁבְתִּי שָׁם עַל שְׂפַת הַבְּרֵכָה, צוֹפֶה
בְּחִידַת שְׁנֵי עוֹלָמוֹת, עוֹלָם תְּאוֹמִים,
מִבְּלִי לָדַעַת מִי מִשְּׁנֵיהֶם קוֹדֵם,
וּמַטֶּה רֹאשִׁי תַּחַת בִּרְכַּת שְׁבֵי חֹרֶשׁ
מַרְעִיפֵי צֵל וָאוֹר וְשִׁיר וּשְׂרָף כְּאֶחָד —
הָיִיתִי מַרְגִּישׁ בַּעֲלִיל בְּנֹבַע חֶרֶשׁ
כְּעֵין שֶׁפַע רַעֲנָן חָדָשׁ אֶל נִשְׁמָתִי,
וּלְבָבִי, צְמֵא תַעֲלוּמָה רַבָּה, קְדוֹשָׁה,

אַיֵּה אֶמְצָאֵךְ וְאַיֵּה לֹא אֶמְצָאֵךְ.
ווּ קאָן איך דיך יאָ געפֿינען,
און ווּאָ קאָן איך דיך נישט געפֿינען.

אַז — ווּאָ איך גיי — דו,
און ווּאָ איך שטיי — דו,
רק דו, נאָר דו, ווידער דו, אבער דו —
דו — דו — דו, דו — דו.

מִזְרָח — דו, מַעֲרָב — דו,
צָפוֹן — דו, דָרוֹם — דו
דו — דו — דו.

שָׁמַיִם דו, אֶרֶץ דו
מַעֲלָה דו, מַטָּה דו,
ווּאָ איך קער מיך ווּאָ איך ווענד מיך
רק דו, נאָר דו, ווידער דו, אבער דו —
דו, דו, דו.

Page 238
כֹּלָא קַמֵּיהּ כְּלָא מַמָּשׁ חָשִׁיב —
תִּתְלַהֵט וְתִתְלַהֵב הַנֶּפֶשׁ לִיקַר תִּפְאֶרֶת גְּדֻלָּתוֹ
וּלְאִסְתַּכָּלָא בִּיקָרָא דְמַלְכָּא
כְּרִשְׁפֵּי אֵשׁ שַׁלְהֶבֶת עַזָּה הָעוֹלָה לְמָעְלָה
וְלִפָּרֵד מֵהַפְּתִילָה וְהָעֵצִים שֶׁנֶּאֱחֶזֶת בָּהֶן:

Pages 246–248
הַבְּרָכָה

וַאֲנִי בִּימֵי נְעוּרַי, חֶמְדַּת יָמַי,
אַךְ רִפְרְפָה עָלַי רִאשׁוֹנָה כְּנַף הַשְּׁכִינָה,

צְבִי אֶרֶץ חֶמְדָּה / יְפֹאַר בִּזְבוּלָךְ
כְּמֵאָז בָּנָה לָךְ / שְׁלֹמֹה בִיהוּדָה.
וְתָשֵׁב הָעֲבוֹדָה / כְּבַשָּׁנִים הָהֵן
וְיוֹסֵף הַכֹּהֵן / לְעוֹרֵר הַחִבָּה.
לְעַמָּךְ מַן טוֹבָה / וְנָשִׁיב בִּמְשִׁיחָךְ
וְתָצִיץ הוֹד זַרְחָךְ, / בְּאוֹרָךְ נִרְאֶה אוֹר: הַכִּינוֹת מָאוֹר

Page 228

הַבֵּן פּוֹרָת יוֹסֵף / יַקִּיר אֶפְרָיִם
יֶלֶד שַׁעֲשׁוּעִים / מַטַּע תִּפְאָרֶת
תָּשִׂישׂ תִּשְׂמַח תָּגִיל / כִּי שִׁבְעָתָיִם
יוּקַם צַדִּיק / וְקָם עַל בֵּית עֲקֶרֶת:

עֵת בֹּא עַל רֹאשׁ צַדִּיק / לָשִׁית עֲטֶרֶת
בִּרְכוֹת הָרִים הוֹרִים / בִּרְכוֹת שָׁדָיִם
בִּרְכוֹת גִּבְעוֹת עוֹלָם / הֲדָרַת כֹּתֶרֶת
כָּל מֶגֶד לָךְ צָפוּן / בִּרְכוֹת שָׁמָיִם:

יָרוּם הֲדַר שׁוֹרוֹ / עִם לָבִיא יָחַד
יָבוּז הֲמוֹן זָרִים / יִשְׁקֹט יָנוּחַ
יִשְׁפֹּט נָחָשׁ לִסְפוֹת / יִשְׂחַק לַפָּחַד:

תָּפִיץ חֵיל עָרִיצִים / תִּשָּׂאֵם רוּחַ
מִשְּׁמַן שַׁלְוֵי עוֹלָם / תִּמְסֹר לַכָּחַד
תֵּשֵׁב בִּנְוֵה שָׁלוֹם / לָעַד בָּטוּחַ:

Pages 236–237

רִבּוֹנוֹ שֶׁל עוֹלָם, רִבּוֹנוֹ שֶׁל עוֹלָם
רִבּוֹנוֹ שֶׁל עוֹלָם, כוועל דיר א דודעלע זינגען.

דו-דו-דו.

וְאִם הַזִּיו נְעִתָּם / בְּחַטַּאת יִשְׂרָאֵל,
מְאוֹר חַסְדָּךְ, הָאֵל, / תְּצַו תָּמִים אִתָּם,
וְאַף גַּם בִּהְיוֹתָם / בְּאֶרֶץ אוֹיְבֵיהֶם
שְׁכִינָה עִמָּהֶם / לְמִבְטָח, מִגְדַּל עֹז,
וְתוֹךְ מִקְדַּשׁ מָעוֹז / בְּאֵשׁ נֹגַהּ תּוֹפָע,
וְשֶׁפַע טוֹב יַשְׁפַּע / בְּדֶרֶךְ יִשְׁכָּן-אוֹר.   הכינות מאור

כְּמוֹ כֵן, צוּר עוֹלָם, / הֲטִיבוֹתָ בָזֶה
לְקָהָל הַלָּזֶה, / לְכוֹנֵן לָךְ אוּלָם,
שְׁנַת שָׁלֵ"ם נִשְׁלָם / לְחֹדֶשׁ זֶה יִנָעַם.
בְּהִתְאַסֵּף הָעָם / לְחָצֵר זֹאת יַחְדָּו,
רְצֵה פֹעַל יָדָיו / וּבָרֵךְ אֶת חֵילוֹ,
וְתַנְעִים גּוֹרָלוֹ / וְחַיֵּיתוֹ בָאוֹר.   הכינות מאור

וּמֵאָז חֹק נָתַן / לְקַדֵּם אַשְׁמוּרוֹת
וְהַצֵּב מִשְׁמָרוֹת / בְּחַדְרֵי הַבַּיִתָן,
וּמוֹשְׁבָן אֵיתָן / בְּלִמּוּד הֶחָצוֹת,
וּבִסְלִיחוֹת נִרְצוֹת, / בְּשִׁירוֹת וּזְמִירוֹת
וְהָיוּ לִמְאוֹרוֹת / לְעַם בָּךְ יִתְעַנַּג
בְּנֵרוֹת הַדּוֹנַג / וְשֶׁמֶן לַמָּאוֹר.   הכינות מאור

וְאוּלָם אַחַר כֵּן, / שְׁנַת כַּעַשׂ מָרָה
חֲרוֹן הַצּוּר חָרָה / בְּעַמּוֹ הַמִּסְכֵּן.
אֲבָל חַסְדוֹ תִקֵּן / מְהֵרָה אֶת פִּצְעוֹ
וְחִישׁ פִּדְיוֹן יִשְׁעוֹ / שְׁנַת הוֹשִׁיעַ בָּא,
וְשָׁב רֹב הַצָּבָא / כְּנֶסֶת וּגְדֵלָה
בְּהָצִיץ בַּאֲפֵלָה / אֱלֹהִים אֶת הָאוֹר !   הכינות מאור

אֱלֹהֵי אַבְרָהָם, / חֲמֹל עַל דַּךְ נִכְלָם,
בְּלֵב זַךְ וּמִשְׁלָם / לְעֶמָּתָךְ יִנְהָג.
בְּצָרוֹת הוּא נִדְהָם / וְשׁוֹמֵר דָּת מֹשֶׁה,
בְּרִיתָךְ לֹא יִנְשֶׁה / וְתָמִיד לָךְ יוֹחִיל.
וְאַף כִּי צַר יוֹחִיל / בְּחָזְקוֹ יִתְכּוֹנָן,
כְּזֵית רַעֲנָן / וְכָתִית לַמָּאוֹר.   הכינות מאור

מָגֵן דָּוִד הַקְשֵׁב שִׁיר רְנָנִי
לְמַעַן שִׁמְךָ, אֲדֹנָי:

וְזִיו שִׁפְעֲךָ לִשְׂרָפִים תָּבִיא
עַל חַיּוֹת וְאוֹפַנִּים בְּדִגְלְךָ תַצְבִּיא
שֹׂבַע שְׂמָחוֹת לְאֶרֶץ הַצְּבִי
יִהְיוּ לְרָצוֹן אִמְרֵי פִי וְהֶגְיוֹן לִבִּי:

Pages 221–227

הֲכִינוֹתָ מָאוֹר, / אֲדֹנָי, אֶל עַמְּךָ,
וּבִדְבִיר אוּלַמְּךָ / הֲכִינוֹתָ מָאוֹר.
הֲכִינוֹתָ מָאוֹר! / יְדִידֵנוּ אָתָּה,
וְהֵן לָנוּ עַתָּה / הֲכִינוֹתָ מָאוֹר.

מְכוֹן הָעוֹלָמִים, / מְשַׁכְלָל מֵעוֹלָם!
בְּסֵתֶר הַנֶּעְלָם / בְּרָזֵי צְמֻצוּמִים,
שְׁפוּנֵי רְשׁוּמִים / שְׁיָרֵי צִיּוּרִים,
מְאִירִים, מַזְהִירִים, / בְּעֹמֶק הַחֶבְיוֹן —
הֲלֹא אָז, אֵל עֶלְיוֹן, / הִגִּיגְךָ שָׁם הִזְהִיר
בְּשֶׁפֶר הַבָּהִיר: / יְהִי אוֹר! וַיְהִי אוֹר.   הכינות מאור

זְכוּת צִדְקַת עַמְּךָ / זְכוּרָה לִתְהִלָּה,
וְרַק הִיא הָעוֹלָה / בְּמַחְשַׁב תַּעְצוּמְךָ —
אֱמוּנָה שָׁם עִמְּךָ / תְּעוּדַת שַׁעֲשׁוּעִים,
לְעַמְּךָ הַנָּעִים / עֲתִידָה וּנְכוֹנָה,
וּבָהּ שֵׁם טוֹב קָנָה / וּמִכָּל עַם נַעֲלָה
בְּסֵדֶר הַבְדָּלָה / לְהַבְדִּיל בֵּין הָאוֹר.   הכינות מאור

לְבָדָד הִשְׁכַּנְתּוֹ / בְּאֶרֶץ הַחַיִּים
וְגֵרַשְׁתָּ גוֹיִים / וְכָל טוּב הִסְכַּנְתּוֹ.
וּמִקְדָּשׁ תִּכַּנְתּוֹ / לְמִשְׁכָּן לִיקָרֶךָ,
וְצִמְצַמְתָּ אוֹרְךָ / בְּבֵין בַּדֵּי אָרוֹן,
וְצִוָּה בֵית אַהֲרֹן / לְהַמְשִׁיךְ זִיו אוֹרוֹת
בְּהֵיטִיבוֹ נֵרוֹת / מְנוֹרַת הַמָּאוֹר.   הכינות מאור

הָאֵר נְתִיבוֹת חָכְמָה וְתוּשִׁיָּה
אַבָּא-בָם אוֹדֶה יָהּ:

הַצּוּר הַשּׁוֹלֵט עַל כָּל הַבְּרוּאִים
מֵבִין פְּתָאִים, מַשְׂכִּיל נְבִיאִים
פְּתַח שַׁעֲרֵי בִינָה הַנִּפְלָאִים
אָבוֹא בִּגְבוּרוֹת אֲדֹנָי אֱלֹהִים:

זְכֹר חַסְדְּךָ לְיִשְׂרָאֵל
לָתֵת גְּדֻלָּה לְדַל שׁוֹאֵל
מָגֵן אַבְרָהָם, שְׁלַח נָא גוֹאֵל
וְקָרָאתָ שְׁמוֹ עִמָּנוּ אֵל:

כַּבִּיר, חַזֵּק עֲדָתְךָ תָהִים
מֵעֹז גְּבוּרָתְךָ רַעְיוֹנֶיהָ רוֹהִים
פַּחַד יִצְחָק, הַצֵּל הַנּוֹהִים
יֻדַּע כִּי אַתָּה אֱלֹהִים:

וָתִיק, זְכֹר מַעֲמַד סִינַי
בְּהִגָּלוֹת תִּפְאַרְתְּךָ לְעַם אֱמוּנַי
אֲבִיר יַעֲקֹב, שְׁמַע קוֹל תַּחֲנוּנַי
וַאֲנִי תְפִלָּתִי לְךָ, אֲדֹנָי:

תָּמוֹךְ רַגְלֶיךָ עַל כֵּס הַפְּלָאוֹת
בְּנֶצַח הוֹדְךָ עֲנֵנִי נוֹרָאוֹת
כִּימֵי מֹשֶׁה וְאַהֲרֹן עֲשֵׂה לְטוֹבָה אוֹת
אַתָּה אֲדֹנָי אֱלֹהִים צְבָאוֹת:

יַקִּיר, אֱמֹר לְצָרוֹתַי דַּי
נוֹהֵג כַּצֹּאן יוֹסֵף, הוֹסֵף מַחֲמַדַּי
יַסֵּד בְּצִיּוֹן, אֵל חַי, יְקָרַת יְסוֹדַי
וְנַחֲלַת עָרִיצִים שַׁדַּי:

צֶמַח בְּמַלְכוּת יִרְאוּ עֵינַי
עַמּוֹ אֵלִיָּהוּ, קַנַּאי בֶּן קַנַּאי

הו״א הַמֵּכִין / הו״א שְׁבָחִין / הו״א גוֹזֵר כֵּן / לֹא אַחֵר
נו קאנסאראס / אי נו ייראס / איל דייו נו מאס /
אֶלָּא הו״א:

הו״א איס רְאשׁוֹן / הו״א איס אַחֲרוֹן / הו״א איס רִבּוֹן / עוֹלָמִים
אי מילדאראס / איסקריטוראס / ב׳יראס נו מאס /
אֶלָּא הו״א:

טוב״ה, מיל ב׳יזיס / פ׳אב׳לאראס / אי איל כְּלָל איס / איסטו:
אי אוטרו מאס / נו פ׳אייאראס / לָא אֱלָהָא אֶלָּא הו״א:

Pages 218–220

אוֹר הַגָּנוּז בְּלִבֵּן הַמַּחְשׁוֹף
אֲצִילֵי קַדְשׁוֹ לוֹ רוּחָם יִכְסֹף
אִישׁ עַל דִּגְלוֹ שִׁפְעוֹ יֶאֱסֹף
בְּתִקְוַת חוּט זֹהַר אֵין סוֹף:

נֶטַע שַׁעֲשׁוּעִים שָׁם אֶצְלוֹ אָמוֹן
שֶׁבַע צַחְצָחוֹת גִּנְזֵי הַמַּטְמוֹן
בּוֹ צָר עוֹלָמִים וְכָל הֶהָמוֹן
לְכָל שֵׂכֶל וּלְכָל אָדָם קַדְמוֹן:

יָצַק אֲדָנִים שָׁם בַּמְּרוֹמִים —
רָאשֵׁי עַמּוּדִים וְשִׁבְעָה קַיָּמִים
בָּם נָכוֹן כִּסֵּא מַלְכוּת עוֹלָמִים
אַוָּה לְמוֹשָׁב לוֹ עַתִּיק-יָמִים:

מֻכְתָּר בְּכֶתֶר לֹא נוֹדַע אַיֵּה
נוֹצֵר חֶסֶד, קוֹנֵה הַכֹּל וּמְחַיֶּה
אֶרֶךְ-אַפַּיִם, אֵל רַחוּם הֱיֵה !
כֹּה תֹאמַר אֶל בְּנֵי יִשְׂרָאֵל אֶהְיֶה:

שֵׂכֶל טוֹב חוֹנֵן לְנֶפֶשׁ חַיָּה
אַתָּה אָבִינוּ, רַב הָעֲלִילִיָּה

אדיינטרו די שו גולים

די שו אלמה בי`נדיג`ו: תם

ב`ינו גואיל שבת"י

אי ישמעאיל קי איס גאי

האפ`ירו תוראתיחה

עאד ליעאשות לאדוני: תם

Page 207

אור שאיין בו מאחאשאב`ה איל איס שיקריטו פ`ונרו

אי קון אילייה אפ`יגורו לוקי איי איניל מונדו

אי נו איי איניל מאחאשאב`ה שיינפרי אישטה שוב`יינדו

קי נו איי אאיל ניקאב`ו ני פרישיפייו דיל טורו:

ביקואח ב`יני אריזיר איל איס שַׁבְּתַי צְבִי

שי טיב`אח קי איס דירוקאר די איל יאחיני אואי

אי אבאשו דישו לוגאר אין קיליפָּה ריב`יעי

קי ריריקו אלוס מיזב`ור פארה אלשאר לה היי:

Page 208

אטורגאראס / אי קריאיראס / קי נו איי מאס / אֶלָא הוּ"א

סאב`יר סאב`ראס / אי סירב`יראס / נו פ`אייאראס /

אֶלָא הוּ"א:

הוּ"א וּשְמוֹ / קי איס אונו / אי אוטרו נו / קרייאדור

ב`ין אי ב`יראס / אינטינדיראס / אוטרו נו מאס /

אֶלָא הוּ"א:

קון הוּ"א כְּלָל / קריב`אנטה מאל / קי איס סַמָּאֵל / בְּלִיָּעַל

לו אינג`יראס / אי לו ב`יראס / דיראס נו מאס /

אֶלָא הוּ"א:

הוּ"א סיראדו / הוּ"א פ`אייאדו / נו קרייאדו / חָלִילָה

נו דימאנדאס / נו טי פריב`אס / נו פיינסאס מאס /

אֶלָא הוּ"א:

Pages 205–206

נא

קרייו איל דייו אה אדם
קי ביב׳ירה לי עולאם
אי קומייו עץ הדאעאת
לי דייו קואח אאיל סאם: תם

מור שיקריטו די אב׳רהם
טודוס ביהי ביראאם
סינוי מאקום סינוי שם
סינוי מאשי סוד נואם: תם

יצחק קי איס גיב׳ורה
שי אטו אטאדורה
שארה שוב׳ייו אין קיטיר
נו שאלייו אפ׳ואירה: תם

יעקב׳ קי איס ישראיל
אינו איי תאם קומואיל
דישקוב׳רייו לו בלאנקו
איליס מואישטרו גואיל: תם

אלמה די איל אמירה
אנטיס די טודו אירה
קואנדו שאלייו איל פ״ילו
קוניל איגואל אירה: תם

אֵי״ן סו״פ׳ אשו לוז טירו
קידו מונג׳ו טיהירו
די איל איזו ב׳ישטירו
דיינטרו די תיהום פורו: תם

קואנדו אֵי״ן סו״פ׳ אינקוז׳ו
באך ליטראס שי קואז׳ו

מואישטראס אלמאס שי קונפלייו
אין לוזיס אלטאס אינפ׳לויין
טוב״ה קומייו אי שירבייו: קון

Page 204
קלו

יה ראב׳ נאתאן אב׳יזה
שיקריטו די קאדישה
קומו אב׳יירטה רוזה: שיקריטו די קאדישה

איל שאלי אפ׳ואירה
קוזה ג׳יקה נו מירה
איש שוריץ די אמירה: שיקריטו

אינטרה אין טודו לוגאר
נו איי אה איליייה פ׳ולגאר
איזו אנוס אפלאזאר: שיקריטו

שו רומיז קי איס בינה
ביאד אור שי אאונה
איליייה מואישטרה אמונה: שיקריטו

דירוקו שלוס מיזוות
באלדו אלוס קיליפות
אדוב׳ו לאס עולאמות: שיקריטו

איס לוז קי נו אפ׳ירה
שיקריטו די אישטירה
טוב׳ה טו אוז׳ו ב׳ירה: שיקריטו

צְבִי גּוֹאֵיל אמירה
אדוב׳ו לה טחירה
איניל לוגאר קי מורה
איש ביסוד גאיי ישמאל

טית קאייו אונה שיב׳דאד
נו איי מוּאירטו ב׳ידראד
איניל פ׳אייה לה בונדאד
איש ביסוד גאיי ישמאל

לאש אב׳לאש מוי שיראדאש
ב׳יגאם מונג׳וש שייאדאש
פ׳איי איניל פ׳אייאדאש
איש ביסוד גאיי ישמאל:

Page 203
צה

יה אדוב׳ו אונה מיזה
אב׳יירטו קומו און רוזה
קומיד קון מונג׳ו לינפייזה:

קון אימונה שי אגוזה
בישירה דישפירטה ריזה:

שו פאן איס פאן דילוס שיילוס
קין קומי ביין קאדוס קאדוס
קון איליייה אאונה טודוס: קון

איליייה קומו ניפ׳קאד בארה
פ׳אס צ׳יראקה קאדה אורה
איזו היטיר ריי אמירה: קון

חיסיד יבינה
איס לה אמונ״ה
זיחרי אישטרינה
תם   :פ׳איי ב׳ינטורה

יה קומי פ׳רוטו
דישו גואירטו
מי אלמה פ׳ארטו
תם   :פ׳איי ב׳ינטורה

קונפלייו טובה
קוניל שים אהבה
זכ״רי אל[א]ב׳ה
תם   :פ׳איי ב׳ינטורה

Pages 201–202
רמא

בְּךָ יְבָרֵךְ יִשְׂרָאֵל
איש ביסוד גאיי ישמאל
קי אדוב׳ו איל גואיל
איש ביסוד גאיי ישמאל

דיש׳ו אוייו אדונאיי
אאיל מוסו ביואדאי
איל קי דיי[נ]טרו די איל איי
איש ביסוד גאיי ישמאל

ראשי טיב׳ות גואיל איש
קי איש יוב׳יל שו שוריז
לה טאמי איזו קודיש
איש ביסוד גאיי ישמאל

Page 198

בַּעֲלוֹתִי אֶל הָהָר
בְּרִדְתִּי לַנַּחַל
פָּגַשְׁתִּי אֶת מֵילִיזֶילְדָּה
בִּתּוֹ שֶׁל הַקֵּיסָר
אֲשֶׁר בָּאָה מִן מֶרְחָץ
מֵרְחִיצָתָהּ
פָּנֶיהָ מַבְהִיקוֹת כְּחֶרֶב
עַפְעַפֶּיהָ כְּקֶשֶׁת פְּלָדָה
שְׂפָתֶיהָ כְּאַלְמֻגִּים   בְּשָׂרָהּ – חָלָב

Pages 199–200

עא

בואין לה ה אורה
קי לה לוז מורה
אין און אישקורה
פ׳איי ב׳ינטורה: תם

אי איס און שיב׳דאד
טית קאייו ב׳ידראד
קון אקיל בונדאד
פ׳איי ב׳ינטורה: תם

ואדאי קון אמור
טומי קון טימור
קון דיג׳ו די מור
פ׳איי ב׳ינטורה: תם

רימיז אבאשטה
אלמה קי גושטה
קוניל אג׳ושטה
פ׳איי ב׳ינטורה: תם

בַּר-יוֹחַאי, בְּקֹדֶשׁ הַקֳּדָשִׁים,
קַו יָרֹק מְחַדֵּשׁ חֲדָשִׁים,
שֶׁבַע שַׁבָּתוֹת סוֹד חֲמִשִּׁים,
קָשַׁרְתָּ קִשְׁרֵי שִׁי״ן קְשָׁרֶיךָ:　　בר-יוחאי, נמשחת

בַּר-יוֹחַאי, יוֹ״ד חָכְמָה קְדוּמָה,
הִשְׁקַפְתָּ לִכְבוּדָּה פְּנִימָה,
לָ״ב נְתִיבוֹת רֵאשִׁית תְּרוּמָה,
אַתְּ כְּרוּב מִמְשַׁח זִיו אוֹרֶךָ:　　בר-יוחאי, נמשחת

בַּר-יוֹחַאי, אוֹר מֻפְלָא רוּם מַעְלָה,
יָרֵאתָ מִלְהַבִּיט כִּי רַב לָהּ,
תַּעֲלוּמָה וְאַיִן קוֹרָא לָהּ,
נַמְתָּ – עַיִן לֹא תְשׁוּרֶךָ:　　בר-יוחאי, נמשחת

בַּר-יוֹחַאי, אַשְׁרֵי יוֹלַדְתֶּךָ,
אַשְׁרֵי הָעָם הֵם לוֹמְדֶיךָ,
וְאַשְׁרֵי הָעוֹמְדִים עַל סוֹדֶךָ,
לְבוּשֵׁי חֹשֶׁן תֻּמֶּיךָ וְאוּרֶיךָ:　　בר-יוחאי, נמשחת

Pages 183–184

אֲזַמֵּר אֵל אֲהַלֵּל אֵל / שְׁמוֹ קָדוֹשׁ בִּמְעוֹנָה
בְּאוֹת יוֹד וְגַם קוֹץ יוֹד / בְּסוֹד הַיּוֹד הִיא צְפוּנָה
וְתוֹךְ יוֹד עִם סוֹף יוֹד / בְּחִבּוּרָם הֵם סוֹד בִּינָה
וְגַם סוֹד הֵא בְּתוֹךְ הֵהֵא / שָׁם גְּנוּזָה וְהִיא טְמוּנָה
וְרִאשׁוֹנָה וְתִיכוֹנָה / וְעֶלְיוֹנָה וְתַחְתּוֹנָה
וְגַם סוֹד וָאו וְקַצְוֵי וָאו / בְּמֶשֶׁךְ וָאו לָאַחֲרוֹנָה
וְסוֹד אַרְבַּע סָמוּךְ לְאַרְבַּע / בְּסוֹד אַרְבַּע הֵם שְׁמוֹנָה
בְּסוֹד עֶשֶׂר הַדְּבוּקִים / הָאֲדוּקִים בְּסוֹד שְׁכִינָה
הַנִּקְבָּע בְּשֵׁם נִקְבָּע / בִּנְפִילַת נוּן רִאשׁוֹנָה
בְּתֵת עַיִן מְקוֹם סוֹף עַיִן / וְגַם תּוֹךְ עַיִן רִאשׁוֹנָה
זֶה הַדָּל לֹא יֶחְדַּל / מֵחֲזוֹת אוֹר הַשְּׁכִינָה
קוֹלוֹ יִקְרַב שִׂיחוֹ יֶעֱרַב / כְּמוֹ תוֹרִים וּבְנֵי יוֹנָה
הַסְּפוּרִים הַסְּדוּרִים / הַקְּבוּעִים בְּסוֹד מִשְׁנָה:

Pages 180–182

בַּר-יוֹחַאי, נִמְשַׁחְתָּ אַשְׁרֶיךָ,
שֶׁמֶן שָׂשׂוֹן מֵחֲבֵרֶיךָ:

בַּר-יוֹחַאי, שֶׁמֶן מִשְׁחַת קֹדֶשׁ,
נִמְשַׁחְתָּ מִמִּדַּת הַקֹּדֶשׁ,
נָשָׂאתָ צִיץ נֵזֶר הַקֹּדֶשׁ,
חָבוּשׁ עַל רֹאשְׁךָ פְּאֵרֶךָ:   בַּר-יוֹחַאי, נִמְשַׁח

בַּר-יוֹחַאי, מוֹשַׁב טוֹב יָשַׁבְתָּ,
יוֹם נַחְתָּ, יוֹם אֲשֶׁר בָּרַחְתָּ,
בִּמְעָרוֹת צוּרִים שֶׁעָמַדְתָּ,
שָׁם קָנִיתָ הוֹדְךָ וַהֲדָרֶךָ:   בַּר-יוֹחַאי, נִמְשַׁח

בַּר-יוֹחַאי, עֲצֵי שִׁטִּים עוֹמְדִים,
לִמּוּדֵי יְיָ הֵם לוֹמְדִים,
אוֹר מֻפְלָא אוֹר הַיְקוֹד הֵם יוֹקְדִים,
הֲלֹא הֵמָּה יוֹרוּךָ מוֹרֶיךָ:   בַּר-יוֹחַאי, נִמְשַׁח

בַּר-יוֹחַאי, וְלִשְׂדֵה תַפּוּחִים
עָלִיתָ לִלְקֹט בּוֹ מֶרְקָחִים,
סוֹד תּוֹרָה כְּצִיצִים וּפְרָחִים,
נַעֲשֶׂה אָדָם נֶאֱמַר בַּעֲבוּרֶךָ:   בַּר-יוֹחַאי, נִמְשַׁח

בַּר-יוֹחַאי, נֶאֱזַרְתָּ בִּגְבוּרָה,
וּבְמִלְחֶמֶת אֵשׁ-דָּת הַשַּׁעֲרָה,
וְחֶרֶב הוֹצֵאתָ מִתַּעְרָהּ,
שָׁלַפְתָּ נֶגֶד צוֹרְרֶיךָ:   בַּר-יוֹחַאי, נִמְשַׁח

בַּר-יוֹחַאי, לִמְקוֹם אַבְנֵי שַׁיִשׁ,
הִגַּעְתָּ לִפְנֵי אַרְיֵה לַיִשׁ,
גַּם גֻּלַּת כּוֹתֶרֶת עַל עַיִשׁ,
תָּשׁוּרִי וּמִי יְשׁוּרֶךָ:   בַּר-יוֹחַאי, נִמְשַׁח

Page 176

מִי נִשְׁקַנִי מִנְּשִׁיקוֹת אַהֲבָה / בִּגְוֵה חֲדַר מֶלֶךְ גְּבוּלִי נָסְבָה
שַׁחַר וְהִנֵּה בָא יְדִיד נַפְשִׁי בְחֵן / וַתֶּהֱמֶה נַפְשִׁי לְמוּלוֹ קָרְבָה
לוּלֵי הֱעִירַנִי בְחֶמְלָה לַעֲמֹד / נִתְפָּרְדָה מֶנִּי וְגוּפִי עָזְבָה
מַה-זֶּה, יְחִידָתִי, מְזַגֵּי תִּרְכְּסִי / וַאֲנִי גְוִיָּתִי בְּחַסְדֵּךְ נִצְּבָה
בִּינוּ שְׂרִידֵי הַזְּמַן הִתְחַבְּרוּת / הַגּוּף וְהַנֶּפֶשׁ בְּיוֹם שֶׁשָּׂגְבָה
נַחַת בְּסוֹד תּוֹרָה וּמִצְווֹת, קָנְתָה / שַׁלְמוּת וְגַם שֵׁם טוֹב, לְשִׂכְלִי הִרְחַבָה
יוֹם תִּכְסָפָה לַחֲזֹר תְּסוֹבֵב גַּלְגָּלִי /בֵּין מַלְאֲכֵי רֶגֶל, מְטַטְרוֹן שַׂר צָבָא
וִדּוּי דְּבָרִים קַבְּלָה, יָהּ, יוֹצְרִי / עַבְדְּךָ בְּעֵת רָצוֹן לְחַיִּים תִּכְתְּבָה
סְפֵק לְגוֹזָלִי תִּזְמַן לִי בָטוֹב / גַּם תֶּאֱפֵן, יָהּ, בִּי וְשַׁוְעִי תַקְשְׁבָה
פּוֹדֶה וּמַצִּיל לַעֲנִיִּים כּוֹאֲבִים / חוּן עַל יְלוּד מַשְׁתָּא בְּפִתְחָךְ יִסְבְּבָה:

אנא ה׳ הושיעה-נא

Pages 177–179

רֵיחַ הַדַּס עָלָה / וְנַפְשִׁי נִבְהָלָה / קַמְתִּי חֲצוֹת לַיְלָה / וְדוֹד יַנְחֵנִי
שַׁבְתִּי נְאוֹת מִדְבָּר / וְהֵיךְ דּוֹד יַעֲבָר- / אֵלַי, וְיִתְחַבָּר / וְיִכְלִימֵנִי
לוֹבֵשׁ כְּלֵי חֶמְדָּה / וְרַעְיָה נוֹדְדָה / וַאֲנִי בְשִׁיר תּוֹדָה / אֲהַלֵּל קוֹנִי
מִבֵּין עָפָאִים / מַלְאֲכֵי רוֹם צוֹבְאִים / נִרְאִים וְאֵין רוֹאִים / לְצוּר עוֹשֵׂנִי
בָּהֶם נְשָׁמָה / מִלְמַעְלָה נֶעְלָמָה / הַנִּקְרָאָה חָכְמָה / בְּסוֹד הֶגְיוֹנִי
נָחוֹת וְנִכְלָלוֹת / שְׁלֹשִׁים מַעֲלוֹת / הֹוֶה וּמוּצָלוֹת / בְּגוּף רַעְיוֹנִי
יוֹם יֶאֱתֶה / צַד הַשְּׂמֹאל אֵשׁ יַחְתֶּה / עָרוּךְ תְּמוֹל תָּפְתֶּה / לְהוֹרִידֵנִי
וְאֶבְחֲרָה יָמִין / אֲשֶׁר בּוֹ אַאֲמִין / נַפְשִׁי בְחֵן יַזְמִין / לְהוֹכִיחֵנִי
סוּרִי, יְחִידָתִי / שְׂמֹאל רַע הַצַּמְתִּי / אָז תַּעֲלִי אוֹתִי / לְרֹאשׁ אַרְמוֹנִי
פִּתְחֵי תְשׁוּבָה / בַּעֲבוֹתוֹת אַהֲבָה / רוּחִי אֲזַי תּוּבָא / וְתַשְׂכִּילֵנִי
שִׁפְעַת רְבִיבִים / מִנְּהָרִים סוֹבְבִים / וּמְטֹהָרִים, שָׁבִים / בְּבֵית חֶזְיוֹנִי
בִּינוּ, יְדִידַי, זֹאת / וְתִזְכּוּ לַחֲזוֹת / סֻכּוֹת מְפֹרָשְׁזוֹת / בְּאוֹר קַדְמוֹנִי
זָכְרָה בְזִכְרוֹן טוֹב, / יְדִידִי, וַחֲטֹב / רַעְיָה כְּגַן רָטֹב / שֶׁהִיא בַת עֵינִי
יַעֲלוּ גְדוּדִים / כָּל שְׁבָטִים נִפְרָדִים / וּבְשִׁיר שֶׁבַח מוֹדִים / לְהַזְכִּירֵנִי
שָׁלוֹם כְּנָהָר / יִסְבְּבָה בִקְעָה וָהָר / אֶרְחַץ וְאֶטְהָר / וְאֶשְׁקָה צֹאנִי:

אנא ה׳ הושיעה-נא

חוּסִי נוֹפְלִים בְּמִכְמֶרֶת / חִשְׁקֵךְ, לִבְלִי יֵרְדוּ שַׁחַת
בּוֹעֲרִים הֵם בְּאֵשׁ אַהֲבָה / כְּמוֹ גַחֶלֶת לוֹחֶשֶׁת: הֵילֵל

Pages 166–167

יִגְּלֶה כְּבוֹד מַלְכוּתָךְ / עַל עַם עָנִי וָהֵלֶךְ
וּמְלֹךְ לְעוֹלָם, צוּר, אֲשֶׁר מָלָךְ / לִפְנֵי מְלָךְ־מֶלֶךְ
מָלָךְ לִפְנֵי מְלָךְ־מֶלֶךְ:

שׁוּב קְנֵה עַם לָךְ כְּמֵהִים / צוּר שׁוֹכֵן בִּשְׁמֵי גְבוֹהִים
שָׂרִיתָ עַל כָּל אֱלֹהִים / מִי לֹא יִרָאֲךָ מֶלֶךְ
מִי לֹא יִרָאֲךָ מֶלֶךְ:

רָצוֹן תַּעְטְרֵנִי אֵל חָי / וְיִיטַב לְךָ שִׁיר שְׁבָחָי
לְעִירְךָ קַבֵּץ נִדָּחָי / כִּי בְרָב־עָם הַדְרַת מֶלֶךְ
כִּי בְרָב־עָם הַדְרַת מֶלֶךְ:

אוֹחִיל עֵת גְּאֻלָּתָךְ / אֲצַפֶּה לִישׁוּעָתָךְ
וְאִם יִתְמַהְמַהּ, בִּלְתְּךָ / לֹא אָשִׂימָה עָלַי מֶלֶךְ
לֹא אָשִׂימָה עָלַי מֶלֶךְ:

לוּלֵי הֶאֱמַנְתִּי לִרְאוֹת טוֹב / כִּמְעַט־קָט הָיִיתִי קָטֵב
נָא צִיץ יִשְׁעִי יְהִי רָטֹב / אֱלֹהִים חַיִּים וּמֶלֶךְ
אֱלֹהִים חַיִּים וּמֶלֶךְ:

חַזֵּק בְּרִיחֵי שְׁעָרָי / וְשַׂגֵּב יֶתֶר עֲדָרָי
לְצִיּוֹן כּוֹנֵן אֲשׁוּרָי / לְאוֹר בְּאוֹר פְּנֵי מֶלֶךְ
לְאוֹר בְּאוֹר פְּנֵי מֶלֶךְ:

שָׁמָּה מַדּוּחַי תְּשׁוֹבֵב / וּמִזְבַּחֲךָ אֲסוֹבֵב
בְּשִׁיר חָדָשׁ לְךָ אֲנוֹבֵב / אוֹדְךָ, אֱלֹהַי הַמֶּלֶךְ
אוֹדְךָ, אֱלֹהַי הַמֶּלֶךְ:

יָהּ, זְכוּת אָבוֹת יָגֵן עָלֵינוּ
נֶצַח יִשְׂרָאֵל מִצָּרוֹתֵינוּ גְאָלֵנוּ
וּמִבּוֹר גָּלוּת דְּלֵנוּ וְהַעֲלֵנוּ
לְנַצֵּחַ עַל מְלֶאכֶת בֵּית יְיָ:

מִיָּמִין וּמִשְּׂמֹאל יְנִיקַת הַנְּבִיאִים
נֵצַח וָהוֹד בָּהֶם נִמְצָאִים
יָכִין וּבֹעַז בְּשֵׁם נִקְרָאִים
וְכָל בָּנַיִךְ לִמּוּדֵי יְיָ:

וִיסוֹד צַדִּיק בְּשִׁבְעָה נֶעֱלָם
אוֹת בְּרִית הִיא לְעוֹלָם
מֵעְיַן הַבְּרָכוֹת צַדִּיק יְסוֹד עוֹלָם
צַדִּיק אַתָּה יְיָ:

נָא הָקֵם מַלְכוּת דָּוִד וּשְׁלֹמֹה
בַּעֲטָרָה שֶׁעִטְּרָה לוֹ אִמּוֹ
כְּנֶסֶת יִשְׂרָאֵל כַּלָּה קְרוּאָה בִנְעִימוֹ
עֲטֶרֶת תִּפְאֶרֶת בְּיַד יְיָ:

חָזָק מְיַחֵד כְּאֶחָד עֶשֶׂר סְפִירוֹת
מַפְרִיד אַלּוּף לֹא יִרְאֶה מְאוֹרוֹת
סַפִּיר גִּזְרָתָם יַחַד מְאִירוֹת
תִּקְרַב רִנָּתִי לְפָנֶיךָ יְיָ:

Page 165

יָפָתִי, לָמָּה עֵינַיִךְ / לְעֵין כֹּל דּוֹרְכִים קֶשֶׁת
יִתְגּוֹדְדוּ כָל רוֹאֵי בָם / יִהְיוּ כְדָגִים תּוֹךְ רֶשֶׁת
קָרְבָתֵךְ שׁוֹאֲפִים, אֲבָל / לְאוֹרֵךְ יִירְאוּ מִגֶּשֶׁת
הֵילֵל אֲשֶׁר כָּל מְאוֹרִים / לְנֶגְדֵּךְ יִלְבְּשׁוּ בֹשֶׁת: הילל

שָׁם לַחֲרָדָה נֶשֶׁף חוֹשְׁקִים / אוֹר לְחָיֵךְ אֲשֶׁר זוֹרַחַת
וְאוֹר עֵינַיִךְ אֲשֶׁר תּוֹךְ / סְגוֹר לִבָּם מִתְלַקַּחַת

צוּף דְּבַשׁ אִמְרֵי נֹעַם חִכֵּךְ לִי
הֵן בְּחַכָּה עַד דַּכָּא תִּמְשְׁכֵנִי :   מַה לָּךְ...

Pages 162–164
אֵל מִסְתַּתֵּר בְּשַׁפְרִיר חֶבְיוֹן
הַשֵּׂכֶל הַנֶּעְלָם מִכָּל רַעְיוֹן
עִלַּת הָעִלּוֹת מֻכְתָּר בְּכֶתֶר עֶלְיוֹן
כֶּתֶר יִתְּנוּ לְךָ יְיָ :

בְּרֵאשִׁית תּוֹרָתְךָ הַקְּדוּמָה
רְשׁוּמָה חָכְמָתְךָ הַסְּתוּמָה
מֵאַיִן תִּמָּצֵא וְהִיא נֶעְלָמָה
רֵאשִׁית חָכְמָה יִרְאַת יְיָ :

רְחוֹבוֹת הַנָּהָר נַחֲלֵי אֱמוּנָה
מַיִם עֲמֻקִּים יִדְלֵם אִישׁ תְּבוּנָה
תּוֹצְאוֹתֶיהָ חֲמִשִּׁים שַׁעֲרֵי בִינָה
אֱמוּנִים נוֹצֵר יְיָ :

הָאֵל הַגָּדוֹל עֵינֵי כֹל נֶגְדֶּךָ
רַב-חֶסֶד גָּדוֹל מֵעַל שָׁמַיִם חַסְדֶּךָ
אֱלֹהֵי אַבְרָהָם, זְכֹר דָּבָר לְעַבְדֶּךָ
חַסְדֵי יְיָ אַזְכִּיר תְּהִלּוֹת יְיָ :

מָרוֹם נֶאְדָּר בְּכֹחַ וּגְבוּרָה
מוֹצִיא אוֹרָה מֵאֵין תְּמוּרָה
פַּחַד יִצְחָק מִשְׁפָּטֵנוּ הָאִירָה
אַתָּה גִבּוֹר לְעוֹלָם יְיָ :

מִי אֵל כָּמוֹךָ עוֹשֶׂה גְדוֹלוֹת
אַבִּיר יַעֲקֹב נוֹרָא תְהִלּוֹת
תִּפְאֶרֶת יִשְׂרָאֵל שֹׁמֵעַ תְּפִלּוֹת
כִּי שֹׁמֵעַ אֶל אֶבְיוֹנִים יְיָ :

יְשַׁוֵּי לוֹן
בְּנִקְבֵּיהוֹן
וְיִטַמְרוּן
בְּגוֹ כֵּפִין:

אֲרֵי הָשְׁתָּא
בְּמִנְחָתָא
בְּחֶדְוָתָא
דִּזְעֵיר־אַנְפִּין:

אַשְׁלִימוּ סְעוּדָתָא דָא
דִּמְהֵימָנוּתָא שְׁלִימְתָא
דְּוַרְעָא קַדִּישָׁא דְיִשְׂרָאֵל:

Pages 160–161

מַה־לָּךְ יִצְרִי תָּמִיד תִּרְדְּפֵנִי
וּלְאוֹיֵב לָךְ כָּל יוֹם תְּשִׂימֵנִי: מה לך...

יוֹם לְיוֹם תִּטְמֹן חִנָּם פַּח יְקוּשִׁים
עַד אֲשֶׁר תּוֹךְ פַּח מוֹקְשָׁךְ תִּלְכְּדֵנִי: מה לך...

צַר וְאוֹיֵב לִי אַתָּה מִנְּעוּרַי
תַּחֲרֹק עָלַי שֵׁן וְתִשְׁטְמֵנִי: מה לך...

חָשְׁקָה נַפְשִׁי לִנְטוֹת אַחֲרֶיךָ
כִּי בְצֵל יָדְךָ מִצַּר תִּצְרֵנִי: מה לך...

קִדְּמוּ עֵינַי לִבְכּוֹת בְּאַשְׁמוּרוֹת
כִּי בְאַף סַכּוֹתָ וַתִּרְדְּפֵנִי: מה לך...

אִם אֲדַמֶּה כִּי תִהְיֶה לִי לְעֶזְרָה
כִּי בְיוֹם צָרָה אֶקְרָא וְתַעֲנֵנִי: מה לך...

יְהוֹן הָכָא
בְּהַאי תַּכָּא
דְּבֵהּ מַלְכָּא
בְּגִלּוּפִין:

צְבוּ לַחְדָּא
בְּהַאי וַעְדָּא
בְּגוֹ עִירִין
וְכָל גַּדְפִּין:

חֲדוּ הָשָׁתָּא
בְּהַאי שָׁעֲתָא
דְּבֵיהּ רַעֲוָא
וְלֵית זַעֲפִין:

קְרִיבוּ לִי
חֲזוּ חֵילִי
דְּלֵית דִּינִין
דְּתַקִּיפִין:

לְבַר נָטְלִין
וְלָא עָלִין
הֲנֵי כַּלְבִּין
דְּחַצִּיפִין:

וְהָא אַזְמִין
עַתִּיק יוֹמִין
לְמִצְחֲיהּ עַד
יְהוֹן חָלְפִין:

רְעוּ דִי-לֵהּ
דְּגַלֵּי לֵהּ
לְבַטָּלָה
לְכָל קְלִפִין:

רִבּוּ יַתִּיר יִסְגֵּי
לְעֵילָא מִן דַּרְגֵּיהּ
וְיִסַּב בַּת זוּגֵּיהּ
דַּהֲוַת פְּרִישָׁא:

יְדַי אַסְחֵי אֲנָא
לְגַבֵּי חַד מָנָא
לְסִטְרָא חוֹרָנָא
דְּלֵית בֵּיהּ מְשָׁשָׁא:

אֲזַמֵּן בִּתְלָתָא
בְּכָסָא דִבְרָכָתָא
לְעֵלַּת עֵלָתָא
עַתִּיקָא קַדִּישָׁא:

Pages 157–159

אַתְקִינוּ סְעוּדָתָא
דִּמְהֵימְנוּתָא שְׁלִימָתָא
חֶדְוְתָא דְּמַלְכָּא קַדִּישָׁא
אַתְקִינוּ סְעוּדָתָא דְּמַלְכָּא:

דָּא הִיא סְעוּדָתָא
דִּזְעֵיר-אַנְפִּין
וְעַתִּיקָא קַדִּישָׁא
וַחֲקַל תַּפּוּחִין קַדִּישִׁין
אַתְיָן לְסַעֲדָא בַהֲדַהּ:

*

בְּנֵי הֵיכְלָא
דְּכַסִּיפִין
לְמֶחֱזֵי זִיו
זְעֵיר-אַנְפִּין:

יְשַׁדַּר לַן שְׁפְרֵיהּ
וְנִחְזֵי בִּיקָרֵיהּ
וְיַחֲוֵי לַן סִתְרֵיהּ
דְּמִתְמַר בִּלְחִישָׁא:

יְגַלֵּי לַן טַעֲמֵי
דְּבִתְרֵיסַר נַהֲמֵי
דְּאָנּוּן אָת בִּשְׁמֵיהּ
כְּפִילָא וּקְלִישָׁא:

צְרוֹרָא דִלְעֵילָא
דְּבֵיהּ חַיֵּי כֹלָּא
וְיִתְרַבֵּי חֵילָא
וְתִסַּק עַד רֵישָׁא:

חֲדוּ חָצְדֵי חַקְלָא
בְּדִבּוּר וּבְקָלָא
וּמַלְּלוּ מִלָּה
מְתִיקָא כְּדֻבְשָׁא:

קֳדָם רִבּוֹן עָלְמִין
בְּמִלִּין סְתִימִין
תְּגַלּוֹן פִּתְגָמִין
וְתֵימְרוּן חִדּוּשָׁא:

לְעַטֵּר פָּתוֹרָא
בְּרָזָא יַקִּירָא
עֲמִיקָא וּטְמִירָא
וְלָאו מִלְּתָא אַוְשָׁא:

וְאִלֵּין מִלַּיָּא
יְהוֹן לִרְקִיעַיָּא
חֲדַתִּין וּשְׁמַיָּא
בְּכֵן הַהוּא שִׁמְשָׁא:

וְנִגְדִּין נַחֲלַיָּא
בְּגַוַּהּ בִּלְחִישִׁין:

הֲלָא נֵימָא רָזִין
וּמִלִּין דְּגָנִיזִין
דְּלֵיתְהוֹן מִתְחַזִין
טְמִירִין וּכְבִישִׁין:

לְאַעְטָרָא כַלָּה
בְּרָזִין דִּלְעֵילָא
בְּגוֹ הַאי הִלּוּלָא
דְּעִירִין קַדִּישִׁין:

Pages 154–156

אַתְקִינוּ סְעוּדָתָא
דִּמְהֵימְנוּתָא שְׁלִימָתָא
חֶדְוָתָא דְּמַלְכָּא קַדִּישָׁא
אַתְקִינוּ סְעוּדָתָא דְּמַלְכָּא:

דָּא הִיא סְעוּדָתָא
דְּעַתִּיקָא קַדִּישָׁא
וּזְעֵיר-אַנְפִּין דַּחֲקַל תַּפּוּחִין קַדִּישִׁין
אָתְיָן לְסַעֲדָא בַהֲדַהּ:

*

אֲסַדֵּר לִסְעוּדָתָא
בְּצַפְרָא דְּשַׁבְּתָא
וְאַזְמִין בַּהּ הָשְׁתָּא
עַתִּיקָא קַדִּישָׁא:

נְהוֹרֵיהּ יִשְׁרֵי בַהּ
בְּקִדּוּשָׁא רַבָּה
וּמַחַמְרָא טָבָא
דְּבֵהּ תֶּחֱדֵי נַפְשָׁא:

דְּיִתְעַנַּג לִשְׁמֵיהּ
בְּמִתְקִין וְדֻבְשִׁין:

אֲסַדֵּר לִדְרוֹמָא
מְנָרְתָּא דִסְתִימָא
וְשֻׁלְחָן עִם נַהֲמָא
בְּצִפּוּנָא אַדְשִׁין:

בְּחַמְרָא גוֹ כָסָא
וּמַדָּנֵי אָסָא
לְאָרוּס וַאֲרוּסָא
לְאַתְקָפָא חַלְשִׁין:

נְעַבֵּד לוֹן כִּתְרִין
בְּמִלִּין יַקִּירִין
בְּשִׁבְעִין עִטּוּרִין
דְּעַל גַּבֵּי חַמְשִׁין:

שְׁכִינְתָּא תִתְעַטַּר
בְּשִׁית נַהֲמֵי לִסְטַר
בְּוָוִין תִּתְקַטַּר
וְזֵינִין דִּכְנִישִׁין:

שְׁבִיתִין וּשְׁבִיקִין
מְסָאֲבִין דְּדָחֲקִין
חֲבִילִין דִּמְעִיקִין
וְכָל זֵינֵי חַרְשִׁין:

לְמִבְצַע עַל רִפְתָּא
כְּזֵיתָא וּכְבֵיעֲתָא
תְּרֵין יוֹדִין נָקֶטָא
סְתִימִין וּפְרִישִׁין:

מְשַׁח זֵיתָא דָכְיָא
דְּטַחֲנִין רֵיחַיָּא

דְּעָבֵד נְיָחָא לַהּ
יְהֵא כָתֵשׁ כְּתִישִׁין:

צְוָחִין אוּף עָקְתִין
בְּטִילִין וּשְׁבִיתִין
בְּרַם אַנְפִּין חַדְתִּין
וְרוּחִין עִם נַפְשִׁין:

חֲדוּ סַגִּי יֵיתֵי
וְעַל חֲדָה תַּרְתֵּי
נְהוֹרָא לַהּ יִמְטֵי
וּבִרְכָן דִּנְפִישִׁין:

קְרִיבוּ שֽׁוֹשְׁבִינִין
עֲבִידוּ תִקּוּנִין
לְאַפָּשָׁה זֵינִין
וְנוּנִין עִם רַחֲשִׁין:

לְמֶעְבַּד נִשְׁמָתִין
וְרוּחִין חַדְתִּין
בְּתַרְתֵּי וּתְלָתִין
וּבִתְלָתָא שְׁבְשִׁין:

וְעִטְרִין שַׁבְעִין לַהּ
וּמַלְכָּא דִּלְעֵילָא
דְּיִתְעַטַּר כֹּלָּא
בְּקַדִּישׁ קַדִּישִׁין:

רְשִׁימִין וּסְתִימִין
בְּגַוַּהּ כָּל עָלְמִין
בְּרַם עַתִּיק יוֹמִין
הֲלָא בָטֵשׁ בַּטְשִׁין:

יְהֵא רַעֲוָא קַמֵּיהּ
דְּתִשְׁרֵי עַל עַמֵּיהּ

הִגָּלֵה נָא וּפְרֹשׂ, חָבִיב, / עָלַי אֶת סֻכַּת שְׁלוֹמֶךְ
תָּאִיר אֶרֶץ מִכְּבוֹדָךְ / נָגִילָה וְנִשְׂמְחָה בָךְ
מַהֵר, אָהוּב, כִּי בָא מוֹעֵד / וְחָנֵּנִי כִּימֵי עוֹלָם:

Pages 149–153

אַתְקִינוּ סְעוּדָתָא
דִּמְהֵימְנוּתָא שְׁלֵימָתָא
חֶדְוָתָא דְמַלְכָּא קַדִּישָׁא
אַתְקִינוּ סְעוּדָתָא דְמַלְכָּא:

דָּא הִיא סְעוּדָתָא
דַּחֲקַל תַּפּוּחִין קַדִּישִׁין
וּזְעֵיר אַנְפִּין וְעַתִּיקָא קַדִּישָׁא
אָתְיָן לְסַעֲדָא בַהֲדַהּ:

*

אֲזַמֵּר בִּשְׁבָחִין
לְמֵעַל גּוֹ פִתְחִין
דְּבַחֲקַל תַּפּוּחִין
דְּאִנּוּן קַדִּישִׁין:

נְזַמֵּן לַהּ הַשְׁתָּא
בְּפָתוֹרָא חַדְתָּא
וּבִמְנַרְתָּא טָבְתָּא
דְּנָהֲרָא עַל רֵישִׁין:

יַמִּינָא וּשְׂמָאלָא
וּבֵינַיְהוּ כַלָּה
בְּקִשּׁוּטִין אָזְלָא
וּמָנִין וּלְבוּשִׁין:

יְחַבֵּק לַהּ בַּעֲלַהּ
וּבִיסוֹדָא דִּי לַהּ

עַל יַד אִישׁ בֶּן פַּרְצִי
וְנִשְׂמְחָה וְנָגִילָה: לכה דודי...

בּוֹאִי בְשָׁלוֹם עֲטֶרֶת בַּעְלָהּ
גַּם בְּשִׂמְחָה וּבְצָהֳלָה
תּוֹךְ אֱמוּנֵי עַם סְגֻלָּה
בּוֹאִי כַלָּה, בּוֹאִי כַלָּה: לכה דודי...

Page 136

שָׁלוֹם עֲלֵיכֶם / מַלְאֲכֵי הַשָּׁרֵת [הַשָּׁלוֹם] / מַלְאֲכֵי עֶלְיוֹן
מִמֶּלֶךְ מַלְכֵי הַמְּלָכִים הַקָּדוֹשׁ בָּרוּךְ הוּא.

בּוֹאֲכֶם לְשָׁלוֹם / מַלְאֲכֵי הַשָּׁרֵת [הַשָּׁלוֹם] / מַלְאֲכֵי עֶלְיוֹן
מִמֶּלֶךְ מַלְכֵי הַמְּלָכִים הַקָּדוֹשׁ בָּרוּךְ הוּא.

בָּרְכוּנִי לְשָׁלוֹם / מַלְאֲכֵי הַשָּׁרֵת [הַשָּׁלוֹם] / מַלְאֲכֵי עֶלְיוֹן
מִמֶּלֶךְ מַלְכֵי הַמְּלָכִים הַקָּדוֹשׁ בָּרוּךְ הוּא.

צֵאתְכֶם לְשָׁלוֹם / מַלְאֲכֵי הַשָּׁרֵת [הַשָּׁלוֹם] / מַלְאֲכֵי עֶלְיוֹן
מִמֶּלֶךְ מַלְכֵי הַמְּלָכִים הַקָּדוֹשׁ בָּרוּךְ הוּא:

Pages 137–138

יְדִיד נֶפֶשׁ, אָב הָרַחֲמָן / מְשֹׁךְ עַבְדְּךָ אֶל רְצוֹנֶךָ
יָרוּץ עַבְדְּךָ כְּמוֹ אַיָּל / יִשְׁתַּחֲוֶה מוּל הֲדָרָךְ
כִּי יֶעֱרַב לוֹ יְדִידוּתָךְ / מִנֹּפֶת צוּף וְכָל טָעַם:

הָדוּר, נָאֶה, זִיו הָעוֹלָם / נַפְשִׁי חוֹלַת אַהֲבָתָךְ
אָנָּא, אֵל נָא, רְפָא נָא לָהּ / בְּהַרְאוֹת לָהּ נֹעַם זִיוָךְ
אָז תִּתְחַזֵּק וְתִתְרַפֵּא / וְהָיְתָה לָךְ שִׁפְחַת עוֹלָם:

וָתִיק, יֶהֱמוּ רַחֲמֶיךָ / וְחוּס נָא עַל בֵּן אוֹהֲבָךְ
כִּי זֶה כַּמֶּה נִכְסֹף נִכְסַף / לִרְאוֹת בְּתִפְאֶרֶת עֻזָּךְ
אָנָּא אֵלִי, מַחְמַד לִבִּי / חוּשָׁה-נָּא, וְאַל תִּתְעַלָּם:

יְיָ אֶחָד וּשְׁמוֹ אֶחָד
לְשֵׁם וּלְתִפְאֶרֶת וְלִתְהִלָּה: לכה דודי...

לִקְרַאת שַׁבָּת לְכוּ וְנֵלְכָה
כִּי הִיא מְקוֹר הַבְּרָכָה
מֵרֹאשׁ מִקֶּדֶם נְסוּכָה
סוֹף מַעֲשֶׂה בְּמַחֲשָׁבָה תְּחִלָּה: לכה דודי...

מִקְדַּשׁ מֶלֶךְ עִיר מְלוּכָה
קוּמִי צְאִי מִתּוֹךְ הַהֲפֵכָה
רַב לָךְ שֶׁבֶת בְּעֵמֶק הַבָּכָא
וְהוּא יַחֲמֹל עָלַיִךְ חֶמְלָה: לכה דודי...

הִתְנַעֲרִי מֵעָפָר קוּמִי
לִבְשִׁי בִגְדֵי תִפְאַרְתֵּךְ עַמִּי
עַל יַד בֶּן יִשַׁי בֵּית הַלַּחְמִי
קָרְבָה אֶל נַפְשִׁי גְאָלָהּ:   לכה דודי...

הִתְעוֹרְרִי הִתְעוֹרְרִי
כִּי בָא אוֹרֵךְ קוּמִי אוֹרִי
עוּרִי עוּרִי שִׁיר דַּבֵּרִי
כְּבוֹד יְיָ עָלַיִךְ נִגְלָה: לכה דודי...

לֹא תֵבוֹשִׁי וְלֹא תִכָּלְמִי
מַה-תִּשְׁתּוֹחֲחִי וּמַה-תֶּהֱמִי
בָּךְ יֶחֱסוּ עֲנִיֵּי עַמִּי
וְנִבְנְתָה עִיר עַל תִּלָּהּ:   לכה דודי...

וְהָיוּ לִמְשִׁסָּה שֹׁאסָיִךְ
וְרָחֲקוּ כָּל מְבַלְּעָיִךְ
יָשִׂישׂ עָלַיִךְ אֱלֹהָיִךְ
כִּמְשׂוֹשׂ חָתָן עַל כַּלָּה: לכה דודי...

יָמִין וּשְׂמֹאל תִּפְרֹצִי
וְאֶת יְיָ תַּעֲרִיצִי

רַק פִּתְרוֹן הַנֶּעְלָם יְבִינֵהוּ הַמֵּבִין
מַדָּעְתוֹ: וְעַתָּה אַתָּה, בְּנִי רוֹאִיאֵל,
כֹּה אָמַר לְךָ יְהוָה אֱלֹהֵי יִשְׂרָאֵל:
"כְּתֹב אֶת אֲשֶׁר רָאִיתָ בַּסֵּפֶר,
וְקָרֵאתָ שְׁמוֹ סֵפֶר הָאוֹת: וְהָיָה
לְאוֹת לְכָל רוֹאֵהוּ לָדַעַת כִּי יְהוָה
דִּבֶּר טוֹב עַל עַמּוֹ יִשְׂרָאֵל, וּכְבָר
הוֹאִיל לְהוֹשִׁיעָם. וּשְׁלַח הַסֵּפֶר
לִסְפָרַד, וְאַל תִּירָא מֵאִישׁ וְאַל
תֵּבוֹשׁ מֵאָדָם, כִּי הִנֵּה יְהוָה אֱלֹהֶיךָ,
אֲשֶׁר בָּטַחְתָּ בּוֹ לְבַדּוֹ, מַחֲזִיק זְרוֹעֶךָ
לְמַעַן יְסַפֵּר שְׁמוֹ הַנּוֹרָא בְּאַפְסֵי
אָרֶץ": וָאַעַשׂ כְּכָל אֲשֶׁר צִוַּנִי
הַזָּקֵן עַל פִּי יְהוָה, וָאֶכְתְּבָה הַסֵּפֶר
הַזֶּה: וְהִנֵּה שְׁלַחְתִּיהוּ לָכֶם הַיּוֹם
[...] לְמוֹשִׁיעַ לֵאמֹר: יְהוָה עִמָּכֶם
בְּשׁוּבְכֶם אֵלָיו. בִּשְׁנַת
הַמַ"ח זֶה בְּלֵב שָׁלֵם.

Page 121

בְּגִנַּת הָאֱגוֹז מֶרְגָּשׁ וּמֻשְׂכָּל
וְסִינַי הוּא וְלַבַּת אֵשׁ סְבִיבָיו
וְהוּא מָקֵף לָאַרְבָּעָה רְבָעָיו
וְאָמְנָם כִּי לְצַד מִזְרָח פְּתָחָיו
וְיִשְׁלַח יָד וְיִקַּח מֵאֱגוֹזָיו

וְהַהֶרְגֵּשׁ לְמִשְׂכָּלוֹ כְּהֵיכָל
וְהוּא בּוֹעֵר וְלֹא בָאֵשׁ יֵאָכֵל
וְאֵין פֶּתַח לְכָל פֶּתִי וְסָכָל
לְאִישׁ נָבוֹן אֲשֶׁר יַעַשׂ וְיוּכָל
וְיִשְׁבֹּר קְלִפָּתוֹ וְיֹאכַל:

Pages 133–135

לְכָה דוֹדִי לִקְרַאת כַּלָּה
פְּנֵי שַׁבָּת נְקַבְּלָה:

שָׁמוֹר וְזָכוֹר בְּדִבּוּר אֶחָד
הִשְׁמִיעָנוּ אֵל הַמְיֻחָד

תְּכֵלֶת וְאַרְגָּמָן. וַיֹּאמֶר: "לֵךְ, שְׁאַל
הָאִישׁ הַהוּא, הַיּוֹשֵׁב בְּהַר הַדִּין,
וְהוּא יַגִּדְךָ וִיוֹדִיעֲךָ מָה הֵמָּה
הַמִּלְחָמוֹת הָאֵלֶּה וּמָה אַחֲרִיתָם
אֲשֶׁר הוּא מִבְּנֵי עַמֶּךָ: וָאַעַל אֶל
הַר הַמִּשְׁפָּט וָאֶקְרַב לִפְנֵי הַזָּקֵן
וָאֶכְרַע וָאֶשְׁתַּחֲוֶה וָאֶפֹּל עַל פְּנֵי
אַרְצָה לִפְנֵי רַגְלָיו. וַיִּסְמֹךְ שְׁתֵּי
יָדָיו עָלַי, וַיַּעֲמִידֵנִי עַל רַגְלַי לְפָנָיו,
וַיֹּאמֶר אֵלַי: "בְּנִי, שָׁלוֹם בֹּאֲךָ !
שָׁלוֹם שָׁלוֹם לְךָ וּלְכָל אֹהֲבֶיךָ ! כִּי [...]
מֵהַמִּלְחָמָה נִצַּלְתָּ, וְכָל מִלְחֲמוֹתַי
נִצַּחְתָּ: וְעַתָּה דַּע וְהָבֵן כִּי יָמִים
רַבִּים וְשָׁנִים קִוִּיתִיךָ פֹּה עַד בֹּאֲךָ,
וְעַתָּה הִנְנִי מַגִּידְךָ מַה-פִּתְרוֹן
הַמִּלְחָמוֹת אֲשֶׁר רָאִיתָ: שְׁלֹשֶׁת
הַגִּבּוֹרִים הָרֹדְפִים זֶה אֶת זֶה שְׁלֹשָׁה
מְלָכִים הֵמָּה אֲשֶׁר יָקוּמוּ [...]
[....] שֵׁם הָאֶחָד קַדְרִיאֵל,
וְשֵׁם הַשֵּׁנִי מַגְדִּיאֵל, וְשֵׁם הַשְּׁלִישִׁי
אַלְפִּיאֵל. וְשֵׁם הַגִּבּוֹר אֲשֶׁר חָזִיתָ
בַּמַּחֲזֶה בַּתְּחִלָּה הוּא תּוֹרִיאֵל,
וּשְׁמִי אֲנִי יְהוֹאֵל אֲשֶׁר הוֹאַלְתִּי
לְדַבֵּר אִתָּךְ זֶה כַּמֶּה שָׁנִים. עַל
כֵּן יִקָּרֵא שְׁמֵךְ אַתָּה בְיִשְׂרָאֵל
עוֹד רוֹאִיאֵל הַחוֹזֶה בֶּן מְקוֹרָאֵל
הַחַי ; כִּי מִמְּקוֹם הַחַיִּים נִגְזַרְתָּ,
וְהַחַיִּים בָּחַרְתָּ. וְעִם הַחַיִּים תִּחְיֶה
וְחַיִּים, הֵם בְּנֵי אַבְרָהָם וְיִצְחָק
וְיִשְׂרָאֵל אֲבֹתֵינוּ, וְכָל הַדְּבֵקִים בָּם
יִדְבְּקוּ בֵאלֹהֵי הָאֱמֶת וְיִחְיוּ עִמָּנוּ.
וְהִנֵּה גִבּוֹר חֲמִישִׁי הוּא מְשִׁיחִי
אֲשֶׁר יִמְלֹךְ אַחַר מְלֹאת יְמֵי אַרְבַּע
מַלְכֻיּוֹת. זֶה פִּתְרוֹן הַנִּגְלֶה לַכֹּל,

אֶל צַד, וַיִּגַּע בְּרַגְלוֹ וַיִּדְבַּק בָּהּ,
וַיָּחֶל הָאִישׁ וַיִּצְעַק צְעָקָה
גְדוֹלָה וּמָרָה עַד מְאֹד, וַיֹּאמֶר:
"אֲהָהּ, יְהוָה, אֱלֹהֵי אֲבוֹתַי, כִּי
יְמִיתֵנִי הַחֵץ, אֲשֶׁר הֻכֵּנִי בַסַּם
אֲשֶׁר בּוֹ". עוֹדֶנּוּ מְדַבֵּר וְרַגְלוֹ
נָפְ<חָ<ה כְנֹאד נָפוּחַ מָלֵא רוּחַ
וּכְרֶגַע גָּבַר הַכְּאֵב וְכָל גּוּפוֹ הִרְגִּישׁ,
עַד אֲשֶׁר נָפְחוּ אֵבָרָיו וּנְתָחָיו
כִּשְׁאוֹר. וּכְשָׁמְעִי קוֹל צַעֲקָתוֹ,
נִכְמְרוּ רַחֲמַי עָלָיו. אָרוּץ וָאֶקְרַב
אֵלָיו, וָאֶלְחַשׁ בְּאָזְנוֹ, וַיִּבְרַח כְּאֵבוֹ
מִכָּל גּוּפוֹ מִפְּנֵי לַחֲשִׁי. וַיְהִי כִרְאוֹת
הָאִישׁ הַגִּבּוֹר הָרִאשׁוֹן אֲשֶׁר הֻכָּהוּ
בְרַגְלוֹ בְחִצּוֹ, כִּי נִרְפָּא מַכְאוֹבוֹ
עַל יְדֵי לַחֲשִׁי; רָץ עָלָיו בַּחֲנִיתוֹ,
וַיַּכֵּהוּ עַל טַבּוּרוֹ, וַיִּתְקָעֶהָ בְּכֵרְסוֹ,
וַיַּפֵּל אֶת בְּנֵי מֵעָיו עַל הָאָרֶץ, וַיִּפֹּל ...
שָׁם וַיָּמָת....

*

וְכִרְאוֹת הַשְּׁלִישִׁי, אֲשֶׁר
הָרִאשׁוֹן הָרַג אֶת הַשֵּׁנִי, רָץ אַחַר
הָרִאשׁוֹן וְחַרְבּוֹ שְׁלוּפָה בְּיָדוֹ [...]
פַּעַם אַחַת וְשֵׁנִית וּשְׁלִישִׁית [...]
עֶשֶׂר מַכּוֹת וַיָּמָת
עֲשִׂירִית. וָאִגַּשׁ אֶל הַמְ[...]
וָאֶשְׁאָלֵהוּ לְשָׁלוֹם
וָאֹמַר לוֹ...: "אֲדוֹנִי, סַפְּרָה-נָּא
לִי פִּתְרוֹנוֹת הַמִּלְחָמָה הַזֹּאת,
אֲשֶׁר רָאִיתִי אֲנִי בַּ׳מַּ׳ר׳אֶ׳ה".
וַיַּרְאֵנִי אִישׁ זָקֵן בַּעַל שֵׂיבָה,
יוֹשֵׁב עַל כִּסֵּא מִשְׁפָּט, וּבְגָדָיו —

וּתְהִי זֹאת לְךָ לְאוֹת בְּיוֹם הַלָּחֲמִי
בְּיֹשְׁבֵי הָאָרֶץ, אֲשֶׁר אַגַּלֶּה לְאָזְנֶיךָ,
וְתֵרָאֶה בְעֵינֶיךָ, וְתָבִין בִּלְבָבְךָ, הָאוֹת
הַנֶּעְלָם הֶחָתוּם בְּמִצְחִי מְפֹרָשׁ;
זֹאת תּוֹרַת הָאוֹת וְחֻקּוֹתֶיהָ – מִקֵּץ
לִקְצִים מִתְחַלֶּפֶת, וּמִדּוֹר לְדוֹרִים
מִתְהַפֶּכֶת, וּמִלְחֶמֶת מַעַרְכוֹת
מְרוֹמִים לוֹחֶמֶת....
כֻּלָּם בִּדְבָרוֹ יוֹרוּ חִצֵּי תוֹרָה,
בְּקֶשֶׁת דַּעַת מוֹרָה בִינָה אֶל
מַטָּרַת חָכְמָה, כִּי כֹחַ דָּם בַּלֵּב
סָתוּם וְחָתוּם; לֵב כָּל חָכָם לֵב
שָׁלֵם הוּא, הַמֵּבִין אֲשֶׁר דָּמוֹ חַי
וְטִיטוֹ מֵת, וְעַל כֵּן חֲתוּמִים בְּלִבּוֹ
טִיט וָדָם; מַר מִמָּוֶת הוּא טִיטוֹ,
וּבוֹ נִטְבַּע כֹּחוֹ; וּמָתוֹק מִדְּבַשׁ
הוּא דָמוֹ, וּבוֹ שָׁכְנָה רוּחוֹ בְמִשְׁכַּן
הַלֵּבָב; נֶפֶשׁ כָּל חַי מַשְׂכִּיל נוֹסַעַת
מֵאֹהֶל הַטִּיט אֶל אֹהֶל הַדָּם
וּמִמִּשְׁכַּן הַדָּם נֹסַעַת אֶל מִשְׁכַּן
לֵב הַשָּׁמַיִם וְשָׁמָּה שָׁכְנַת כָּל
יְמֵי חַיֶּיהָ....

*

וָאֶשָּׂא עֵינַי וָאֵרֶא וְהִנֵּה
שְׁלֹשָׁה גִבּוֹרִים רֹדְפִים זֶה לָזֶה,
וְרָצִים זֶה אַחַר זֶה, רָחוֹק
כִּמְטַחֲוֵי קֶשֶׁת זֶה מִזֶּה, וְאוֹמֵר
אִישׁ אֶל רֵעֵהוּ: "רוּץ, הִלָּחֵם
כְּנֶגְדִּי!" – וָאֵרֶא וְהִנֵּה רָץ הָאֶחָד
הָרִאשׁוֹן לִקְרַאת הַשֵּׁנִי, וּבְנוּסוֹ
יָרָה אַחֲרָיו חֵץ שָׁנוּן,
וַיִּפֹּל הַחֵץ לִפְנֵי רַגְלוֹ,
וַיַּךְ כְּאֶבֶן זוֹחֶלֶת וַיַּעֲבִירֶנָּה מִצַּד

וָאֶפְקְחָה עֵינַי וָאַבִּיט וָאֵרֶא
וְהִנֵּה מַעְיָן עִי"ן לְשׁוֹנוֹת נוֹבֵעַ מִבֵּין
אוֹת מִצְחוֹ ; אוֹת מִצְחוֹ סַם
הַמָּוֶת קָרְאוּ הָאִישׁ וַאֲנִי קְרָאתִיו
סַם הַחַיִּים, כִּי הֲפַכְתִּיו מִמֵּת לְחָי ;

*

וַיִּירָא הָאִישׁ הַהֲפֵכָה, אֲשֶׁר הָפַכְתִּי
לִכְבוֹד אֱלֹהֵי יִשְׂרָאֵל, וַיִּשְׂמַח בִּי
מְאֹד וַיְבָרְכֵנִי בִּרְכַּת עוֹלָם, וַיִּפְתַּח
פִּיו עָלַי וַיֹּאמֶר קוֹל רָם :

"אַשְׁרֵי צֶמַח צַדִּיק, וְאַשְׁרֵי
הוֹרָיו וּמוֹרָיו, וְאַשְׁרֵי הָעָם הַבָּא
אִתּוֹ, וְאַשְׁרֵי הָאֲנָשִׁים הַסָּרִים אֶל
מִשְׁמַעְתּוֹ. וּבָרוּךְ יְדָוָד אֱלֹהִים,
אֱלֹהֵי יִשְׂרָאֵל, אֱלֹהָיו אֲשֶׁר בֵּרְכוֹ ;
בִּרְכַּת עוֹלָם בִּרְכָתוֹ, כִּי מִמֶּנָּה הַכֹּל
נִהְיָה ; וְחֵן וָחֶסֶד סְבִיבָהּ, וּצְדָקָה
וּמִשְׁפָּט תּוֹכָהּ, וְחִצֵּי רַחֲמִים קַשְׁתָּהּ
מוֹרָה, וְעַל דַּם הַלְּבָבוֹת חַרְבָּהּ מְנִיעָה ;
גִּבּוֹר, לִבְּךָ – פֶּרַח נָטוּעַ בְּעֵדֶן, צִיץ
צֶמַח מִמְּרוֹמֵי מָרוֹם, אֲשֶׁר מִלְחַמְתִּי
נִצַּחְתָּ, וּדְמֵי מִצְחִי וְטִבְעָם וְצִבְעָם
הָפַכְתָּ, וְעַל כָּל נְסִיּוֹנֵי מַחְשְׁבוֹתַי
עָמַדְתָּ ; דְּיוֹ גָדַלְתָּ וְעַל דְּיוֹ תִּתְגַּדַּל,
אוֹת קָדַשְׁתָּ וְעַל יַד אוֹת וּמוֹפֵת
תִּתְקַדַּשׁ, בְּשֵׁם גָּדוֹל וְקָדוֹשׁ זֶה, הַנִּקְרָא
יהו"א, ידו"ד, יאו"ה –
מְחַדֵּשׁ מְחֻדָּשׁ ; הַשֵּׁם הַנִּכְבָּד
וְהַנּוֹרָא הַזֶּה יִהְיֶה בְּעֶזְרֶךָ, וְאוֹת
הַמֵּצַח יוֹדִיעֶךָ, וּמִמְּקוֹר הַלֵּב יְכַלְכֵּל
רוּחֶךָ, וְיוֹשִׁיט לְךָ אֶת שַׁרְבִיט הַזָּהָב
אֲשֶׁר בְּיַד הַכָּבֵד לְהַחֲיוֹתְךָ חַיֵּי עוֹלָם ;

*

מַחֲזֵה חָדָשׁ הֶרְאַנִי אֱלֹהַי בְּשֵׁם
מְחַדֵּשׁ עַל רוּחַ מִתְחַדֵּשׁ, יוֹם
רְבִיעִי לַחֹדֶשׁ הַשְּׁבִיעִי, אֲשֶׁר הוּא
הַיָּרֵחַ הָרִאשׁוֹן לְרֵאשִׁית שְׁמֹנֶה-
עֶשְׂרֵה שָׁנָה לְמַרְאוֹתַי, חוֹזֶה
הָיִיתִי וְהִנֵּה אִישׁ בָּא מִן הַמַּעֲרָב
בְּחַיִל כָּבֵד מְאֹד, וּמִסְפַּר גִּבּוֹרֵי מַחֲנֵהוּ
– שְׁנַיִם וְעֶשְׂרִים אֶלֶף אִישׁ:

הוֹד הָאִישׁ הַהוּא וַהֲדָרוֹ וְכֹחַ
גְּבוּרַת לִבּוֹ מַרְעִישׁ כָּל הָאָרֶץ
וּמַגְעִישׁ לְבוֹת אַנְשֵׁי חַיִל, וְעִמּוֹ בַּעֲלֵי
זְרוֹעַ פָּרָשִׁים וְרַגְלִים אֵין קֵץ בִּלְתִּי
גִּבּוֹרָיו, וּבְמִצְחוֹ אֵת
חָתוּם בְּדָם וּבְדִיּוֹ לַפְּאוֹת הַשְּׁתַּיִם,
וּדְמוּת אוֹת כִּדְמוּת מַקֵּל מַכְרִיעַ
בִּנְתַיִם, וְהוּא אוֹת נֶעְלָם מְאֹד:
צֶבַע הַדָּם שָׁחוֹר הָיָה וְנֶהְפַּךְ לְאָדָם,
וְצֶבַע הַדְּיוֹ הָיָה אָדֹם וְהִנֵּה
הוּא שָׁחוֹר, וּמַרְאֵה הָאוֹת הַמַּכְרִיעַ
בֵּין שְׁתֵּי הַמַּרְאוֹת – לָבָן : פְּלָאוֹת
הוּא מְגַלֶּה הַחוֹתָם, הַמַּפְתֵּחַ תּוֹךְ
מֵצַח הַבָּא וְעַל פִּיהוּ מִתְגַּלְגֵּל
וְנֹסֵעַ כָּל צְבָא הֶחָיִל: וַאֲנִי בִּרְאוֹתִי
פָּנָיו בַּמַּרְאֶה – נִבְהַלְתִּי, וְנִרְתַּע לִבִּי
בְּקִרְבִּי וְנִתַּר מִמְּקוֹמוֹ, וָאֶחְפְּצָה
לְדַבֵּר לִקְרֹא בְשֵׁם אֱלֹהַי לְעָזְרֵנִי,
וַיָּנָס הַדָּבָר מֵרוּחִי:
וַיְהִי בְּעֵת רְאוֹת
הָאִישׁ עֹצֶם פַּחְדִּי וְחֹזֶק יִרְאָתִי,
פָּתַח פִּיו וַיְדַבֵּר, וַיִּפְתַּח אֶת פִּי
לְדַבֵּר, וָאַעַן לוֹ כִּדְבָרוֹ : וּבְדַבְּרִי
הִתְעַצַּמְתִּי וָאֶתְהַפְּכָה לְאִישׁ
אַחֵר...

Pages 113–120

הָאוֹת תַּאֲוָה הִיא
וְהַשַּׂחַק הוּא הַחוֹשֵׁק
לָדַעַת חֵפֶץ מְנִיעוֹ, הַנּוֹתֵן חַסְדּוֹ
לְרוּחוֹ וְרַחֲמָיו לְכֹחוֹ
לְמַעַן יִישַׁר פָּעֳלוֹ —
מַלְכוּת בְּרֹאשָׁהּ
וְתוֹרָה בִּזְנָבָהּ עֵת,
וְתוֹרָה בְּרֹאשָׁהּ
וּמַלְכוּת בִּזְנָבָהּ בְּעֵת,
וְהָאוֹת וְהַנִּקּוּד וְהַנִּגּוּן
מְגַלִּים סוֹד הַדָּם ...

*

וַיְדַבֵּר יְהֹוָה אֵלַי בְּעֵת רְאוֹתִי
שְׁמוֹ מְפֹרָשׁ וּמְיֻחָד בְּדָם
לִבִּי מַבְדִּיל בֵּין דָּם לְדִיּוֹ וּבֵין
דְּיוֹ לְדָם: וַיֹּאמֶר אֵלַי יְהֹוָה:
"הִנֵּה נַפְשְׁךָ — דָּם שְׁמָהּ, וּדְיוֹ —
שֵׁם רוּחֲךָ, וְהִנֵּה אָבִיךָ וְאִמְּךָ
כֵּלִים לִשְׁמִי זֶה וּלְזִכְרִי זֶה":
וָאֶשְׁמַע הַהֶבְדֵּל הַגָּדוֹל, אֲשֶׁר
בֵּין נַפְשִׁי וְרוּחִי, וָאֶשְׂמְחָה
בּוֹ שִׂמְחָה גְדוֹלָה מְאֹד, וָאֵדַע
כִּי נַפְשִׁי שֶׁכְנָה עַל צִבְעָהּ
בַּמַּרְאָה הָאֲדֻמָּה כַדָּם, וְרוּחִי
שֶׁכְנָה עַל צִבְעָהּ בַּמַּרְאָה
הַשְּׁחוֹרָה כַדְּיוֹ: וְהַמִּלְחָמָה
הָיְתָה חֲזָקָה מְאֹד בַּלֵּב בֵּין
הַדָּם וּבֵין הַדְּיוֹ, וְהַדָּם הָיָה מִן
הָרוּחַ וְהַדְּיוֹ מִן הֶעָפָר, וְנָצַח
הַדְּיוֹ לַדָּם, וְהַשַּׁבָּת גָּבְרָה עַל
כָּל יְמֵי הַחֹל: וַיָּנַח לִבִּי בְּקִרְבִּי
עַל זֶה, וָאֶתֵּן שֶׁבַח בְּפִי
לְשֵׁם יְהֹוָה, וְאֲהוֹדֶה בְּלִבִּי לַיהֹוָה לָעַד...

דְּחָמֵאן וְלָא חָמֵאן, אֲטִימִין אָדְנִין, סְתִימִין עַיְנִין. לָא חָמֵאן וְלָא
שָׁמְעִין, לָא יָדְעִין בְּסָכְלְתָנוּ חַד דְּכְלִילָא בְּתְרֵין בְּגַוַּיְהוּ, דְּחַיִּין לֵיהּ
לְבַר. אִנּוּן מִתְדַּבְּקִין בֵּין אִנּוּן תְּרֵי. חַד, אֲמֵנָא דְאֻמָּנָא לָא שַׁרְיָא
בְּגַוַּיְהוּ. לָא אִכְּתְבוּ בְּסִפְרֵי דַּכְרָנַיָּא. אִתְמְחוֹן מִסִּפְרָא דְּחַיַּיָּא.

זוהר 3

גּוּפָא דְּמַתְנִיתִין: אֲנַן קְרֵיבִין הֲוֵינָא. שְׁמַעֲנָא קָלָא מִתְהַפַּךְ מִלְּעֵילָא
לְתַתָּא. אִתְפַּשְּׁטַת בְּעָלְמָא קַל מְחַבַּר טוּרִין וּמְחַבַּר טִנָּרִין תַּקִּיפִין.
עֲלֵוֹלִין וְרַבְרְבִין סָלְקִין. אָדְנִינָא פְּתִיחָן. הֲוָה אָמַר בְּמַטְלָנוֹי: קוֹץ
קוֹצִיתָא דְּמִיכָן דְּמִיכִין שֵׁינָתָא בְּחוֹרֵיהוֹן, קַיְמִין בְּקִיּוּמֵיהוֹן... כֻּלְּהוּ לָא
מַרְגְּשִׁין וְלָא יָדְעֵי דְּסִפְרָא פְּתִיחַ וּבִשְׁמָא אִכְּתִב...

זוהר 4

קָלָא אַהֲדַר כְּמִלְּקַדְמִין וַאֲמַר: "עִלָּאִין, טְמִירִין סְתִימִין, פְּקִיחֵי עֵינָא,
אִנּוּן דִּמְשַׁטְּטִין בְּכָל עָלְמָא, אִסְתַּכַּלוּ וַחֲמוּ! תַּתָּאִין, דְּמִיכִין, סְתִימִין
בְּחוֹרֵיכוֹן, אִתְּעָרוּ! מַאן מִנְּכוֹן דִּי חֲשׁוֹכָא מְהַפְּכִין לִנְהוֹרָא, וְטַעֲמִין
מְרִירָא לְמִתְקָא עַד לָא יֵיתוּן הָכָא. מַאן מִנְּכוֹן דִּמְחַכָּאן בְּכָל יוֹמָא
לִנְהוֹרָא דְּנָהַר, בְּשַׁעֲתָא דְּמַלְכָּא פָּקֵד לְאַיַּלְתָּא, וְאִתְיַקַּר וְאִתְקְרֵי מַלְכָּא
מִכָּל מַלְכִין דְּעָלְמָא. מַאן דְּלָא מְצַפֵּא דָא בְּכָל יוֹמָא בְּהַהוּא עָלְמָא,
לֵית לֵיהּ חוּלָקָא הָכָא".

Page 107

עֲטִיפָא בְּקִטְפָא אִזְדַּמֵּנֶת,
שָׁרֵי שָׁרֵי
לָא תֵעַל
וְלָא תִנְפֹּק
לָא דִידָךְ וְלָא בְעַדְבָּךְ,

תּוּב תּוּב

יַמָּא אִתְרַגְגָשֶׁת
גַּלְגְּלוֹי לָךְ קָרַאן,
בְּחוּלָקָא קַדִּישָׁא אֲחִידְנָא
בְּקֻדְשָׁא דְּמַלְכָּא אִתְעַטְּפְנָא.

3

וְכֹחַ שִׁמְךָ הַנֶּעְלָם אֶהְיֶה
אֲשֶׁר הַיּוֹדֵעַ סוֹד – לְעוֹלָם יִחְיֶה:

וְהוּא הַמַּזִּיל שֶׁפַע וּבְרָכָה עַל הַכֹּל
וְכָל הָעוֹלָמוֹת תְּלוּיוֹת בּוֹ כְּאֶשְׁכֹּל:

וְתַזִּיל טַל יְשׁוּעָה, טַל חֶסֶד, טַל בְּרָכָה
לְחַדֵּשׁ מַזָּלִי לְטוֹבָה וּמַרְפֵּא וַאֲרוּכָה:

וְתָאִיר עֵינִי בְּתוֹרָתֶךָ
וְאַל נָא יְעַכְּבוּנִי הַקְּלִפּוֹת הַחִיצוֹנוֹת, הַסּוֹבְבוֹת סְבִיב מַחֲנוֹתֶיךָ:

וְתִתְּנֵנִי לְחֶסֶד וּלְרַחֲמִים בְּעֵינֵי אֱלֹהִים וְאָדָם
וְסַמְּכוּנִי בְכָל מְאֹדָם, מָמוֹנָם
וְאַל תַּצְרִיכֵנִי לִידֵי מַתְּנוֹת בָּשָׂר וָדָם:

Pages 105–106

זוהר 1

מַתְנִיתִין. רְעוּתָא דְעוּבָדָא, קִטְרֵי דִמְהֵימְנוּתָא, קָל קָלָא דְקַלְיָא אִתְּעַר
מֵעֵילָא לְתַתָּא. אַנַן פְּתִיחִין עַיְנִין הֲוֵינַן, גִּלְגּוֹלָא אַסְחַר מֵעֵילָא לְכַמָּה
סִטְרִין. קָל נְעִימוּתָא אִתְּעַר: "אִתְּעַרוּ נָיְמִין דְּמִיכִין דִּשְׁדִינָתָּא בְּחַרֵיהוֹן
וְלָא יָדְעֵי וְלָא מִסְתַּכְּלָן וְלָא חָמָאן, אֲטִימִין אָדְנִין, כְּבֵדִין דְּלִבָּא, נָיְמִין
וְלָא יָדְעִין; אוֹרַיְתָא קַיְמָא קַמַּיְהוּ וְלָא מַשְׁגִּיחִין, וְלָא יָדְעֵי בְּמָה
מִסְתַּכְּלִין, חָמָאן וְלָא חָמָאן, אוֹרַיְתָא רְמָאת קָלִין: אִסְתַּכַּלּוּ, טִפְּשִׁין!
פְּתַחוּ עַיְנִין וְתִנְדְּעוּן! לֵית מַאן דְּיַשְׁגַּח וְלֵית מַאן דְּיַרְכֵּן אָדְנֵיהּ. עַד
מָה תֶּהֱווֹן בְּגוֹ חֲשׁוֹכָא דִרְעוּתַיְיכוּ. אִסְתַּכַּלּוּ לְמִנְדַּע וְאִתְגְּלֵי לְכוֹן
נְהוֹרָא דְנָהַר".

זוהר 2

תּוֹסְפָתָּא. קְטוּרֵי רָמָאי דְּקַסְטְרֵי דְּקַסְטְרָא. אִנּוּן פְּתִיחָן עַיְנִין, פְּתִיחָן
אָדְנִין. קָל מִן קָלַיָּא נָחַת מֵעֵילָא לְתַתָּא, מִתְחַבַּר טוּרִין וְטִנָּרִין. מַאן אִנּוּן

בְּטֶרֶם אֶקְרָא הֲלֹא תַעֲנֶה
כִּי בֹשְׁתִּי לִשְׁאֹל מִן הַמֶּלֶךְ.

דְּרָכֶיךָ יְנַחֲמוּנִי, כִּי שָׁמַעְתִּי עֲוֹנוֹת תִּכְבֹּשׁ
וּבְךָ חָסָיָה נַפְשִׁי וְלֹא חֲבוֹשׁ:
כִּי הַגּוּף בַּמַּסְגֵּר תִּכְבֹּשׁ,
וְהִיא – בְּהֵיכְלֵי מֶלֶךְ !

יוֹדַעַת אָז בַּשַּׁחַת אוֹתִי תִטְבֹּל
הֲלֹא אִם שַׂלְמָתָה חָבוֹל תַּחְבֹּל –
תְּשִׁיבֶנּוּ לָהּ, אַחֲרֵי תִסְבֹּל
הַמִּשְׁפָּט אֲשֶׁר שָׁפַט הַמֶּלֶךְ.

חַזֵּק יַד חֲלוּשָׁה וְתֵשֵׁב לָהּ בְּאֵיתָן
וּבְעֵת יָשׁוּבוּ הַדְּבָרִים לַהֲוָיָתָן
תְּשַׁנֶּה לְטוֹב מִגְּנַת הַבַּיִתָן
הַפַּרְדֵּס אֲשֶׁר לַמֶּלֶךְ.

Pages 97–98

1

יִשְׁלַח הַשֵּׁם אוֹרוֹ הַנֶּעְלָם
לִפְתֹּחַ שַׁעֲרֵי עֶזְרָה לַעֲבָדָיו
וּלְהָאִיר לְבָן נָתוּן בָּאֹפֶל וְנֶאְלָם:

יִתְעַשֵּׁת הַמֶּלֶךְ הַגָּדוֹל יִצְדַּק וְיִשְׁלַם
וְיִפְתַּח לָנוּ שַׁעֲרֵי חָכְמָה
וִיעוֹרֵר אַהֲבַת קֶדֶם וִימוֹת עוֹלָם:

2

בְּשֵׁם הַנֶּעְלָם אֶהְיֶה אֲשֶׁר אֶהְיֶה
אֲשֶׁר בְּטַלְלֵי רָצוֹן וּבְרָכָה מֵתִים יְחַיֶּה
וְכֹחַ בָּנֶיךָ – הַקּוֹרְאִים בִּשְׁמֶךָ – תַּגְבִּיר כְּאַרְיֵה
וְתִשְׁלַח לָנוּ אֵלִיָּהוּ וּמָשִׁיחַ צִדְקֵנוּ, אֲשֶׁר בְּצִלּוֹ נִחְיֶה:

וְאִם לְרָעָה – יִהְיֶה לַעַג וָקֶלֶס,
כִּי לֹא הָיְתָה מֵהַמֶּלֶךְ.

חָגוּר חֲרָדוֹת לְהוֹדוֹת פְּשָׁעַי אָחִישׁ
בְּטֶרֶם לְבֵית-מוֹעֵד כְּבוֹדִי גַז חִישׁ.
שָׁם תָּוַי בְּפָנַי יַעֲנֶה – וּמִי יַכְחִישׁ
אֶת אִגְּרוֹת הַמֶּלֶךְ ?

מֵעֻצַּת נֶפֶשׁ אֶל אֶרֶץ תַּלְאוּבוֹת סָחַרְתִּי
וְכִמְעַט בְּקִבְרוֹת הַתַּאֲוָה נִקְבַּרְתִּי,
וְאַחֲרֵי שׁוּבִי נִחַמְתִּי, כִּי לֹא שָׁמַרְתִּי
אֲנִי פִּי מֶלֶךְ.

נָתַן בְּלִבִּי חֵשֶׁק הָעוֹלָם
לִרְדֹּף אַחֲרֵי יָמִים וְהֶבְלָם.
אָכֵן, בְּהִשָּׁפְטִי עַל כָּל נֶעְלָם
יָרֵא אֲנִי אֶת אֲדוֹנִי הַמֶּלֶךְ.

יוֹדֵעַ עֲוֹנוֹ וְחָרֵד לַחוֹבוֹ
יְצַפֶּה חַסְדְּךָ וְלֹא יָחִיל טוּבוֹ,
נִבְעַת מִלְּפָנֶיךָ, כִּי אֵיךְ יָבוֹא
רָשָׁע לִפְנֵי מֶלֶךְ ?

רַחֲמֶיךָ לְכַף זְכוּת שִׂימָה קַלְבּוֹן
בְּהִשָּׁקֵל עֲוֹן עֶבֶד מוֹדֶה לְרִבּוֹן –
וְעַל-כָּרְחוֹ יִתֵּן אֶת הַחֶשְׁבּוֹן
לִפְנֵי הַמֶּלֶךְ.

וּלְךָ, יְיָ, הַחֶסֶד – וּבוֹ מַחְסֵהוּ
וּלְךָ, יְיָ, הַצְּדָקָה – וְהִיא מִכְסֵהוּ
וּלְךָ, יְיָ, הַסְּלִיחָה – כִּי תַשְׁלִים מַעֲשֵׂהוּ
לְמִדַּת הַמֶּלֶךְ.

נִסְמַכְתִּי עָלֶיךָ וְלֹא לְמַעֲשַׂי אֶפְנֶה,
כִּי אָמַרְתִּי : עוֹלָם חֶסֶד יִבָּנֶה !

וּבְבִרְכָתִי תְּנַעֲנַע לִי רֹאשׁ / וְאוֹתָהּ קַח לְךָ כְּבְשָׂמִים רֹאשׁ
יֶעֱרַב נָא שִׂיחִי עָלֶיךָ / כִּי נַפְשִׁי תַעֲרֹג אֵלֶיךָ:

Pages 94–96

מֵרֹאשׁ מִקַּדְמֵי עוֹלָמִים
נִמְצֵאתִי בְמִכְמַנָּיו הַחֲתוּמִים,
מֵאַיִן הִמְצִיאַנִי, וּלְקֵץ יָמִים
נִשְׁאַלְתִּי מִן הַמֶּלֶךְ.

שַׁלְשֶׁלֶת חַיַּי מִיסוֹד הַמַּעֲרָכָה
לִמְשֹׁךְ תַּבְנִית בִּתְמוּנָה עֲרוּכָה
לִשְׁקֹל עַל יְדֵי עוֹשֵׂי הַמְּלָאכָה
לְהָבִיא אֶל גִּנְזֵי הַמֶּלֶךְ.

הוֹפִיעַ לְגַלּוֹת אֲשֶׁר הִטְמִין
הֵן מִשְּׂמֹאל הַגֻּלָּה וּמֵהַיָּמִין
מִמַּעֲלוֹת הַיּוֹרְדוֹת מִן
בְּרֵכַת הַשֶּׁלַח לְגַן הַמֶּלֶךְ.

בֶּעָפָר רְקַמְתִּי וְאִם רוּחֲךָ בִּי נָשׁוּב
בַּנְתָּ לְרֵעִי כְּגֵר בָּאָרֶץ אֶהְיֶה חָשׁוּב.
עַד מָתַי יִהְיֶה מַהֲלָכְךָ וּמָתַי תָּשׁוּב
וַיִּיטַב לִפְנֵי הַמֶּלֶךְ?

נֵר לְרַגְלִי שַׂמְתָּ וְלִנְתִיבָתִי,
תְּחַפֵּשׂ כָּל חַדְרֵי בֶטֶן בְּרוּחַ נְדִיבָתִי,
וּבְצֵאתִי מִלְּפָנֶיךָ הִזְהַרְתָּ אוֹתִי:
יְרָא אֶת יְיָ, בְּנִי, וָמֶלֶךְ!

נָתַתָּ בְיָדַי לֵב — מֹאזְנֵי מִשְׁפָּט וָפֶלֶס,
אִם לְחֶסֶד יַמְצִיאַנִי — בּוֹ אֶתְעַלֵּס

Pages 81–86

אַנְעִים זְמִירוֹת וְשִׁירִים אֶאֱרֹג / כִּי אֵלֶיךָ נַפְשִׁי תַעֲרֹג

נַפְשִׁי חִמְּדָה בְּצֵל יָדֶךָ / לָדַעַת כָּל רָז סוֹדֶךָ

מִדֵּי דַבְּרִי בִּכְבוֹדֶךָ / הוֹמֶה לִבִּי אֶל דּוֹדֶיךָ

עַל כֵּן אֲדַבֵּר בְּךָ נִכְבָּדוֹת / וְשִׁמְךָ אֲכַבֵּד בְּשִׁירֵי יְדִידוֹת

אֲסַפְּרָה כְבוֹדְךָ וְלֹא רְאִיתִיךָ / אֲדַמְּךָ אֲכַנְּךָ וְלֹא יְדַעְתִּיךָ

בְּיַד נְבִיאֶיךָ, בְּסוֹד עֲבָדֶיךָ / דִּמִּיתָ הֲדַר כְּבוֹד הוֹדֶךָ

גְּדֻלָּתְךָ וּגְבוּרָתֶךָ / כִּנּוּ לְתֹקֶף פְּעֻלָּתֶךָ

דִּמּוּ אוֹתְךָ וְלֹא כְפִי יֶשְׁךָ / וַיְשַׁוּוּךָ לְפִי מַעֲשֶׂיךָ

הִמְשִׁילוּךָ בְּרֹב חֶזְיוֹנוֹת / הִנְּךָ אֶחָד בְּכָל דִּמְיוֹנוֹת

וַיֶּחֱזוּ בְךָ זִקְנָה וּבַחֲרוּת / וּשְׂעַר רֹאשְׁךָ בְּשֵׂיבָה וְשַׁחֲרוּת

זִקְנָה בְּיוֹם דִּין וּבַחֲרוּת בְּיוֹם קְרָב / כְּאִישׁ מִלְחָמוֹת יָדָיו לוֹ רָב

חָבַשׁ כּוֹבַע יְשׁוּעָה בְּרֹאשׁוֹ / הוֹשִׁיעָה-לוֹ יְמִינוֹ וּזְרוֹעַ קָדְשׁוֹ

טַלְלֵי אוֹרוֹת רֹאשׁוֹ נִמְלָא / וּקְוֻצּוֹתָיו רְסִיסֵי לָיְלָה

יִתְפָּאֵר בִּי, כִּי חָפֵץ בִּי / וְהוּא יִהְיֶה לִי לַעֲטֶרֶת צְבִי

כֶּתֶם טָהוֹר פָּז דְּמוּת רֹאשׁוֹ / וְחַק עַל מֵצַח כְּבוֹד שֵׁם קָדְשׁוֹ

לְחֵן וּלְכָבוֹד צְבִי תִפְאָרָה / אֻמָּתוֹ לוֹ עִטְּרָה עֲטָרָה

מַחְלְפוֹת רֹאשׁוֹ כְּבִימֵי בַחֲרוּת / קְוֻצּוֹתָיו תַּלְתַּלִּים שְׁחוֹרוֹת

נְוֵה הַצֶּדֶק צְבִי תִפְאַרְתּוֹ / יַעֲלֶה-נָּא עַל רֹאשׁ שִׂמְחָתוֹ

סְגֻלָּתוֹ תְּהִי בְיָדוֹ עֲטֶרֶת / וּצְנִיף מְלוּכָה צְבִי תִפְאֶרֶת

עֲמוּסִים נְשָׂאָם עֲטֶרֶת עִנְּדָם / מֵאֲשֶׁר יָקְרוּ בְעֵינָיו כִּבְּדָם

פְּאֵרוֹ עָלַי וּפְאֵרִי עָלָיו / וְקָרוֹב אֵלַי בְּקָרְאִי אֵלָיו

צַח וְאָדֹם לִלְבוּשׁוֹ אָדֹם / פּוּרָה בְדָרְכוֹ בְּבוֹאוֹ מֵאֱדוֹם

קֶשֶׁר תְּפִלִּין הֶרְאָה לֶעָנָיו / תְּמוּנַת יְיָ לְנֶגֶד עֵינָיו

רוֹצֶה בְעַמּוֹ עֲנָוִים יְפָאֵר / יוֹשֵׁב תְּהִלּוֹת בָּם לְהִתְפָּאֵר

רֹאשׁ דְּבָרְךָ אֱמֶת קוֹרֵא מֵרֹאשׁ / דּוֹר וָדוֹר עַם דּוֹרֶשְׁךָ דְּרֹשׁ

שִׁית הֲמוֹן שִׁירַי נָא עָלֶיךָ / וְרִנָּתִי תִקְרַב אֵלֶיךָ

תְּהִלָּתִי תְּהִי לְרֹאשְׁךָ עֲטֶרֶת / וּתְפִלָּתִי תִּכּוֹן קְטֹרֶת

תִּיקַר שִׁירַת רָשׁ בְּעֵינֶיךָ / כְּשִׁיר יוּשַׁר עַל קָרְבָּנֶיךָ

בִּרְכָתִי תַעֲלֶה לְרֹאשׁ מַשְׁבִּיר / מְחוֹלֵל וּמוֹלִיד צַדִּיק כַּבִּיר

Pages 73–74

אֲדֹנָי, נֶגְדְּךָ כָל תַּאֲוָתִי, / וְאִם לֹא אַעֲלֶנָּה עַל שְׂפָתִי.

רְצוֹנְךָ אֶשְׁאָלָה רֶגַע – וְאֶגְוָע, / וּמִי יִתֵּן וְתָבוֹא לִי שְׁאֵלָתִי,

וְאַפְקִיד אֶת שְׁאָר רוּחִי בְּיָדֶךָ / וְיָשַׁנְתִּי וְעָרְבָה לִי שְׁנָתִי !

בְּרָחְקִי מִמְּךָ – מוֹתִי בְּחַיָּי, / וְאִם אֶדְבַּק בְּךָ – חַיַּי בְּמוֹתִי,

אֲבָל לֹא אֶדְעָה בַּמֶּה אֲקַדֵּם, / וּמַה-תִּהְיֶה עֲבוֹדָתִי וְדָתִי.

דְּרָכֶיךָ, אֲדֹנָי, לַמְּדֵנִי, / וְשׁוּב מִמַּאֲסַר סִכְלוּת שְׁבוּתִי,

וְהוֹרֵנִי בְּעוֹד יֶשׁ בִּי יְכֹלֶת / לְהִתְעַנּוֹת, וְאַל תִּבְזֶה עֱנוּתִי,

בְּטֶרֶם יוֹם אֱהִי עָלַי לְמַשָּׂא, / וְיוֹם יִכְבַּד קְצָתִי עַל קְצָתִי,

וְאֶכָּנַע בְּעַל-כָּרְחִי, / וְיֹאכַל / עֲצָמַי עָשׁ וְנִלְאוּ מִשְּׂאֵתִי,

וְאֶסַּע אֶל מְקוֹם נָסְעוּ אֲבוֹתַי, / וּבִמְקוֹם תַּחֲנוֹתָם תַּחֲנוֹתִי.

כְּגֵר-תּוֹשָׁב אֲנִי עַל גַּב אֲדָמָה, / וְאוּלָם כִּי בְּבִטְנָהּ נַחֲלָתִי.

נְעוּרַי עַד הֲלֹם עָשׂוּ לְנַפְשָׁם, /וּמָתַי גַּם אֲנִי אֶעֱשֶׂה לְבֵיתִי ?

וְהָעוֹלָם אֲשֶׁר נָתַן בְּלִבִּי / מְנָעַנִי לְבַקֵּשׁ אַחֲרִיתִי !

וְאֵיכָה אֶעֱבֹד יוֹצְרִי – בְּעוֹדִי / אֲסִיר יִצְרִי וְעֶבֶד תַּאֲוָתִי ?

וְאֵיכָה מַעֲלָה רָמָה אֲבַקֵּשׁ – / וּמָחָר תִּהְיֶה רִמָּה אֲחוֹתִי ?

וְאֵיךְ יִיטַב בְּיוֹם טוֹבָה לְבָבִי, / וְלֹא אֵדַע – הֲיִיטַב – הֲיִיטַב מָחֳרָתִי ?

וְהַיָּמִים וְהַלֵּילוֹת עֲרֵבִים / לְכַלּוֹת אֶת שְׁאֵרִי עַד כְּלוֹתִי,

וְלָרוּחַ יְזָרוּן מַחֲצִיתִי, / וְלֶעָפָר יְשִׁיבוּן מַחֲצִיתִי.

וּמָה אֹמַר – וְיִצְרִי יִרְדְּפֵנִי / כְּאוֹיֵב מִנְּעוּרַי עַד בְּלוֹתִי ?

וּמַה-לִּי בַזְּמַן – אִם לֹא רְצוֹנֶךָ ? / וְאִם אֵינֶךָ מְנָתִי – מַה-מְּנָתִי ?

אֲנִי מִמַּעֲשִׂים שׁוֹלָל וְעָרֹם, / וְצִדְקָתְךָ לְבַדָּהּ הִיא כְּסוּתִי.

וְעוֹד מָה אַאֲרִיךְ לָשׁוֹן וְאֶשְׁאָל ? / אֲדֹנָי, נֶגְדְּךָ כָל תַּאֲוָתִי !

Pages 75–76

יוֹנַת רְחוֹקִים נָדְדָה יַעֲרָה / כָּשְׁלָה וְלֹא כָלְתָה לְהִתְנַעֲרָה.

הִתְעוֹפְפָה, הִתְנוֹפְפָה, חוֹפְפָה / סָבִיב לְדוֹדָהּ סוֹחֲרָה, סוֹעֲרָה,

וַתַּחֲשֹׁב אֶלֶף לְקֵץ מוֹעֲדָהּ – / אַךְ חָפְרָה מִכֹּל אֲשֶׁר שִׁעֲרָה.

דּוֹדָהּ – אֲשֶׁר עִנָּהּ בְּאֶרֶךְ נְדוֹד / שָׁנִים, וְנַפְשָׁהּ אֶל שְׁאוֹל הֶעֱרָה –

הֵן אָמְרָה: "לֹא אֶזְכְּרָה עוֹד שְׁמוֹ !" / וַיְהִי בְתוֹךְ לִבָּהּ כְּאֵשׁ בּוֹעֲרָה.

לָמָּה כְאוֹיֵב תִּהְיֶה לָהּ ? – וְהִיא / פִּיהָ לְמַלְקוֹשׁ יֶשְׁעֲךָ פָּעֲרָה,

וַתַּאֲמִין נַפְשָׁהּ וְלֹא נוֹאֲשָׁה – / אִם כָּבְדָה בִשְׁמוֹ וְאִם צָעֲרָה.

יָבוֹא אֱלֹהֵינוּ וְאַל יֶחֱרָשׁ – / עַל כָּל סְבִיבָיו אֵשׁ מְאֹד נִשְׂעֲרָה !

Page 70

לִקְרַאת מְקוֹר חַיֵּי אֱמֶת אָרוּצָה — / עַל כֵּן בְּחַיֵּי שָׁוְא וְרִיק אָקוּצָה
לִרְאוֹת פְּנֵי מַלְכִּי מְנַמַּתִי לְבָד, / לֹא אֶעֱרֹץ בִּלְתּוֹ וְלֹא אַעֲרִיצָה
מִי יִתְּנֵנִי לַחֲזוֹתוֹ בַחֲלוֹם ! / אִישַׁן שְׁנַת עוֹלָם וְלֹא אָקִיצָה
לוּ אֶחֱזֶה פָנָיו בְּלִבִּי בָיְתָה — / לֹא שָׁאֲלוּ עֵינַי לְהַבִּיט חוּצָה:

Pages 71–72

יָהּ אָנָה אֶמְצָאֲךָ ?   מְקוֹמְךָ נַעֲלֶה וְנֶעְלָם !
וְאָנָה לֹא אֶמְצָאֲךָ ?   כְּבוֹדְךָ מָלֵא עוֹלָם !

הַנִּמְצָא בַּקְּרָבִים   אַפְסֵי אֶרֶץ הֵקִים,
הַמִּשְׂגָּב לַקְּרוֹבִים,   הַמִּבְטָח לָרְחוֹקִים,
אַתָּה יוֹשֵׁב כְּרוּבִים,   אַתָּה שׁוֹכֵן שְׁחָקִים.
תִּתְהַלֵּל בִּצְבָאֲךָ — וְאַתְּ עַל רֹאשׁ מַהֲלָלָם,
גַּלְגַּל לֹא יִשָּׂאֲךָ — אַף כִּי חַדְרֵי אוּלָם !

וּבְהִנָּשְׂאֲךָ עֲלֵיהֶם   עַל כֵּס נִשָּׂא וָרָם,
אַתָּה קָרוֹב אֲלֵיהֶם   מֵרוּחָם וּמִבְּשָׂרָם,
פִּיהֶם יָעִיד בָּהֶם,   כִּי אֵין בִּלְתְּךָ יוֹצְרָם.
מִי זֶה לֹא יִירָאֲךָ — וְעֹל מַלְכוּתְךָ עֻלָּם ?
אוֹ מִי לֹא יִקְרָאֲךָ — וְאַתָּה נוֹתֵן אָכְלָם ?

דָּרַשְׁתִּי קֻרְבָתְךָ,   בְּכָל לִבִּי קְרָאתִיךָ,
וּבְצֵאתִי לִקְרָאתְךָ —   לִקְרָאתִי מְצָאתִיךָ,
וּבְפִלְאֵי גְבוּרָתְךָ   בַּקֹּדֶשׁ חֲזִיתִיךָ.
מִי יֹאמַר לֹא רָאֲךָ ? הֵן שָׁמַיִם וְחֵילָם
יַגִּידוּ מוֹרָאֲךָ   בְּלִי נִשְׁמָע קוֹלָם !

הַאָמְנָם כִּי יֵשֵׁב   אֱלֹהִים אֶת הָאָדָם ?
וּמַה־יַּחְשֹׁב כָּל חוֹשֵׁב,   אֲשֶׁר בֶּעָפָר יְסוֹדָם —
וְאַתָּה קָדוֹשׁ יוֹשֵׁב   תְּהִלּוֹתָם וּכְבוֹדָם !
חַיּוֹת יוֹדוּ פִלְאֲךָ   הָעוֹמְדוֹת בְּרוּם עוֹלָם,
עַל רָאשֵׁיהֶם כִּסְאֲךָ—וְאַתָּה נוֹשֵׂא כֻלָּם !

וְשָׁם יָנוּחוּ יְגִיעֵי כֹחַ —
וְאֵלֶּה בְּנֵי נֹחַ.

וּבוֹ נֹעַם בְּלִי תַכְלִית וְקִצְבָּה,
וְהוּא הָעוֹלָם הַבָּא.

וְשָׁם מַעֲמָדוֹת וּמַרְאוֹת
לַנְּפָשׁוֹת הָעוֹמְדוֹת בְּמַרְאוֹת הַצּוֹבְאוֹת,
אֶת פְּנֵי הָאָדוֹן לִרְאוֹת וּלְהֵרָאוֹת.

שׁוֹכְנוֹת בְּהֵיכְלֵי מֶלֶךְ,
וְעוֹמְדוֹת עַל שֻׁלְחַן הַמֶּלֶךְ,
וּמִתְעַדְּנוֹת בְּמֶתֶק פְּרִי הַשֵּׂכֶל —
וְהוּא יִתֵּן מַעֲדַנֵּי מֶלֶךְ.

זֹאת הַמְּנוּחָה וְהַנַּחֲלָה,
אֲשֶׁר אֵין תַּכְלִית לְטוּבָהּ וְיָפְיָהּ —
וְגַם זָבַת חָלָב וּדְבַשׁ הִיא וְזֶה-פִּרְיָהּ.

כט
מִי יָכִיל עָצְמָתָךְ?
בְּבָרְאֲךָ מִזִּיו כְּבוֹדְךָ יִפְעַת טְהוֹרָה,
מִצּוּר הַצּוּר נִגְזָרָה,
וּמִמַּקֶּבֶת בֹּר נְקָרָה.

וְאָצַלְתָּ עָלֶיהָ רוּחַ חָכְמָה,
וְקָרָאתָ שְׁמָהּ נְשָׁמָה.
עֲשִׂיתָהּ מִלַּהֲבוֹת אֵשׁ הַשֵּׂכֶל חֲצוּבָה,
וְנִשְׁמָתוֹ כְּאֵשׁ בּוֹעֲרָה בָהּ.

וְשִׁלַּחְתָּהּ בַּגּוּף לְעָבְדֵהוּ וּלְשָׁמְרֵהוּ,
וְהִיא כְּאֵשׁ בְּתוֹכוֹ וְלֹא תִשְׂרְפֵהוּ.

כִּי מֵאֵשׁ הַנְּשָׁמָה נִבְרָא הַגּוּף
וְיָצָא מֵאַיִן לַיֵּשׁ —
מִפְּנֵי אֲשֶׁר יָרַד עָלָיו יְיָ בָּאֵשׁ.

לַעֲרֹךְ תְּהִלּוֹת וְשִׁירוֹת —
לְנֶאְזָר בִּגְבוּרוֹת.

כֻּלָּם בַּחֲרָדָה וּרְעָדָה כּוֹרְעִים וּמִשְׁתַּחֲוִים לָךְ,
וְאוֹמְרִים: "מוֹדִים אֲנַחְנוּ לָךְ.

שֶׁאַתָּה אֱלֹהֵינוּ,
אַתָּה אֲדוֹנֵינוּ —
וַאֲנַחְנוּ עֲבָדֶיךָ,
וְאַתָּה בּוֹרְאֵנוּ —
וַאֲנַחְנוּ עֵדֶיךָ.
אַתָּה עֲשִׂיתָנוּ,
וְלֹא אֲנַחְנוּ —
וּמַעֲשֵׂה יָדְךָ כֻּלָּנוּ".

כו

מִי יָבוֹא עַד תְּכוּנָתֶךָ?
בְּהַגְבִּיהֶךָ לְמַעְלָה מִגַּלְגַּל הַשֵּׂכֶל כִּסֵּא הַכָּבוֹד,
אֲשֶׁר שָׁם נְוֵה הַחֶבְיוֹן וְהַהוֹד,
וְשָׁם הַסּוֹד וְהַיְסוֹד,
וְעָדָיו יַגִּיעַ הַשֵּׂכֶל וְיַעֲמֹד.

וּמִלְמַעְלָה גָּאִיתָ וְעָלִיתָ עַל כֵּס תַּעֲצוּמָךְ —
וְאִישׁ לֹא יַעֲלֶה עִמָּךְ.

כז

מִי יַעֲשֶׂה כְמַעֲשֶׂיךָ?
בַּעֲשׂוֹתְךָ תַּחַת כִּסֵּא כְבוֹדֶךָ,
מַעֲמָד לְנַפְשׁוֹת חֲסִידֶיךָ.

וְשָׁם נְוֵה הַנְּשָׁמוֹת הַטְּהוֹרוֹת,
אֲשֶׁר בִּצְרוֹר הַחַיִּים צְרוּרוֹת.

וַאֲשֶׁר יִיגְעוּ וְיִיעָפוּ,
שָׁם כֹּחַ יַחֲלִיפוּ.

כֻּלָּם גְּזָרוֹת פְּנִינִיּוֹת,
וְחַיּוֹת עֶלְיוֹנִיּוֹת,
חִיצוֹנִיּוֹת וּפְנִימִיּוֹת,
הֲלִיכוֹתֶיךָ צוֹפִיּוֹת.

מִמְּקוֹם קָדוֹשׁ יְהַלֵּכוּ,
וּמִמְּקוֹר הָאוֹר יִמָּשֵׁכוּ.

נֶחְלָקִים לְכִתּוֹת,
וְעַל דִּגְלָם אוֹתוֹת,
בְּעֵט סוֹפֵר מָהִיר חֲרוּתוֹת.
מֵהֶם נְסִיכוֹת,
וּמֵהֶם מְשָׁרְתוֹת;

מֵהֶם צְבָאוֹת,
רָצוֹת וּבָאוֹת,
לֹא עֲיֵפוֹת וְלֹא נִלְאוֹת,
רוֹאוֹת וְלֹא נִרְאוֹת.

מֵהֶם חֲצוּבֵי לֶהָבוֹת,
וּמֵהֶם רוּחוֹת נוֹשְׁבוֹת,
מֵהֶם מֵאֵשׁ וּמִמַּיִם מָרְכָּבוֹת;

מֵהֶם שְׂרָפִים,
וּמֵהֶם רְשָׁפִים;

מֵהֶם בְּרָקִים,
וּמֵהֶם זִקִּים.

וְכָל כַּת מֵהֶם מִשְׁתַּחֲוָה לְרוֹכֵב עֲרָבוֹת,
וּבְרוּם עוֹלָם נִצָּבִים לַאֲלָפִים וְלִרְבָבוֹת.

נֶחְלָקִים לְמִשְׁמָרוֹת,
בַּיּוֹם וּבַלַּיְלָה לְרֹאשׁ אַשְׁמוּרוֹת,

וְכֹחָהּ נוֹגַעַת עַד שְׂפַת הַבְּרִיאָה הַשְּׁפָלָה הַחִיצוֹנָה —
הַיְרִיעָה הַקִּיצוֹנָה בַּמַּחְבֶּרֶת.

כד

מִי יָבִין סוֹדוֹת בְּרִיאוֹתֶיךָ ?
בַּהֲרִימְךָ עַל גַּלְגַּל הַתְּשִׁיעִי גַּלְגַּל הַשֵּׂכֶל,
הוּא הַהֵיכָל לְפָנַי —
הָעֲשִׂירִי יִהְיֶה קֹדֶשׁ לַיְיָ !

וְהוּא הַגַּלְגַּל הַנַּעֲלָה עַל כָּל עֶלְיוֹן,
אֲשֶׁר לֹא יַשִּׂיגֵהוּ רַעְיוֹן,
וְשָׁם הַחֶבְיוֹן,
אֲשֶׁר הוּא לִכְבוֹדְךָ לְאַפִּרְיוֹן.

מִכֶּסֶף הָאֱמֶת יָצַקְתָּ אוֹתוֹ
וּמִזְּהַב הַשֵּׂכֶל עָשִׂיתָ רְפִידָתוֹ
וְעַל עַמּוּדֵי צֶדֶק שַׂמְתָּ מְסִבָּתוֹ
וּמִכֹּחֲךָ מְצִיאוּתוֹ
וּמִמְּךָ וְעָדֶיךָ מְגַמָּתוֹ
וְאֵלֶיךָ תְּשׁוּקָתוֹ.

כה

מִי יַעֲמִיק לְמַחְשְׁבוֹתֶיךָ ?
בַּעֲשׂוֹתְךָ מִזִּיו גַּלְגַּל הַשֵּׂכֶל
זֹהַר הַנְּשָׁמוֹת,
וְהַנְּפָשׁוֹת הָרָמוֹת.

הֵם מַלְאֲכֵי רְצוֹנֶךָ,
מְשָׁרְתֵי פָנֶיךָ.

הֵם אַדִּירֵי כֹחַ וְגִבּוֹרֵי מַמְלֶכֶת,
בְּיָדָם לַהַט הַחֶרֶב הַמִּתְהַפֶּכֶת,
וְעוֹשֵׂי כָל מְלָאכֶת —
אֶל אֲשֶׁר יִהְיֶה-שָׁמָּה הָרוּחַ לָלֶכֶת.

Pages 62–69

ט

אַתָּה חָכָם,
וְהַחָכְמָה מְקוֹר חַיִּים מִמְּךָ נוֹבַעַת,
וְחָכְמָתְךָ נִבְעָר כָּל אָדָם מִדָּעַת.

אַתָּה חָכָם,
וְקַדְמוֹן לְכָל קַדְמוֹן,
וְהַחָכְמָה הָיְתָה אֶצְלְךָ אָמוֹן.

אַתָּה חָכָם,
וְלֹא לָמַדְתָּ מִבִּלְעָדֶיךָ,
וְלֹא קָנִיתָ חָכְמָה מִזּוּלָתֶךָ.

אַתָּה חָכָם,
וּמֵחָכְמָתְךָ אָצַלְתָּ חֵפֶץ מְזֻמָּן,
שַׂמְתּוֹ כְפוֹעֵל וְאָמָּן.

לִמְשֹׁךְ מֶשֶׁךְ הַיֵּשׁ מִן הָאַיִן,
כְּהִמָּשֵׁךְ הָאוֹר הַיּוֹצֵא מִן הָעָיִן.

וְשׁוֹאֵב מִמְּקוֹר הָאוֹר מִבְּלִי דְלִי,
וּפוֹעֵל הַכֹּל בְּלִי כֶלִי.

וְחָצֵב וְחָקַק,
וְטִהַר וְזִקַּק.

וְקָרָא אֶל הָאַיִן – וְנִבְקַע,
וְאֶל הַיֵּשׁ – וְנִתְקַע,
וְאֶל הָעוֹלָם – וְנִרְקַע,

וְתִכֵּן שְׁחָקִים בַּזֶּרֶת,
וְיָדוֹ אֹהֶל הַגַּלְגַּלִּים מְחַבֶּרֶת,
וּבִלְלָאוֹת הַיְכֹלֶת יְרִיעוֹת הַבְּרִיאוֹת קוֹשֶׁרֶת,

קוֹל יְצַפְצֵף / וְשִׁיר יְרַצֵּף / צְבָא מַחֲנֶה / שְׁלִישִׁיָּה,
וְנוּרִיאֵל / שַׂר הָאֵל / עוֹמֵד בָּם / לְתַלְפִּיָּה.
לְשַׁאֲטָתָם / וְשַׁעֲטָתָם / יְרוֹפֵף חוּג / הָעֲלִיָּה
בְּקוֹל "אַיֵּה / מְקוֹם אֶהְיֶה, יוֹצֵר רוּם / וְתַחְתִּיָּה?"
רְאוֹת נֶאְדָּר / הַנֶּהְדָּר / יוֹם וָלֵיל / יִתְאָבוּ:
הָבוּ לַאֲדֹנָי, בְּנֵי אֵלִים, הָבוּ !

טְכוּסֵי הוֹד / לְךָ שָׁהוֹד / בָּרְבִיעִית / יָעִידוּ,
וְאִמְרָתְךָ / וְזִמְרָתְךָ / עִם רְפָאֵל / יַגִּידוּ,
וְצִיץ מָעֹז / וְכֶתֶר עֹז / לְךָ יְקַשְּׁרוּ / וְיַעֲנִידוּ,
וְאַרְבַּעְתָּם / שִׁיר מִכְתָּם / יַתְמִידוּ / וְיַצְמִידוּ.
וְחַבְּרִתָּם / וְגִבְּרִתָּם / לְבַל יִיגְעוּ / וְיִדְאָבוּ:
הָבוּ לַאֲדֹנָי, בְּנֵי אֵלִים, הָבוּ !

נִיצוֹצִים / נִקְבָּצִים / לְךָ יַחַד / יְרַנְּנוּ,
בְּעַד עֲמוּסִים / הַחֲמוּסִים / לְךָ קוֹלָם / יְחַנְּנוּ,
בְּאֵימָתְךָ / וְיִרְאָתְךָ / רַגְלֵיהֶם / יְכוֹנֵנוּ.
בְּקוֹל חָזָק / כְּמוֹ בָזָק / קְדֻשָּׁתְךָ / יְשַׁנְּנוּ,
עֲנוֹת קָדוֹשׁ / לְאֵל קָדוֹשׁ / לְמוּל קָדוֹשׁ / יַעֲרְבוּ:
הָבוּ לַאֲדֹנָי, בְּנֵי אֵלִים, הָבוּ!

Page 61

אֲהַבְתִּיךָ כְּאַהֲבַת אִישׁ יְחִידוֹ / בְּכָל לִבּוֹ וְנַפְשׁוֹ וּמְאֹדוֹ
וְשַׁשְׁתִּי עַל לְבָבְךָ אֲשֶׁר תָּר / לְהָבִין סוֹד פְּעֻלַּת אֵל יְלָדוֹ
וְהַדָּבָר מְאֹד עָמֹק וְרָחוֹק / וּמִי יָבִין וּמִי יֵדַע יְסוֹדוֹ
אֲבָל אַגִּיד לְךָ דָבָר שְׁמַעְתִּיו / וְעָלֶיךָ לְהִתְבּוֹנֵן בְּסוֹדוֹ
חֲכָמִים אָמְרוּ, כִּי סוֹד הֱיוֹת כֹּל— / לְמַעַן כֹּל אֲשֶׁר הַכֹּל בְּיָדוֹ
וְהוּא נִכְסָף לְשׁוּמוֹ יֵשׁ כְּמוֹ יֵשׁ / כְּמוֹ חוֹשֵׁק אֲשֶׁר נִכְסָף לְדוֹדוֹ
וְאוּלַי זֶה יְדָמוּ הַנְּבִיאִים / בְּאָמְרָם כִּי בְרָאוֹ עַל כְּבוֹדוֹ.
הֲשִׁיבוֹתִי לְךָ דָבָר, וְאַתָּה / קְנֵה מוֹפֵת לְמַעַן הַעֲמִידוֹ.

הוּא אֲשֶׁר יְסוֹכֵךְ הָעֲצָמִים   הוּא אֲשֶׁר יְקְרֹם הַגֵּלֶד
הוּא אֲשֶׁר יְכוֹנְנֵהוּ בְּעָצְמָה   הוּא אֲשֶׁר יְפַח בַּגּוּף נְשָׁמָה
הוּא אֲשֶׁר יְעוֹרֵר נִרְדָּמִים   הוּא אֲשֶׁר יְשִׁיבֵהוּ לָאֲדָמָה

Pages 59–60

שִׁנְאַנִּים / שַׁאֲנַנִּים / כְּנִיצוֹצִים / יְלַהֲבוּ,
לַהֲטֵיהֶם / וּמַעֲטֵיהֶם / כְּעַיִן קָלָל / יִצְהָבוּ,
מוּל כִּסֵּא / מִתְנַשֵּׂא / בְּקוֹל רַעַשׁ / יִרְהָבוּ,
הֵן בְּמַחֲזֶה / זֶה לָזֶה / לְהַקְדִּישׁ אֵל / יֶאֱהָבוּ:
הָבוּ לַאדֹנָי, בְּנֵי אֵלִים, הָבוּ !

לָךְ חַיּוֹת / עֶלְיוֹת / בְּתַחְתִּית כֵּס / הַנִּקְבָּע,
וְאֶרְאֵלִים / וְחַשְׁמַלִּים / אַזוֹרֵי זִיו / הַנִּצְבָּע,
תְּהִלָּתָךְ / וְהִלָּתָךְ / יְהוֹדוּן מַ- / חֲנוֹת אַרְבַּע,
זֶה יַעֲרִיץ / וְזֶה יַמְרִיץ / לָךְ זֶמֶר / וְשִׁיר יַבַּע,
בְּנֵי חַיִל / יוֹם וְלַיִל / בְּמִשְׁמְרוֹתָם / נִצָּבוּ:
הָבוּ לַאדֹנָי, בְּנֵי אֵלִים, הָבוּ !

מְכוֹן מִשְׁמָר / הַנֶּאֱמָר / בְּרֹאשׁ מַחֲנוֹת / הֲמוֹנֶיךָ
הֲלֹא נִמְסָר / בְּיַד הַשָּׂר / מִיכָאֵל / גְּאוֹנֶךָ.
בְּמֶרְכָּבוֹת / לִרְבָבוֹת / יַעֲמֹד עַל / יְמִינֶךָ,
וְיָקוּ / וְיִלָּווּ / דְּרֹשׁ אַיֵּה / מְעוֹנֶךָ,
וְשָׁם סָגוֹד / לְמוּל פַּרְגּוֹד / לָךְ יִסְגְּדוּ / וְיִקְרָבוּ:
הָבוּ לַאדֹנָי, בְּנֵי אֵלִים, הָבוּ !

הֲמוֹן מַחֲנֶה / הַמִּשְׁנֶה / עַל יָרֵךְ / שְׂמֹאל נִזְקָף,
וְעַל צְבָאוֹ / וּנְשִׂיאוֹ / גַּבְרִיאֵל / הַנִּשְׁקָף,
בִּשְׂרָפִים / לַאֲלָפִים, / בְּחֵיל כָּבֵד / מְאֹד נִתְקָף,
זֶה אֵיפֹה / וְאֵלֶּה פֹּה, / וְכִסֵּא קָד- / שְׁךָ מֻקָּף.
גְּזוּרֵי אֵשׁ / אַזוֹרֵי אֵשׁ / וְסוּסֵי אֵשׁ / יִרְכָּבוּ —
הָבוּ לַאדֹנָי, בְּנֵי אֵלִים, הָבוּ !

Pages 55–58

מַלְכוּתְךָ מַלְכוּת כָּל עוֹלָמִים

שֵׁם מַלְכוּתוֹ מְיֻחָד וְאֵין שֵׁנִי לְצִדּוֹ
בִּשְׁלֹשָׁה סְפָרִים נֶחְתָּמִים
לַהֲקַת עֶשֶׂר סְפִירוֹת יָזַם לַחְשֹׂף
וְחָמֵשׁ בְּחָמֵשׁ מְהֻסְכָּמִים
מֵהֶם יַשְׂכִּיל כִּי הַיּוֹצֵר מְיֻחָד
וְהוּא רֹאשׁ לְכָל רֹאשׁ וְרֹם עַל כָּל רָמִים
הַמַּשְׂכִּיל בָּהֶם יֵדַע וְיָצוּר
וְעֵדָיו גְּלוּיִים וּמְפֹרָסָמִים
הִגְבִּיל אֵשׁ לְמַעֲלָה וּלְמַטָּה מָיִם
וּשְׁנַיִם-עָשָׂר מַזָּלוֹת בַּמְּרוֹמִים
קִיֵּם עַמּוּדִים גְּדוֹלִים מֵאֵין כָּמוֹהוּ
וּמֵהֶם יוֹצְאִים מֵימֵי תְהוֹמִים
טִלְטֵל אֵשׁ מִמַּיִם בְּתָקְפוֹ וְעָצְמוֹ
לְאוֹתוֹת וּלְמוֹעֲדִים וּלְיָמִים
נִתְלָה עוֹלָם בְּיָדוֹ כְּאֶשְׁכּוֹל
כִּי בְיָהּ יְיָ צוּר עוֹלָמִים
בּוֹ כְּבוֹד מַלְכוּתוֹ מֵאָז יִשְׁכֹּן
הוּא רוּחַ אֱלֹהִים חַי הָעוֹלָמִים
רוֹאֶה הַכֹּל וְעַל הַכֹּל מַשְׁקִיף
וְכָל הַיְצוּרִים בִּשְׁמוֹ קַיָּמִים
יָחִיד מַנְהִיג הַכֹּל כְּרֶגַע
לוֹכֵד בְּעָרְמָם חֲכָמִים
הוּא הַתּוֹלֶה אֲגֻדַּת אֲרָקִים
וְיוֹצִיא לָאוֹר כָּל תַּעֲלוּמִים
וְהוּא אֲשֶׁר יַעֲשִׁיר וְיוֹרִישׁ
וְיַחְבִּיר תְּמוּנוֹת לַגְּלָמִים
וְהוּא אֲשֶׁר יָרִים וְיַשְׁפִּיל
כָּל הֶהָרִים הָרָמִים
הוּא אֲשֶׁר יַטְרִיפֵם לֶחֶם חֻקָּם
הוּא אֲשֶׁר יוֹרִיד הַגְּשָׁמִים
הוּא אֲשֶׁר יְכוֹנֵן גּוּף הַיֶּלֶד

שׁוֹכֵן עַד מֵאָז נִשְׂגָּב לְבַדּוֹ
שֶׁכְּלֵל עוֹלָמוֹ מֵאוֹר לְבוּשׁ מַדּוֹ
לַעֲצַת אָמוֹן נִכְסַף נִכְסוֹף
לִבְרֹר כְּנֶגְדָם עֲשָׂרָה בְּאֵין סוֹף
מֵבִין סוֹדָם יָבֵהַל וְיִפְחָד
מָה אַתָּה סוֹפֵר לִפְנֵי אֶחָד
הֲכִי עֶשֶׂר הֵם אֲחוּזוֹת בְּמָצוֹר
הוּא הַיּוֹצֵר אֲשֶׁר בָּם יַעֲצוֹר
הֵן בְּאוֹתִיּוֹת עֶשְׂרִים וּשְׁתָּיִם
הִבְדִּילָם בְּרוּחַ חֹק מַכְרִיעַ בֵּינְתָיִם
קָנָה מֵאַיִן יֵשׁ וְיָצַר מֶמֶשׁ מִתֹּהוּ
קָבַע בְּתוֹךְ קַו יָרֹק אַבְנֵי בֹהוּ
טָבַע שֵׁשׁ קְצָווֹת חֲתוּמִים בִּשְׁמוֹ
טִכֵּס בָּם כִּסְאוֹ וְצָבָא מְרוֹמוֹ
נִשָּׂא עַל כֹּל שְׁמוֹ אֲשֶׁר שָׁת בַּכֹּל
נִשְׂגָּב מִמָּקוֹם וְהוּא מָקוֹם לַכֹּל
בְּרוּחַ מָרוֹם אֲשֶׁר שָׁת כִּסְאוֹ נָכוֹן
בְּכֵן מוֹשֵׁל בַּכֹּל וְתִיכוֹן
רָם עַל כֹּל וּמֵהַכֹּל תַּקִּיף
רוֹדֶה בַכֹּל וְעַל הַכֹּל מַקִּיף
יוֹצֵר הַכֹּל בְּמַאֲמָר בְּלִי פֶגַע
יָהּ סוֹבֵל הַכֹּל בְּלִי יֶגַע
הוּא הַמְגַלְגֵּל אֲפֻדַּת שְׁחָקִים
הוּא הָאוֹמֵר יְהִי כֵן וְיָקִים
וְהוּא אֲשֶׁר יַקְהִיל וְיַפְרִישׁ
וְהוּא אֲשֶׁר יְפַצֵּץ וְיַקְרִישׁ
דְּעוּ כִּי הוּא אֲשֶׁר יָאִיר וְיַאְפִּיל
וְהוּא אֲשֶׁר יִסְמֹךְ וְיַפִּיל
הוּא אֲשֶׁר יְמַלֵּא לַיְצוּרִים סִפְקָם
הוּא אֲשֶׁר יִתֵּן מַאֲכָלָם וּמַשְׁקָם
הוּא אֲשֶׁר יְחַיֶּה מְתֵי חָלֶד

פָּנִים וְאָחוֹר
וְסִימָן לַדָּבָר —
אֵין בְּטוֹבָה לְמַעְלָה מֵעֹנֶג
וְאֵין בְּרָעָה לְמַטָּה מִנֶּגַע

כֵּיצַד צְרָפָן
וּשְׁקָלָן וַהֲמִירָן—
א עִם כֻּלָּן
וְכֻלָּן עִם א
ב עִם כֻּלָּן
וְכֻלָּן עִם ב
וְחוֹזְרוֹת חֲלִילָה
בְּרל״א שְׁעָרִים
וְנִמְצָא כָל הַיְצוּר
וְכָל הַדִּבּוּר
יוֹצֵא מִשֵּׁם אֶחָד

יָצַר מַמָּשׁ מִתֹּהוּ
וְעָשָׂה אֵינוֹ — יֶשְׁנוֹ
וְחָצַב עַמּוּדִים גְּדוֹלִים
מֵאֲוִיר שֶׁאֵינוֹ נִתְפָּס
צֵרֵף וְהֵמִיר וְעָשָׂה
אֵת כָּל הַיְצוּר
וְאֵת כָּל הַדִּבּוּר
בְּשֵׁם אֶחָד
וְסִימָן לַדָּבָר —
עֶשְׂרִים וּשְׁנַיִם חֲפָצִים בְּגוּף אֶחָד

מִכָּאן וְאֵילָךְ צֵא וַחֲשֹׁב
מַה-שֶּׁאֵין הַפֶּה יָכוֹל לְדַבֵּר
וְלֹא הָאֹזֶן יְכוֹלָה לִשְׁמֹעַ

כְּשַׁלְהֶבֶת קְשׁוּרָה בְּגַחֶלֶת
וְאָדוֹן יָחִיד
וְאֵין לוֹ שֵׁנִי
וְלִפְנֵי אֶחָד מָה אַתָּה סוֹפֵר

עֶשֶׂר סְפִירוֹת בְּלִימָה
בְּלֹם פִּיךָ מִלְּדַבֵּר
וְלִבְּךָ מִלְּהַרְהֵר
וְאִם רָץ פִּיךָ לְדַבֵּר
וְלִבְּךָ לְהַרְהֵר
שׁוּב לַמָּקוֹם
שֶׁלְּכָךְ נֶאֱמַר:
'וְהַחַיּוֹת רָצוֹא וָשׁוֹב'
וְעַל דָּבָר זֶה נִכְרְתָה בְרִית

עֶשְׂרִים וּשְׁתַּיִם אוֹתִיּוֹת יְסוֹד
חֲקָקָן, חֲצָבָן, צְרָפָן, שְׁקָלָן וֶהֱמִירָן
וְצָר בָּהֶן אֶת כָּל הַיְצוּר
וְאֶת כָּל הֶעָתִיד לָצוּר

עֶשְׂרִים וּשְׁתַּיִם אוֹתִיּוֹת
חֲקָקָן בְּקוֹל
חֲצָבָן בְּרוּחַ
וּקְבָעָן בַּפֶּה בַּחֲמִשָּׁה מְקוֹמוֹת
אחה״ע — בַּגָּרוֹן
גיכ״ק — בַּחֵךְ
דטלנ״ת — בַּלָּשׁוֹן
זסצר״ש — בַּשִּׁנַּיִם
בומ״ף — בַּשְּׂפָתַיִם

עֶשְׂרִים וּשְׁתַּיִם אוֹתִיּוֹת
קְבוּעוֹת בְּגַלְגַּל כְּמִין חוֹמָה
בְּרל״א שְׁעָרִים
חוֹזֵר הַגַּלְגַּל

עֶשֶׂר סְפִירוֹת בְּלִימָה
עֶשֶׂר וְלֹא תֵשַׁע
עֶשֶׂר וְלֹא אַחַת-עֶשְׂרֵה
הָבֵן בְּחָכְמָה
וְחַכֵּם בְּבִינָה
בְּחֹן בָּהֶן
וַחֲקֹר מֵהֶן
וְהַעֲמֵד דָּבָר עַל בֻּרְיוֹ
וְהוֹשֵׁב יוֹצֵר עַל מְכוֹנוֹ

עֶשֶׂר סְפִירוֹת בְּלִימָה
מִדָּתָן עֶשֶׂר שֶׁאֵין לָהֶן סוֹף:

עֹמֶק רֵאשִׁית   וְעֹמֶק אַחֲרִית
עֹמֶק טוֹב   וְעֹמֶק רַע
עֹמֶק רוּם   וְעֹמֶק תַּחַת
עֹמֶק מִזְרָח   וְעֹמֶק מַעֲרָב
עֹמֶק צָפוֹן   וְעֹמֶק דָּרוֹם

וְאָדוֹן יָחִיד
אֵל מֶלֶךְ נֶאֱמָן
מוֹשֵׁל בְּכֻלָּן מִמְּעוֹן קָדְשׁוֹ
עַד עֲדֵי עַד

עֶשֶׂר סְפִירוֹת בְּלִימָה
צְפִיָּתָן כְּמַרְאֵה הַבָּזָק
וְתַכְלִיתָן אֵין לָהֶן קֵץ
וּדְבָרוֹ בָהֶן בְּרָצוֹא וָשׁוֹב
וּמַאֲמָרוֹ כְּסוּפָה יִרְדֹּפוּ
וְלִפְנֵי כִסְאוֹ הֵם מִשְׁתַּחֲוִים

עֶשֶׂר סְפִירוֹת בְּלִימָה
נָעוּץ סוֹפָן בִּתְחִלָּתָן
וּתְחִלָּתָן בְּסוֹפָן

Page 34

אָנָּא, בְּכֹחַ גְּדֻלַּת יְמִינְךָ, תַּתִּיר צְרוּרָה
קַבֵּל רִנַּת עַמְּךָ, שַׂגְּבֵנוּ טַהֲרֵנוּ, נוֹרָא
נָא גִבּוֹר, דּוֹרְשֵׁי יִחוּדְךָ – כְּבָבַת שָׁמְרֵם
בָּרְכֵם, טַהֲרֵם – רַחֲמֵי צִדְקָתְךָ תָּמִיד גָּמְלֵם
חֲסִין קָדוֹשׁ, בְּרֹב טוּבְךָ נַהֵל עֲדָתֶךָ
יָחִיד גֵּאֶה, לְעַמְּךָ פְּנֵה, זוֹכְרֵי קְדֻשָּׁתֶךָ
שַׁוְעָתֵנוּ קַבֵּל, וּשְׁמַע צַעֲקָתֵנוּ, יוֹדֵעַ תַּעֲלוּמוֹת:

Pages 42–47

בִּשְׁלֹשִׁים וּשְׁתַּיִם נְתִיבוֹת פְּלִיאוֹת חָכְמָה
חָקַק יָהּ
יְהֹוָה צְבָאוֹת
אֱלֹהִים חַיִּים
אֵל שַׁדַּי
רָם וְנִשָּׂא
שׁוֹכֵן עַד וְקָדוֹשׁ שְׁמוֹ
מָרוֹם וְקָדוֹשׁ הוּא
וּבָרָא אֶת עוֹלָמוֹ בִּשְׁלֹשָׁה סְפָרִים:
בִּסְפָר, סֵפֶר וְסִפּוּר

עֶשֶׂר סְפִירוֹת בְּלִימָה
וְעֶשְׂרִים וּשְׁתַּיִם אוֹתִיּוֹת
שָׁלֹשׁ אִמּוֹת
וְשֶׁבַע כְּפוּלוֹת
וּשְׁתֵּים-עֶשְׂרֵה פְּשׁוּטוֹת

עֶשֶׂר סְפִירוֹת בְּלִימָה
כְּמִסְפַּר עֶשֶׂר אֶצְבָּעוֹת
חָמֵשׁ כְּנֶגֶד חָמֵשׁ
וּבְרִית יָחִיד מְכֻוֶּנֶת בָּאֶמְצַע
בְּמִלַּת הַלָּשׁוֹן
וּבְמִילַת הַמָּעוֹר

מֶלֶךְ תָּר בְּכָל פֹּעַל / כָּל מַה־יִּפְעַל / בְּמַטָּה וּבְמַעַל.
מֶלֶךְ בַּעֲשָׂרָה מַלְבּוּשִׁים / יִתְאַזַּר בִּקְדוֹשִׁים / אֵל נַעֲרָץ בְּסוֹד קְדוֹשִׁים. קָדוֹשׁ.
מֶלֶךְ אֱלֹהֵי עוֹלָם / הִמְלִיכוּהוּ עַם עוֹלָם / יְיָ יִמְלֹךְ לְעוֹלָם. קָדוֹשׁ.

Pages 32–33

וְחַיּוֹת אֲשֶׁר הֵנָּה מְרֻבָּעוֹת כִּסֵּא
בְּמָאתַיִם וַחֲמִשִּׁים וָשֵׁשׁ מַכְנִיפוֹת כִּסֵּא
גּוֹעֲשׁוֹת בּוֹ בְּסוֹכְכָם פָּנִים בְּפָנִים בַּכִּסֵּא
דְּמוּת רָקִיעַ בְּרֹאשָׁם נָטוּי לַכִּסֵּא
הוּא כְּעֵין הַקֶּרַח וּבוֹ שָׁבִיב כִּסֵּא
וּמִמַּעַל לָרָקִיעַ כְּמַרְאֵה דְמוּת כִּסֵּא
זוֹעֲוֹת בְּלִי לֵאוּת מֵחִיל כִּסֵּא
חָשׁוֹת בִּרְצוֹא וָשׁוֹב וּמַרְעִישׁוֹת כִּסֵּא
טָסוֹת כַּבָּזָק וְלֹא מְזִיזוֹת הוֹד כִּסֵּא
יוֹדְעוֹת כִּי כָל מָקוֹם לֹא יָכִיל מְקוֹם כִּסֵּא
כַּף רֶגֶל חֲמֵשׁ מֵאוֹת וַחֲמֵשׁ־עֶשְׂרֵה יְשָׁרָה לַכִּסֵּא
לְעֵת תֶּרְשֵׁינָה לְפָאֵר קוֹפְצוֹת מִתַּחַת לַכִּסֵּא
מִתְעַלְּפוֹת מִפַּחַד רָם יוֹשֵׁב עַל כִּסֵּא
נִרְאוֹת נוֹשְׂאוֹת וְהֵם נִשָּׂאוֹת מִתַּחַת כִּסֵּא
סְבוּלוֹת מִתַּחַת זְרוֹעוֹת עוֹלָם כִּסֵּא
עֲתִירַת זוֹ כְתַעַל תְּרַפֶּינָה כָּנָף בַּכִּסֵּא
פְּשָׁעִים אִם עָצְמוּ מַשִּׁיקוֹת כִּסֵּא
צוֹרֵר כִּי יַשְׁטִין יְפָרְשֵׁז עָנָן כִּסֵּא
קוֹל שׁוֹפָר כִּי יַעַל מְאַחֵז פְּנֵי כִּסֵּא
רַחֲמִים יָלִין בְּעַד רְשׁוּמִים עַל כִּסֵּא
שׁוֹפֵט יִרְצֶה מְשֶׁבֶת בְּאוּלָם כִּסֵּא
תַּבְנִית תָּם יְפֵן חֲקוּקָה בַכִּסֵּא
אַרְבַּע חַיּוֹת נוֹשְׂאוֹת נְשׂוּאַת כִּסֵּא
לְבִלְתִּי לְנַבֵּל לְמַעֲנוּ כִסֵּא
עוֹד יְפְצֶה פֶּה וְיַפְגִּיעַ בַּכִּסֵּא
זְכֹר לְיוֹשְׁבֵי נְטָעִים אֲשֶׁר עִמְּךָ בַכִּסֵּא
רַחֵם מְצוּקִים אֲשֶׁר שַׂמְתָּ עֲלֵיהֶם הֲדוֹם כִּסֵּא
וְאָז יִתְרָעֵשׁ הַגַּלְגַּל, וּכְרוּב לִכְרוּב וְחַיָּה לְעוֹף לְעֻמַּת כִּסֵּא
בָּרוּךְ כְּבוֹד יְיָ מִמְּקוֹמוֹ.

הַמֶּלֶךְ

יוֹשֵׁב עַל־כִּסֵּא רָם וְנִשָּׂא.
שׁוֹכֵן עַד מָרוֹם וְקָדוֹשׁ שְׁמוֹ.
וְכָתוּב: "רַנְּנוּ צַדִּיקִים בַּיָי, לַיְשָׁרִים נָאוָה תְהִלָּה":

תִּתְרוֹמָם	יְשָׁרִים	בְּפִי
תִּתְבָּרַךְ	צַדִּיקִים	וּבְדִבְרֵי
תִּתְקַדָּשׁ	חֲסִידִים	וּבִלְשׁוֹן
תִּתְהַלָּל:	קְדוֹשִׁים	וּבְקֶרֶב

מֶלֶךְ אָזוּר גְּבוּרָה / גָּדוֹל שִׁמְךָ בִּגְבוּרָה / לְךָ זְרוֹעַ עִם גְּבוּרָה.
מֶלֶךְ בִּגְדֵי נָקָם / לָבֵשׁ בְּיוֹם נָקָם / לְצָרָיו יָשִׁיב אֵל חֵיקָם.
מֶלֶךְ גֵּאוּת לָבֵשׁ / יַמִּים מְיַבֵּשׁ / וְגַאֲוַת אֲפִיקִים מְכַבֵּשׁ.
מֶלֶךְ בַּעֲשָׂרָה לְבוּשִׁים / הִתְאַזַּר בְּקָדוֹשִׁים / אֵל נַעֲרָץ בְּסוֹד קְדוֹשִׁים. קָדוֹשׁ.
מֶלֶךְ דָּר בְּנִהוֹרָא / עוֹטֶה אוֹרָה / מִשְׁפָּטֶנּוּ יוֹצִיא לָאוֹרָה.
מֶלֶךְ הִתְאַזַּר עֹז / יָמִינוֹ תָעֹז / וֶאֱנוֹשׁ אֵל יָעֹז.
מֶלֶךְ וַיִּלְבַּשׁ צְדָקָה / נִקְדָּשׁ בִּצְדָקָה / לְךָ יְיָ הַצְּדָקָה.
מֶלֶךְ זֶה הָדוּר בִּלְבוּשׁוֹ / וְכוֹבַע יְשׁוּעָה בְּרֹאשׁוֹ / אֱלֹהִים יָשַׁב עַל כִּסֵּא קָדְשׁוֹ.
מֶלֶךְ חֲמוּץ בְּגָדִים / זָעוּם בְּדַרְכוֹ בּוֹגְדִים / יִבְצֹר רוּחַ נְגִידִים.
מֶלֶךְ טַלִּיתוֹ כַּשֶּׁלֶג מְצַחְצָח / צַח וּבְצַחְצָחוֹת יִצַחְצָח / מְצַחְצְחִים פָּעֳלָם לָנֶצַח.
מֶלֶךְ יָעַט קִנְאָה / קָנֹא קִנֵּא / גָּאֹה גָּאָה / כְּאִישׁ מִלְחָמוֹת עָיִיר קִנְאָה.
מֶלֶךְ כָּל אַפְסֵי אֶרֶץ / יִשְׁתַּחֲווּ לְמֶלֶךְ עַל כָּל הָאָרֶץ / כִּי בָא לִשְׁפֹּט הָאָרֶץ.
מֶלֶךְ לְיוֹם קוּמוֹ לָעַד / כָּל יְצוּר יִרְעַד / רָם וְנִשָּׂא שׁוֹכֵן עַד.
מֶלֶךְ מוֹשֵׁל עוֹלָם בִּגְבוּרָתוֹ / יִרְעֲשׁוּ הָרִים בְּגַאֲוָתוֹ / וּכְאֵילִים יְרַקְּדוּ מִגַּעֲרָתוֹ.
מֶלֶךְ נוֹרָא לְמַלְכֵי אֶרֶץ / חוֹל תָּחוֹל הָאָרֶץ / מִיּוֹשֵׁב הַכְּרוּבִים תָּנוּט הָאָרֶץ.
מֶלֶךְ שְׂאֵתוֹ מִי יַעֲצָר־כֹּחַ / וְהוּא נוֹשֵׂא כֹל בַּכֹּחַ / נוֹתֵן לַיָּעֵף כֹּחַ.
מֶלֶךְ עָמְדוּ לַדִּין / בְּיוֹם הַדִּין / שׁוֹפֵט גֵּאִים בַּדִּין.
מֶלֶךְ פִּלֵּשׁ סוֹד הַמַּעֲמִיקִים / לַסְתִּיר עֵצָה בְּמַעֲמַקִּים / יַחְשֹׂף וִיגַלֶּה עֲמָקִים.
מֶלֶךְ צִוָּה מִכָּל־רוּחַ / עָרִיצֵי גַּסֵּי הָרוּחַ / לְאַסְּפָם בְּשֶׁטֶף רוּחַ.
מֶלֶךְ קְהַל מַלְכֵי אֲדָמָה / בְּסַעֲרוֹ מַשָּׂא דוּמָה / יִפְקֹד כָּל צְבָא מְרוֹמָה.
מֶלֶךְ רָם וְנִגְבַּהּ בַּמִּשְׁפָּט / וְעֹז מֶלֶךְ אָהֵב מִשְׁפָּט / מְכוֹן כִּסְאוֹ צֶדֶק וּמִשְׁפָּט.
מֶלֶךְ שׁוֹפֵט צֶדֶק / לְפָנָיו יְהַלֵּךְ צֶדֶק / לְהָלִיץ בְּעַד רוֹדְפֵי צֶדֶק.
מֶלֶךְ תַּקִּיף בַּמֶּמְשָׁלָה / כִּסְאוֹ לְמַעֲלָה תָּלָה / וּמַלְכוּתוֹ בַּכֹּל מָשָׁלָה.
מֶלֶךְ תַּחַת גֵּיא מִמַּבָּטוֹ / מַרְעִיד יְסוֹד בְּהַבִּיטוֹ / בַּכֹּל מְשׁוֹטֵט מַבָּטוֹ.

אֵשׁ הַמַּרְאָה כְּמוֹ מַרְאוֹת   אֵשׁ וַדַּאי כִּי לֹא כָבָה
אֵשׁ זוֹרַחַת וּמְשׁוֹטֶטֶת   אֵשׁ חוֹשֶׁשֶׁת וּמִתְלַקַּחַת
אֵשׁ טָסָה בְרוּחַ סְעָרָה   אֵשׁ יוֹקֶדֶת בְּאֶפֶס עֵצִים
אֵשׁ כִּי כָל יוֹם מִתְחַדֶּ[שֶׁת]   אֵשׁ לֹא נִפְחָה מֵאֵשׁ
אֵשׁ מַעֲלָה לוּלְבִּין   אֵשׁ נִיצוֹצֶיהָ הֵם הַבְּרָקִים
[אֵשׁ סוּפָה מַרְכְּבוֹתָיו]   אֵשׁ עָנָן וַעֲרָפֶּל]
אֵשׁ פְּלָד[וֹת] פל...   אֵשׁ [צְרָיו תְּלָהֵט]
[אֵשׁ קוֹדַחַת] עַ[ד שֶׁ]אוֹל תַּחְתִּית   [אֵשׁ ר]................קרה
אֵשׁ שְׁחוֹרָה כָעוֹרֵב   אֵשׁ תַּלְתַּלִּים כְּצִבְעֵי קֶשֶׁת

Pages 25–26

מִשָּׁמַיִם לִשְׁמֵי הַשָּׁמָיִם / מִשְּׁמֵי שָׁמַיִם לַעֲרָפֶל /
מֵעֲרָפֶל לִזְבוּלָה / מִזְּבוּלָה לִמְעוֹנָה /
מִמְּעוֹנָה לִשְׁחָקִים / מִשְּׁחָקִים לַעֲרָבוֹת /
מֵעֲרָבוֹת לְרוּם כִּסֵּא / וּמֵרוּם כִּסֵּא לְמֶרְכָּבָה:

מִי יִדְמֶה-לָּךְ / מִי יִשְׁוֶה-לָּךְ /
מִי רָאָה / מִי הִגִּיעַ /
מִי יִתְלֶה רֹאשׁ / מִי יָרִים עָיִן /
מִי יַקְשֶׁה / מִי יָעִיז /
מִי יָזִיד / מִי יְחַשֵּׁב בַּלֵּב /
מִי יִגְאֶה / מִי יִּסַ / מִי יַעֲרֹךְ:

וּרְכוּבָךְ עַל כְּרוּב / וְדִיאָתָךְ עַל רוּחַ /
וְאָרְחָךְ בְּסוּפָה / וְדַרְכֵּךְ בִּסְעָרָה /
וּשְׁבִילָךְ בְּמַיִם / וּשְׁלִיחוּתָךְ בָּאֵשׁ /
אֶלֶף אֲלָפִים וְרִבֵּי רְבָבוֹת:
נַעֲשִׂים אֲנָשִׁים / נַעֲשִׂים נָשִׁים /
נַעֲשִׂים רוּחוֹת / נַעֲשִׂים זִיקִים /
נַעֲשִׂים כָּל דְּמוּת / וְעוֹשִׂים כָּל שְׁלִיחוּת /
בְּאֵימָה, בְּיִרְאָה, בְּפַחַד, בְּרַעַד, בִּרְתֵת, בְּזִיעַ —
יִפְתְּחוּ פֶה לְהַזְכִּיר זֵכֶר קָדְשָׁךְ כַּכָּתוּב:
"וְקָרָא זֶה אֶל זֶה וְאָמַר —
קָדוֹשׁ, קָדוֹשׁ, קָדוֹשׁ יְהוָה צְבָאוֹת":

מַרְאֵה כֹהֵן	כִּדְמוּת הַקֶּשֶׁת בְּיוֹם הֶעָנָן
מַרְאֵה כֹהֵן	כְּהוֹד אֲשֶׁר הִלְבִּישׁ צוּר לַיְצוּרִים
מַרְאֵה כֹהֵן	כְּוֶרֶד הַנָּתוּן בְּתוֹךְ גַּן חֶמֶד
מַרְאֵה כֹהֵן	כְּזֵר הַנָּתוּן עַל מֵצַח מֶלֶךְ
מַרְאֵה כֹהֵן	כְּחֶסֶד הַנִּתָּן עַל פְּנֵי חָתָן
מַרְאֵה כֹהֵן	כְּטֹהַר הַנָּתוּן בִּצְנִיף טָהוֹר
מַרְאֵה כֹהֵן	כְּיוֹשֵׁב בַּסֵּתֶר לְחַלּוֹת פְּנֵי מֶלֶךְ
מַרְאֵה כֹהֵן	כְּכוֹכַב הַנֹּגַהּ בִּגְבוּל מִזְרָח
מַרְאֵה כֹהֵן	כִּלְבוּשׁ מְעִיל וְשִׁרְיָן צְדָקָה
מַרְאֵה כֹהֵן	כְּמַלְאָךְ הַנִּצָּב עַל רֹאשׁ דֶּרֶךְ
מַרְאֵה כֹהֵן	כְּנֵר הַמֵּצִיץ מִבֵּין הַחַלּוֹנוֹת
מַרְאֵה כֹהֵן	כְּשָׂרֵי צְבָאוֹת בְּרֹאשׁ עַם-קֹדֶשׁ
מַרְאֵה כֹהֵן	כְּעֹז אֲשֶׁר הִלְבִּישׁ טָהוֹר לַמִּטַּהֵר
מַרְאֵה כֹהֵן	כְּפַעֲמוֹנֵי זָהָב עַל שׁוּלֵי הַמְּעִיל
מַרְאֵה כֹהֵן	כְּצוּרַת הַבַּיִת וּפָרֹכֶת הַמָּסָךְ
מַרְאֵה כֹהֵן	כִּקְהִלָּה הַמְכֻסָּה תְּכֵלֶת וְאַרְגָּמָן
מַרְאֵה כֹהֵן	כִּרְוֹאֵי זְרִיחַת שֶׁמֶשׁ עַל הָאָרֶץ
מַרְאֵה כֹהֵן	כְּשׁוֹשַׁנַּת גַּן בֵּין הַחוֹחִים
מַרְאֵה כֹהֵן:	כְּתַבְנִית עָשׁ, כְּסִיל וְכִימָה מִתֵּימָן

Page 23

חַלּוֹנוֹת בַּקָּשָׁה	חַלּוֹנוֹת תְּפִלָּה
חַלּוֹנוֹת שִׂמְחָה	חַלּוֹנוֹת בְּכִיָּה
חַלּוֹנוֹת רָעָב	חַלּוֹנוֹת שֹׂבַע
חַלּוֹנוֹת עֲנִיּוּת	חַלּוֹנוֹת עֹשֶׁר
חַלּוֹנוֹת שָׁלוֹם	חַלּוֹנוֹת מִלְחָמָה
חַלּוֹנוֹת לֵדָה:	חַלּוֹנוֹת הֵרָיוֹן

וּרְאֵה הַחַלּוֹנוֹת עַד אֵין חֵקֶר וְאֵין מִסְפָּר:

Page 24

אֵשׁ בּוֹעֶרֶת בִּיבֵשִׁים וּבְלַחִים	אֵשׁ אֲשֶׁר הִיא אוֹכְלָה אֵשׁ
אֵשׁ דּוֹמָה לַאֲרִי רוֹבֵץ	אֵשׁ גּוֹחֶלֶת בְּשֶׁלֶג וְקִיטוֹר

לְמֶחְקַר תֵּבֵל
לִמְהַלָּכָא בְּיַבֶּשְׁתָּא
לְמִסְתַּכְּלָא בְּזִיוָא
לְאַשְׁרָאָה בְתַגָּא
לְמִשְׁתַּבָּחָא בְּאִיקָרָא
לְמֵימַר שְׁבָחָא
לִמְדַבָּקָא אָתִין
לְמֵימַר שְׁמָהָן
לְמִצְפֵּי לְעֵילָא
וּלְמִצְפֵּי לְתַתָּא
לְמִדַּע בְּפֵרוּשׁ חַיָּיא
וּלְמִחְזֵי בְּחֶזְוַת מִיתַיָּא
לִמְהַלָּכָא בְּנַהֲרֵי נוּרָא
וּלְמִדַּע בְּבַרְקָא.

Page 14

שֶׁרָאֲתָה	אַשְׁרֵי עַיִן
שֶׁזָּכָה לְכָךְ	אַשְׁרֵי הַגֶּבֶר
שֶׁקִּבְּלָה אוֹתוֹ	אַשְׁרֵי הָאֵם
שֶׁיָּנַק מֵהֶם	אַשְׁרֵי הַדַּדַּיִם
שֶׁגָּדַל בָּהֶם	אַשְׁרֵי מֵעַיִם
שֶׁלָּמַד בָּהּ	אַשְׁרֵי תוֹרָה
שֶׁעָרַךְ	אַשְׁרֵי בִינָה
שֶׁחִבְּקוּ אוֹתוֹ	אַשְׁרֵי זְרוֹעוֹת
שֶׁרָדַף	אַשְׁרֵי שָׁלוֹם
שֶׁהֱצִיצָה-בּוֹ	אַשְׁרֵי עַיִן
אַשְׁרֶיךָ יִשְׁמָעֵאל שֶׁזָּכִיתָ לְכָךְ.	

Pages 20–22

מַרְאֵה כֹהֵן	כְּאֹהֶל הַנִּמְתָּח בְּדָרֵי מַעֲלָה
מַרְאֵה כֹהֵן	כִּבְרָקִים הַיּוֹצְאִים מִזִּיו חַיּוֹת
מַרְאֵה כֹהֵן	כְּגֹדֶל גְּדִילִים בְּאַרְבַּע קְצָווֹת

וּמְפָרְעוֹת אֶת פְּנֵיהֶם
הֵן מְפָרְעוֹת
וּמֶלֶךְ הַכָּבוֹד מְכַסֶּה פָנָיו
וְהָיָה עֲרָבוֹת רָקִיעַ מִתְבַּקֵּעַ
מִפְּנֵי הֲדַר זִיו יְפִי תֹאַר
חֶמְדַּת חֶמְלַת תַּאֲוַת זֹהַר
זֹהַר הַנֶּזֶר מַרְאֶה פְּנֵיהֶם.
כְּדָבָר שֶׁנֶּאֱמַר: "קָדוֹשׁ, קָדוֹשׁ, קָדוֹשׁ":

Page 12

מֶלֶךְ מַלְכֵי הַמְּלָכִים
אֱלֹהֵי הָאֱלֹהִים וַאֲדוֹנֵי הָאֲדוֹנִים
הַמְסֻבָּב בְּקִשְׁרֵי כְתָרִים
הַמֻּקָּף בְּעַנְפֵי נְגִידֵי נֹגַהּ
שֶׁבְּעַנְפוֹ הוֹדוֹ כִּסָּה שָׁמַיִם
וּבַהֲדָרוֹ יוֹפִיעַ מְרוֹמִים
וּמִזִּיווֹ יִתְבַּעֲרוּ תְהוֹמוֹת
וּמִתָּאֳרוֹ נִתְזוּ שְׁחָקִים
וְגֵאִים מַפְלִיט תָּאֳרוֹ
וְאֵיתָנִים מְפוֹצֵץ כִּתְרוֹ
וִיקָרִים טוֹרֵד חֲלוּקוֹ
וְכָל עֵצִים יִשְׂמְחוּ בִדְבָרוֹ
יְרַנְּנוּ דְשָׁאִים בְּשִׂמְחָתוֹ
וּבְדַבְּרוֹ יִזְּלוּ בְשָׂמִים
טוֹרְדִין וְיוֹצְאִין בְּלַהֲבֵי אֵשׁ
חֶדְוָה נוֹתְנִין לְשׁוֹחֲרֵיהֶם
וְשַׁלְוָה לִמְקַיְּמֵיהֶם:

Page 13

לְמִסַּק לְעֵילָא
לְמֵחַת לְתַתָּא
לְמִרְכַּב גַּלְגַּלִּין

Pages 10–11

1

בְּכָל יוֹם וָיוֹם
בְּהַגִּיעַ עֲלוֹת הַשַּׁחַר
מֶלֶךְ הָדוּר יוֹשֵׁב
וּמְבָרֵךְ לַחַיּוֹת:
"לָכֶם חַיּוֹת, אֲנִי אוֹמֵר
לָכֶם בְּרִיּוֹת, אֲנִי מַשְׁמִיעַ
חַיּוֹת חַיּוֹת נוֹשְׂאוֹת כִּסֵּא כְבוֹדִי
בְּלֵב שָׁלֵם וּבְנֶפֶשׁ חֲפֵצָה.
תִּתְבָּרֵךְ שָׁעָה שֶׁיָּצַרְתִּי אֶתְכֶם בָּהּ
יִתְרוֹמַם הַמַּזָּל שֶׁיָּצַרְתִּי אֶתְכֶם בּוֹ
יָאִיר אוֹרוֹ שֶׁל אוֹתוֹ הַיּוֹם
שֶׁעֲלִיתֶם בַּמַּחְשָׁבָה עַל לְבָבִי
שֶׁאַתֶּם כְּלֵי חֶמְדָּה
שֶׁהֱכַנְתִּי וְשִׁכְלַלְתִּי אֶתְכֶם בּוֹ
הַחֲרִישׁוּ לִי קוֹל,
כָּל יְצוּרִים שֶׁבָּרָאתִי
וְאֶשְׁמַע וְאַאֲזִין לִתְפִלַּת בָּנָי.

2

בְּכָל יוֹם וָיוֹם
בְּהַגִּיעַ תְּפִלַּת הַמִּנְחָה
מֶלֶךְ הָדוּר יוֹשֵׁב וּמְרוֹמֵם לַחַיּוֹת
עַד שֶׁלֹּא יְכֻלֶּה דָּבָר מִפִּיו
חַיּוֹת הַקֹּדֶשׁ יוֹצְאוֹת מִתַּחַת כִּסֵּא כָבוֹד.
בְּפִיהֶם מְלוֹא רִנָּה
בְּכַנְפֵיהֶם מְלוֹא גִילָה
יְדֵיהֶם מְנַגְּנוֹת
וְרַגְלֵיהֶם מְרַקְּדוֹת
וְעוֹקְפוֹת וְסוֹבְבוֹת אֶת מַלְכָּם
אַחַת מִימִינוֹ וְאַחַת מִשְּׂמֹאלוֹ
אַחַת מִלְּפָנָיו וְאַחַת מֵאַחֲרָיו
וּמְגַפְּפוֹת וּמְנַשְּׁקוֹת אוֹתוֹ

לֹא עֵינֵי בָשָׂר וָדָם וְלֹא עֵינֵי מְשָׁרְתָיו.
וְהַמִּסְתַּכֵּל בּוֹ וְהַמֵּצִיץ וְהָרוֹאֶה אוֹתוֹ
אוֹחֲזוֹת מַחֲזָרְאוֹת לְגַלְגַּלֵּי עֵינָיו.
וְגַלְגַּלֵּי עֵינָיו מְפַלְּטִין וּמוֹצִיאִין לַפִּידֵי אֵשׁ
וְהֵן מְלַהֲטִין אוֹתוֹ, וְהֵן שׂוֹרְפִין אוֹתוֹ ;
כִּי הָאֵשׁ הַיּוֹצֵא מִן הָאָדָם הַמִּסְתַּכֵּל
הִיא מְלַהֶטֶת אוֹתוֹ, וְהִיא שׂוֹרֶפֶת אוֹתוֹ.
מִפְּנֵי מַה ? – מִפְּנֵי מִדָּה שֶׁל חָלוּק שֶׁל זְהַרְרִיאֵל, יְהֹוָה אֱלֹהֵי יִשְׂרָאֵל
שֶׁמְּעַטֵּר וּבָא עַל כִּסֵּא כְבוֹדוֹ

Page 9

לְחַי עוֹלָמִים	הָאַדֶרֶת וְהָאֱמוּנָה
לְחַי עוֹלָמִים	הַבִּינָה וְהַבְּרָכָה
לְחַי עוֹלָמִים	הַגַּאֲוָה וְהַגְּדֻלָּה
לְחַי עוֹלָמִים	הַדֵּעָה וְהַדִּבּוּר
לְחַי עוֹלָמִים	הַהוֹד וְהֶהָדָר
לְחַי עוֹלָמִים	הַוַּעַד וְהַוָּתִיקוּת
לְחַי עוֹלָמִים	הַזָּךְ וְהַזֹּהַר
לְחַי עוֹלָמִים	הַחַיִל וְהַחֹסֶן
לְחַי עוֹלָמִים	הַטֶּכֶס וְהַטֹּהַר
לְחַי עוֹלָמִים	הַיִּחוּד וְהַיִּרְאָה
לְחַי עוֹלָמִים	הַכֶּתֶר וְהַכָּבוֹד
לְחַי עוֹלָמִים	הַלֶּקַח וְהַלִּבּוּב
לְחַי עוֹלָמִים	הַמְּלוּכָה וְהַמֶּמְשָׁלָה
לְחַי עוֹלָמִים	הַנּוֹי וְהַנֵּצַח
לְחַי עוֹלָמִים	הַשִּׂגּוּי וְהַשֶּׂגֶב
לְחַי עוֹלָמִים	הָעֹז וְהָעֲנָוָה
לְחַי עוֹלָמִים	הַפְּדוּת וְהַפְּאֵר
לְחַי עוֹלָמִים	הַצְּבִי וְהַצֶּדֶק
לְחַי עוֹלָמִים	הַקְּרִיאָה וְהַקְּדֻשָּׁה
לְחַי עוֹלָמִים	הָרֹן וְהָרוֹמְמוּת
לְחַי עוֹלָמִים	הַשִּׁיר וְהַשֶּׁבַח
לְחַי עוֹלָמִים :	הַתְּהִלָּה וְהַתִּפְאֶרֶת

Page 6

מְבַטְּלֵי גְזֵרָה, מְפֵרֵי שְׁבוּעָה,
מַעֲבִירֵי חֵמָה, מְשִׁיבֵי קִנְאָה,
מַזְכִּירֵי אַהֲבָה, מְסַדְּרֵי רֵעוּת
לִפְנֵי הֲדַר-גְּאוֹן-הֵיכַל-נוֹרָא:

מַה-לָּכֶם שֶׁאַתֶּם נוֹרָאִים,
וּפְעָמִים לָכֶם שֶׁאַתֶּם שְׂמֵחִים?
מַה-לָּכֶם שֶׁאַתֶּם מְרַנְּנִים,
וּפְעָמִים לָכֶם שֶׁאַתֶּם מְבֹהָלִים?

אָמְרוּ: כְּשֶׁאוֹפַנֵּי גְבוּרָה מַקְדִּירִין,
עוֹמְדִים אָנוּ בְּבֶהָלָה גְדוֹלָה;
וּכְשֶׁזָּהֳרֵי שְׁכִינָה מְאִירִין,
אָנוּ שְׂמֵחִים שִׂמְחָה רַבָּה !

Pages 7–8

מִדָּה שֶׁל קְדֻשָּׁה, מִדָּה שֶׁל גְּבוּרָה
מִדָּה נוֹרָאָה, מִדָּה מְבֹהָלָה
מִדָּה שֶׁל רְתֵת, מִדָּה שֶׁל זִיעַ
מִדָּה שֶׁל בֶּהָלָה, מִדָּה שֶׁל חַלְחָלָה
מִדָּה שֶׁל חָלוּק שֶׁל זַהַרְרִיאֵל, יְהֹוָה אֱלֹהֵי יִשְׂרָאֵל
שֶׁמְּעֻטָּר וּבָא עַל כִּסֵּא כְבוֹדוֹ
וְחָקוּק וּמָלֵא כֻּלּוֹ מִבִּפְנִים וּמִבַּחוּץ יְהֹוָה יְהֹוָה
וְעֵינֵי כָל בְּרִיָּה אֵינָהּ יְכוֹלָה לְהִסְתַּכֵּל בּוֹ ;

ACKNOWLEDGMENTS

This book began to take shape some fifteen years ago, and a number of people have contributed to the selection and preparation of the material it now includes. In particular, I'm grateful for the assistance, guidance, goading, correction, encouragement, and above all the conversation offered in person and on the page by Daniel Abrams, Ammiel Alcalay, Patrick Alexander, Shahar Bram, Dvora Bregman, David Caligiuri, Julie Cohen, John Donatich, Shulamit Elizur, Steven Fraade, Eli Gottlieb, Michal Govrin, Yehoshua Granat, Matti Huss, James Kugel, Susan Laity, Gabriel Levin, Laura Lieber, Ivan Marcus, Daniel Matt, María Rosa Menocal, Robert Schine, Ileene Smith, Howard Sobel, Nanette Stahl, Sandra Valabregue-Perry, Mary Valencia, Assia Vilenkin, Steven Wasserstrom, Elliot Wolfson, and Joseph Yahalom. Unalphabetical acknowledgment is due to Adina Hoffman, as always, for everything. Thanks are also due to Haviva Pedaya for detailed discussion of the work here. And my debt is especially deep to Boaz Huss, whose thorough review of the manuscript was indispensable. It goes without saying that all errors, of fact and fabrication, are mine.

The Poetry of Kabbalah was first conceived of by Aminadav Dykman, who, with Moshe Idel, drew up its initial outline. That plan evolved considerably over time, and the final selection of the poems was made by the translator. Both editors would like to thank Moshe Idel for his enthusiastic support of this project from the start, and for his contribution to it early on. They would also like to acknowledge the work of Dr. Uri Melammed, of the Academy of Hebrew Language in Jerusalem, who prepared and proofread the vocalization of the Hebrew texts with devotion and precision, and provided helpful information pertaining to the textual sources.

Earlier versions of some of these translations were first printed in the following journals: Conjunctions, Lvng, The Paris Review, and Poetry. Translations of the poems by Shelomoh Ibn Gabirol, Yehudah HaLevi (apart from "Where Will I Find You"), Moshe ben Nahman, Avraham Abulafia, and Joseph Gikatilla come from The Dream of the Poem: Hebrew Poetry from Muslim and Christian Spain, c. 950–1492, copyright © 2007 by Princeton University Press, and appear courtesy of the press. "Angel of Fire" (by Yannai) was first published in Sacred Trash: The Lost and Found World of the Cairo Geniza, by Adina Hoffman and Peter Cole (New York, 2011), and appears courtesy of Schocken/Nextbook. To the editors of those journals and volumes—Bradford Morrow, Robyn Creswell, Peter O'Leary, Christian Wiman, Hanne Winarsky, Jonathan Rosen, Altie Karper—my thanks.

Finally, grateful acknowledgment is due to the Pritzker Family Philanthropic Fund, the Lucius N. Littauer Foundation, and the John D. and Catherine T. MacArthur Foundation for their generous and generative support of this work.

PETER COLE'S most recent book of poems is *Things on Which I've Stumbled*. His many volumes of translations from Hebrew and Arabic include *The Dream of the Poem: Hebrew Poetry from Muslim and Christian Spain, 950–1492* and *War & Love, Love & War*, by Aharon Shabtai. With Adina Hoffman, he is the author of a book of nonfiction, *Sacred Trash: The Lost and Found World of the Cairo Geniza*. Cole has received numerous honors for his work, including the PEN Translation Prize, the National Jewish Book Award for Poetry, an American Academy of Arts and Letters Award for Literature, and fellowships from the NEA, the NEH, and the Guggenheim Foundation. In 2007, he was named a MacArthur Foundation Fellow.

AMINADAV DYKMAN collaborated on *The English Homer* (Penguin) with George Steiner. He has published translations of French, Russian, English, Greek, Latin, and Italian poetry into Hebrew, including volumes of Renaissance and baroque poetry, as well as selected poems by Ovid, Joseph Brodsky, and W. H. Auden. He teaches comparative literature and directs the Translation Studies Program at the Hebrew University in Jerusalem.